Capitalism, Innovations, and Health after Covid-19

Sébastien Lechevalier • Jean-Paul Gaudillière •
Kathryn Ibata-Arens • Kayo Takuma
Editors

Capitalism, Innovations, and Health after Covid-19

An Asian Perspective

palgrave
macmillan

Editors
Sébastien Lechevalier
Ecole des Hautes Etudes en Sciences Sociales (EHESS)
Paris, France
German Institute for Japanese Studies (DIJ)
Tokyo, Japan

Jean-Paul Gaudillière
Ecole Hautes Etudes en Sciences Sociales (EHESS)
Paris, France

Kathryn Ibata-Arens
Department of Political Science
DePaul University
Chicago, IL, USA

Kayo Takuma
Faculty of Law
Keio University
Tokyo, Japan

ISBN 978-3-032-24478-9 ISBN 978-3-032-24479-6 (eBook)
https://doi.org/10.1007/978-3-032-24479-6

This Palgrave Macmillan imprint is published by the registered company Springer Nature Switzerland AG.
The registered company address is: Gewerbestrasse 11, 6330 Cham, Switzerland

Preface

This book is the outcome of a long-term project supported by the Ecole des Hautes Etudes en Sciences Sociales (EHESS, Paris), to which we would like to express our gratitude. In 2020, Jean-Paul Gaudillière and Sébastien Lechevalier submitted a proposal entitled “Capitalisms, technologies, societies and Health. An Euro-Asian research project” (CTSH project: https://ctsh.hypotheses.org/) to beneficiate from an EHESS funding under the label “Three years international research team” and were selected. We are grateful to Caroline Chu (EHESS International Office) and Jérôme Malois (EHESS Research Office) for their great advice and friendship. Then, despite the difficulties originating in the COVID-19 Pandemic, this funding scheme allowed all the contributing authors to meet at the Social Sciences Campus Condorcet, near Paris, in Aubervilliers, in May 2021, in July 2022, and in July 2024. These meetings facilitated the design of our joint framework as well as the collective writing of the chapters included in this book. During the last two years of the project, monthly webinars allowed for further lively discussions. These efforts were decisive in assuring for the coherence of an enterprise gathering colleagues from different countries and disciplines, which rarely meet. We are very grateful to all the authors for their commitment to the project. We would like also to thank sincerely the staff of the Fondation France-Japon de l’EHESS—Jodie Cazau, Fabien Michel, Céline Caliaro, and Yukiko Itoh—for their support, kindness, and professionalism.

Besides the initial financial support from EHESS, the publication of this book has beneficiated from several additional funding sources that we would like to acknowledge:

- a French government grant managed by the Agence Nationale de la Recherche (ANR) under the France 2030 programme (Reference: ANR-23- PAVH-0005) (INNOVCARE Project).
- The Sakurada-kai foundation;
- Bordeaux University through the Changes Research Department;

Last but not least, we would like to thank Steven Casper for his great questions, two anonymous for their extremely useful comments, and the whole editorial and production team of Palgrave MacMillan, beginning with Ellie Duncan and Shanmathi Priya Sampath for their great support.

Paris, Tokyo, Kyoto
February 2026

Sébastien Lechevalier
Jean-Paul Gaudillière
Kathryn Ibata-Arens
Kayo Takuma

Contents

1 Capitalism, Innovations, and Health After Covid-19. An Asian Perspective: An Introduction 1
Sébastien Lechevalier, Jean-Paul Gaudillière, Kathryn Ibata-Arens, and Kayo Takuma

Part I Systems in Crisis? Capitalism, Innovation, and Health 21

2 Anthropogenetic Development: Long Unnoticed and Already in Crisis 23
Robert Boyer and Olivier Boylaud

3 The Crisis of Capitalism and Health Innovation: Symptoms of a Crisis or of Success? 69
Philippe Gorry and Matthieu Montalban

4 The Mission-Oriented Science, Technology and Innovation (STI) Policies in Japan and Korea with a Focus on Health 113
Hideaki Shiroyama, Jeehoon Ki, Makiko Matsuo, and Hyeonoh Kim

Part II A Critical Moment and Its Openings: Covid Responses 171

5 Innovation Systems Under Crisis: Vaccine Development in Asia and Europe 173
Cornelia Storz, Keun Lee, Wen-Hua Kuo, and Franziska Dorothea Velte

6 Glocal Health Governance: Organizational Innovations in the Era of COVID-19 215
Wen-Hua Kuo and Kayo Takuma

7 Frugal Innovations and Health System Resilience. The Conceptualization, Policy Support and Forms of Frugality During Covid-19 in South India 243
Harilal Madhavan and Jean-Paul Gaudilliere

Part III Knowledge in Action: Asian Experiences 279

8 Care Systems in Crisis and Innovative Welfare Technologies: Stakeholders' Views Regarding Care Robots in Hong Kong SAR (China), Ireland and Japan 281
Naonori Kodate, Mei-chun Cheung, Akiyo Yumoto, Sarah Donnelly, Yurie Maeda, Mayuko Tsujimura, Hasheem Mannan, Wenwei Yu, Sayuri Suwa, Kazuko Obayashi, Shigeru Masuyama, W. C. H. Chan, Boris Hauray, and Diarmuid O'Shea

9 Care-led Innovation. A New Paradigm and an Application in the Japanese Context of Society 5.0 313
Sébastien Lechevalier

10 *Appropriate Technologies*, Primary Health Care and the Integration of Traditional Medicines in India 363
Jean-Paul Gaudillière and Harilal Madhavan

11 Commons and the Political Economy of Access: Generics, Neo-traditional Formulations and the Dominant Intellectual Property Regime of Medicines 389
Kathryn Ibata Arens, Jean-Paul Gaudillière, Harilal Madhavan, and Etienne Nouguez

12 General Conclusion 427
Sébastien Lechevalier, Jean-Paul Gaudillière, Kathryn Ibata-Arens, and Kayo Takuma

Glossary 441

List of Contributors

Robert Boyer is an economist, former Senior Researcher at CNRS and former Professor at EHESS (France)

Olivier Boylaud holds a PhD in economics and is an independent economist and statistician (France)

W. C. H. Chan is Associate Professor in Social Work at Northumbria University (United Kingdom)

M. C. Cheung is Associate Professor, Department of Social Work at The Chinese University of Hong Kong (Hong Kong SAR, China)

Sarah Donnelly is Associate Professor in Social Work at University College Dublin (Ireland)

Jean-Paul Gaudillière is an historian of science and medicine. He is Senior Researcher at Inserm, (French National Institute for Health and Medical Research) and Professor at EHESS (France)

Philippe Gorry is Associate Professor of cell biology, past director of technology transfer, and a researcher in the economics of innovation in health at Bordeaux School of Economics (France)

Boris Hauray is Research Fellow in Sociology at Inserm/National Institute of Health and Medical Research (France)

Kathryn Ibata-Arens is Vincent de Paul Professor of Political Science, DePaul University (USA)

Jeehoon Ki serves as an associate research fellow at Korea Institute of S&T Evaluation and Planning (KISTEP, Korea)

Hyeonoh Kim is an associate research fellow at Korea Institute of S&T Evaluation and Planning (KISTEP, Korea)

Naonori Kodate is Associate Professor in Social Policy and Welfare Technology at University College Dublin (Ireland)

Wen-Hua Kuo is Professor at National Yang Ming Chiao Tung University, Taiwan, where he teaches medicine in society.

Sébastien Lechevalier is an economist and a Professor at EHESS (France) and Visiting research fellow at DIJ (German Institute for Japanese Studies, Japan)

Keun Lee is an economist and Distinguished Professor of Chung-Ang University and Seoul National University (emeritus)

Harilal Madhavan is an economist, Director and Associate Professor at Centre for Studies in Population and Development, Department of Economics, CHRIST University (India)

Yurie Maeda is Lecturer in Business and IT at Technological University Dublin (Ireland)

Hasheem Mannan is Associate Professor in Health Systems at University College Dublin (Ireland)

Shigeru Masuyama is Professor at the Travelers Medical Center, Tokyo Medical University Hospital (Japan)

Makiko Matsuo is Project Associate Professor at the Graduate School of Public Policy, The University of Tokyo (Japan)

Matthieu Montalban is Associate Professor in economics at Université de Bordeaux, attached to Bordeaux School of Economics (France)

Etienne Nouguez is a sociologist and CNRS Researcher at the Center for the Sociology of Organizations (Sciences Po-CNRS, France)

Kazuko Obayashi is Professor in Healthcare Management at Nihon Fukushi University (Japan)

Diarmuid O'Shea is President of the Royal College of Physicians of Ireland (Ireland)

Hideaki Shiroyama is Professor of Public Administration at the Graduate School of Public Policy and the Graduate Schools for Law and Politics, The University of Tokyo (Japan)

Cornelia Storz is Professor of Innovation and Entrepreneurship at Goethe University Frankfurt (Germany)

Sayuri Suwa is Professor, Graduate School of Nursing at Chiba University (Japan)

Kayo Takuma is a Professor at the Faculty of Law, Keio University (Japan)

Mayuko Tsujimura is Professor, Department of Visiting Nursing at Shiga University of Medical Science (Japan)

Franziska Dorothea Velte works as Senior Assistant Manager at KPMG AG WPG, supporting the department Risk & Treasury with focus in Recovery & Resolution Planning (Germany)

Wenwei Yu is Professor, Center for Frontier Medical Engineering at Chiba University (Japan)

Akiyo Yumoto is Associate Professor at Kawasaki City College of Nursing (Japan)

List of Figures

Fig. 2.1	Health and education at the heart of the anthropogenetic development model	28
Fig. 2.2	The evolution of life expectancy 2019, 2020 and 2021. https://www.Nature.Com/articles/s41562-022-01450-3/figures/1	31
Fig. 2.3	Vaccination tends to reduce the fall in life expectancy. https://www.Nature.Com/articles/s41562-022-01450-3/figures/5. *Source* Schöley Jonas et al. (2022), pp. 1651 and 1655	32
Fig. 2.4	The recent evolutions since Covid in historical perspective. *Source* Elaborated by the author from OECD data	33
Fig. 2.5	The recent rise in preventive care spending. *Source* Elaborated by the author from OECD data	34
Fig. 2.6	The aging has become a central issue. *Source* Elaborated by the author from "United Nations, Department of Economic and Social Affairs, Population Division (2022). World Population Prospects 2022, Online Edition" data	35

Fig. 2.7 Towards a negative impact of productivity and thus growth. *Note* The vertical axis represents the annual average growth rate of GDP per capita in OECD countries for the 10-year period. The horizontal axis represents the old dependency ratio at the beginning of each period. *Source* Hyun-Hoon Lee, Kwanho Shin; Decomposing Effects of Population Aging on Economic Growth in OECD Countries. Asian Economic Papers 2021; 20 (3): 138–159. https://doi.org/10.1162/asep_a_00839 36
Fig. 2.8 The long-term evolution of publications. Shares of scientific publications by scientific field, 1840–2019. *Source* World Intellectual Property Report 2022: The Direction of Innovation, https://doi.org/10.34667/tind.45356 (figure 1.3 p. 23) 38
Fig. 2.9 The growth of patent applications for health care 2013–2022. *Source* Elaborated by the author from European Patent Office (EPO) data 38
Fig. 2.10 The growth of patent granted for health care 2013–2022. *Source* Elaborated by the author from European Patent Office (EPO) data 39
Fig. 2.11 Acquisitions by Gafam since their creation until 2020. *Source* Special recollection from public data by the authors (see technical appendix) 39
Fig. 2.12 Cumulative amount of main acquisitions in healthcare sectors, in millions of US$. *Source* Special recollection from public data by the authors (see technical appendix) 44
Fig. 2.13 The surprising decline of Venture capital and agreements after the Covid-19. *Source* SVB (2023), Healthcare Industry Trends—Mid-Year 2023, Update. https://www.svb.com/trends-insights/reports/healthcare-investments-and-exits 45
Fig. 2.14 EU, US, Japan: A common trend. *Source* Own elaboration 50
Fig. 2.15 The anthropogenetic sector is replacing manufacturing. *Source* Own elaboration (see technical appendix) 51
Fig. 2.16 1950–2022: The long-term rise of anthropogenetic logic (UE, US, Japan). *Source* Own elaboration (see technical appendix) 53
Fig. 2.17 The United States have reached the limit of the anthropogenetic mode of development. *Source* Own elaboration (see technical appendix) 54
Fig. 2.18 One century long transformation of the United States economy towards the anthropogenetic mode. *Source* Own elaboration (See technical appendix) 55

Fig. 2.19 The engines of US growth: from fordism to anthropogenetic mode via financialization. *Source* Own elaboration (see technical appendix) 56
Fig. 3.1 Trend in patent applications for the top five offices (in number of patent applications), 1883–2023. *Sources* authors; data: WIPO 75
Fig. 3.2 Slowdown of labor productivity gains in % in some OECD countries, 1971–2022. *Sources* authors; data: OECD 76
Fig. 3.3 Healthcare expenditures vs GDP 2019. *Sources* authors; data: OECD 80
Fig. 3.4 Life expectancy in France, Germany, Japan, South Korea and USA, 1855–2025. *Sources* authors; data: OurWorldindata 81
Fig. 3.5 Self-reported life satisfaction vs GDP per capita, 2022. *Sources* authors; data: OurWorldindata 82
Fig. 3.6 Government health expenditure as a share of GDP, 1880–2024. *Sources* authors; data: OurWorldindata 83
Fig. 3.7 Total health expenditures as percentage of GDP in OECD, 2023. *Sources* authors; data: OECD 84
Fig. 3.8 Percentage of aged people in some OECD countries, 1950–2022. *Sources* authors; data: OECD 85
Fig. 3.9 Fertility rate: Children per woman, 1960–2020. *Sources* authors; data: OECD 86
Fig. 3.10 Price index changes in consumer goods and services in the USA, 1997–2024. *Sources* authors; data: OurWorld in data 87
Fig. 3.11 The "Eroom law" or the declining trend of drug R&D efficiency, 1950–2023. *Sources* authors; data: Scannell et al. (2012), Schuhmacher et al. (2025), IQVIA (https://www.iqvia.com/insights/the-iqvia-institute/reports-and-publications/reports/global-trends-in-r-and-d-2025.) 94
Fig. 3.12 Projected global digital health market size in billions of USD, 2019–2025. *Sources* Authors, Data: Statista 100
Fig. 3.13 The Moore Law: Computations per second per computer over time, 1971–2021. *Sources* authors; data: OurWorld in data 101
Fig. 4.1 Changing structure of science, technology innovation governance in Japan. *Source* Authors 138
Fig. 4.2 Evolution of Korea's comprehensive plans: From pilot and ecosystem to hybrid model 148
Fig. 4.3 Average percentage of programs with at least one social performance indicator (2018–2022), by R&D program group. *Source* Translated from Figure 5–1 in Ki, et al. (2024b) 152

Fig. 4.4 Yearly Changes in the Percentage of Programs with at Least One Social Performance Indicator (2018–2022), by R&D Program Group. *Source* Translated from Figure 5–2 in Ki et al. (2024b) 152
Fig. 4.5 Changes in the Proportion of Five Performance Indicator Types (2018–2022) in the Social Problem-Solving R&D Program Group. *Source* Translated and Adapted from Figure 5–3 in Ki et al. (2024b) 153
Fig. 4.6 Average Share of Programs Including Each Outcome Type in Representative Performance (2018–2022), Social Problem-Solving R&D Group (Unit: Percentage (%)). *Source* Translated from Figure 5–4 in Ki, et al. (2024b) *Note* A program is counted as including an outcome type if at least one of its representative achievements corresponds to that type. For example, the 75.7% for social outcomes means that 75.7% of programs included at least one social achievement in their representative performance over the 2018–2022 period. Totals exceed 100% because multiple outcome types can be reported per program 154
Fig. 4.7 Yearly Share of Programs Including Each Outcome Type in Their Representative Performance (2018–2022), Social Problem-Solving R&D Group. *Source* Translated from Figure 5–5 in Ki et al. (2024b) *Note* A program is counted as including a given outcome type if at least one of its representative achievements submitted at midterm evaluation falls under that type. Since each program can present multiple representative achievements, the total across outcome types may exceed 100%. For example, in 2020, 80% for social outcomes means that 80% of social problem-solving programs included at least one social outcome among their representative performance results 155
Fig. 4.8 Mission 1 Roadmap: Enhancing Safety for Older Adults. *Source* OECD (2025, p. 25) 158
Fig. 4.9 Mission 2 Roadmap: Closing the Digital Divide for Older Adults. *Source* Translated and adapted from the figure on p. 55 in Joint Ministries (2023) 159
Fig. 5.1 Vaccine value chain. *Source* Own representation 178
Fig. 8.1 Robots mentioned in the interviews 291
Fig. 9.1 A bird-eye view on Society 5.0. *Source* Cabinet office 324
Fig. 9.2 Health related-issues in Society 5.0. *Source* Cabinet office 326
Fig. 9.3 Moonshot goal 7. *Source* AMED 330

List of Tables

Table 2.1	How ecological crises generate illnesses and affect health	41
Table 2.2	How GAFAM enter healthcare 2010–2020	45
Table 4.1	SIP Program 1st phase (2014 ~ 2018)	125
Table 4.2	SIP Program 2nd phase (2019 ~ 2022)	128
Table 4.3	SIP Program 3rd phase (2023 ~)	132
Table 4.4	Evolution of governance approaches across Korea's comprehensive plans (2013–2027)	147
Table 5.1	Vaccine safety and efficacy of common COVID-19 vaccines	177
Table 5.2	Time-to-market of common COVID-19 vaccines	181
Table 5.3	Availability of common COVID-19 vaccines	182
Table 5.4	Summary of the cases	201
Table 7.1	Innovations, stakeholders and frugal components	266
Table 8.1	Profiles of three jurisdictions	288
Table 8.2	Background data of the interviewees	290
Table 8.3	Key stakeholders mentioned in the interviews	293
Table 8.4	Facilitating factors for the diffusion of care robots	300
Table 8.5	Hindering factors for the diffusion of care robots	302
Table 9.1	The innovcare grid	337
Table 9.2	The innovcare grid—applied to the analysis of Potaro	345
Table 9.3a	The innovcare grid—an alternative version and an application to the analysis of HomeAssist	349
Table 9.3b	Care-led Innovation Analysis (CLIA)	352

CHAPTER 1

Capitalism, Innovations, and Health After Covid-19. An Asian Perspective: An Introduction

Sébastien Lechevalier, Jean-Paul Gaudillière, Kathryn Ibata-Arens, and Kayo Takuma

Abstract In this introductory chapter, we present the focus of the book, which is twofold. On the one hand, we revisit the Covid-19 crisis, as it reveals two underlying crises of the innovation and capitalist systems, in relation

We are extremely grateful to two anonymous referees and to Matthieu Montalban for their useful critical comments.

S. Lechevalier (✉)
Ecole des Hautes Etudes en Sciences Sociales (EHESS), Paris, France;
German Institute for Japanese Studies (DIJ), Tokyo, Japan
e-mail: sebastien.lechevalier@ehess.fr

J.-P. Gaudillière
Inserm & EHESS, Paris, France

K. Ibata-Arens
DePaul University, IL, Chicago, USA

K. Takuma
Keio University, Tokyo, Japan

S. Lechevalier et al. (eds.), *Capitalism, Innovations, and Health after Covid-19*,
https://doi.org/10.1007/978-3-032-24479-6_1

with health. This is why this book offers an interdisciplinary exploration of the intertwined crises of innovation and capitalism exposed by the Covid-19 pandemic. We interpret it not merely as a health emergency but as a revealing rupture in the dominant models of technological innovation and capitalist accumulation, particularly in health systems. On the other hand, we propose in-depth case studies of healthcare innovations in Asia that are often successful yet contrast markedly in how actors employ market and non-market mechanisms to create healthcare solutions. These cases vary, from studies of how community based intellectual property rights develop surrounding traditional medicines, to alternative national regulatory regimes to encourage the promotion of generic medicines, to detailed studies of how the Japanese healthcare system has embraced robots as a partial solution to its demographic challenges in the area of geriatric care. These and other case studies in the book synergize to promote the following general message: alternative innovation systems surrounding healthcare are disruptive but viable. As a whole, this book is framed as a critique of the healthcare innovation system that dominates the US and, in parts, Europe. This system focuses heavily on market-based innovation driven by strong intellectual property rights, an ecosystem supporting healthcare entrepreneurship, healthcare provision containing strong market elements as means of access, and strong commitments to the use of biomolecular pharmaceutical products rather than the organization of care as a human-based service. By contrast to previous works, we propose here to foster new thinking about the future of innovation and health needs.

1.1 Introduction

On February 11th, 2021 the *New York Times* featured a long article on what it labeled the "newest diplomatic currency: Covid-19 vaccines" insisting on the strategic uses of vaccines purchases and, donations by countries, which were not among the usual global health players, from China to the UAE, while in parallel the US, Britain, and EU countries had cleared the shelves reserving doses of the most innovative vaccines that far outnumbered their populations. Vaccine innovation was then quickly replacing the 2020 debates about the feasibility, utility, and adverse consequences of the public health measures aiming at controlling the spread of Covid-19 by reducing contacts between people. The design and development by Pfizer and Moderna of highly original mRNA vaccines, as well as that of half a dozen of more conventional vaccines in Britain, China,

Brazil or India in less than a year was indeed a spectacular achievement that deeply changed the responses to the pandemic.

In 2001 however, public discussions, which had not yet the benefits of insight, insisted on the problems facing a paradigmatic case of paralleled biomedical innovations. Two registers of inadaptations between vaccines as market-oriented technological products and the health needs of many people were then on the agenda. The most visible one was no surprise to economists and public health observers. It regarded issues of access and inequalities resulting from intellectual property rights and their consequences on prices with ensuing calls for similar interventions as those, which—after 2000—had permitted the production of generic versions of anti-HIV drugs and their circulation in the global South, namely open-license, technology transfers and public purchase. Much less expected—and rarely discussed within the innovation literature—were however questions about the quick disinvestment of public health and social interventions like the testing, tracing, isolating infrastructures many countries had put in place in 2020 and what may be called a "pharmaceuticalization" of Covid-19 control with the risk of placing all our eggs in the same basket and of further reducing the role of care and social interventions in the search for innovative policies.

Pharmaceuticalization is a social science more than a public health category. It has first emerged in the social studies of health and medicine as an analogue to the concept of medicalization (Conrad & Schneider, 1992) in order to analyze the processes through which the consumption of drugs and industrial medical products has become, in Europe and North America, the preferred if not the unique way biomedicine contributes to the prevention and the treatment of health disorders. In the literature on health in the global North, pharmaceuticalization has therefore often been associated with studies of drugs' markets and political economy with peculiar interests in the role of multinational pharmaceutical compagnies. These major players in the growth of drug uses dominate research and development, define indications and actively promote their products to prescribers and health practitioners. For example, it has been argued that the generalization of preventive drug consumption to control symptoms like hypercholesterolemia, osteoporosis, or overweight in order to reduce the risks of serious chronic disorders, is an epistemic and cultural change that would not have happened if industrial capitalism had not deeply transformed pharmacy in the twentieth century. In contrast, the pharmaceuticalization of care in the global South has marginally been associated with the prevention and the treatment of chronic disorders even if—as the Global Burden of Disease metrics as repeatedly shown since the late 1990s—non-communicable diseases (NCDs) are the first cause of mortality and morbidity in a majority of low-and-middle-income countries Gaudilliere & Chabrol (2026). When applied to the global South, the pharmaceuticalization of care and public health focuses on infectious diseases. Global health actors have indeed nurtured this pattern through their massive investments in drug access programs as appropriate responses to needs unmet because of processes that are in the first place understood as market failures.

Covid-19 started to redistribute these cards as the debates about the various registers of responses to the pandemic pointed the urgency of building new bridges between innovation regimes, health practices, and population needs.

Although times have changed and the SARS-Cov-2 virus seems forgotten by all except the experts of emerging diseases and pandemic preparedness, this is the challenge our collective book seeks to address. *Capitalism, innovations, and health after Covid-19. An Asian perspective* is framed as a critique of the healthcare innovation system that dominates the US and, in parts, Europe. This system focuses heavily on market-based innovation driven by strong intellectual property rights, an ecosystem supporting healthcare entrepreneurship, healthcare provision containing strong market elements as means of access, and strong commitments to the use of biomolecular pharmaceutical products rather than the organization of care as a human-based service. While in our past work, we have criticized this system for many reasons, including its consequences in terms of high costs (relative to the benefits, i.e. the quality of healthcare provision) and strong inequalities in healthcare outcomes, we propose here to foster new thinking about the future of innovation and health needs through two moves. The first one is to take into account the pharmaceuticalization challenge or—better said—the forms of care that the dominant model of innovation favors. The second displacement we propose is to nurture the critique with a positive contribution to research on healthcare innovation through presenting empirical research from Asia on alternative trajectories by which organizations, groups, and governments can create meaningful healthcare innovations. Major countries in Asia—from South Korea and Japan to Vietnam and specific regions of India—have indeed better fared during the early stages of the Covid-19 pandemic than wealthy European and

North American countries, starting with the United States; at least when basic health indicators like mortality are concerned. We build on the hypothesis that such unexpected contrast is the result of history and previous investments in public health and care-oriented forms of innovations the book investigates. In doing so, we do not focus strictly on health systems, care and innovation but incorporate also some analyses of the underlying innovation systems and the capitalistic political economy they are inserted in, given the interactions between them.

Our focus is therefore twofold. On the one hand, we revisit the Covid-19 crisis, as it reveals two underlying crises of the innovation and capitalist systems, in relation with health. This is why this book offers an interdisciplinary exploration of the intertwined crises of innovation and capitalism exposed by the Covid-19 pandemic. We interpret it not merely as a health emergency but as a revealing rupture in the dominant models of technological innovation and capitalist accumulation, particularly in health systems.

On the other hand, we propose in-depth case studies of healthcare innovations in Asia that are often successful yet contrast markedly in how actors employ market and non-market mechanisms to create healthcare solutions. These cases vary, from studies of how community based intellectual property rights develop surrounding traditional medicines, to alternative national regulatory regimes to encourage the promotion of generic medicines, to detailed studies of how the Japanese healthcare system has embraced robots as a partial solution to its demographic challenges in the area of geriatric care. These and other case studies in the book synergize to promote the following general message: alternative innovation systems surrounding healthcare are disruptive but viable.

1.2 How to Make Sense of the Covid-19 Pandemic and Its Challenges of the Dominant Model?

Our main contention is that the pandemic, understood as a "critical moment" (Koselleck 2006), has exposed decisive issues regarding the future of our societies. Underlying the pandemic path and the heterogeneous responses to it, is a dual crisis in innovation as breakdown in the introduction and collective utility of the new, and in capitalism as an arbiter of societal needs. The two crises are intertwined, and interrogating these connections is a theme of this book although not its most original one. To enrich the existing literature on innovation systems, their capitalistic framing and bearing on health, we further propose that focusing our lens on Asia provides powerful lessons about alternative pathways—and as a result tangible evidence-based hopes for a better way forward. This is particularly the case for the relationship between the current economic regime of accumulation and growth, the changing needs of the people, and the organization of innovation within health systems.

The Covid-19 crisis is indeed a major source of discontinuities that should force us to rethink some basic concepts related to the organization of our societies. It is in fact a multi-faceted crisis with economic, political, and sociological dimensions. The fact that the Covid-19 crisis is not simply a medical crisis has of course not been missed by scholars in the social sciences and some of the authors of the book have contributed to its understanding (Boyer, 2020; Gaudillière et al., 2021; Ibata-Arens, 2021). Thus, it should lead us to look for a research agenda that seeks to reconsider the dynamics of innovation, and of capitalism, placing health at the center.

Viewed from a comparative and international perspective, one of the most striking features from the Covid-19 crisis in addition with, and connected to, the pharmaceuticalization of health policies mentioned above, is the existence of pervading discrepancies between, on the one hand, the principles, targets and tools visible in crisis management and, on the other hand, those fostered by global health for more than thirty years, as Beaudevin et al. (2020) suggest.

More precisely, five dimensions of the dual crises are in this respect of great importance and must be kept in mind: (a) the unexpected geo-epidemiology of the disease with a high burden of mortality and morbidity in Europe and North America, which—as already mentioned—contrasted the less severe situation in many Asian countries, especially during the period 2020–2021, challenging the assumption that expertise and resources are in the global North while pressing health needs and risks are in the global South; (b) the visibility and importance of social innovation since—in the absence of vaccines and specific medications the initial responses relied on public health measure of lockdown, isolation and case tracing to reduce transmission; (c) the return of pressing issues of service organization since the bottlenecks in many countries have not been not so much related to technology but rather to the most basic dimension of clinical work: the ability of hospitals and health centers to welcome patients, to care and to cure them. What is missing is not high-tech, but human resources and physical spaces that have been reduced for many years by public policies whose major aims were to curb costs and reduce budgets; (d) the unexpected and adverse consequences of the massive delocalization of industrial production in favor of Asian countries in times of strong competition for the provision of health products; (e) serious political divisions have been greatly reflected in the response to the pandemic, forcing changes and institutional innovation into existing forms of international cooperation.

Based on this assessment of the Covid-19 moment, the major originality of the present book is to approach the pandemic multiple dimensions from the two major underlying crises—of innovation systems and of capitalism. To this effect the book mobilizes and connects two research strands that have heretofore too often been developed separately: firstly, the Science and Technology Studies (STS) and social science studies of innovation and health systems already mentioned for their contribution to our understanding of competing forms of care or global health governance; secondly, the French regulation theory as framework to analyze the diversity of capitalistic regimes of accumulation and their crisis. The latter proposes at the same time a theory of crises, an integrated analysis of capitalisms and innovation systems in their diversity, and has shown its ability to contribute to a better understanding of institutional change of Asian socio-economic systems (Amable, 2003; Boyer, 2005; Lechevalier, 2014; Storz et al., 2013).

1.3 Crisis of the Innovation Model

The first crisis we need to explore is related to the innovation model, and its analysis should lead to revisiting some of the fundamental relationship between innovation, technology and society. Here, our premise is the recognition of the paradoxes of innovation in troubled times (Lechevalier, 2019). For more than a half century now, innovation—mainly derived from technological advances—has been considered a driving force of economic and societal development and ultimately, prosperity. In fact, there are plenty of examples that support this view including the very fast elaboration and—in spite of all inequalities—provision of vaccines against COVID-19 through the mobilization of major private actors and governments.

However, as mentioned above in relations with the pandemic, during the last decades, which can be considered as the so-called Golden Age of innovation, there have been mounting doubts about the consequences of the conjunction between the dominant model of liberal capitalism and what may be considered as a hegemonic model of innovation, which we label Neo-Schumpeterian.[1] Both favor forced obsolescence and the design of new industrial products, the extraction of ever more material resources, technological development, and market-based mechanisms to link the systems of innovation and social needs.

While this crisis of innovation is general, it is particularly visible in the health sector, whose significance has been rediscovered in the context of the global pandemic. Our claim here is that major problems have been identified in relations with the importance of care and service relationship to access and quality of care, starting with the ways in which the innovation system has favored the pharmaceuticalization of health interventions while disinvesting the strengthening of health systems and the social dimensions of care.[2] This general pattern has resulted in paradoxes, adverse effects, and failures well-known to the social studies of health and medicine. For instance:

[1] In the context of this book, in using the concept of "Neo-Schumpeterian", we do not refer to a specific school of economic thought but rather to any economic thinking that put technological innovation at the center of economic dynamics, while referring to Joseph Schumpeter. Moreover, the concept of pharmaceuticalization and 'neo-schumpeterian' model of innovation are not equivalent, although they are connected. In the same way, in our view, the level of innovation systems and level of capitalism should be jointly considered by distinctively analyzed. See glossary, as well as Chaps. 2, 3, 9 and 11 for a more precise discussion.

[2] In what follows, it is important to distinguish the system of (healthcare) innovation and what is a healthcare (services provision) system. The first one can be defined as the set of institutions (e.g. research, education, financial system ...) that promote and constrain innovation in the field of healthcare. According to the World health organization (WHO), a healthcare system is an organized network of people, institutions, and resources that work together to deliver health services—including prevention, treatment, and rehabilitation—to meet the health needs of a target population. It integrates components like hospitals, clinics, providers, and financing mechanisms to improve health, promote wellness, and ensure efficient, quality care. In short, the healthcare innovation system is only a part of the healthcare system. This distinction is important to understand that we do not deny the importance of innovations for healthcare. The dominant innovation system (in general and in healthcare in particular) has certainly been efficient for producing many technological innovations. However, we question its ability to answer to the needs of patients in terms of providing and performing treatment for example, especially by comparison with alternative models of frugal or care-led innovations.

- Gaps between the increasing resources dedicated to innovation and decreasing well-being observed in many cases, which illustrate the adverse effects of scaling up and mass consumption (e.g., generalized antimicrobial resistance, spread of nosocomial contaminations in hospitals, inability of global health actors at investing in the prevention and care of chronic disorders);
- Adverse consequences with innovations contributing to rising inequalities through different dimensions including lack of access to services, high out of pocket spending, dissatisfied health personnel or inappropriate technologies (e.g., imposed in the global South);
- Scandals arising from the conjunction between the dynamics of market valorization and the weaknesses of regulation (e.g., conflicts of interests in pharmaceutical industries, lack of investments in "neglected diseases", undone science);
- Rising environmental costs originating in the operations of health systems with their too often non-sustainable use of resources (e.g., fossil fuels, single use plastic and electronic wastes, exhaustion of medicinal plants).

1.4 Crisis of Capitalism

The second crisis is the one of capitalism. During the pandemic, highly effective vaccines were developed as a product of the capitalist economy, greatly helping our fight against the pandemic. On the other hand, developed and developing countries have been at odds over the issue of vaccine patents, creating disparities in access to vaccines. In this way, the pandemic has been overcome in part thanks to the benefits of capitalism, but at the same time, it has brought to light the problems of the same capitalism.

This crisis is fundamentally a productivity crisis, which has not been overcome by innovation (Gorry & Montalban, 2026). What is true for the capitalist system in general is even truer for the health sector, and this is not anecdotal in the context of the long unnoticed emergence of a new mode of development, which is structured in part by the centrality of the health sector, and which is labelled as the "anthropogenetic" mode of development. (Boyer & Boylaud, 2026).[3] From our theoretical

[3] The concept of "anthropogenetic", which literally describes the production *of* men/women *by* men/women (through healthcare, education, culture), is used to characterize a mode of development that is contrasting with the Fordist one, marked by the development of manufacturing production (production of goods by men/women). See also the glossary.

perspective, which is inspired by the French Regulation school, crises are key periods which deepen the destabilization of previous regulation modes and foster the emergence of new ones, as it was the case in the 1970s–1980s, with the crisis of the so-called "Fordist" regulation mode (Boyer, 2005).

Although all the authors of this book do not mobilize the theoretical framework of the French Regulation school, we consider it is a useful and powerful conceptual approach. Our purpose here is not to enter into the details of the theory but to highlight some of its elements that are relevant for the issues we consider in this book. Regulation theory (RT) is a comparative and historical approach to the diversity and transformation of capitalisms that has at least three characteristics that are worth of interest in the context of this book.

The first one is that RT analyzes capitalism not as a stable system, but as changing historical forms, alternating between periods of growth (accumulation regimes) and structural crises. It is in this sense that it is a theory of crises. According to RT, every economy has its own structural crisis, which highlights the variety of forms that crises can take. Furthermore, the Marxist origins of RT lead it to emphasize that in economies dominated by the capitalist logic of profit and accumulation, crises are a recurring phenomenon and undermine the illusion of economic (natural and automatic) regulation maintained by many mainstream economists.

The second major contribution of RT that informs this book is the conception of capitalism as a succession of changing historical forms. Thus, after having analyzed the dominant form of postwar capitalism, namely Fordism, at the time of its entry into crisis in the late 1960s and early 1970s, RT identified a particularly influential form among the many forms that succeeded it, namely financialized capitalism, while pointing to its fundamental instability, later revealed by a remarkable succession of financial crises (Boyer, 2000). Since then, several stylized facts seem to point to the emergence of a new form of capitalism, namely the anthropogenetic mode of development (Boyer & Boylaud, 2026),[4] at the very moment when capitalism was entering a novel kind of crisis, as revealed by the Covid-19 pandemic.

[4] It is worth mentioning here that some other RT researchers have also emphasized the emergence of digital platforms capitalism (Montalban et al., 2019). It is distinct from the anthropogenetic mode of development but not without any relation as Big Tech companies are also investing a lot in health industries.

The third finding of RT relevant to our book is the recognition of the diversity of capitalism at each stage of its transformation. Admittedly, this recognition is far from being the preserve of RT, as evidenced by the success of the Varieties of Capitalism (VoC) approach (Hall & Soskice, 2001) insofar as it relates to the analysis of Asian forms of capitalism in contrast to the European or Anglo-Saxon ones (Amable, 2003). In line with the discussion on the developmentalist state model, RT has sought to explain the growth and development performance of East Asian capitalism through a number of historical institutional constructs, including state involvement in the promotion of capital formation, the use of industrial policy to allocate capital and support nascent industries, and cooperation between the bureaucracy and the private sector, while emphasizing the internal diversity of these Asian capitalist systems (Boyer et al., 2012).

More recently, the challenge for RT (as for other institutionalist approaches) has been to rethink Asian capitalism beyond the paradigms of growth and the developmental state, with the emergence of a model focused on well-being in a post-development context. This is one of the motivations for exploring the Asian experience in this book. However, an often-overlooked characteristic of Asian capitalism concerns the transformation of their social protection systems according to a logic that differs from what has been and is observed in Europe (Storz et al., 2013). Our hypothesis is that social protection is at the heart of institutional change in East Asia, in a context of redefinition of the social compromise, but also in a context of unprecedented pressures on this system due to demographic transition and epidemiological transition (see Lechevalier & Monfort, 2025, for the case of Japan).

In short, considering both the capitalist system and innovation model, our view is that the pandemic as a moment of crisis has revealed the central position of health in our economies. Our perspective in confronting the post-Covid situation and the anthropogenetic hypothesis is to advance a joint analysis of innovation systems and forms of capitalism in crisis. This will reveal a fundamental diversity of models, while making visible the fissures in its façade, exposing underlying weaknesses, but also openings for transformative change. Within this diversity, Asian capitalisms are of particular interest.

1.5 An Asian Perspective

The Asian perspective we have adopted provides a remarkable test-case for the anthropogenetic hypothesis, showing at the same time its validity with the critical importance of health investments and care-led innovation practices, and its limitations with the highly contrasted roles markets and private accumulation play for highly heterogeneous systems, or with the immense difficulty at facing the challenges of the Anthropocene and the unaccounted costs of growth. The anthropogenetic hypothesis therefore comes in the book just as possible pattern and framework, certainly not as a determined and inevitable path. Its importance as a possible alternative lies in the priority granted to human capabilities, social relationships and the provision of services to persons as targets of innovation and investments in parallel with a redefined production of industrial goods. Such anthropogenetic features were visible during the Covid-19 crisis in Asia. The book takes in the idea that their roots lie in three different socio-historical temporalities: (a) the legacy of the twentieth century social states and their public-health oriented management of populations; (b) the health transitions of the second half of the twentieth century and their contemporary consequences in terms of changing health needs, which are powerfully illustrated by the massive burden of chronic diseases and the challenges of quickly aging societies; (c) the legacy of recent experiences in the control of epidemics (SARS-CoV1, MERS …) and the articulation of social and technological innovations.

On that basis, our main question can be summarized as follows: how do contemporary initiatives in Asia to satisfy health and social needs, in responses to crises, challenge the dominant transatlantic models of innovation and capitalism, and in which ways?

1.6 Why Focus on Experiences of Innovations Beyond Technology?

The book explores what we consider to be experiences of innovation in the health sector, which are really existing configurations of actions trying to meet recognized health needs and linking knowledge, markets, and care, in ways alternative to the technology and start-up centered model of capital risk investments, or to the reductionist and linear pipeline model of drug research and marketing pharmaceutical capitalism (Gaudillière et al., 2021; Gorry & Montalban, 2026) has favored.

In this context, experience does not mean a systematic, coherent and full-blown example of successful health problem-solving, but instead reveals a possible path to respond to basic needs and poorly answered health issues, a trajectory of action, teaching lessons with their contradictions, achievements and limitations. The experiences we have selected are therefore, in the first place, *trials* of innovation *beyond technology* (Lechevalier, 2019), for which—the book shows—various categories and concepts have recently been forged and used: organizational innovation, appropriate technologies, frugal innovation, care-led innovation, and the commons. Experience thus means incomplete or partly successful processes whose interest lies in their heuristic value. It means that they are not necessarily supported by alternative *theories* of innovation (Goding et al., 2021). Since there is no "magic bullet" or "one size fits all" solution for alternative innovation, diversity is an asset, revealing differences in the problems selected and the tools mobilized. These provide for complementarities, and thus will open the door to a "systemic" discussion of alternatives to the dominant, pharmaceuticalized, model of health innovation.

The first category emerging from the cases the book investigates is—unsurprisingly—that of *organizational innovation*, eventually labeled institutional innovation. Government bodies and social institutions have indeed been central in the approach of capitalism the regulation theory has developed. Organizational innovation thus appears as direct response to the limitations of market-oriented mechanisms, as expression of the political will to put in place policies targeting less economic performance, which is for instance central when performance is defined through costs-benefits analysis or cost-effectiveness analysis, than health needs as expressed through institutions and political representation.

The importance of institutional or political prioritization (Gaudilliere et al., 2022) is evidently in resonance with the idea of *the commons* as basis for socially more adequate organization of research, production, and use of health goods and services. The commons however bring in much stronger emphasis on the issue of more or less democratic decision-making processes involved when choosing priorities and programs. After all, in the now classical scheme proposed by Ostrom (1990), the commons are the result of a community setting the rules and boundaries of an appropriate (re)production and use of resources or services.

The last categories for innovation beyond technology identified and discussed in the book are those most directly addressing the definition of health needs and the mismatch between these and the dominant innovation model. The notion of ***care-led innovation*** places center-stage the fact that health is a social and relational property, not a simple material fact. Health systems—and therefore innovation within them—of course imply the use and the provision of material goods, but these can only perform as part of a service relationship, which is a personal one based on human work and interactions between people. This is the very basic meaning of care in healthcare before the wording became synonymous of medical treatment. Care-led innovation therefore points to ways of thinking about innovation that prioritize the conditions through which care interactions meet new health needs, for instance those of aging populations, or the massive burden of chronic disorders.

Finally, ***frugal innovation***, the category most discussed in the global South and a kind of reinvention of the idea of (socially) appropriate technology, which was high in currency among development experts before the 1990s, captures many of the above as it resonates with low cost or affordable, with technological simplicity, with adaptation to local needs and means. Moreover, in a context where health, and more generally production systems are confronted with the consequences of multiple ecological crises (climate, biodiversity, mass-pollution) frugality has acquired a new layer of meaning, becoming a synonymous of, or a criteria for, sustainability.

1.7 Structure of the Book

In order to answer our core question about the uniquely Asian challenges to the innovation and capitalism status quo, we have gathered a group of diverse scholars who have collaborated for three years to discuss our Asian perspective on capitalism, innovation and health. The structure of the resulting book includes three parts:

1. *Systems in crisis? Capitalism, innovation and health.*

The first part is a general and more systemic one aimed at complementing the introduction by specifying the nature of the two crises we have identified. The Chapter 2 (Boyer & Boylaud, 2026) introduces some major theoretical insights from the French Regulation theory in illuminating the crisis of capitalism, the specificity of Asian countries, and the validity of the anthropogenetic hypothesis in a post-Covid world. The Chapter 3 (Gorry & Montalban, 2026), which is inspired by the theoretical framework of Chapter 2, focuses on the crisis of innovation, taking the case of the pharmaceutical sector as a paradigmatic situation and insisting on the articulation between the epistemic, economical and institutional dimensions of contemporary tensions. Chapter 4 (Shiroyama et al., 2026) proposes a comparative exploration of the ways in which science, technology, and innovation systems in Japan and South Korea have sought to integrate social issues in their official targets in order to respond to these crises. This is also a transition to part 2 of the book.

2. *A critical moment and its openings: Covid responses.*

The second part gathers chapters on the Covid-19 pandemic taken as a field site and reservoir of interventions addressing health needs in a more social and integrated way than the conventional policies of access to drugs and devices. Chapter 5 (Storz et al., 2026) thus looks at the question of vaccine R&D from an institutional perspective, reminding us that organizational features and managerial capabilities have played a key role in the diversity of vaccines discovered and applied. Chapter 6 (Kuo & Takuma, 2026) follows by examining organizational innovations at a different scale, namely that of global health governance. Although the crisis has seriously challenged the preparedness and biosecurity paradigm advocated by key actors like WHO, the World Bank, UNAIDS, the Global Fund, and private foundations like the Gates it has also revealed strong adaptation based on local initiatives relayed by regional health diplomacy. Chapter 7 (Madhavan & Gaudillière, 2026) follows developments in the South India state of Kerala during the Covid-19 crisis to argue for the practical and theoretical importance of frugal innovation for the ability of low and middle-income countries to foster a culture of innovation that meets basic health needs through state intervention, community participation, and medical pluralism.

3. *Knowledge in action: Asian experiences.*

The third part approaches Asian experiments in innovation beyond technology from a more general perspective since it interrogates the relationship between forms of knowledge, sociotechnical systems, and the specificity of services based upon and targeting corporal bodies and social interactions, following of the key insights from the Regulation theory, according to which each socio-economic system has the crisis of its structure. Chapter 8 (Kodate et al., 2026) follow the mobilization of robots for the care of the elderly in countries—first of all Japan—where the anthropogenetic model has strong relevance. Chapter 9 (Lechevalier, 2026) thus proposes the notion of care-led innovation as an alternative to the idea that robots and digital machines will *per se* provide for the needs of aging societies.

The last two chapters bring in experiences aiming at the advancement and mobilization of local medical knowledge in health and innovation systems, which prioritize basic care. Chapter 10 (Gaudillière & Madhavan, 2026) follows the industrialization of Ayurveda, one of the Indian systems of medicine, and its plant-based therapies as a powerful legacy of twentieth century debates on appropriate technology laden with both promises and limitations. Chapter 11 (Ibata-Arens et al., 2026) investigates policies of access to curative therapies challenging the dominant intellectual property regime of pharmacy following the massive but unequal developments of markets for generics on the hand, plant-based neo-traditional remedies on the other hand, showing that one limitation of such experiences is that they reflect the creation of public rather than common goods.

References

Amable, B. (2003). *The diversity of modern capitalism*. Oxford University Press.

Beaudevin, C., Gaudillière, J. P., Gradmann, C., Lovell, A. M., & Pordié, L. (2020). Global health and the new world order: Introduction. In *Global health and the new world order* (pp. 1–28). Manchester University Press.

Boyer, R. (2000). Is a finance-led growth regime a viable alternative to Fordism? A preliminary analysis. *Economy and Society*, *29*(1), 111–145.

Boyer, R. (2005). How and why capitalisms differ. *Economy and Society*, *34*(4), 509–557.

Boyer, R., Uemura, H., & Isogai, A. (Eds.) (2012). *Diversity and transformations of Asian capitalisms* (Vol. 96). Routledge.

Boyer, R. (2020). *Les capitalismes à l'épreuve de la pandémie*. La Découverte.

Boyer, R., & Boylaud, O. (2026). Anthropogenetic development: Long unnoticed and already in crisis. In S. Lechevalier, J.-P. Gaudillière, K. Ibata-Arens, &

K. Takuma (Eds.), *Capitalism, innovations, and health after Covid-19. An Asian perspective*. Palgrave MacMillan.

Conrad, P., & Schneider, J. W. (1992). *Deviance and medicalization: From badness to sickness*. Temple University Press.

Gaudillière, J. P., Izambert, C., & Juven, P. A. (2021). *Pandémopolitique: Réinventer la santé en commun*. La Découverte.

Gaudilliere, J.-P., McDowell, A., Lang, C., & Beaudevin, C. (2022). *Global health for all: Knowledge, politics, and practices*. Rutgers University Press.

Gaudillière, J.-P., & Madhavan, H. (2026). Appropriate technologies, primary health care and the integration of traditional medicines in India. In S. Lechevalier, J.-P. Gaudillière, K. Ibata-Arens, & K. Takuma (Eds.), *Capitalism, innovations, and health after Covid-19: An Asian perspective*. Palgrave MacMillan.

Gaudilliere, J.-P., & Chabrol, F. (2026b). Pharmaceuticals from and for the Global: South. In D. G. Conor, S. Kleinhout-Vliek, T. Martin, & P. W. S (Eds.), *Handbook of global pharmaceuticals, biotechnology, and society studies*. Edward Eldgar Publishing.

Godin, B., Gaglio, G., & Vinck, D. (2021). *Handbook on alternative theories of innovation*. Edward Elgar Publishing.

Gorry, P., & Montalban, M. (2026). The crisis of capitalism and health innovation: Symptoms of a crisis or of success? In S. Lechevalier, J.-P. Gaudillière, K. Ibata-Arens, & K. Takuma (Eds.), *Capitalism, innovations, and health after Covid-19: An Asian perspective*. Palgrave MacMillan.

Hall, P. A., & Soskice, D., (Eds.). (2001). *Varieties of capitalism: The institutional foundations of comparative advantage*. Oxford University Press.

Ibata-Arens, K. C. (2021). *Pandemic medicine: Why the global innovation system is broken, and how we can fix it*. Lynne Rienner Publishers.

Ibata Arens, K., Gaudillière, J.-P., Madhavan, H., & Nouguez, E. (2026). Commons and the political economy of access: Generics, neo traditional formulations and the dominant intellectual property regime of medicines. In S. Lechevalier, J.-P. Gaudillière, K. Ibata-Arens, & K. Takuma (Eds.), *Capitalism, innovations, and health after Covid-19: An Asian perspective*. Palgrave MacMillan.

Kodate, N., Cheung, M. C., Yumoto, A., Donnelly, S., Maeda, Y., Tsujimura, M., Mannan, H., Wenwei, Y., Suwa, S., Obayashi, K., Masuyama, S., Chan, W. C. H., Hauray, B., & O'Shea, D. (2026). Institutional design, welfare technologies and diffusion of innovation: Stakeholders' views regarding care robots in Hong Kong SAR (China), Ireland and Japan. In S. Lechevalier, J.-P. Gaudillière, K. Ibata-Arens, & K. Takuma (Eds.), *Capitalism, innovations, and health after Covid-19: An Asian perspective*. Palgrave MacMillan.

Kosselleck, R., & Richter, W. (2006). Crisis. *Journal of the History of Ideas*, *67*(2), 357–400.

Kuo, W., & Takuma, K. (2026). Glocal health governance: Organizational innovations in the Era of Covid-19. In S. Lechevalier, J.-P. Gaudillière, K. Ibata-Arens, & K. Takuma (Eds.), *Capitalism, innovations, and health after Covid-19: An Asian perspective*. Palgrave MacMillan.

Lechevalier, S. (2026). Care-led innovation. A new paradigm and an application in the Japanese context of Society 5.0. In S. Lechevalier, J.-P. Gaudillière, K. Ibata-Arens, & K. Takuma (Eds.), *Capitalism, innovations, and health after Covid-19: An Asian perspective*. Palgrave MacMillan.

Lechevalier, S. (Ed.). (2019). *Innovation beyond technology: Science for society and interdisciplinary*. Springer.

Lechevalier, S. (Ed.). (2014). *The great transformation of Japanese capitalism*. Routledge.

Lechevalier, S., & Monfort, B. (2025). Japan at the forefront of the economics of aging? A bibliometric analysis. *The Journal of the Economics of Ageing, 100601*.

Madhavan, H., & Gaudilliere, J.-P. (2026). Frugal innovations and health system resilience: The conceptualization, policy support and forms of frugality during Covid-19 in South India. In S. Lechevalier, J.-P. Gaudillière, K. Ibata-Arens, & K. Takuma (Eds.), *Capitalism, innovations, and health after Covid-19: An Asian perspective*. Palgrave MacMillan.

Montalban, M., Frigant, V., & Jullien, B. (2019). Platform economy as a new form of capitalism: A Régulationist research programme. *Cambridge Journal of Economics, 43*(4), 805–824.

Ostrom, E. (1990). *Governing the commons: The evolution of institutions for collective action*. Cambridge University Press.

Shiroyama, H., Ki, J., Matsuo, M., & Kim, H. (2026). The mission oriented science, innovation and technology (STI) policies in Japan and Korea with a focus on health. In S. Lechevalier, J.-P. Gaudillière, K. Ibata-Arens, & K. Takuma (Eds.), *Capitalism, innovations, and health after Covid-19: An Asian perspective*. Palgrave MacMillan.

Storz, C., Amable, B., Casper, S., & Lechevalier, S. (2013). Bringing Asia into the comparative capitalism perspective. *Socio-Economic Review, 11*(2), 217–232.

Storz, C., Lee, K., Kuo, W., & F. Velte. (2026). Covid-19 and successful vaccine development: Comparative lessons for innovation and policy from East Asia and Europe. In S. Lechevalier, J.-P. Gaudillière, K. Ibata-Arens, & K. Takuma (Eds.), *Capitalism, innovations, and health after Covid-19: An Asian perspective*. Palgrave MacMillan.

PART I

Systems in Crisis? Capitalism, Innovation, and Health

CHAPTER 2

Anthropogenetic Development: Long Unnoticed and Already in Crisis

Robert Boyer and Olivier Boylaud

Abstract Development is conceptualized as the result of the interaction between two processes: on the one hand, training through education, the extension of life expectancy through health, and culture, which socializes individuals; on the other hand, the creation of value, which enables the financing of public goods such as education, health, and culture. The complementarity and synergy between these processes defines a mode of anthropogenic development, in the sense of human creation through work. This mode has quietly asserted itself in contemporary societies as the mode based on mass production and consumption has weakened, even beyond the power of financialization. It takes three contrasting forms in the United States, Japan, and the European Union, depending on contrasting institutionalized compromises: commercial, civic, or strongly state-driven. After nearly a century of growth, the North American anthropogenic model is stumbling over the ineffectiveness of competition to steer the public health sector and extend life expectancy for the greatest number of people. The EU, the home of welfare capitalism, is struggling

R. Boyer (✉) · O. Boylaud
CNRS & EHESS, Paris, France
e-mail: r.boyer2@orange.fr

S. Lechevalier et al. (eds.), *Capitalism, Innovations, and Health after Covid-19*,
https://doi.org/10.1007/978-3-032-24479-6_2

to sustain its model because its poor economic performance limits its public funding. In contrast, Japan seems to have maintained its progress in life expectancy despite near economic stagnation, but its founding compromise is not easy to replicate. In addition to this comparative historical analysis, supported by long-term statistics, this chapter analyzes various contemporary issues. The return of pandemics, aging, the consequences of digital technology and AI on the organization of health, education, and culture. Not to mention the consequences of climate change and biodiversity loss on global health. The imperative of habitability calls for an update of the anthropogenic mode of development.

2.1 Introduction

Since the 1980s, researchers inspired by regulation theory have been looking at possible successors to the post-World War II growth regime. Such regimes are the expression of collective constructs that are not the consequence of hazards or shocks, or of pure economic determinism, let alone technological. It is therefore important to follow the strategy of key players who are likely to impose their logic on all the other players.

Would a service economy aimed at both consumers and companies supplant the dominance of the manufacturing sector and herald a new period for the various capitalisms (Petit, 2013)? On the contrary, should we consider that domestic markets have become too narrow, so that growth is increasingly driven by the exports of innovative industrial products? In retrospect, was it not financial innovation that prevailed to the point of favoring configurations dominated by financial globalization? (Aglietta & Rébérioux, 2004). In fact, these growth factors, which tend to coexist in varying proportions depending on the country, have all reached their limits: productivity gains have dried up as a result of the shift to a tertiary economy, protectionist tensions have risen, and financial crises have recurred on a global scale.

Another hypothesis had long been put forward, that of the transformation of capitalisms under the effect of the rise of social protection (Théret, 1992), but it was far from being a common vision for conventional macroeconomics built on the abstraction of microeconomic foundations. Denying the historicity of growth regimes, it was unlikely to withstand the rise of perils and crises. The emergence of Covid-19 has brutally revived an approach based on an anthropogenic mode of development (Boyer, 2020).

It is important to recognize that this vision of development, centered on the complementary cross-relationship between education and health, could not be recognized by most of the macro-economic theories that have successively dominated the academic field. At the same time, a growing body of research—both field surveys and comparative statistical analysis—was renewing the analysis of development: what had been considered the result of successful development was, in fact, its foundation. Spending on education and healthcare thus became investments, vectors of economic dynamism and improved well-being. There is a convergence with the analysis of development in terms of capability (Armatya, 2001) and empirical research that has confirmed, for example, the decisive role of education in reducing infant mortality and combating poverty. Introducing this paradigm is the subject of the first part of this chapter.

The second part of this chapter looks at how the events and developments of the 2020s affect the recognition of the anthropogenetic regime. Does Covid-19 reflect an awareness of the probable return of pandemics, and therefore a reassessment of public health imperatives? Ageing populations are no longer exclusive to Japan, which should lead to very different socio-economic regimes from those that were based on strong growth. Climate change and threats to biodiversity should logically imply a shift in the hierarchy of government priorities: these are all threats to the planet's habitability and, among other things, the source of new threats to health. Doesn't the speed with which vaccines against Covid-19 can be obtained testify to a breakthrough in a new approach to medicine and therapy? Should we expect a new course in the anthropogenetic regime? Finally, in the age of platform capitalism, do Artificial Intelligence and advances in biology open up a plurality of futures?

A third part extends the time horizon and goes beyond a comparison of Japan and the USA to include members of the European Union. In the light of long historical series (1950–2022 or 1955–2022), is the rise of the anthropogenetic sector general, and has it continued in recent years? Is there still a case for making manufacturing industry the hard core of economic activity, and if this is no longer the case, how can macroeconomic theories be reformulated? How are we to interpret the contrast between a trend deceleration in growth measured by the GDP indicator and the remarkable stability in the rise of life expectancy, if not as the silent victory of a model that is very different from that of the post WWII Golden Age and widely misunderstood? Should we then invoke a form of scientific and technological determinism? Nothing is less certain, since national trajectories over the long term are the expression of contrasting institutional configurations, in terms of both efficiency and social justice. Ultimately, an unexpected and paradoxical result emerges: each of these variants of the anthropogenic mode has recently encountered its limits. Barely recognized at last, it's in crisis!

A brief conclusion summarizes the main results and attempts to shed some light on this paradox.

2.2 Education and Health at the Heart of Anthropogenic Development

2.2.1 *The Need for an Updating of Vision and Theorizing*

The recognition of the anthropogenetic mode of development has been hampered by the influence of successive economic theories since the founding of political economy (Boyer, 2021). For the classical authors, economic activity is reduced to the circuit of producing goods from other goods and labor. For Marxists, money is converted into capital in order to generate surplus-value, thereby initiating a new cycle of accumulation. For Keynes's disciples, education and health care are part of public spending whose function is to stabilize an economy subject to financial instability. Finally, for Schumpeter's followers, a flow of technical and organizational innovations revives a cycle of economic expansion and slowdown.

Each of these theories points to certain issues in education and health. Activities among others in the production of labor power for the classical tradition, the support of profit-seeking for the Marxists, a simple component of demand for the Keynesians, or an area of scientific research and innovation on a par with the digital paradigm. In fact, the hypothesis of an anthropogenetic regime argues that the purpose of work is to produce the human being itself, through education, training, health and culture, which are the central processes of societies seeking the well-being of individuals.

A series of empirical analyses have sought to provide empirical evidence in favor of this view. From the outset, Japan's trajectory after the bursting of the speculative bubble in 1990 attracted the attention of regulation researchers (Boyer & Yamada, 2000). Since the decade of the 1990s, the breakthrough of information and communication technologies in the United States has somewhat obscured the long-term growth trend in the share of education and health spending in GDP (Boyer, 2002). The proliferation of research aimed at explaining why healthcare costs are growing faster than in other sectors for almost all OECD countries can be interpreted as a shift in the growth regime and not as the consequence of decades of inefficient management (Boyer, 2015). The eruption of Covid-19 brutally revealed to governments and public opinion the importance of a functional healthcare system capable of meeting public health challenges. For the first time in the world, most political leaders have decided in favor of health, even at the expense of economic activity: is this not recognition of a fundamental objective, long dominated by that of growth or competitiveness? Finally, the importance of care workers, whose aim is to improve the well-being of the members of a society (Boyer, 2023), has also been recognized.

2.2.2 *Development: A Historical Perspective*

Development theory emerged in the aftermath of the Second World War, when analysts observed that many economies were failing to catch up with the growth path of the industrialized economies. The aim was to diagnose the obstacles to growth: weak market incentives, specialization in raw materials, dominance in the global economy, poor institutional organization and inadequate economic policies. In a second stage, the notion of development was transformed in favor of an analysis in terms of transformations in social, technological and institutional organization, the success of which contributes to accelerated growth. Since the 1990s, an even broader conception has been implemented by international organizations following Amartya Sen's seminal work on development indicators. Alongside average per capita income, a human development indicator incorporates demographic data (infant mortality and life expectancy) and data on the spread of education (school enrolment rate and duration). Nowadays, indicators identifying income inequality and inequality of access to major public services appear as necessary complements in the face of the growing heterogeneity of economic and social situations within most national economies (PNUD, 2014).

2.2.3 *The Originality of the Anthropogenetic Development Model*

This puts education and health back at the heart of development. In the past, analysts tended to consider that improvements in the quality of life and its extension resulted from the enrichment of society, which could devote more resources to education and health. Today, theorists and practitioners also insist on the impact of education and health on the development process. On the one hand, it improves the skills, including health care skills, brought into families by women (Esping Andersen, 2008). On the other hand, reducing infant mortality and overcoming major epidemics changes the demographic regime, enabling a demographic dividend to be achieved through, for example, the rejuvenation of the population. At the same time, investment in general education and training brings additional benefits through longer life-cycles, including working life, which in turn increases the return on education policies (Fig. 2.1).

Successful development is thus the result of a circular, and in some cases cumulative, process. It ranges from business investment, which forms productive capital, to education spending, which contributes to social capital that synergizes with the creation of infrastructure by public authorities. If we adopt this approach, an offensive health strategy can in some cases help to accelerate growth. This is even more the case with education, as it also shapes access to healthcare and interest in child and family welfare.

Is this a conceptual revolution without historical precedent? Not at all, since as early as the mid-nineteenth century, Friedrich List took the following position: "Those who raise pigs and those who make bagpipes are indeed productive, but teachers of youth and maturity, virtuosos, doctors, judges and administrators, are productive to a higher degree. The teacher prepares the next generation for production, the doctor preserves the productive forces of his patient, the judge produces legal certainty and the administrator public order."

At this stage of the analysis, we must add a third component to the anthropogenic mode of development: culture. Culture is understood in

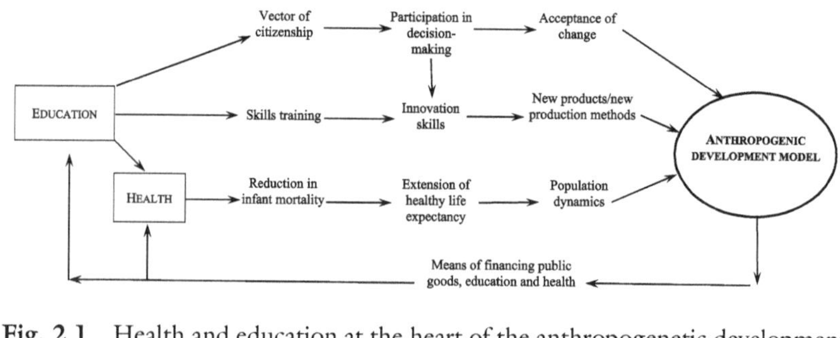

Fig. 2.1 Health and education at the heart of the anthropogenetic development model

a broad sense as the matrix of collective representations that allows members of a society to recognize themselves as belonging to the same community. In fact, it is what allows us to overcome the conflicts and contradictions that any society experiences by negotiating compromises, which are the foundation of political, social, and economic institutions. Without this catalyst, anomie and stagnation in human development threaten to take hold.

To illustrate this, one need only consider the paradox represented by Argentina's trajectory since World War II: endowed with all the attributes of a prosperous and dynamic economy, the country has been unable to forge a political system that favors the emergence of compromises between social blocs with antagonistic projects (César & Ludmer, 2023). On the other hand, it is difficult to statistically identify the contribution of culture, because the activities grouped under this heading in statistical systems are only indirect and uncertain contributions to the formation of collective representations that underpin a mode of development. Beyond this imperfection, the remainder of this chapter will consider education, health, and culture as the tripod of the anthropogenic mode.

This approach has the merit of going beyond the exclusive focus on healthcare costs, as it makes explicit the direct and indirect benefits associated with improved health. On the one hand, the gains in terms of well-being and life expectancy are in fact the real result of activity in the healthcare sector. On the other hand, the corresponding improvements create favorable conditions for economic activity through the enhancement of education, the acceptability of innovation through the extension of skills. In short, health and education are at the origin of the dynamic efficiency that lies at the heart of economic development. In a sense, we find the principles underpinning social-democratic models, which emphasize the contribution of social security systems to the formation of collective capital, which is then mobilized in the quest for competitiveness (Visser & Hemerijck, 1997; Masden, 2008; Campbell et al., 2008).

2.3 How the Transformations of the 2020 Decade Affect the Anthropogenetic Development Patterns?

Does the novelty of the context encourage the development of this original form of socio-economic organization? It's important to sketch out an initial, albeit partial, assessment. Related and interesting findings are provided by various chapters of this book (among them Gorry & Montalban, 2026).

2.3.1 *The Pandemic Has Shown That the Quality of the Healthcare and Education Systems Matters*

Politicians had long been concerned about soaring healthcare costs, and had often taken measures to limit access to doctors by controlling entry to the profession and reducing the number of hospital beds. In a way, the supply of care was supposed to generate a sometime superfluous demand. In the field of education, the quality of teaching and its impact on inequalities posed problems. Covid-19 implied an abrupt reassessment of the place of these two sectors in society (Boyer, 2020).

On the one hand, hospitals save lives, medical research is essential and prevention can play a decisive role in the response to new health risks. On the other hand, having failed to learn the lessons of previous pandemics, some societies have paid a heavy price in terms of excess mortality. In a panic of urgency, many governments decided to confine their populations, even if it meant bringing economic activity to a sudden halt in the least essential sectors. For the first time, health came before the economy. And this is the cornerstone of the anthropogenetic mode.

Closing the schools posed a formidable dilemma: in the name of the fight against the pandemic, did we have the right to deprive the younger generations of education, thus permanently penalizing them in the acquisition of the skills they needed to integrate into the economy and society? The result has been an unprecedented use of distance learning, thanks to the mobilization of information and communication technologies—another step forward in the affirmation of human production through the work deployed in education and healthcare.

In fact, policies to combat the pandemic have ranged along a spectrum from giving absolute priority to fighting the spread of the virus to minimizing economic losses. What emerges is a contrast between societies where the fall in life expectancy has been rapidly offset (basically European countries with good health coverage) and others where it is prolonged (Central European countries and the United States). Broadly speaking, the quality of the healthcare system and its relevance to public health issues seem to define two contrasting trajectories of response to Covid19 (Fig. 2.2). Another differentiation lies in the importance attached respectively to containment and other non-medical measures, and to the search for therapies and vaccines: the governments that were best able to deploy vaccination were able to limit the fall in life expectancy (Fig. 2.3).

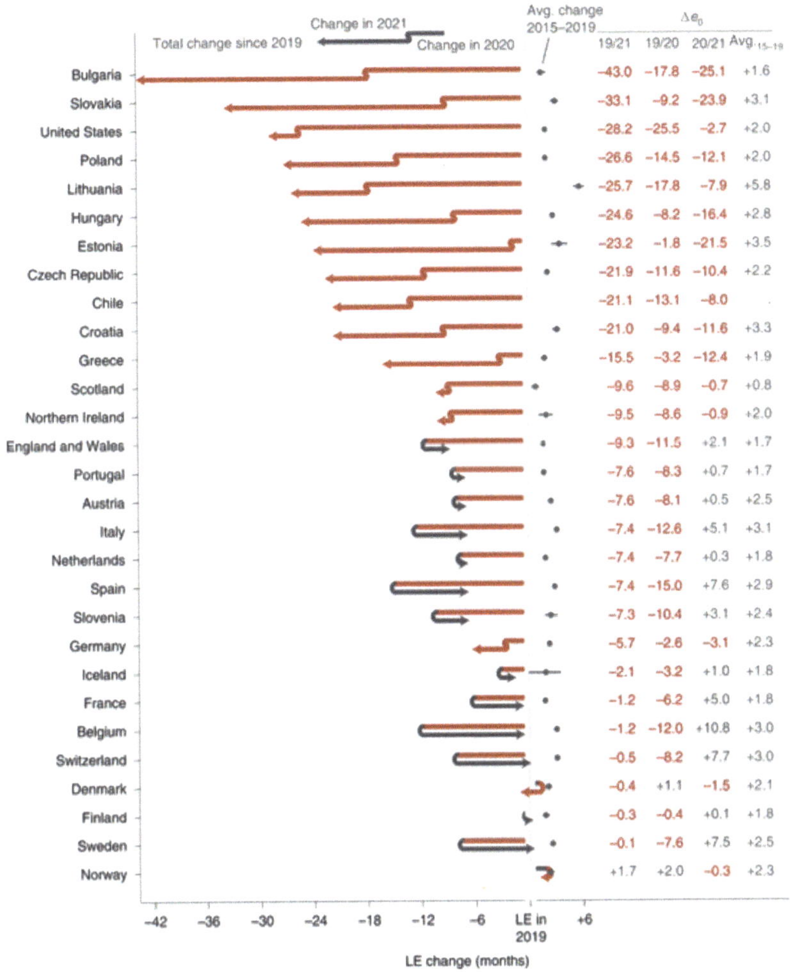

Fig. 2.2 The evolution of life expectancy 2019, 2020 and 2021. https://www.Nature.Com/articles/s41562-022-01450-3/figures/1

In this way, the social utility of not only the health sector, but also education, has become clear (Boyer, 2023). Indeed, countries that have permanently closed their schools have penalized the future of their young generations simply by being unprepared for pandemics and under-investing

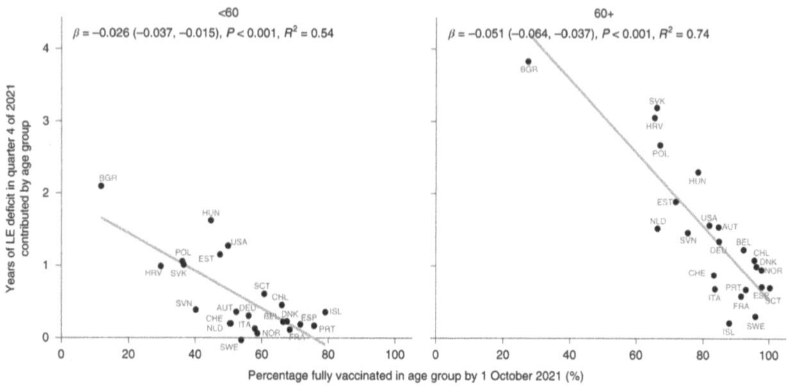

LE deficit is defined as the counterfactual LE from a Lee-Carter mortality forecast based on death rates for the fourth quarter of the years 2015 to 2019 minus observed LE. The points are labelled with ISO three-letter country codes.

Fig. 2.3 Vaccination tends to reduce the fall in life expectancy. https://www.Nature.Com/articles/s41562-022-01450-3/figures/5. *Source* Schöley Jonas et al. (2022), pp. 1651 and 1655

in health. Hence the cancellation of twenty years of progress in the human development index. The Covid-19 reminded us that anthropogenetic logic is part of the long-term development of societies, as opposed to finance, which is part of the short term and which, since deregulation policies, has been guiding government choices.

The pandemic marked a break in the management of the various components of the healthcare sector. This manifested itself in an intensification of hospitalizations under Covid-19, but simultaneously a postponement of other interventions. Statistics for a sample of OECD countries confirm that a larger proportion of GDP has been allocated to healthcare spending, against a backdrop of falling output. Remarkably, this share then stabilized under the dual effect of economic recovery and a return to previous management patterns (Fig. 2.4). The exceptionalism of the United States should be emphasized, as it spends the most on healthcare without achieving good results in terms of life expectancy. European countries occupy a median position, while South Korea is witnessing an acceleration in healthcare spending. Contrasting national trajectories in response to the same global event.

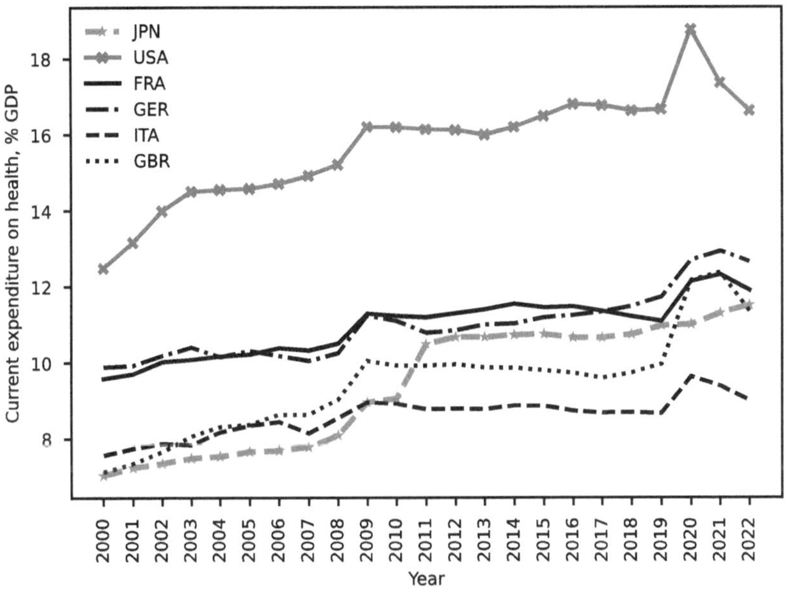

Fig. 2.4 The recent evolutions since Covid in historical perspective. *Source* Elaborated by the author from OECD data

This dramatic episode highlighted the degree of unpreparedness of many countries and, more generally, the preponderance of curative care to the detriment of prevention, not least of pandemics. Remarkably, almost all countries have significantly increased their corresponding expenditure since 2020 (Fig. 2.5). Indeed, governments that drew the right conclusions from the H1N1 pandemic have considerably limited human and economic losses. We do not have enough hindsight to determine whether or not the prevention imperative will define a new priority for healthcare policies.

2.3.2 The Effects of Ageing: Rising Needs but Financing Difficulties

The transformation of the age pyramid has become a preoccupation for many governments in the 2020s: with the lag in aging, European countries will join Japan and even the United States in facing the problem of

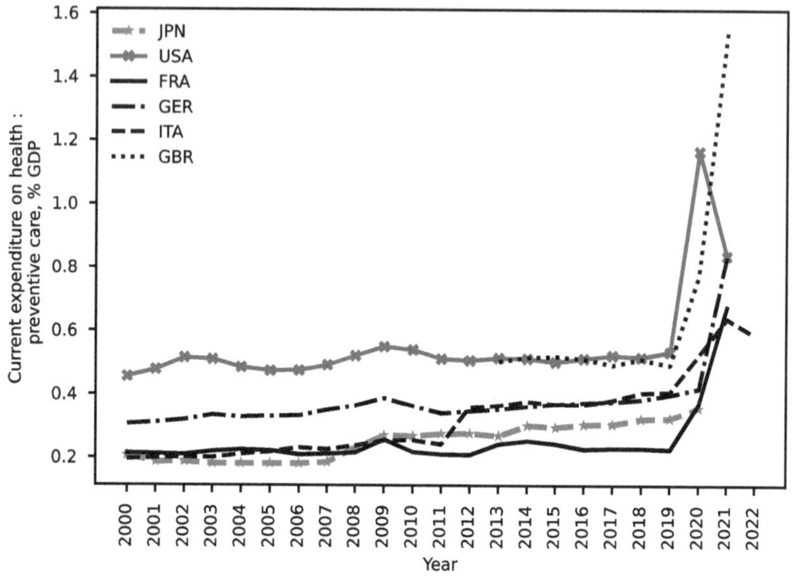

Fig. 2.5 The recent rise in preventive care spending. *Source* Elaborated by the author from OECD data

aging. This is particularly evident in the rising proportion of over-65s in the 15–64 age group (Fig. 2.6).

The result is a series of tensions in the various growth regimes, including anthropogenetic ones. First of all, it's well established that healthcare costs are rising sharply for the elderly. We can even imagine that the generalization of dependency implies an extension of the coverage of this risk according to original modalities, that of care, i.e. varied care implying a new direction for innovation, as suggested by Japanese policy (Lechevalier, 2026). These are two factors extending the anthropological logic. However, there's nothing mechanical about it, since it's important to find the funding and anticipate the training of caregivers.

Logically, innovation, which cannot be reduced to technology alone (Lechevalier, 2019), should be stimulated to find treatments and medicines, as well as institutional arrangements to organize this new sector. Is it realistic to anticipate a revolution enabling a cumulative drop in costs? In the light of previous medical breakthroughs and disappointments with the

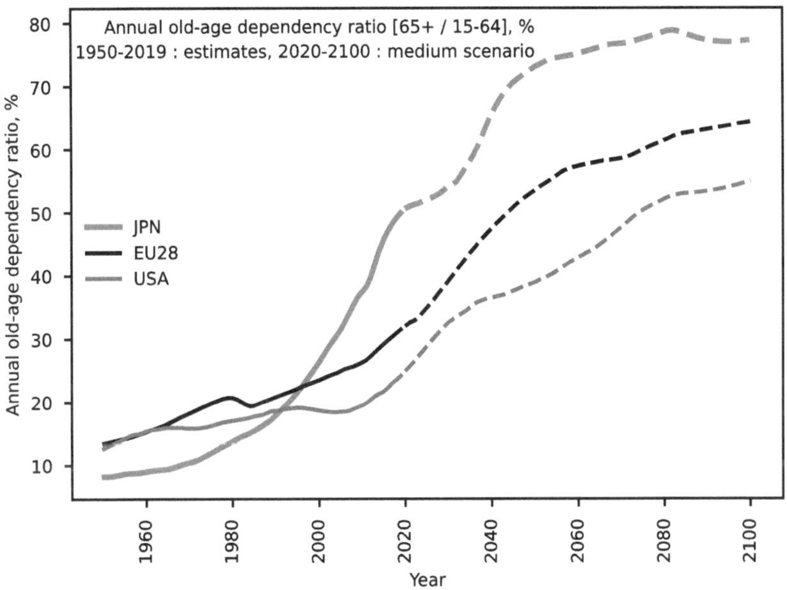

Fig. 2.6 The aging has become a central issue. *Source* Elaborated by the author from "United Nations, Department of Economic and Social Affairs, Population Division (2022). World Population Prospects 2022, Online Edition" data

hope of an effective treatment for Alzheimer's disease, for example, this is unlikely. Consequently, it's prudent to anticipate an extension of the field covered by development focused on health, education and culture.

Provided that the economy generates sufficient resources to finance the expenses incurred by ageing. However, the shrinking proportion of the working population is weighing on wealth creation, and raises the question of intergenerational justice. The vigor of the conflicts surrounding the adaptation of pension schemes augurs well for future difficulties. In a way, the anthropogenetic perspective is encountering its limits by the very fact of its success. Is a revival in productivity conceivable? It would be highly desirable, but it comes up against the fact that in the current organization of work, the economy's productivity tends to decrease with the size of the older generations (Fig. 2.7).

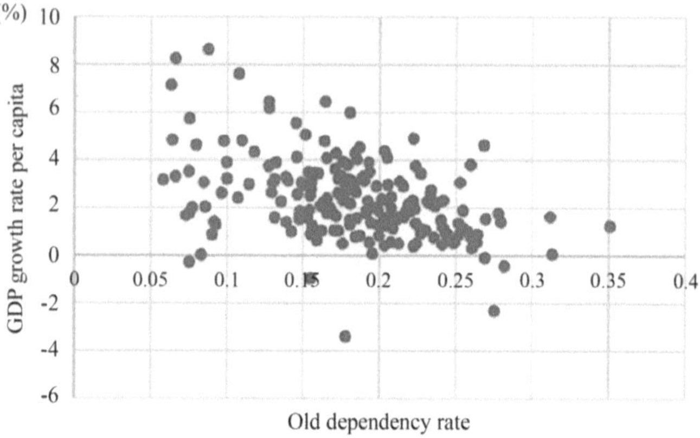

Fig. 2.7 Towards a negative impact of productivity and thus growth. *Note* The vertical axis represents the annual average growth rate of GDP per capita in OECD countries for the 10-year period. The horizontal axis represents the old dependency ratio at the beginning of each period. *Source* Hyun-Hoon Lee, Kwanho Shin; Decomposing Effects of Population Aging on Economic Growth in OECD Countries. Asian Economic Papers 2021; 20 (3): 138–159. https://doi.org/10.1162/asep_a_00839

This is undoubtedly a sign that this mode of development is entering a crisis: the private sector is proving incapable of taking charge of dependency, especially for the most modest, and the public sector is stumbling over limited funding for social protection due to the multiplicity of priorities and the persistence of low growth, if not the persistence of a trend towards stagnation (Gorry & Montalban, 2026).

2.3.3 New Medical Techniques: A Bifurcation or a Continuation of Diminishing Returns?

The history of medicine shows that its advances derive from responses to the emergence of new health threats and the opportunities opened up by the development of techniques, including those in other sectors. Faced with the major transformations of the 2020s, will new directions emerge for medical research? Throughout history, medical research has gone through various phases. Scientific publications were first dominated by the natural sciences and humanities, then by engineering and technology from the twentieth century[e] onwards. The medical and health sciences experienced a boom around 1900 and again in the 1950s, but their share of publications tended to stabilize (Fig. 2.8).

Patents are an important gateway, and show a multiplicity of applications. The gap between patent applications and their recognition shows the uncertainty that affects all R&D expenditure in terms of results (Figs. 2.9 and 2.10). The 2020s seem to indicate a slowdown in the number of biotechnology patents granted, despite the fact that these are expected to bring new approaches to finding idiosyncratic treatments for both old and emerging diseases (Fig. 2.11). The fall in pharmaceutical patents is undoubtedly due to the rising cost of developing new drugs (Gorry & Montalban, 2026). The combination of these two trends, if confirmed, does not augur well for the long-awaited revolution in medical progress that will translate into lower costs, as observed in most industrial sectors, but not in services. What's more, the high labor content of healthcare makes such a bifurcation unlikely.

In contrast to this prognosis, the speed with which messenger RNA techniques have made it possible to develop effective vaccines against Covid-19 seems to be ushering in a new era. According to the WHO, the 80 billion in private profits would correspond to a social return of 71 trillion thanks to the limitation of economic losses (WHO, 2023a). Clearly, such a return is exceptional and cannot be extrapolated to other drugs. Reducing the cost of treating certain diseases does not necessarily follow the path of high medical technology: a low-cost traditional drug has been shown to provide remarkable protection against recurrent strokes. Similarly, while no miracle drug has yet proved effective in the fight against Alzheimer's and other degenerative diseases, the combination of physical activity, cholesterol reduction and blood pressure control has reduced the incidence of the disease (Neville, 2023).

This means recognizing that lifestyles play a role in the onset, spread and treatment of many diseases. We know that education is a factor in prevention, that dietary practices are important, and that a growing number of ailments stem from the environment. This is a reminder of the holistic nature of the anthropogenetic mode. Unsurprisingly, its future depends to a large extent on the choices made in response to the ecological crisis.

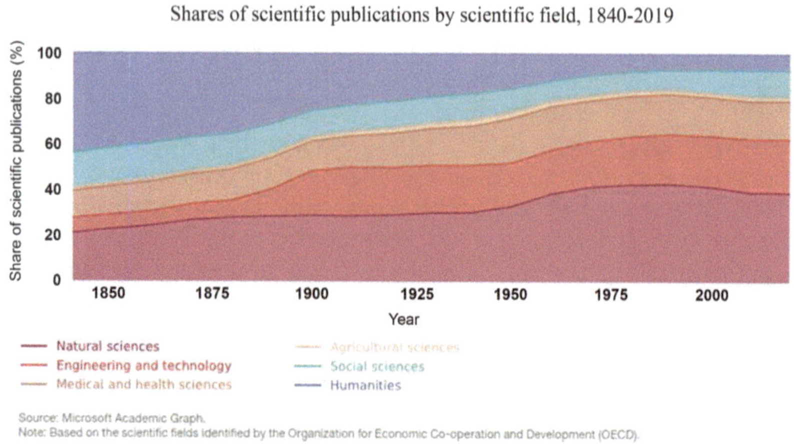

Fig. 2.8 The long-term evolution of publications. Shares of scientific publications by scientific field, 1840–2019. *Source* World Intellectual Property Report 2022: The Direction of Innovation, https://doi.org/10.34667/tind.45356 (figure 1.3 p. 23)

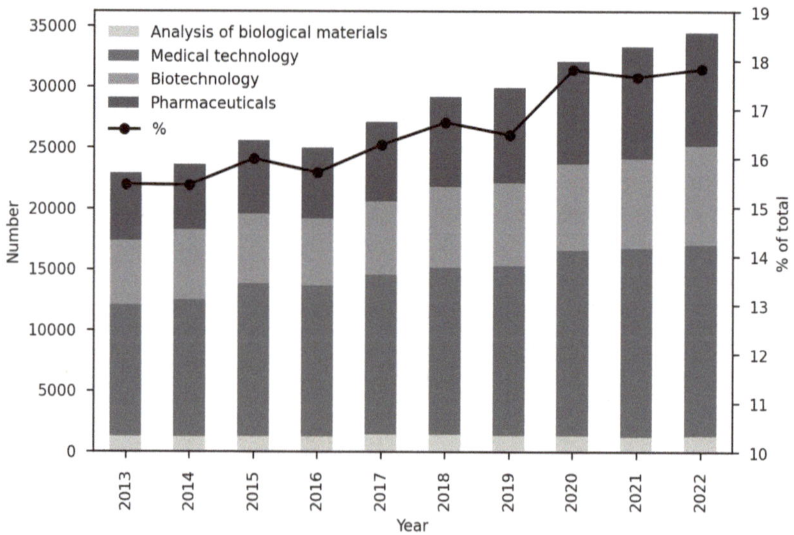

Fig. 2.9 The growth of patent applications for health care 2013–2022. *Source* Elaborated by the author from European Patent Office (EPO) data

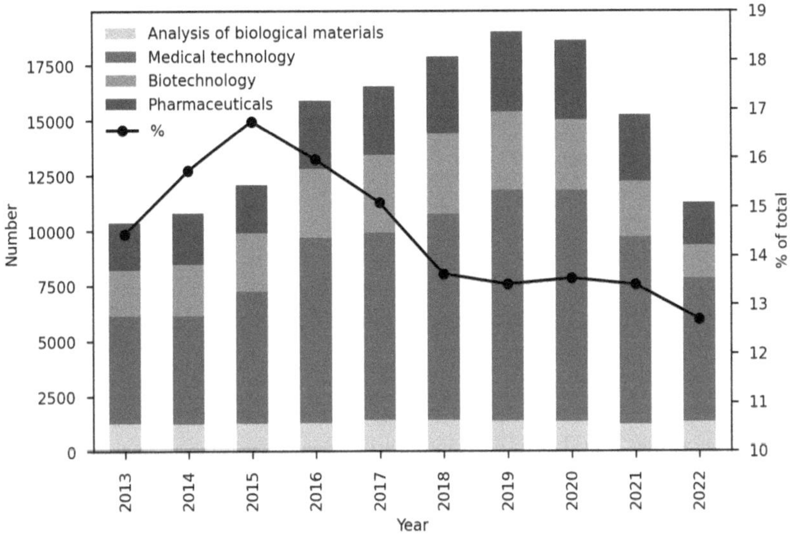

Fig. 2.10 The growth of patent granted for health care 2013–2022. *Source* Elaborated by the author from European Patent Office (EPO) data

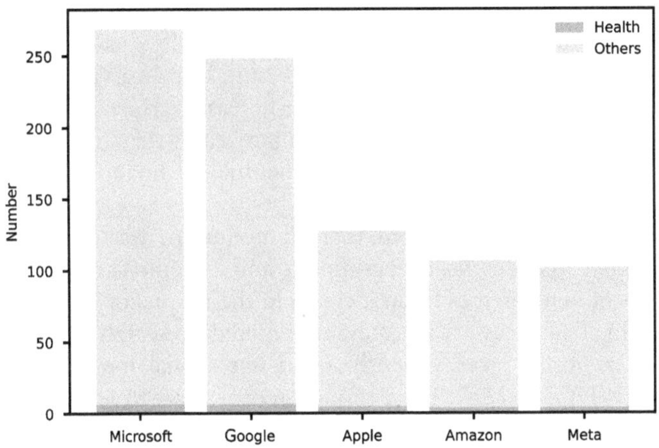

Fig. 2.11 Acquisitions by Gafam since their creation until 2020. *Source* Special recollection from public data by the authors (see technical appendix)

2.3.4 *Climate and Ecological Crises: No Possibility of Wellbeing on an Uninhabitable Earth*

These crises are major obstacles to the continuation of the modes of growth that have succeeded one another since 1945, all of which prospered at the expense of resource depletion, the destruction of ecological niches, pollution and climate sustainability. They bring to the fore the question of survival for a growing number of people. On the face of it, this is an opportunity to forge an alliance between anthropogenetic logic and the preservation of the biosphere. On reflection, the same transformations that argue in favor of a change in development mode make it more difficult, for at least four reasons.

Extreme climatic events are becoming more frequent and often more severe: hurricanes in unusual locations, long droughts in other regions, meteorological instabilities everywhere, drastic reductions in biodiversity, all threaten security, lifestyles, production methods and, ultimately, health (Genton, 2022). For the poorest countries, agricultural productivity is reduced, leading to malnutrition and even famine (FAO, 2023), which are sources of conflict and migration. To a lesser extent, these problems also affect the wealthier societies of the North. To the point of suggesting that food should be included as a fourth component of the anthropogenetic mode (Allaire, 2023), an absolutely necessary addition for societies dominated by the rural sector. A society close to the subsistence level must first overcome this obstacle before generating a sufficient surplus to invest in education and health. Even for the most affluent societies, we must anticipate an increase in the costs of responding to extreme climatic events, and in many cases negative productivity shocks. All these factors add to the difficulties of financing the anthropogenetic mode.

It has now been established that air pollution, waste, deteriorating water quality, frequent heatwaves, floods and extreme climatic events are all sources of new diseases or an increase in the frequency of existing ones (Table 2.1). The necessary investment in medical research and care makes maintaining health more expensive, and is essential for the viability of societies (WHO, 2023b). Even though recent years have seen the limits of funding possibilities being reached, due in particular to a trend towards secular stagnation.

While anthropogenetic logic and ecological projects both contribute to maintaining the well-being of populations, their practical

Table 2.1 How ecological crises generate illnesses and affect health

Cause	*Health impacts*
Air pollution	Air pollution Respiratory diseases, cardiovascular damage, fatigue, headaches and anxiety, irritation of the eyes, nose and throat, damage to reproductive organs, nervous system damage. Cardiovascular diseases in development stages of infants and cancer later in life, as well as impact on cognitive performance.
Solid waste	High incidence of cancer and lymphoma has been found in populations living near contaminated sites and landfills (e.g. kidney, larynx, pancreas, liver, lung cancer) as well as higher risks for congenital malformations, lowbirth weight and neural tube defects. Other health problems concern noise, smell and issues due to annoyance, lowering the quality of life of affected residents.
Wastewater	Microorganisms in water can cause diarrhea, skin and tissue infections and dysentery, while other disease-causing bacteria such as E. coli O157:H7, Salmonella, Vibrio and Leptospirosis can be found in untreated wastewaters.
Heatwaves	Exhaustion, cramps, syncope, strokes, kidney disorders, psychiatric illness, chronic pulmonary illness, diabetes and cerebrovascular accidents. Lost productivity, which will impact developing countries.
Vector-borne diseases	Modification of geographical range of the habitat of animal vectors of diseases such as malaria, dengue fever, chikungunya, yellow fever and the Zika virus.
Floods	Responsible for the emergence of waterborne diseases, as well as for the destruction of key infrastructure that in vulnerable areas can increase the displacement of refugees and dislocated people. Drowning, injuries and hypothermia, health risks are related to evacuation of patients, loss of health workers of health infrastructure such as essential drugs. Medium-term implications include infected wounds, poisoning, affected mental health, communicable diseases and starvation. In the long term, chronic diseases and poverty-related diseases such as malnutrition can impact severely on the affected population.
Droughts	Malnutrition and undernutrition.
Extreme weather events	Deaths, physical injuries, mental health issues, water and food scarcity, water- and vector-borne diseases, forced migration, and damage to health facilities.
Sea surface temperature	Fish stocks and fisheries production are decreasing, affecting the protein intake of many people. It is also affecting the nutritional values of the available seafood, leading to a reduction of lipids and proteins in some species.

(continued)

Table 2.1 (continued)

Cause	*Health impacts*
Ozone depletion	Exposure to ultraviolet (UV) radiation leads to skin cancer, premature ageing of skin, signs of sun damage such as wrinkles, leathery skin and liver spots. Eye problems due to UV rays leading to the cornea becoming inflamed or burned, increased risk of cataracts. Exposure to UV rays can also weaken the immune system, which leads to the body having a harder time fending off infections.

Source World health organization (2023b)

implementation can come into conflict. In theory, reliable data would be needed to assess the effectiveness of each measure, but uncertainty and imperfect knowledge of the processes at work make this difficult. How, then, can governments steer these transformations, without the equivalent of bets that run the risk of being contradicted by subsequent developments? This is a far cry from the model based on the development of digital technology, which is much more certain thanks to Moore's amazing law, which has not been disproved since it was formulated at the dawn of digital technology (Gorry & Montalban, 2026). As a result, ecological planning is unprecedentedly difficult in comparison with the processes that enabled the transition to mass production during and after the Second World War, first for the military, then for the civilian sector.

There is also a temporal conflict. The horizon of investments aimed at maintaining the biosphere, a condition of human habitability, does not a priori correspond to that of the fight to treat both traditional and new diseases. History shows that such conflicts of time horizons are the source of major crises. Over the past four decades, it is the time of finance that has come into conflict with that of the economy and production (Boyer, 2013). In the decades to come, those in charge will be tempted to give priority to either anthropogenetic logic or ecological preservation. This will undoubtedly lead to considerable delays and inefficiencies.

Ultimately, these are all obstacles to the orderly evolution of the Great Transformation underway. Moreover, a second contradiction arises: education, health and culture are usually organized within a national space, whereas the new challenges of health and climate protection operate on a global scale (Global Health Care Outlook, 2023). Given the decline of the international organizations inherited from Bretton-Woods, and the difficulty of building new ones, we must reject the hypothesis of an easy transition from a world where the imperative of growth was paramount to one where the preservation of the biosphere is crucial.

2.3.5 *Will Digital Capitalism Revolutionize Healthcare?*

The power of digitization has opened up new possibilities in response to Covid-19. On the one hand, tracking the mobility of individuals using cell phone data has enabled governments to fine-tune policies to combat the spread of the virus, as have non-medical tools such as masks. On the other hand, data on banking transactions and the activity of digital platforms made it possible to monitor economic activity in real time, useful information for deciding on measures to confine populations. They also made up for the delay inherent in compiling statistics within national accounting systems. In this way, political leaders who had been able to draw conclusions from previous pandemics and organize health information accordingly were able to limit human losses (Boyer, 2020).

As a result, the pandemic revealed healthcare as a global public good (Gaudillière et al., 2021). At the same time, it has accelerated the rise of GAFAMs and other new companies as the bearers of innovative solutions and the beneficiaries of their advances. One example is the organization of telecommuting. While traditional industries continued to decline, the digital sector recorded considerable profits and rapid stock market valuations. The result has been a flurry of acquisitions by GAFAMs in a whole range of sectors. The surprise, however, is that healthcare represents a tiny fraction of the total flows observed up to 2020 (Fig. 2.11). In terms of stocks, only Microsoft and Oracle have significant stakes in the healthcare sector (Fig. 2.12).

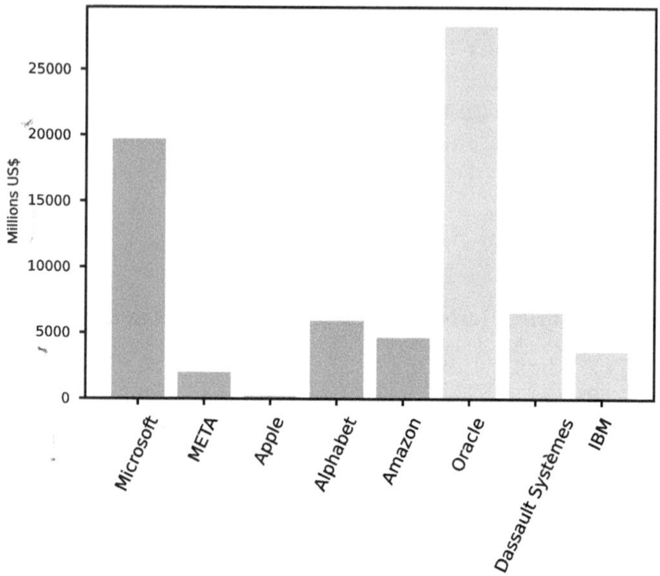

Fig. 2.12 Cumulative amount of main acquisitions in healthcare sectors, in millions of US$. *Source* Special recollection from public data by the authors (see technical appendix)

More recent data on venture capital and mergers & acquisitions show, firstly, strong growth in venture capital investment in medical technology in 2021, but a marked reduction once the pandemic has passed, a trend which also affects biopharmaceuticals (Fig. 2.13). This can be seen as an expression of the short-termism typical of financial market players, which leaves the future of the relationship between digital and healthcare open (Fig. 2.13).

This is an invitation to take a closer look at the ways in which digital technology can intervene in healthcare. We are struck by the multiplicity of legal forms used by Google, Apple, Facebook, Amazon and Microsoft: commercial or research partnership, joint venture, service provision, acquisition (Table 2.2). Similarly, the points of application are multiple. They can range from simple IT and logistics services to

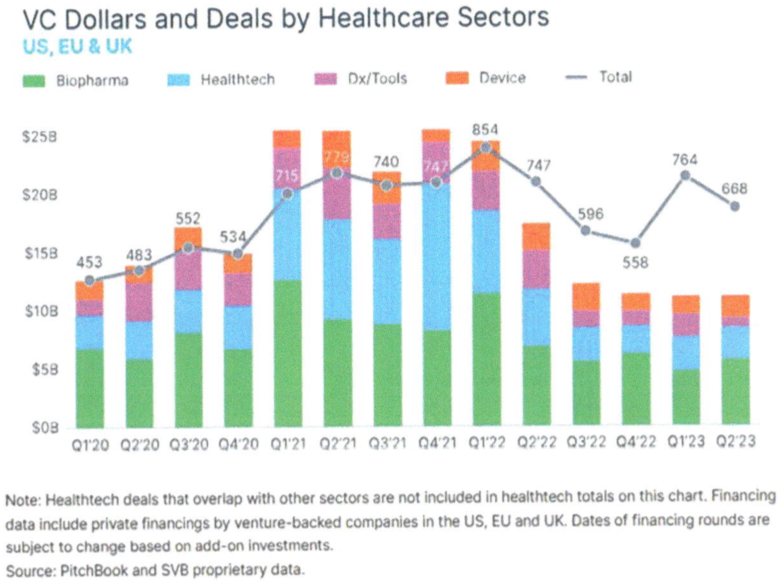

Fig. 2.13 The surprising decline of Venture capital and agreements after the Covid-19. *Source* SVB (2023), Healthcare Industry Trends—Mid-Year 2023, Update. https://www.svb.com/trends-insights/reports/healthcare-investments-and-exits

Table 2.2 How GAFAM enter healthcare 2010–2020

	Google	*Apple*	*Facebook*	*Amazon*	*Microsoft*
Commercial partnership	13	5	1	3	20
New ventures	6	1			
New products of services					
Announced	11	3	2	1	1
Launched	5	7	2	6	
Acquisitions	6	2		1	3
Research partnerships	2	3	4	2	8
Service termination	2		1	1	1

Source Elaborated from Ozalp et al. (2022)

the supply of high-performance systems, as in the case of Microsoft. At another extreme, Amazon offers healthcare services and insurance (Hodgson, 2023), while Google has a subsidiary to facilitate healthcare R&D (Table 2.3).

Table 2.3 The healthcare subsectors in which the GAFAM do invest. *Source* Gleiss, A., Kohlhagen, M., & Pousttchi, K. (2021). An apple a day—how the platform economy impacts value creation in the healthcare market. Electronic markets, 31(4), 849–876. https://doi.org/10.1007/s12525-021-00467-2

	smart devices	systems & apps	digital health & health-IT	IT infrastructure & collaboration	commerce & logistics	healthcare services	health insurance	health R&D
Google	Fitbit Nest Pixel	**Android (Things)** [h] **Assistant** [t] **Fit** [h] **Search** [t]	**Workspace** [h]	**Cloud Life** [h]	**Play Store** [t] Wing			Calico DeepMind Verily
Apple	iPad iPhone HomePod Watch	**iOS** [h] **Siri** [t]	**Health App** [i] **Health Records** [t] **CareKit** [i]	**HealthKit** [h] **ResearchKit** [i]	**App Store** [t]	AC Wellness		
Facebook	Oculus	**Facebook** [t] **WhatsApp** [t]						fastMRI CTRL-kit
Amazon	Echo	**Alexa** [h]	Comprehend	AWS	Basic Care **Business** [t] Logistics **Marketplace** [t] PillPack Prime Air	Care	(Haven)	
Microsoft	HoloLens Surface	**Windows** [h]	HC NeXT HC Bot ehCOS EHR	**365** [h] Azure **Teams** [i]				

bold: platform services (t: transaction; i: innovation; h: hybrid/integrative)

From these initial investigations, a number of hypotheses emerge that need to be verified by more in-depth research. Firstly, it is essentially on the basis of their competitive advantage in information processing that the digital giants are investing in healthcare. Their impact on the dynamics of healthcare costs is not such that GAFAMs can significantly influence trends that ultimately derive from breakthroughs, or otherwise, in medical research (Gorry & Montalban, 2026). Secondly, digital technology enables people to work remotely, which can be applied to medical consultations, thus mitigating the uneven geographical distribution of GPs. However, it is not clear that this will lead to cost moderation, given the acute shortage of doctors in some countries, even though this is the hope of governments (Gallois & Rauly, 2018). Finally, Artificial Intelligence (AI) can undoubtedly accelerate the search for new biotechnologies, but they can prove extremely expensive. This is the case with treatments that use genetic scissors to intervene at cell level. They open up a new stage in medicine, but costs in the million-dollar range (Loder, 2023) will inevitably come up against the financing possibilities of both private and public insurance companies.

In short, the hope of a cost-cutting anthropogenetic mode is unlikely to materialize.

2.3.6 *Education and Culture in the Age of AI*

Many education systems are faced with three imperatives: to improve the effectiveness of teaching methods, and not just to allocate more resources to teaching; to reduce inequalities in access to education, as this is the breeding ground for the polarization of society and politics; and to review the list of knowledge required by contemporary structural changes (UNESCO, 2023). To what extent does AI provide solutions? The literature is unanimous in attributing four potentialities to AI. Firstly, to provide access to a mass of information, which is a resource for learners. Secondly, to enable personalized learning tailored to each student, in the hope of boosting their interest and commitment. What's more, AI offers instant solutions that are akin to the online games so popular with the younger generation, who are immersed in a "presentational" society. Finally, virtual tutorials can be designed to complement, if not replace, teachers (UNESCO, 2021).

In a sense, the switch from Google to ChatGPT amounts to entrusting a software program with the task of synthesizing a considerable mass of information (Sarrion, 2023). This may be a good starting point for personal investigation, but for many learners, it also runs the risk of actually being the end point, eliminating all personal effort and delegating knowledge and even reasoning to a machine. In effect, the intellectual work of analysis, synthesis and summary is delegated to an automaton (Andler, 2023): it never stops improving, but this is not the case for the student, who becomes the passive receptacle of processes of which he has not the slightest idea! Moreover, is it acceptable for answers to be unable to cite the sources used? It's enough to disqualify them academically. In fact, an experiment comparing the quality of answers to the same question from two groups of students—one using AI, the other not—showed that, on average, the quality of answers from the first group was inferior. The relevance of the power of AI in terms of renewing teaching methods needs to be reassessed. In fact, the attempt to replace face-to-face teaching with virtual teaching goes back several decades, without having been successful in reducing costs or stimulating student interest.

Is AI helping to democratize access to quality education? Two recent observations merit consideration. Covid-19 has been associated with a rather unexpected boom in distance learning thanks to high-performance tools. On the upside, this has reduced the number of children falling behind at school; on the downside, it has deepened the digital divide. In wealthy societies, children from disadvantaged backgrounds have often been penalized for lack of equipment. On an international scale, school attendance has fallen in the poorest countries, due to a lack of resources. As a result, the human development index has recorded an unprecedented decline. The second observation may seem more anecdotal: players in the new economy and digital capitalism of Silicon Valley entrust their children's education to schools where the quality of teachers prevails, far from the routine learning of AI!

Once again, we need to challenge the technological determinism that holds that whatever the problem—be it economic, social, energy-related or environmental—a scientifically-based solution can be found through technical innovation. Actually, reducing inequalities in education is a matter of political choices, followed by the deployment of appropriate organizations and procedures. To take just one example, Finland has successfully reformed its education system to ensure efficiency and social justice, with digital technology playing a key role. They are adjuncts to an overall strategy. By contrast, in the United States and the United Kingdom, access to quality education has become the discriminating variable when it comes to social position and political participation.

Third question: what should be taught in the age of AI? What machines are not capable of conceiving: analytical reasoning, critical thinking, responding to randomness, teamwork to respond to unprecedented situations (Andler, 2023). This position may seem surprising at a time when AI is taking over cultural goods such as literature, cinema, TV series and music, and not just all automatable economic activities. Indeed, in the anthropogenetic logic, culture is not just a booming economic sector. Fundamentally, it is the symbolic foundation of society, enabling individuals to define themselves as belonging to a collective capable of deliberating and forging the rules, conventions and institutions that govern it.

In this respect, two characteristics of AI are problematic. Firstly, who are the players involved, and does it serve the general interest? In fact, under the pretext of the inevitability of all-digital technology, they intend to shape societies to their own advantage, and thus exercise a power that goes beyond the economic and financial sphere. Artificial intelligence thus risks exacerbating inequalities and accentuating the already considerable financial instability by generalizing mimetic behavior (Boyer, 2023b). So much so that some see it as a threat to democracy, and call for public authorities to take control (Acemoglu, 2021). Secondly, we must challenge the dematerialization that AI is said to bring about, since training software requires a considerable amount of work by a myriad of operators, and is extremely energy-intensive, consuming many non-renewable resources (Crawford, 2021). In short, AI's conflict with the ecological and climatic imperative is obvious, and it is more a danger than an ally of the anthropogenetic project.

2.4 A Historical and International Perspective

The preceding developments have sought to identify how contemporary transformations affect the likelihood of emergence and maturation of this original mode of development based on education, health and culture. What emerges is a number of long-term continuities that need to be characterized. At the same time, it is important to broaden the analysis beyond the trajectories of Japan and the United States, to include the European Union and the diversity of its member states.

2.4.1 Long-term Rise of Anthropogenetic Logic in All Three Regions of the World Economy

It is possible to reconstruct long historical statistical series for Japan, the United States and a Euro-zone grouping the main economies (Fig. 2.14). What emerges is a remarkable commonality of long-term trends. From 1975 to mid-2010, the anthropogenetic sector's share of employment and value added grew steadily.

The most striking result is undoubtedly that this cumulative movement has reached its limits, with the share of values added stagnating at roughly equivalent levels in both the USA and Europe. Japan remains the most

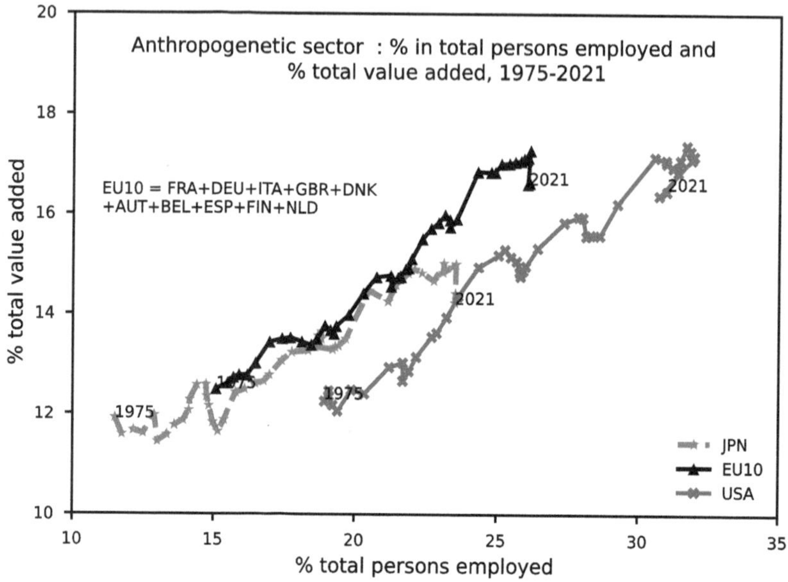

Fig. 2.14 EU, US, Japan: A common trend. *Source* Own elaboration

parsimonious country, while showing good results in terms of life expectancy, while the USA is the most expensive and unequal (Deaton, 2013; Case & Deaton, 2020).

In all three cases, recent years have seen the end of this model. In the United States, competition between insurers and healthcare providers is proving to be more wasteful than efficient. So much so, in fact, that attempts at reform aimed at socializing healthcare have failed, given the zeitgeist in favor of a market-based approach. In the European Union, these same expenses are largely socialized by public systems that are struggling to ensure financing, which has been made more difficult by the succession of crises and the downward trend in productivity and growth. There is no longer any doubt, therefore, that the anthropogenetic mode has taken hold—this is a general phenomenon in wealthy economies—but it has entered a crisis, except perhaps in Japan, which has long been able to reconcile the disappearance of growth prospects with continued investment in the well-being of populations, including the elderly, all without excessive costs.

2.4.2 *From the Domination of Industry to That of Anthropogenic Mode*

John Maynard Keynes once said that public policy-makers often draw so much inspiration from the theories of the past that they fail to understand the issues at stake in each new era. Yet it is remarkable that, implicitly or explicitly, economists—and macroeconomists in particular—build their analyses on what was the regime in force at the time their conceptualizations were constructed. To give just one example, both real-cycle models and post-Keynesian formalizations seek to identify evolutions driven by investment-driven industrial cycles. But the rise of services shifts the economy's center of gravity, to the point of introducing an entirely different dynamic. It is from this perspective that we can see the inadequacy of most theorizations when we relate the share of the manufacturing sector to the share of the anthropogenetic mode (Fig. 2.15).

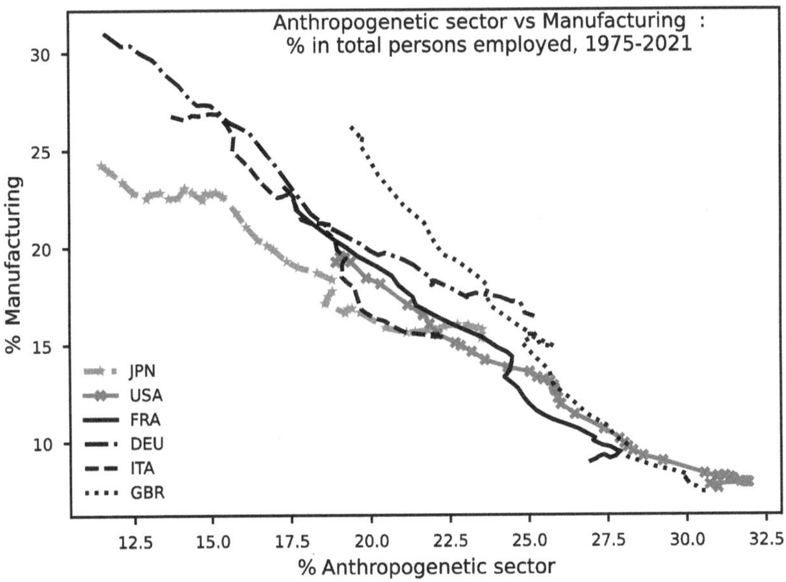

Fig. 2.15 The anthropogenetic sector is replacing manufacturing. *Source* Own elaboration (see technical appendix)

Deindustrialization appears to be a general phenomenon, albeit with varying degrees of delay depending on the country. Even within the European Union, there are notable differences between Italy and France, or the UK and Germany. This stylized fact calls for an aggiornamento in macroeconomic theorizing. Assuming that the anthropogenetic logic is dominant, what is the architecture of institutional forms (form of competition, wage relations, relationship to the state, integration into the international economy) and what does it imply for the accumulation regime? This is undoubtedly a promising research program proposed by regulation theory (Boyer et al., 2023).

2.4.3 *Exhaustion of Growth, Permanent Extension of Life Expectancy*

We also need to return to the objectives that every economy is supposed to pursue. For market fundamentalists, the essential thing is to maintain competition which, through the maximization of profits by companies and utility by individuals, guarantees the most efficient use of resources. This postulate is invalidated when we note the public-good aspects associated with education, health and, in a sense, culture. The American example illustrates the extent of the gap between theorizing and observational data in terms of results. In the post-World War II socio-economic regime, growth emerged as the main criterion of economic success. On the other hand, public health indicators—such as falling infant mortality, healthy life expectancy and people's perception of their well-being—are rarely invoked in general policy debates.

This is a serious mistake, since the statistics from 1950 to 2022 show an inexorable slowdown in growth trend, particularly through the succession of crises, but a steady improvement in average life expectancy, interrupted by Covid-19, except in Japan (Fig. 2.16).

The hierarchy between these three zones of the world economy needs to be reconsidered: they share the same trend towards economic stagnation, but their public health performance is very uneven. The worst performer is none other than the United States, a trend exacerbated by the Covid-19 episode. Japan, on the other hand, is continuing its anthropogenetic progression, even though its growth momentum has run out. As the country is better prepared to cope with pandemics,

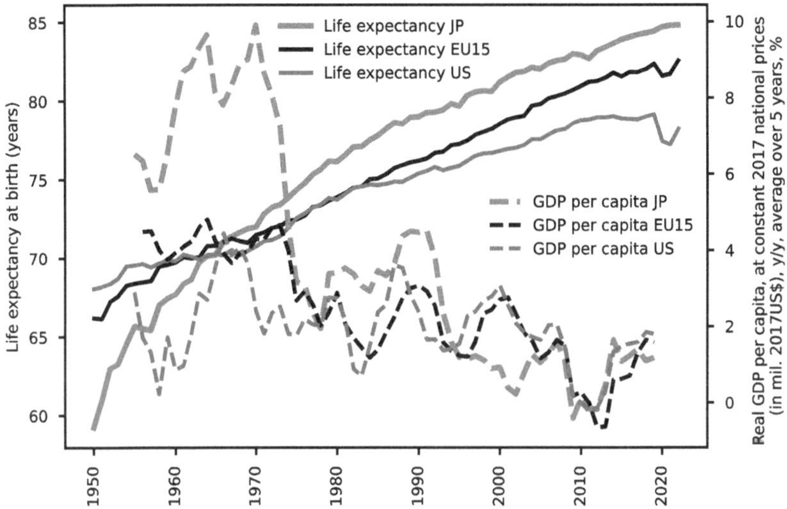

Fig. 2.16 1950–2022: The long-term rise of anthropogenetic logic (UE, US, Japan). *Source* Own elaboration (see technical appendix)

Covid-19 did not mark a pause in the progression of life expectancy. In part, the seriousness of today's crises stems from the fact that most governments are keen to boost growth without taking into account the new anthropogenetic and ecological requirements.

2.4.4 No Medical Technological Determinism: as Many Variants as Types of Capitalism

All too often, theorists are tempted to invoke determinisms that impose themselves on the economy, to the point of implying a single configuration of institutional forms. This overlooks the fact that the emergence of coordination mechanisms is endogenous to the economy. The diversity of social protection systems bears witness to this openness to founding institutional compromises, all endowed with a certain contingency and national idiosyncrasies. The anthropogenetic mode is no exception to this rule (Fig. 2.17).

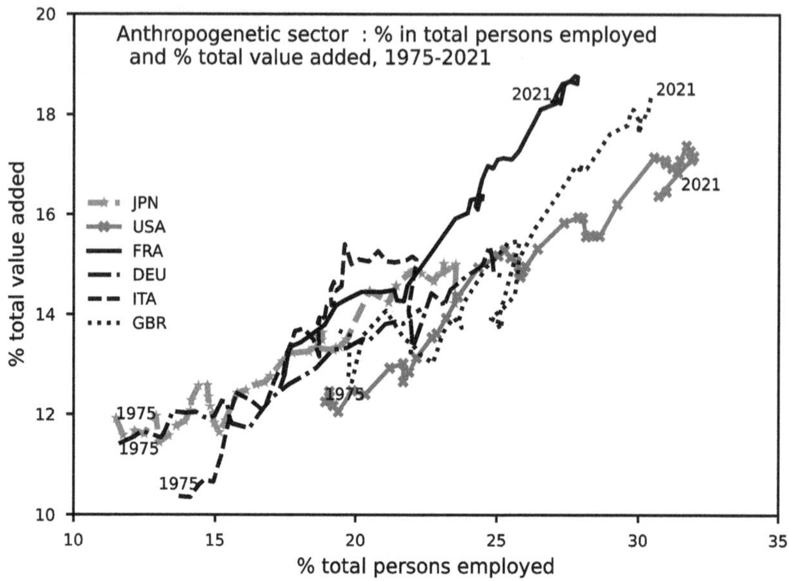

Fig. 2.17 The United States have reached the limit of the anthropogenetic mode of development. *Source* Own elaboration (see technical appendix)

Within a general trend of growth in the share of employment and added value, we note that certain countries, such as the United States, are seeing a limit to their progress, while in France, on the other hand, the trend is continuing despite an unfavorable context in terms of productivity and growth. Italy is following yet another trajectory, since its structural difficulties since joining the Euro and the peculiarities of a family-type social security system limit the expression of anthropogenetic logic (Boyer, 2020).

2.4.5 *This Mode of Development Has Already Reached Its Limits.*

The USA is a case in point. The anthropogenetic mode took off after the Second World War, undergoing an initial downturn in the early 1970s, then rapid growth from 2000 onwards, before stagnating since the great financial crisis of 2008 (Fig. 2.18).

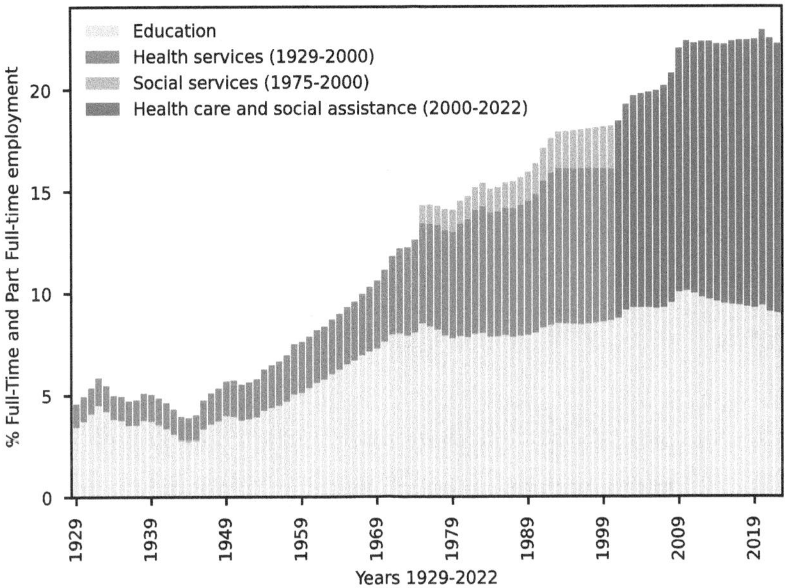

Fig. 2.18 One century long transformation of the United States economy towards the anthropogenetic mode. *Source* Own elaboration (See technical appendix)

We find confirmation of the ramp-up and maturation of this mode of development, so particular that it is rarely recognized as such. Since 1995, the Fordist dynamic based on manufacturing has been steadily declining, then stabilizing. Many heterodox macroeconomic analyses insist on the transition to a regime of accumulation driven by innovation and financial globalization. It is clear that, from 2005 onwards, value added by the financial sector outstripped that of industry. On the other hand, since 1995, the anthropogenetic sector has outstripped industry, but since 2010, its share of value added has stagnated (Fig. 2.19).

This confirms the central finding of this chapter: as soon as this mode of development is detected, it is already in crisis.

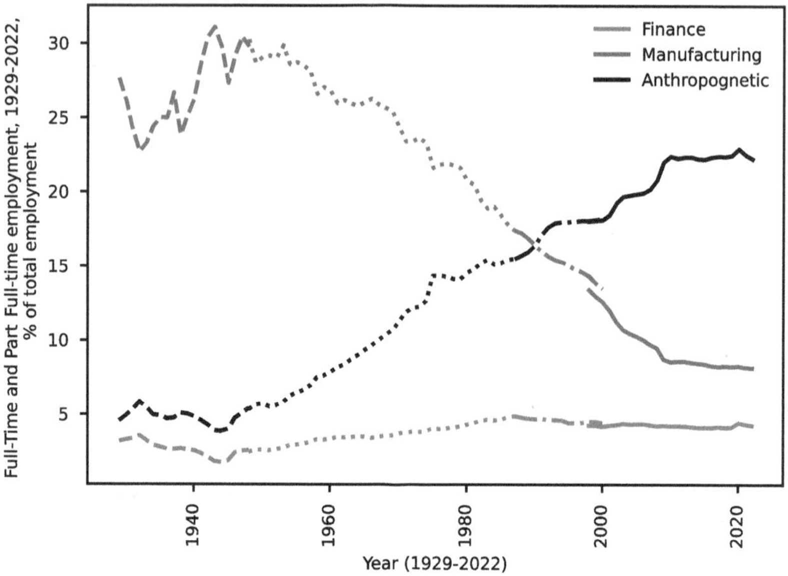

Fig. 2.19 The engines of US growth: from fordism to anthropogenetic mode via financialization. *Source* Own elaboration (see technical appendix)

2.5 Conclusion

The empirical analyses in this chapter provide new arguments in favor of the silent emergence of a mode of development based on human production through education, training, health and culture.

1. This hypothesis was put forward by combining a general taxonomy of social protection systems with a study of Japanese society since the 1990s, characterized by quasi-economic stagnation but continued improvement in well-being, particularly among the elderly, whose life expectancy has continued to rise. A similar trend has since been observed both in the USA and in the various countries of the European Union: a gradual slowdown in growth but continuing improvement in life expectancy, including in good health, throughout the period 1950–2022.

2. This structural transformation invalidates the relevance of conventional growth models, which consider only technical innovations that improve economic efficiency. Indeed, these models make improvements in life expectancy the direct and exclusive consequence of strong growth, and assume that in the long term all sectors evolve at the same speed. On the contrary, statistical observations show that spending on education, training and healthcare is systematically rising faster than other areas of expenditure. Medical and public health innovations play a decisive role in improving people's quality of life. In fact, the spread of medical techniques invented in the richest economies has effectively extended life expectancy in most other countries, in addition to allocating growth dividends to public health and education. It is therefore misleading to reduce the analysis of socio-economic regimes to the GDP indicator alone. This is one of the obstacles to recognizing anthropogenetic development as a sui generis socio-economic regime.
3. It would be questionable to reduce its emergence to a purely scientific and medical determinism. In fact, it is the synergy between widespread education, advances in medical knowledge and techniques, and the invention of social security and/or private insurance systems that has driven the dynamism of all spending and investment that contributes to well-being, and therefore the possibility of living a long and healthy life in a society rich in interaction and exchange. The dynamism of the post-World War II growth regime freed up the resources needed to forge skills, invest in the health sector, but also in culture, the catalyst for social and political interactions that can thus lead to the founding compromises of original socio-economic regimes. The arrival at the limits of this mode based on the synchronization of mass production and consumption has led to an uncertain period of trial and error in the search for a successor. In retrospect, the recurrence of government efforts to limit the rising cost of public services points to the power of the anthropogenic mode of development. Yesterday it was dominated by the imperative of performance and competitiveness, today it is the response to citizens' demands for a decent life supported by access to fundamental goods such as education, health and culture.
4. The anthropogenetic logic has thus manifested itself in almost all OECD countries, but in different ways depending on the exact nature of the political and institutional configurations. These are

all modulations. In the United States, this mode is exceptionally costly, inefficient and unequal, as financialization and confidence in market mechanisms dominate. Not surprisingly, in Japan, the principle of socialization by the state implies a relatively egalitarian mode—especially in education—and a holistic approach to health care allows for a certain frugality, while allowing life expectancy to continue to rise. The European Union is dominated by forms of capitalism incorporating universal social protection systems, with notable variations in the role of education in reducing inequality. Citizens' demands to maintain extensive public services are met with reluctance by governments sensitive to the competitive demands of big business and the valuation of financial markets.

5. This chapter provides an important update on previous research. By the end of the 2010 decade, the anthropogenic mode had itself reached its limits, but these differed from country to country. In the United States, the pandemic highlighted the flaws in the organization of the healthcare sector, its neglect of prevention and its extremely unequal nature (Case & Deaton, 2020). The divergence in life expectancy between the richest and the most disadvantaged is spectacular. The limit lies in the ineffectiveness of market competition to regulate both health and education, marked by excessive student debt in response to increasingly expensive university courses. In Europe, the slowdown in growth is even more marked than in the United States, so that this loss of dynamism is reducing funding possibilities for education, research and healthcare. Many governments are in open conflict with the social groups that have suffered most from policies to "rationalize" public spending and reduce corporate taxation. Only public indebtedness has made it possible to reconcile these two imperatives, a strategy made increasingly problematic by the tightening of monetary policies since 2022. Public health spending remains strong, but for how long? Paradoxically, Japan seems to have found a cruising speed: despite recurrent stimulus policies, quasi stagnation has not been overcome, but life expectancy continues to rise and inequalities have not exploded. This is undoubtedly because social integration, particularly for the elderly, contributes to maintaining their well-being and health. Successive governments, for their part, have found a certain legitimacy in their arbitration in favor of the well-being of the elderly and the adaptation of society to aging and stagnation.

6. How ironic! Not yet recognized as such by macro-economists, poorly taken into account by health economists, the anthropogenetic mode has already entered a crisis in most countries. Is it not surprising that approaches still persist which make the manufacturing industry the driving force of the economy, when this assumption has long been outdated in advanced countries? Similarly, the succession of speculative bubbles generated by financial liberalization and globalization has long concealed the trend towards stagnation. The return of high-intensity warfare has highlighted the importance of the national security imperative. All these events are delaying the realization of the power of the synergy between education, health and culture. We can't help but recall Joan Robinson's observation from the 1970s that, as soon as economists think they've understood a growth regime, it goes into crisis and they're lost.
7. The events and surprises that have marked the beginning of the 2020s are numerous: the perception of the consequences of aging, the probable return of pandemics, the irruption of climate, energy and ecological issues, and the coming back of open armed conflicts. All these factors complicate the aggiornamento of anthropogenetic development. Preventing the earth from becoming uninhabitable for humanity and preserving peace are imperatives and preliminaries to the pursuit of human development.

Technical Appendix

Current expenditure on health (Figs. 2.4 and 2.5)

We use the « Classification of Health Care Functions » (ICHA-HC) who's a grouping of health care goods and services by purpose. The first-digit categories identify the purpose of health care, or the various potential needs of a consumer of health care. The first digit are: HC.1 Curative care HC.2 Rehabilitative care HC.3 Long-term care (health) HC.4 Ancillary services (non-specified by function) HC.5 Medical goods (non-specified by function) HC.6 Preventive care HC.7 Governance, and health system and financing administration HC.9 Other health care services not elsewhere classified (n.e.c.)

Figure 2.3 shows the "current expenditure on health" for all functions. Figure 2.4 gives the expenses of « HC.6 Preventive care » which contains:

Information, education and counseling programs Immunization programs, Early disease detection programs Healthy condition monitoring programs Epidemiological surveillance and risk and disease control programs Preparing for disaster and emergency response program Origin of data: OECD Unit: % of GDP.

Annual old age dependency ratio (Fig. 2.6)

The indicator: The average number of economically dependent population per 100 economically productive population for a given country, territory, or geographic area, at a specific point in time. Economically dependent population is defined as the population 65 years of age and over; economically productive population is defined as the population between 15 and 64 years of age, for the same country, territory, or geographic area, at the same specific point in time. Origin of data: "United Nations, Department of Economic and Social Affairs, Population Division (2022). World Population Prospects 2022, Online Edition" Unit: %, 1950-2019: values, 2020-2100: estimates.

Patent applications granted for health care (Figs. 2.9 and 2.10)

Origin of data: European patents office (EPO), Cover: 2012-2022, situation at: end January 2023.

Units: Number and % of total Granted patents hand the creators and manufacturers of a protected work a monopoly over that work for a set period of time. Published patent applications for inventions do not give these rights to the creators of works, but simply say that the works might be protected in the future. Just because a patent application is published, it won't always be granted. For « Health care », we retain 4 technological subdomains of 2 domains of the International patent classification IPC (see table). The technological classification used is the simplified classification established by the World Intellectual Property Organization (WIPO) which groups the IPC technology classes into 5 technological domains and 35 technological subdomains that correspond to the scope of the invention.

GAFAM acquisitions in healthcare (Figs. 2.11 and 2.12)

The approach adopted to identify GAFAM acquisitions in healthcare.

Initially, we considered as falling within the health sector the companies identified in the "GAFAM Empire" project whose activity description contained: "Health care", "Child care", "Hospital", "Medical », "Medical device", "Biotechnology" "Fitness", "Sports", "Beauty". "GAFAM Empire" (https://gafam.theglassroom.org/) is a project that examines all known acquisitions made by five major technology companies: Google, Amazon, Facebook, Apple and Microsoft, since the time they made the first until the end of summer 2022.

The project provides information on GAFAM acquisitions but also on relationships between companies before and after these acquisitions. For example, the project contains elements on the acquisition by Microsoft of the company "Nuance Communication" in 2021 but also on acquisitions by "Nuance Communication" before this date. In the section devoted to methodology, the project website offers a table with the main data for 1327 companies. The table contains in particular the year of the operation, the location of the company, the sector(s) and activities. Secondly, based on consultation of articles, sites and studies on BigTech acquisitions in the health sector, we completed the list by adding health-related companies that were classified in the project in other sectors as well as the most recent acquisitions.

This additional research also allowed us to note the existence of significant acquisitions made in digital health and life sciences by other BigTechs and in particular by IBM, Oracle and Dassault Systèmes. Finally, for each of the companies on the list and for those of IBM, Oracle and Dassault Systems, we looked for the amount of the operation. In total, we examined 58 operations, including 47 for GAFAM.

Anthropogenetic sectors in the long term (Figs. 2.14, 2.15 et 2.17)

Anthropogenic sector = Education (P) + Human health and social work activities (Q) + Arts, entertainment and recreation (R) + Accommodation and food service activities.

Data mobilized: the database containing the weight of anthropogenic sectors in employment and added value was built from several sources:

- EUROSTAT: national accounts aggregates by industry
- EUROSTAT: national accounts employment data by industry
- OECD: national accounts by industry
- OECD: structural analysis database (STAN)

- KLEMS database (https://www.rug.nl/ggdc/productivity/eu-klems/?lang=en)
  - KLEMS23: Bontadini F., Corrado C., Haskel J., Iommi M., Jona-Lasinio C. (2023), EUKLEMS & INTANProd: industry productivity accounts with intangibles—Sources of growth and productivity trends: methods and main measurement challenges
  - KLEMS12
  - KLEMS13 for US: Dale W. Jorgenson, Mun S. Ho, and Jon Samuels, "A Prototype Industry-Level Production Account for the United States, 1947-2010," Second World KLEMS Conference, Harvard University, August 9, 2012; for Japan « The Japan Industrial Productivity Database 2012 » -RIETI
- RIETI23: Database « The Japan Industrial Productivity Database 2023 »—RIETI
- BEA: table 6.4A to D (Full-time and part time employees by industry)
- STAN/TAB6A ou STAN/TAB6B: indicates that Stan and national accounts are compatible (we use STAN for the oldest period and TAB6A or TAB7A for recent years)
- KLEMxx for KLEMS milesime xx
- R indicate retopolation
- E Indicate extrapolation Anthropogenetic sectors in the long term (Figs. 2.14, 2.15 et 2.17)

The long term rise of anthropogenetic logic (Fig. 2.16)

Sources: Real GDP per capita at constant 2017 national prices (in mil. 2017US$): Penn World Table, version 10.01, Feenstra, Robert C., Robert Inklaar and Marcel P. Timmer (2015), "The Next Generation of the Penn World Table" American Economic Review, 105(10), 3150–3182, available for download at http://www.ggdc.net/pwt.

Life expectancy: United Nations, Department of Economic and Social Affairs, Population Division (2022). World Population Prospects 2022, Online Edition Smoothing of GDP per capita growth rate between two rolling 5-year periods.

This mode of development has already reached its limits (Figs. 2.18 and 2.19)

Source of data: BEA: table 6.4A to D (Full-time and part time employees by industry) The tables take into account breaks in the sectoral series

Sectoral composition:

1929–1948 (tab 6.4A): Anthropogenetic = health services + education services + education (gov) Finance = "Finance, insurance, and real estate"-"real estate" Manufacturing = Manufacturing

1948–1987 (tab 6.4B): Anthropogenetic (1948–1974) = health services + education services + education (gov) Anthropognetic (1975–1987) = health services+social service + education services + education (gov) Finance = "Finance, insurance, and real estate"-"real estate" Manufacturing = Manufacturing

1987–2000 (tab 6.4C): Anthropogenetic = Health care services + social assistance + education services + education (gov) Manufacturing – Manufacturing Finance = "Finance, insurance, and real estate"—"Real estate"

1998–2022 (tab 6.4D): Anthropogenic = Health care and social assistance + education services + education (gov) Finance = Finance and insurance Manufacturing = Manufacturing

References

Acemoglu, D. (2021). Redesigning AI: Work, democracy and justice in the age of automation. *Boston Review*, *18*, spring.

Andler, D. (2023). *Intelligence artificielle, intelligence humaine: La double énigme.* Gallimard.

Aglietta, M., & Rébérioux, A. (2004). *Les Dérives du capitalisme financier.* Albin Michel.

Allaire, G. (2023). Régimes d'accumulation et socialisation de l'agriculture et de l'alimentation dans Boyer Robert, Jean-Pierre Chanteau, Agnès Labrousse et Thomas Lamarche. In *Théorie de la régulation, un nouvel état des savoirs.* Dunod.

Armatya, S. (2001). *Development as freedom.* Oxford University Press.

Boyer, R. (2002). *La croissance début de siècle. De l'octet au gène.* Albin Michel.

Boyer, R. (2013). Les crises financières comme conflit de temporalités. *Vingtième Siècle: Revue d'histoire*, *117*, 69–88. https://doi.org/10.3917/vin.117.0069

Boyer, R. (2015). L'essor du secteur de la santé annonce-t-il un modèle de développement anthropogénétique ? *Revue de la Régulation*, [En ligne], 17 1er semestre/Spring 2015. https://doi.org/10.4000/regulation.11159

Boyer, R. (2020). *Les capitalismes à l'épreuve de la pandémie.* La Découverte.

Boyer, R. (2021). *Une discipline sans réflexivité peut-elle être une science ? Epistémologie de l'économie.* Presses de la Sorbonne.

Boyer, R., Chanteau, J.-P., Labrousse, A., & Lamarche, T. (2023). *Théorie de la régulation : Un nouvel état des savoirs.* Dunod.

Boyer, R. (2023a), Développement anthropogénétique et reconnaissance de l'utilité sociale du travail. *Sociologie du Travail* [En ligne], Vol. *64* 1–2 | Janvier-Juin 2022, mis en ligne le 02 mai 2022, consulté le 01 novembre 2023. http://journals.openedition.org/sdt/40685; https://doi.org/10.4000/sdt.40685

Boyer, R. (2023b, Novembre). Spéculation et inégalités: Les mirages de l'intelligence artificielle. *Alternatives Economiques.* https://www.alternatives-economiques.fr/speculation-inegalites-mirages-de-lintelligence-artificielle/00107813

Boyer, R., & Yamada, T. (2000). *Japanese capitalism in crisis.* Routledge.

Campbell, J., Hall, J., & Pedersen, O. K. (2008). *National identity and the varieties of Capitalism: The danish experience.* DJOF publishing.

Case, A., & Deaton, A. (2020). *Deaths of despair and the future of capitalism.* Princeton University Press.

César, N. J., & Ludmer, G. (2023). Argentine: Conflits entre deux logiques et récurrence des crises, dans Boyer Robert, Jean-Pierre Chanteau, Agnès Labrousse et Thomas Lamarche (coord.). *Théorie de la régulation, un nouvel état des savoirs*, 577–583. Dunod.

Crawford, K. (2021). *Atlas of AI.* Yale University Press.

Cohen, D., Hung, A., Weinberg, E & Zhu, D. (2020). *Healthtech in the fast lane: What is fueling investor excitement?* McKinsey. https://www.mckinsey.com/industries/life-sciences/our-insights/healthtech-in-the-fast-lane-what-is-fueling-investor-excitement

Deaton, A. (2013), *The great escape: Health, wealth and the origin of inequality*, Princeton University Press, Princeton

Esping Andersen, G. (2008). Childhood investments and skill formation. *International Tax and Public Finance, 15*, 14–49.

FAO. (2023), La sécurité alimentaire et de la nutrition dans le monde, https://www.fao.org/3/cc6550fr/cc6550fr.pdf

Gallois, F., & Rauly, A. (2018). Complémentarité des systèmes de production et de régulation: Une mise en évidence par la télémédecine. *Revue de la Régulation.* https://doi.org/10.4000/regulation.12692

Gaudillière, J-P ., Izambert, C., & Juven, P.-A. (2021). *Pandémopolitique.* La Découverte.

Genton, V. (2022, Novembre). Impact global du dérèglement climatique sur la santé. *Santé et environnement: Revue médicale Suisse.* https://www.revmed.ch/livres/sante-et-environnement/partie-2-environnement-sante-et-societe-perspectives-multidisciplinaires/perspective-de-la-sante-publique/17-impact-global-du-dereglement-climatique-sur-la-sante#tab=tab-toc

Global Health Care Outlook. (2023). https://www.deloitte.com/content/dam/assets-shared/legacy/docs/gx-UPDATED-Health-care-Outlook-2023_Consolidated.pdf

Gorry, P., & Montalban, M. (2026). The crisis of capitalism and health innovation: Symptoms of a crisis or of success? In S. Lechevalier, J.-P. Gaudillière, K. Ibata-Arens, & K. Takuma (Eds.), *Capitalism, innovations, and health after Covid-19: An Asian perspective*. Palgrave MacMillan.

Hodgson, C. (2023, November 8). Amazon expands healthcare push with one medical benefits for Prime members. *Financial Times*. https://www.ft.com/content/90fdcadf-7ec4-4fcc-9847-c6f96e445de2

Jonas, S., Aburto, J. M., Kashnitsky, I., Kniffka, M. S., Luyin, Z., Hannaliis, J., Dowd, J. B., & Kashyap, R. (2022, December). Life expectancy changes since COVID-19. *Nature Human Behaviour*, *6*, 1649–1659.

Lechevalier, S. (2019). *Innovation beyond technology: Science for society and interdisciplinary approaches*. Springer.

Lechevalier, S. (2026). Care-led innovation: A new paradigm and an application in the Japanese context of Society 5.0. In S. Lechevalier, J.-P. Gaudillière, K. Ibata-Arens, & K. Takuma (Eds.), *Capitalism, innovations, and health after Covid-19: An Asian perspective*. Palgrave MacMillan.

Loder, N. (2023, November 18–24). Treatments arriving in 2024 will use genetic scissors and other new tricks, *The economist*, p. 91.

Masden, K. (2008). How can it fly? The paradox of a dynamic labour market in a Scandinavian Welfare State. In J. Campbell, J. Hall, & O. K. Pedersen (Eds.), *National identity and the varieties of Capitalism: The danish experience* (pp. 321–355). DJOF publishing.

Neville, S. (2023, October 30). What is behind the unexpected decline in dementia? *Financial Times*.

OECD (2022), *Investir dans les systèmes de santé pour protéger la société et stimuler l'économie: Priorités et estimations de l'ordre de grandeur des coûts* (version abrégée). https://www.oecd.org/coronavirus/policy-responses/investir-dans-les-systemes-de-sante-pour-proteger-la-societe-et-stimuler-l-economie-priorites-et-estimations-de-l-ordre-de-grandeur-des-couts-version-abregee-38389499/

Ozalp, H., Ozcan, P., Dinckol, D., Zachariadis, M., & Gawer, A. (2022). Digital Colonization" of highly regulated industries:An analysis of big tech platforms' entry into health care and education. *California Management Review*, *64*(4), 78–107.

Petit, P. (2013). *Slow growth and the service economy*. Bloomsburry.

PNUD. (2014). *Rapport sur le développement humain 2013. L'essor du Sud: Le progrès humain dans un monde diversifié*.

Sarrion, E. (2023). *La révolution ChatGPT*. Editions Eyroles.

The Economist (2023). *The world largest health care research study in Britain.* https://www.economist.com/britain/2023/10/18/the-worlds-largest-health-research-study-is-under-way-in-britain?utm_content=article-link-5&etear=nl_today_5&utm_campaign=r.the-econom

Théret, B. (1992). *Régimes économiques de l'ordre politique: Esquisse d'une théorie régulationniste des limites de l'Etat* (pp. 319). PUF—Presses Universitaires de France.

UNESCO. (2021). *Comprendre l'impact de l'intelligence artificielle sur le développement des compétences.* Edition de l'Unesco.

UNESCO. (2023, octobre–décembre). *Education in the age of artificial intelligence.* The UNESCO Courier.

Van Daalen, K., et al. (2022). The 2022 Europe report of the Lancet countdown on health and climate change: Towards a climate resilient future, *The Lancet Public Health*, *7*(11), e942–e965 https://www.thelancet.com/action/showPdf?pii=S2468-2667%2822%2900197-9

Visser, J., & Hemerijck, A. (1997). *'A Dutch Miracle'—Job growth, welfare reform and corporatism in the Netherlands.* Amsterdam University Press.

World Health Organization. (2023a), *2023 Emerging technologies and scientific innovations: A global public health perspective.* WHO global health foresight series. World Health Organization. https://apps.who.int/iris/rest/bitstreams/1515446/retrieve

World Health Organization. (2023b). A framework for the quantification and economic valuation of health outcomes originating from health and non-health climate change mitigation and adaptation action. https://apps.who.int/iris/rest/bitstreams/1499830/retrieve

World Intellectual Property Report 2022: The Direction of Innovation. *WIPO.* https://www.wipo.int/edocs/pubdocs/en/wipo-pub-944-2022-en-world

CHAPTER 3

The Crisis of Capitalism and Health Innovation: Symptoms of a Crisis or of Success?

Philippe Gorry and Matthieu Montalban

Abstract In this chapter, we examine the issue of the "innovation crisis" and the productivity paradox of advanced capitalist economies by looking at the transformations in the healthcare and pharmaceutical sectors. We show that Fordism and its crisis have had an equivalent in the health sectors, and that a substantial part of the slowdown in productivity gains observed in developed countries is due to a growing share of low-productivity services,

We are grateful to our colleagues from CTSH project, especially Sébastien Lechevalier, Jean-Paul Gaudillière. Kathryn Ibata-Arens, Kayo Takuma for their help in editing, and all the team for the interesting exchanges. The remaining errors are ours.

P. Gorry
Bordeaux University, Bordeaux, France
e-mail: philippe.gorry@u-bordeaux.fr

M. Montalban (✉)
Institut d'Etudes Politiques de Bordeaux alias Sciences Po Bordeaux, Bordeaux, France
e-mail: matthieu.montalban@u-bordeaux.fr

S. Lechevalier et al. (eds.), *Capitalism, Innovations, and Health after Covid-19*,
https://doi.org/10.1007/978-3-032-24479-6_3

including healthcare services. At the same time, the pharmaceutical sector experienced a declining marginal productivity on innovation, called now "Eroom's law". We show that this medical and pharmaceutical Fordism crisis is in fact the consequence of his own success in improving the health and life expectancy of OECD populations. In order to reduce the costs of healthcare systems, a neoliberal regime was put in place. The new strategy now turns to digital health, in the hope of reducing the cost of health services, improving care and solving the problem of medical Fordism crisis beyond pharmaceutical innovation. However, despite hopes and initial successes, this strategy has to prove its efficiency because it could amplify some problems revealed by the neoliberal policy applied to healthcare.

3.1 Introduction

Capitalism, as a mode of production, is often associated with its ability to reward innovations. This economic system encourages economic agents to invest in research and development for developing new products or services toward a profit maximization through temporary monopolies. Technological progress, such as automation, computerization, robotics, artificial intelligence is seen in economic theory as a way to accelerate growth (Solow, 1956) and to increase profit rate (Ricardo, 1819; Marx, 2008) by transforming the conditions of production, increasing efficiency and productivity. Usually, innovations and technologies are associated with more qualitative and/or cheaper products and/or more efficient process and organization of production (Schumpeter, 1934). Marx (2008) emphasized the process of automation and the permanent transformation of conditions of production related to competition and accumulation of capital. The economic changes brought about by innovations have been characterized and theorized by Joseph Schumpeter under the concept of creative destruction: a new product will destroy obsolete activities, leading to substitution of new products over old ones. Successful innovators will capture market share and the competition will foster innovations in the market. Access to capital is essential for R&D risk-taking and venture capital play a crucial role. But at the same time, Schumpeter (1942) believed that capitalism would gradually weaken itself and eventually collapse: it is the success of capitalism that would undermine it, because the rise of living standards would change expectations of people, increase the demand of regulation and reduce its innovativeness. This process is called endometabolic crisis in Regulation Theory (Boyer, 2015): the better a system functions, the more it generates transformations that will undermine its own dynamics. But for Regulation Theory, the final crisis of capitalism is rarely the rule: capitalism passed different periods, called mode of development (combination of mode of regulation and accumulation regime) and endo-metabolic crises, transiting one system to another.

The last four decades in advanced economies give the feeling of a succession of multiple crises following the end of Fordism, although continuous reforms—neoliberal or not—were implemented by governments to solve those crises. Slowdown of growth and productivity, financial crises, high unemployment rate, crisis of Welfare State, crisis of public debt and environmental crisis, all of them seem to be related to the crisis of Fordism or to the reforms implemented to solve this original crisis. But others believe that it is not the crisis of Fordism or neoliberal mode of development, but the crisis of capitalism or technical progress which is in question.

In the healthcare sector, although innovation and higher living standards improved health conditions of populations of advanced economies, we can observe some symptoms of this crisis between capitalism, innovation and health evoked by Schumpeter: during the COVID19 pandemic and the critical response has raised many concerns about the relations between economic and healthcare system. Among them, some political discourses from lay people but also from researchers have questioned the responsibility of capitalism, globalization and techno-science in the health crisis, or even questioned the ability of pharmaceutical companies to solve it, with the growth of anti-vaccines arguments. The deindustrialization and relocation of pharmaceutical facilities has increased the dependency of France and many other western countries on imported drugs, leading to the lack of efficient response to the pandemic (supply of medicines, masks...) and prompting calls for a new industrial policy (Aghion et al., 2021; Coris et al., 2021; Gorry, 2023).

Although many scholars expect a new "coherent" regime (see for example Clévenot, 2008), Boyer (2015) proposes another hypothesis: the problems encountered by advanced economies are the consequences of the invisible emergence of an anthropogenetic mode of development, in which healthcare, education and all the activities linked to the reproduction and "maintenance" of human would be the main drivers of innovation, demand and growth. This mode of development is referred to as "anthropogenetic" (Boyer, 2015; Boyer & Boylaud, 2026). The Japanese 5.0 society project seems to describe a political will to move in this direction (Lechevalier, 2026).

Taking this hypothesis seriously, this chapter will show that the endometabolic crisis of Fordism also has its health counterparts and that the current problems of low productivity and innovation now includes the healthcare and pharmaceutical sectors and can still be linked to the crisis of Fordism and neoliberal solutions. But contrary to the idea of a coherent model, we would show that anthropogenetic model is not sustainable because of productivity problems, and that digitalizing the economy including health and pharmaceutical sectors, is a way of trying to make it sustainable. In our view, the productivity slowdown is partly a consequence of the shift from manufacturing to services such as healthcare in advanced economies, and an endometabolic crisis of the earlier success of what we call medical Fordism in the healthcare sector and the failure of medical neoliberalism to address these problems. We will give some insights by looking at the healthcare and pharmaceutical sectors, allowing at the same time to understand how these sectors contribute to Fordism and neoliberal growth and crises, and how the successive regimes and modes of regulation have led to productivity and costs diseases in those sectors. As we shall see, the current hopes come from digitalization in health and pharmaceutical sectors as a way to boost productivity, but it has yet to prove its worth.

In Sect. 3.2, we summarize the transformations of capitalism following the crisis of Fordism, showing the role of the decline of productivity gains in this crisis and its causes in the process: capitalism is a very efficient system for innovation, but we observed for the last decades a decline of productivity gains at the core of a different crisis. In Sect. 3.3, we analyze the path of anthropogenetic mode of development and the crisis of the relation between healthcare services and capitalism. We will show how capitalism has raised the level of health of the population, and how the specificities of health services lead to an endometabolic crisis of productivity, leading to (some attempts at) neoliberal reforms in healthcare. In Sect. 3.4, we focus on innovation, especially in the pharmaceutical industry, to understand the "crisis" of innovation ("Eroom law") and its causes and we will show, once again, its endometabolic nature. In Sect. 3.5, we analyze how digitalization could help to solve those crises and the remaining limits of digital innovations. Section 3.6 concludes.

3.2 From the Crisis of Fordism to Failure of Neoliberalism: The "Secular Stagnation"

Fordism, which emerged in the early twentieth century, is characterized by mass production of standardized products, inducing economies of scale, a vertical division of labor through assembly-line work and wages increasing at the same speed as the productivity to develop consumption. In the classic works of the Regulation Theory, Fordism was a mode of development, combining the previous organization with a monopolist mode of regulation, including the development of collective bargaining, the creation of the welfare and interventionist State, monopolistic regulation of competition and markets and a larger socialization of incomes and expenditures. Fordism was also characterized by a weak international trade openness at its beginning but years after years of GATT and EEC agreements by a greater openness allowing to exploit economy of scale at international level without disrupting the national economies under a certain period of time.

The crisis was largely an endometabolic process: on one side, as workers became richer and markets of household goods saturated, household consumption shifted towards high-quality, customized and complex products and services. On the other side, we observed a growing internationalization of economy. At the beginning, the demand for diversity (scope) and economic openness could be combined with economy of scale, but the productivity gains were decreasing. As a result, the mode of regulation invented in the post-war period and which supported the growth regime became a problem, as wages and social costs continued to grow while productivity and growth slowed.

The neoliberal regime emerged as a consequence of the crisis of Fordism especially for solving the productivity crisis and restructuring the conditions of production (Duménil et Lévy, 2014): the crisis of Fordism was characterized by a fall of profit rate due to a slowdown of productivity gains and an obsolete mode of regulation. The post-Fordist regimes are the neoliberal-financialized accumulation regime, followed by two possible regimes, the digital platforms capitalism and the anthropogenetic regime in development, or a hybrid form of the three. The neoliberal regime and reforms are based on globalization, deregulation of markets, rationalization of public expenditures, taxation and public services with some forms of privatization but with relative resilience of social protection—a compromise sometimes referred to as "social (neo)liberalism" (Cabannes, 2012, 2015). In fact, neoliberalism and financialization have been ways of reducing the bargaining power of workers and the cost of "democratic capitalism", but also a way to "buy time" through debt (Streeck, 2014). Indeed, while several forms of privatizations occurred, social and public expenditures remained high to manage economic cycles and their social consequences, generating debt.

Since the brutal crisis of financialized accumulation regime (Boyer, 2000, 2009), capitalism has taken a Schumpeterian and digital turn with the transformations implemented by Big Tech, Silicon Valley and start-ups, sometimes described by critics as "techno-solutionists" (Morozov, 2013): technological innovation, whether digital or not, is seen as the main way to solve the major socio-economic challenges. Indeed, in most growth models, innovation is the means to increase Gross Domestic Product (GDP) per capita and welfare, as it is supposed to decrease costs and/or to increase quality of product and/or to increase productivity, and it can avoid a steady state or stagnation. The belief that technology, particularly digital technology, has the potential to drive economic growth, solve societal problems and improve well-being, gave rise to techno-optimism. Techno-optimism emphasizes the potential of digital technologies to increase efficiency and productivity across all sectors, including health market, by reducing cost and enabling disruptive new business models, toward a better market efficiency while maximizing economic output. It promotes a culture of entrepreneurships with a strong belief in individual initiative and market-driven innovation. In this context, the dominance of digital platform, exemplified by Big Tech, gave birth to a new form of capitalism, the digital platform capitalism (Srnicek, 2017; Montalban et al., 2019; Boyer, 2022; Montalban, 2023). Moreover, related to this process a new regime of IP came to birth, generating a patent race (Fig. 3.1).

But almost 30 years after it was formulated, the empirical facts still do not contradict the famous paradox of Solow: we are seeing a lot of computers and innovations, even a strong increase in patenting, but productivity gains remain low and decreasing (Fig. 3.2), leading to a possible secular stagnation in advanced economies (Gordon, 2012, 2018).

Post-Fordist modes of development have therefore not solved the problem of the slowdown in productivity gains that was at the source of the Fordist crisis and the unsustainable regulations invented to "solve" this

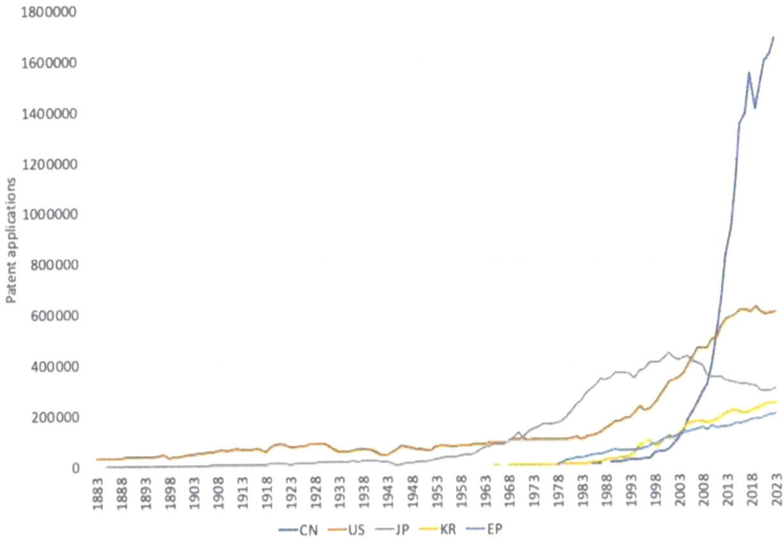

Fig. 3.1 Trend in patent applications for the top five offices (in number of patent applications), 1883–2023. *Sources* authors; data: WIPO

productivity problem. Boyer (2015) considers that an anthropogenetic model based on health and education sectors is slowly emerging as a new possible mode of development. But as Boyer & Boylaud pointed out (2026), we raise many doubts about the sustainability of such model. We will call "medical Fordism" the development of healthcare sectors made possible by strong growth and productivity, mass production, large consumption and large socialization of healthcare and the increasing standardization of healthcare product and services. In the following sections, the crisis should not to be understood in the sense of a sudden fall in activity and accumulation, but as a mode of development that is becoming less and less sustainable, due to a growing divergence between the mode of regulation and the regime of accumulation.

As we shall see in the next two sections, the health and pharmaceutical sectors are in fact undergoing their own version of the endometabolic slowdown in productivity and the Fordist and post-Fordist crises, due to the cost of socialization, the growing cost of innovation and health services and the endometabolic transformations linked to the success achieved in healthcare sectors.

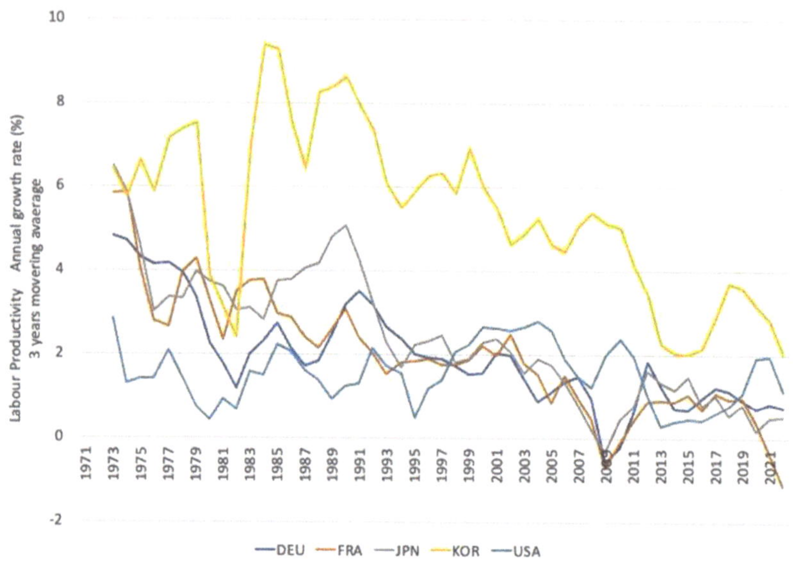

Fig. 3.2 Slowdown of labor productivity gains in % in some OECD countries, 1971–2022. *Sources* authors; data: OECD

3.3 The Case of Health: An Endometabolic Crisis of Welfare State and Anthropogenetic Mode of Development?

The welfare State was widely institutionalized after the Great Depression and the Second World War, providing public pensions, social protection such as healthcare and forming part of the Fordist social compromise and mode of the regulation. It had taken many different forms in different the countries, with different level and forms of socialization (Esping-Andersen, 1990), but it is a common trend. As a consequence, access to healthcare services and products has improved almost continuously since 1945, with regulations and service provisions for patients/citizens, partly because of the specificity of health goods and because of this social compromise in a context of high growth. There is a strong correlation between high GDP per capita and better health, which was part of the Fordist growth model, but the "crisis of Welfare State" (Rosanvallon, 2015) is largely a consequence of the endometabolic productivity's Fordist crisis, but also of the demographic transition that is the consequence of long-term growth. The specificities of health goods and sectors also explain some pathologies—the "cost disease" of healthcare sectors and the consequences of "over-consumption" problems linked to public goods—that the neoliberal policies have tried (and failed) to cure since the 90's.

3.3.1 *Specificities of Health Goods*

Health goods are distinguished from other types of goods and services by their unique characteristics and purposes. They are designed to prevent (vaccines), diagnose (tests) or treat (drugs and medical devices) health diseases. They are strictly regulated by governments to ensure efficacy and safety for patients through regulatory agencies such as FDA or EMA and are distributed by specific authorized healthcare providers (pharmacies or hospital): they require certified healthcare professionals to prescribe or administer health goods because final consumer (patient) does not have sufficient knowledge to make the decision.

3.3.1.1 *Externalities*

In general, health goods generate positive externalities by improving health of individual and of the population. For example, vaccinating a person, not only protects them from the disease but also prevents the spread of the disease in the population. In general, improving individual health has a positive impact on productivity and the economy through increasing the workforce and human capital. Moreover, in the case of infectious diseases, the state of health of one person can affect that of another. This explains why the public sector has taken a large place in the provision of healthcare.

3.3.1.2 *Socialized Demand and Superior Goods*

Health is considered as a superior good, i.e. an economic good that has a growing share in the budget when the income grows—but it also means that households tend to limit their health expenditures when they have a low income. Therefore, access to care is now through insurances schemes that fund reimbursements for health goods or through state-funded providers such as hospitals. In many advanced countries after the Second World War, quasi-universal healthcare systems have been implemented, because of externalities to ensure equitable access to essential health goods and avoid that the classic problems of insurance. Socialized demand involves an insurance system to manage the financial risks collectively. By sharing the cost over a larger population, health insurance system reduces the burden on individuals and is supposed to promote solidarity and social cohesion. The socialization of demand favors continuous growth in expenditures and a growing share of budget, which leads to demand being controlled to avoid infinite growth.

3.3.1.3 Products and Services

Health goods are heterogeneous: they encompass a wide range of products and services, from medicines to supportive services, for the prevention, diagnosis, treatment, or management of diseases with price ranging from a few cents (example: aspirin pill or Personal Protective Equipment) to a million euros (example: gene therapy for rare disease or artificial heart). They could be freely available (over-the-counter) or strictly restricted to prescription by hospital doctors. But health is defined by WHO as "a state of complete physical, mental and social well-being and not merely the absence of disease or infirmity", which means many elements can contribute to it. Typically, access to food and water are of course essential for health, as having a safe environment.

3.3.1.4 No Creative Destruction

While the concept of creative destruction proposed by economist Schumpeter (1934) provides insights into the dynamics of innovation and market evolution, the application of this concept to the healthcare sector is complex. On one side, health market has been subject to continuous innovation and technological advancements. During the last century, research breakthroughs, new drug discoveries, and improvements in medical technologies drive the development of new and more effective therapy, eradicating certain infectious diseases, curing many cancers, transforming the morbidity of certain diseases and contributing greatly to the increase in life expectancy. But at the same time, it is crucial for governments to balance the need for market competition and innovation with considerations of affordability and patient safety.

But in reality, it is clear that therapeutic innovations are not creative destruction because new treatments do not often lead to the disappearance of old molecules: they complete the therapeutic arsenal and at best impose new hierarchies among therapeutic options. Older medicines, such as aspirin or penicillin, like many others, still have their place in the pharmacopoeia and are not obsolete, including in oncology, where many innovative medicines are regularly brought to market. The first chemotherapies, nitrogen mustard or folic acid, developed in 1940s gave up their first place this last decade to targeted therapies such as brought by the biotechnology revolution, but the classical chemotherapies are still in used, associated with tyrosine kinase inhibitors or monoclonal antibodies, in first-line regimen. The healthcare services sectors are labor-intensive and are not really affected (but this could change, see below) by rapid technological change, innovation being mainly organizational or in care practices. The pharmaceutical and medical device sectors, on the other hand, are oligopolies with fringe,[1] where the dominant firms operate under a Schumpeter mark II regime and the dominated start-ups under a Schumpeter mark I regime,[2] but without the turbulence associated with bankruptcies that such a regime usually generates: the least competitive firms in these sectors rarely go bankrupt and are more often than not bought out because, as we will see after, the demand is growing strongly.

3.3.2 The Health and Growth Nexus: The "Medical Fordism" at the Root of Anthropogenetic Model

Health and economic growth are interdependent relationships and influence each other within society. Improvements in health can contribute to economic growth, and economic development can, in turn, impact health outcomes. Understanding the dialectical relation between health and economic growth highlights the importance of investing in health systems, promoting equitable access to healthcare, and implementing policies that address social determinants of health. But the relation between growth

[1] An oligopoly with fringe is a market structure characterized by one or a small number of incumbent sellers and several dominated competing sellers. The Stackelberg model is a typical theoretical example.

[2] Schumpeter mark I and Schumpeter mark II technological regimes are typical patterns of organization of industry and innovation, referring to the situation described by Schumpeter (1934) for Schumpeter I regime and Schumpeter (1942) for Schumpeter II. The typology has been refined by Nelson and Winter (1982) and Breschi et al. (2000): a Schumpeter mark I regime is characterized by many entries and exits from the market, large technological opportunities, radical innovations implemented by a large number of small firms and an important process of creative destruction and bankruptcies; a Schumpeter mark II regime is characterized by an oligopoly of large firms with very few entries and exits, high technological barriers and small technological opportunities, rare bankruptcies and mainly incremental innovations and standardization of technology and products.

and health is not monotonic: over a certain threshold, more health expenditures could generate less growth (Van Zon & Myuken, 2001; Van Zon et al., 2005).

3.3.2.1 A Positive Relation …

There is a positive relation between economic growth and health expenditures (Fig. 3.3). Economic growth typically results in higher government revenues and household incomes. As individuals and governments have more resources, they allocate them to public goods including healthcare. Increased public spending on healthcare lead to access to essential medicines and healthcare services. Similarly, increased household income allows individuals to afford for healthcare and health insurance coverage, but also to access to food, better transport and better environmental conditions. Overall, higher health expenditures are associated with improved health outcomes, especially longer life expectancy in all countries (Fig. 3.4). Better health outcomes can lead to increased well-being (Fig. 3.5).

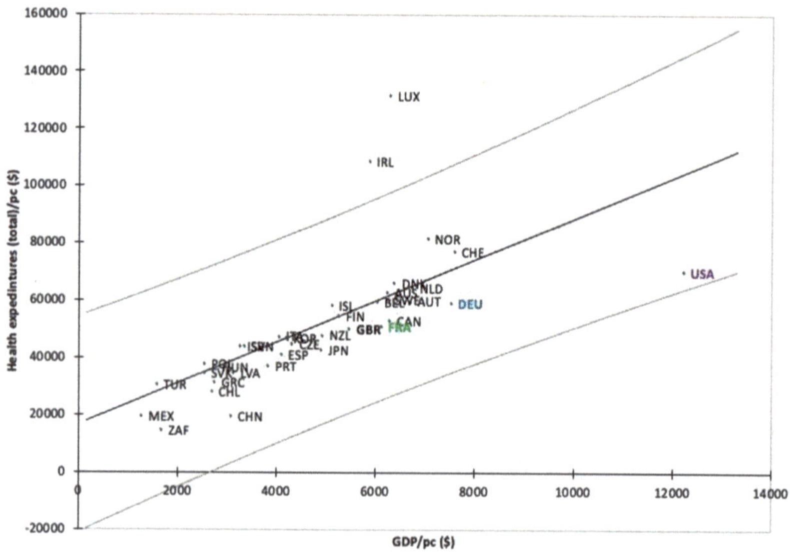

Fig. 3.3 Healthcare expenditures vs GDP 2019. *Sources* authors; data: OECD

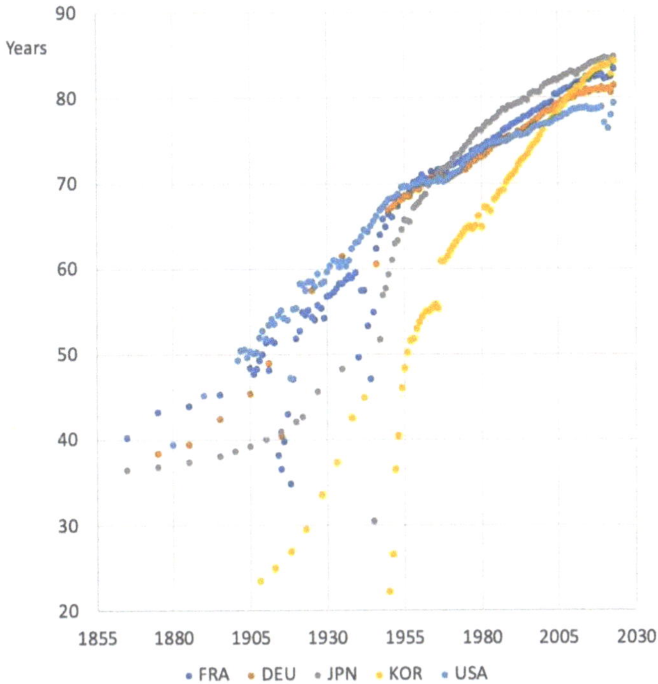

Fig. 3.4 Life expectancy in France, Germany, Japan, South Korea and USA, 1855–2025. *Sources* authors; data: OurWorldindata

The correlation between those variables is bi-directional: higher growth means higher health expenditures and longer, happier life expectancy, but also when individuals are healthy, they are more likely to participate in the labor force, contribute to economic activities and generate income. Then reduction of absenteeism, lowers healthcare costs for employers, will enhances overall labor productivity. This in turn can drive economic growth by stimulating consumption, attracting investments, fostering innovation, and a positive feedback loop is established. As health is part of human capital, this is an endogenous growth dynamic.

Investing in healthcare, promoting disease prevention, and ensuring access to healthcare services can contribute to a healthier population. This, in turn, enhances human capital development. Good health is a crucial

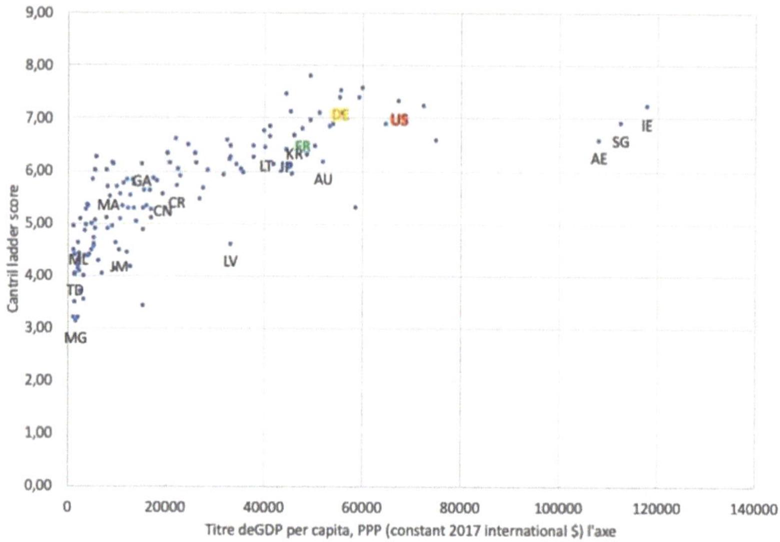

Fig. 3.5 Self-reported life satisfaction vs GDP per capita, 2022. *Sources* authors; data: OurWorldindata

determinant of educational attainment: when individuals are healthy, they are more likely to achieve higher levels of education, and to contribute to productivity and economic growth.

Health is also a source of demand for innovation and health goods that creates activities: the need for improved healthcare services, medical treatments, and technologies drives investment in research and development. Innovations in the healthcare sector not only improve health outcomes but also create employment opportunities, stimulate economic growth, and contribute to the development of human capital in fields such as medicine, biotechnology, and pharmaceutical industry. Health innovations have positive externalities because, as we see before, healthier population will have less absenteeism and can be more productive.

3.3.2.2 *… but with Negative Feedback After Some Thresholds Due to Aging and the Baumol's Disease Costs*

But the dialectical relation between health and economic growth can also be negative. The implementation of Welfare State has been criticized by philosophers and economists, discussing the impact of social expenditures on economic growth, public debt and education. However, as long as the increase in costs was almost offset by a parallel GDP growth, the debate was closed and the Welfare State model was supported by most Western countries with a steady increase of social expenditures as percentage of GDP, due to the increase in government revenues (Figs. 3.6 and 3.7). However, while health expenditure is necessary to maintain and improve health, rising health costs and expenses represent a financial burden for households and governments. Indeed, the share of health expenditures tends to increase in most countries due to the rising life expectancy and the growing proportion of the population that is elderly, inactive and often ill (Fig. 3.8). At the same time, fertility rates have strongly declined in most countries (Fig. 3.9). A decline in the young and active population tends to reduce growth, while at the same time a growing ageing population leads to an increase in costs, particularly for pensions and healthcare for the elderly. According to the OECD (2024),

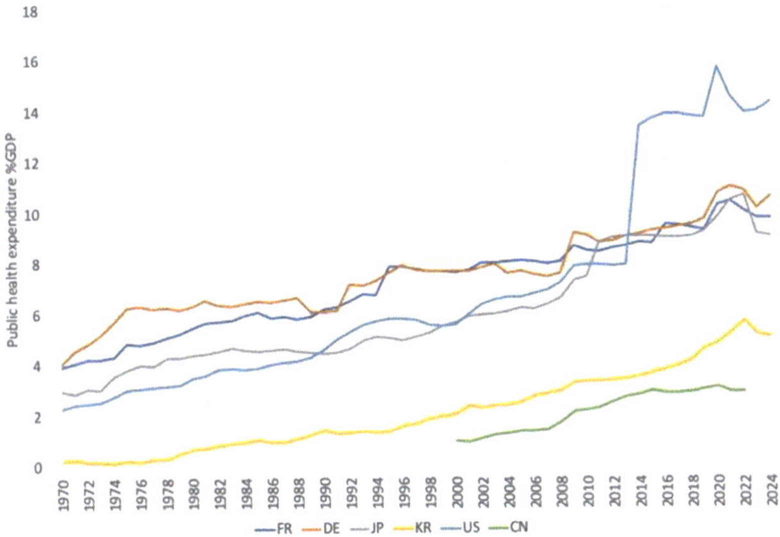

Fig. 3.6 Government health expenditure as a share of GDP, 1880–2024. *Sources* authors; data: OurWorldindata

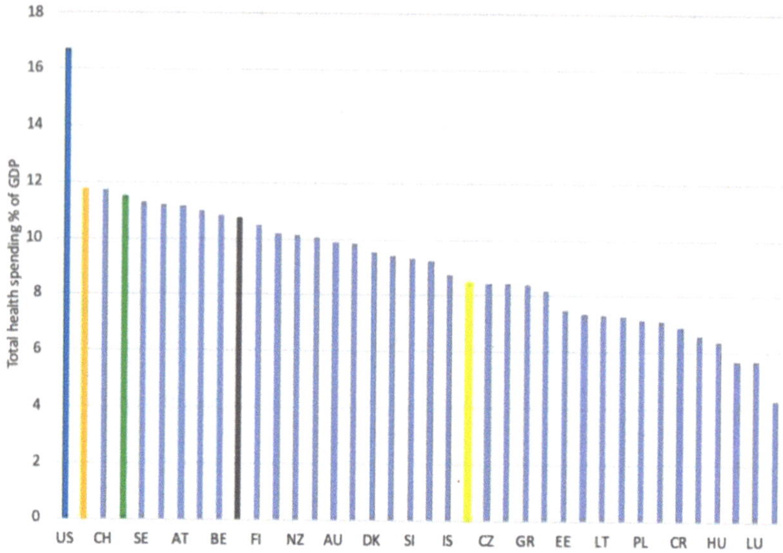

Fig. 3.7 Total health expenditures as percentage of GDP in OECD, 2023. *Sources* authors; data: OECD

growth in public spending on healthcare is expected to be twice as high as the average growth in public revenue in Western countries.

Most countries in the world, whether OECD, BRICS or developing countries are facing, population ageing, driven by declining fertility rates and rising percentage of aged people in population (Figs. 3.8 and 3.9). With an ageing population, there is an increased demand for healthcare services, long-term care, and pension benefits. Especially, elderly population is characterized by high morbidity due to chronic diseases (such as cancer, diabetes or cardiovascular diseases). At the same time, this ageing population is no longer part of the active workforce. The negative relation arises from the fact that as the number of non-active individuals, increases relative to the working-age population, and the financing of the healthcare system falls on a smaller group of taxpayers, challenging sustainability of social, pension and healthcare systems. So, the governments' response to this negative effect is to increase retirement age and to reduce some health expenditures' coverage.

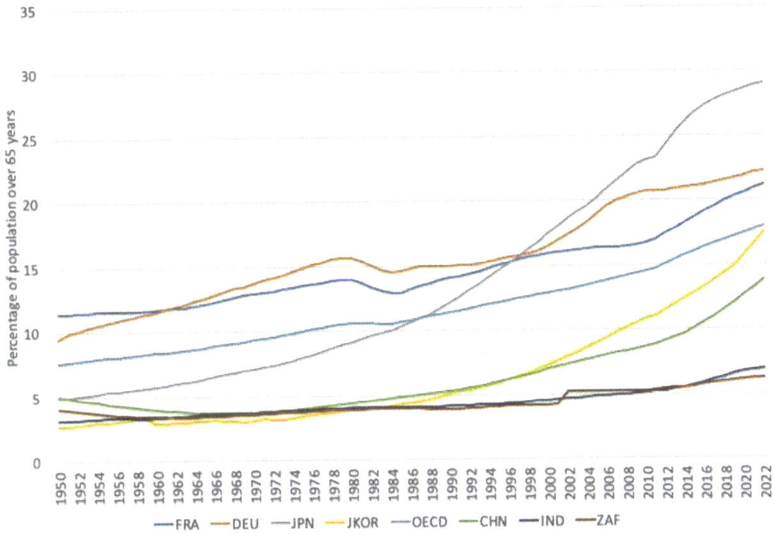

Fig. 3.8 Percentage of aged people in some OECD countries, 1950–2022. *Sources* authors; data: OECD

Finally, higher health costs can potentially limit economic growth by reducing consumption, savings, investments opportunities in others sectors or by allocating more people to less productive jobs. The recent COVID pandemic also illustrates how a disease outbreak can disrupt healthcare systems, decrease productivity, disrupt supply chains, reduce consumer spending, and lead to economic recessions. In the future, the costs associated with environmental health issues and transition to sustainable practices will pose similar economic challenges.

Baumol's disease costs (Baumol & Bowen, 1965) refers to a phenomenon in which sectors characterized by low productivity growth, such as certain service sectors, experience rising costs over time despite limited increases in productivity. This occurs because labor-intensive industries, such as healthcare and education, cannot achieve the same level of productivity gains as sectors that can leverage technological advancements and automation. As a result, the relative price of these services rises, and they are indirectly financed by higher productivity gains in other industries. The costs of pathologies include direct healthcare costs, such

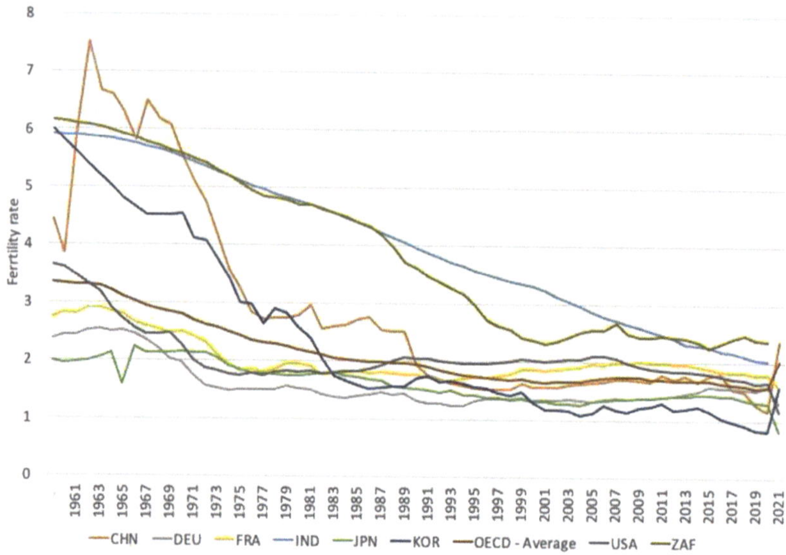

Fig. 3.9 Fertility rate: Children per woman, 1960–2020. *Sources* authors; data: OECD

as medical treatments, hospitalizations, and medications, as well as indirect costs related to lost productivity, absenteeism, and disability caused by diseases. Technological advancements, globalization, shifts in consumer preferences, and changes in economic policies have led to deindustrialization in Western countries. The decline in the relative importance of the manufacturing sector has led to a shift of high productivity employments to low productivity employments in services, although services, including healthcare, can hardly increase their productivity, which are labor intensive. Therefore, the relative price of manufactured products is declining compared to service in the long run (Fig. 3.10). As a result, with the reduction of manufacturing in total employment and the relative growth of services with low productivity will reduce the aggregated macroeconomic productivity gains. Nordhaus (2008) shows how the costs disease has reduced productivity at the macroeconomic level in the US. For Baumol (1993), this cost disease in healthcare raises public concerns for funding those services, because it means a growing share of public budgets will be allocated to those services.

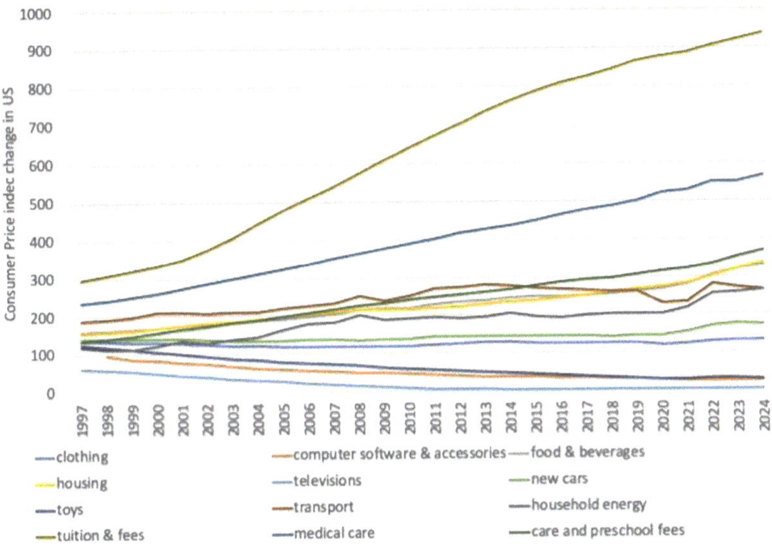

Fig. 3.10 Price index changes in consumer goods and services in the USA, 1997–2024. *Sources* authors; data: OurWorld in data

However, there are still debates about the risks and reality of Baumol disease costs in healthcare sectors. Indeed, Baumol (2012, p. 18) itself did not consider that the cost disease should be a pretext to rationalize the provision of healthcare services: "The updated analysis of the cost disease presented in this book focus on the key conclusion that follows from this: no matter how painful rising medical and educational bills may be, society can afford them, and there is no need to deny them to ourselves or to the less affluent members of our society, or indeed to the world; Overall incomes and purchasing power must rise quickly enough to keep these services affordable, despite their persistently rising costs". In the same vein, an unsustainable increase of welfare expenditures under a disease's costs hypothesis is not warranted and can be compatible with a Pareto improvement (Andersen & Kreiner, 2017). Colombier argues that Baumol effect in healthcare is less important than previously thought because some improvements for reducing the costs are possible for policy-makers and because price index of healthcare services has some flaws (Colombier, 2017). Atanda et al. (2018) contests the existence of a Baumol effect in healthcare. Tabarrok (2022) shows that several healthcare services have been contaminated by the cost disease, but not all. Bailey et al. (2016) consider that cost disease is conceptually confusing, and wrongly conceives of public health services as unable to improve their productivity.

Baumol effects are not the only source of growth of the healthcare expenditure: health goods as superior good, the socialization of expenditures or the existence of rent seeking behavior are also factors in the increase in healthcare expenditures. Whether or not healthcare budget inflation is related to the cost disease, and even if Baumol changed his mind before his death, several neo-liberal cost-containment strategies were implemented due to the growing share of public resources allocated while GDP growth was slowing.

3.3.2.3 Neoliberal Reforms as Cost Containment Strategies and Their Side Effects

As a strategy to contain social costs and promote economic efficiency, many countries have implemented neoliberal reforms since 1990s. Neoliberal reforms involve cutting public spending, privatizing of public services, deregulating markets, and making labor market more flexible. They are associated with increase in income inequality and financialization of the economy (Lazonick, 2009). The neoliberal policies have also been implemented in the field of healthcare (Pierru, 2008; Batifoulier, 2015), even if social protection has been one of the last sectors affected (Cabannes, 2012, 2015).

3.3.3 Neoliberalism in Medicine in Search of Economic Efficiency: A Critique of the 'Over-socialization' of Costs

Neoliberalism argues that excessive government intervention and socialization of costs in healthcare can lead to inefficiencies, like moral hazards, low market competition and public good problems. It usually results in an increase in costs. Whether true or false, this negative perception of socialization was adopted by many OECD countries that then implemented reforms to reduce inefficiency and to increase cost effectiveness.[3]

[3] However, it should be underlined here that it is questionable to blame over-socialization of expenditures, if we consider the very high cost of US system, which is largely private and had for a long time, a very bad coverage.

Since the mid-1990s, the whole of OECD countries and most of middle-income countries have incorporated various Health Technology Assessment (HTA) tools to their decision-making process in order to circumvent the inflation of health expenditures. The institutionalization of this policy resulted in the creation of HTA agency (Example: National Institute of Clinical Excellence (NICE) in UK), which is relying on a scientific discipline, pharmaco-economics,[4] to compare the value of one pharmaceutical drug or drug therapy to another, using different method including cost-effectiveness analysis (CEA). CEA compares the relative costs and outcomes of different treatment. It is measured in monetary terms and expressed as an incremental cost-effectiveness ratio (ICER), the ratio of change in costs to the change in effects, and used as a threshold to establish a willingness-to-pay value (acceptance of reimbursement or formulary listing at a given price). For example, NICE establish in 2007 a cost-per-QALY threshold around £30,000. The implementation of such decision tools by health systems has not been without controversy. Many stakeholders feel that cost-effectiveness is a way of rationing the supply of health care and limiting access of patients to innovative therapy.

While neoliberalism supports market efficiency, cost-effectiveness analysis has been applied in various healthcare system with different degrees of government involvement or socialized healthcare. Its application is influenced by political, social or ethical considerations and different healthcare systems may prioritize different value such as equity or access.

3.3.3.1 Incentivizing Patients, Doctors and Companies

In such context, neoliberal strategies have been implemented to incentivize patients through co-payments mechanisms. It is believed that patients will seek more cost-effective care and help contain healthcare costs. But the efficiency of such a measure remains to be proven because it can lead to a renunciation of care, more health-related problems and a reduced labor force. Neoliberal approaches may also involve incentivizing doctors to provide cost-effective care through payment models that reward physicians for achieving certain quality and cost targets. Companies could also be

[4] Pharmacoeconomics "is the science of measuring *costs* and *outcomes* associated with the use of pharmaceuticals in health-care delivery. Its objective is to improve public health through rational decision making when selecting among alternative therapies, e.g., for formularies and their impact on costs and outcomes." (Rai & Goyal, 2017).

incentivized, classically by stimulating competition and innovation in the healthcare sector. But critics argue that reliance on market incentives can lead to skimming strategies (firms are focusing on high profitable market like cancer) and neglecting underserved population (rare diseases, pediatric population and tropical diseases). In general, the incentivization of economic agents on the demand or supply side, is at the root of concerns about the commodification of health care and the potential for inequities in access and quality of care in market driven.

3.3.3.2 *The Problem of Provision of Healthcare*

Neo-liberalism advocates the privatization of healthcare services, which involves transferring the management of healthcare system from the public sector to private entities, through privatization, out-sourcing and contracting. At the same time, neoliberalism places value on individual choice and consumer empowerment. Despite political debate, in practice, governments play, a role in the provision or funding of healthcare system in many countries. Indeed, the provision of health care is the source of positive externalities. The social benefit of providing healthcare to individual exceeds private benefit; a good example is with immunization programs which prevent outbreak of infectious diseases.

3.4 Medical Fordism Crisis and Pharmaceutical Innovation

Over the last few decades, healthcare systems are facing barriers and new challenges in the development of new medical technologies or treatments: a crisis of innovation in health. These challenges include science complexity and R&D higher costs, promises and disappointments of biotech revolution, patent cliff and generic competition, "pharmerging" country markets, financialized business model, macroeconomic constraints, health technology assessment and lengthy regulatory processes, and scarcity of healthcare labor force since the COVID crisis. All of these hurdles are harder to overcome if the productivity of innovation is declining. Various attempts have been made by firms and governments to address these issues and foster innovation in the healthcare sector.[5] It should be noted that the

[5] Firms have invested for decades in many new technologies: molecular biology, high speed screening, pharmacogenomics, enzyme therapies etc. Some common strategies of

higher cost of R&D and its lower return does not mean that no radical innovations have been achieved: certain new cancer treatments (such as humanized anti-receptor monoclonal antibody in breast cancer or CAR (chimeric antigen receptor) cell immunotherapy), or RNA-base vaccines (such as COVID vaccines; see Velte et al., 2026), represent a major advance. In this section, we will analyze the cause of the R&D crisis in pharmaceutical industry. As we will see, this crisis is not exogeneous but it is an endometabolic crisis of what we will call pharmaceutical Fordism.

3.4.1 *The Antibiotics as a Paradigm Form of "Medical/Pharmaceutical Fordism"*

Until the discovery and diffusion of penicillin and the first antibiotics (ATB) and the first vaccination's campaigns, human species was very fragile against bacteria and virus, leading a lot of humans to die from any acute infectious diseases. ATB was described as a "magical bullet", solving major deadly infectious diseases that killed billion of humans among history. The spread of ATB began after the Second World War, during the post-war era of Fordism. (Aglietta, 1976). During their early development and widespread use, ATB were produced on a large scale to meet the growing demand. It comes with standardization of ATB in terms of formulation dosage and administration. The mass production and widespread use of ATB resulted in economies of scale, and the development of so-called blockbuster business model, leading to lower costs and increased affordability for patients, and so, mass consumption of medicines. This mass production aspect aligns with the principles of Fordism, which emphasized efficient mass production of standardized goods and their mass consumption through extraction of economies of scales. With the manufacturing of ATB, pharma industry implements assembly-line processes with careful controlled all along the line in order to

governments are: (1) tax credits and grants to encourage companies and researchers to pursue innovative solutions. (2) drug regulatory flexibility to accelerate the introduction of innovation, (3) market exclusivity (example: orphan drug legislation) to allows companies to recoup their costs and profit from their innovations, (4) public-private partnerships to facilitate knowledge sharing (Example: Innovative Health Initiative with EU commission), (5) value-based pricing to link reimbursement and payment systems to the value and outcomes delivered by healthcare innovations, and more recently (6) digital health technologies (telemedicine, health apps and artificial intelligence) to revolutionize healthcare delivery.

ensure consistent quality and efficiency akin to the division of labor in a Fordism manufacturing. Moreover, the large socialization of medical expenditures after the development of the Welfare State fueled the large diffusion of these "magic bullets" that have completely changed and improved human life.

It is also during the Fordism era that the first antipsychotic and antidepressants were discovered (Ramachandraiah et al., 2009; Hillhouse & Porter, 2015) and progressively distributed to the population, in a similar way to antibiotics.

Vaccines have similarities with ATB, although the production process is slightly different from that for chemical molecules. Mass production and consumption—sometimes compulsory, and very often socialized—with high levels of standardization enable economies of scale to be achieved. Like antibiotics in the fight against bacteria, vaccines are very efficient to reduce the burden of viral diseases.

However, the name we give to this model is a bit of exaggeration: pharmaceutical firms focus on innovation to obtain monopoly power, as in the "innovation and flexibility" production model (Boyer & Freyssenet, 2000), and so do not really belong to the typical Fordist model. But it was the Fordism and the large increase and socialization of incomes that made mass production and the so-called blockbuster business model possible. And this configuration was only marginally transformed during the post-Fordist regimes, i.e. the neoliberal and current regimes.

At the same time, this very quick diffusion fueled the prosperity of pharmaceutical industry that observed a double-digit growth for decades. In parallel, different therapeutic scandals pushed the government to implement stringent controls over the safety and efficacy of drugs, through the institutionalization of drugs regulations, double-blinded clinical trials and agencies in charge of these controls (Pignarre, 2003; Chauveau, 1999; Montalban, 2007; Bélis-Bergouignan et al., 2014). It was also at that time that patenting of drugs' molecules diffused in some advanced economies, although it was an old story in the USA (Gaudillière, 2008, 2021).

These great medical successes have increased the life expectancy of the population. Therefore, we have slowly observed an endogenous epidemiologic transition in the population. As we will see, this success story will be at the root of the current productivity problems.

3.4.2 *The "Eroom's Law": The Costs Disease of Pharmaceutical Industry*

During the neoliberal era and the financialized accumulation regime, the dominant model became the famous blockbuster business model, that still exploits the economies of scales and mass consumption but is focused on the most profitable diseases where there is a strong monopoly power through patents (Montalban, 2007; Montalban and Sakinç, 2013).

The tremendous success of pharmaceutical industry lasted long. The first radical innovations were followed by incremental ones (with the launch of "me too" drugs) but also new therapeutic areas were developed, like cancer drugs, anticholesterol drugs, related to the progressive epidemiologic transition. Indeed, as long as we can cure more easily most of the infectious diseases and people can live longer, degenerative and life-style diseases become the new therapeutic areas of development. However, over the long term, we have observed a decline in pharmaceutical R&D productivity, linked to an increase in the attrition rate for new drugs and, at the same time, an increase in the cost of drug R&D, which has been called "Eroom's law". by Scannell et al. (2012), for contrasting it with the Moore law in computers.[6] The development cost of drugs has become very high and is almost doubling every 10 years: it was estimated 802 millions of dollars in 2002 (Di Masi et al., 2002), 1318 millions in 2007 (Di Masi & Grabowski, 2007, 2012; Di Masi et al., 2016) to almost 4 billions in 2019 in the most pessimistic studies (Schlander et al., 2021). "Eroom's Law" is indeed related to the crisis of pharmaceutical Fordism and refers to the observation that the cost of developing new drugs has been increasing over time, while the number of new drugs approved by regulatory authorities has been decreasing. The high cost of drug development, coupled with the declining number of successful drug candidates, impacts the sustainability and profitability of traditional pharmaceutical business models. "Eroom law" is also related to the "better than well" or "better than the Beatles" problematic. This is the feeling that new drugs offer only a modest additional benefit compared with drugs that are already widely used.

[6] It is an observation made by Gordon Moore, co-founder of Intel, stating that the number of transistors on a microchip, doubles approximately every two years, leading to a rapid increase in computing power and efficiency.

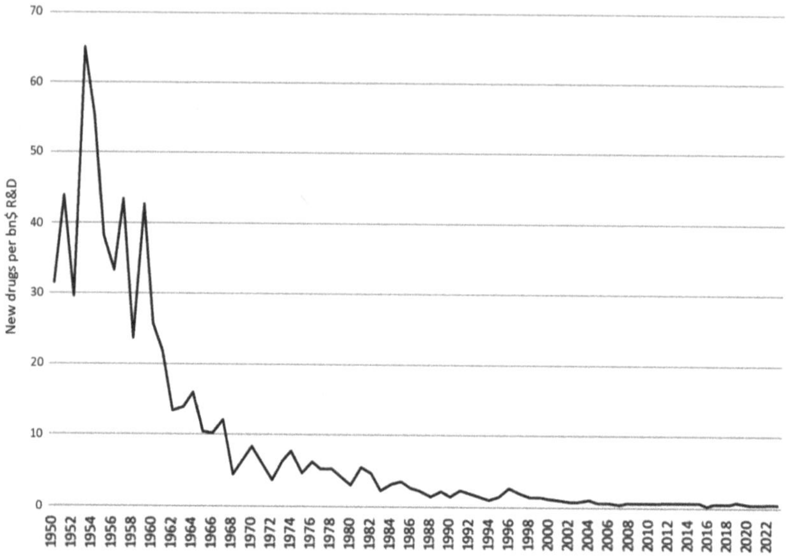

Fig. 3.11 The "Eroom law" or the declining trend of drug R&D efficiency, 1950–2023. *Sources* authors; data: Scannell et al. (2012), Schuhmacher et al. (2025), IQVIA (https://www.iqvia.com/insights/the-iqvia-institute/reports-and-publications/reports/global-trends-in-r-and-d-2025.)

This trend is attributed to various factors, including the increasing complexity of drug discovery and development, stringent regulatory requirements, and a shift towards more challenging therapeutic areas (Fig. 3.11) (Scannell et al., 2012).

3.4.2.1 Growing Risk Aversion, Growing Cost of Regulations and Bureaucracy

The costs of regulations have increased strongly among decades and explain the concentration of the industry (Grabowski & Vernon, 1977; Scannell et al., 2012). It is explained by the complexity of procedures, but also by the growing risk aversion of side effects in a healthy population. When more and more people are in good health, it becomes less and less acceptable to suffer from dangerous side effects of drugs. Therefore, the number of people required in clinical trials tends to increase to detect side effects and the regulation and controls tighter, sometimes with longer monitoring process of the patients, leading to increasing costs of development. It is a well-known example that some old drugs like aspirin would struggle hard to obtain the market authorization if it would have been discovered nowadays, due to its important side effects. Financialization was partly a symptom and a way to solve the growing costs and risks of innovation and bureaucratic problems but it did not substantially increase the R&D productivity. Instead, a growing share of profit were allocated to dividends and share buy-backs (Montalban & Sakinç, 2013). At the same time, in order to circumvent the stringent regulations and bureaucracy while creating shareholder value, pharmaceutical companies have tended to spend large sums on lobbying, engage in ghostwriting (Gagnon, 2021; Gorry, 2015) and use illegal practices that have led to major convictions (Bélis-Bergouignan et al., 2014; Abrams et Wolfe, 2024).

3.4.2.2 With the Epidemiological Transition, the Decreasing Health Benefits of Medicines Innovations

While the WHO defines health as a "a state of complete physical, mental and social well-being and not merely the absence of disease or infirmity", this does not change the fact that medicines are authorized and developed for specific therapeutic indications, i.e. to treat some specific pathologies. Therefore, if an efficient drug already exists, it is very hard to find another one which will be more effective than the previous ones. For example, the first antibiotics or antidepressants were very efficient. The new ones have to prove a marginal increase in efficacy or less side effects, which will imply testing the new drug against the old ones for ethical and scientific reasons. But comparing a new drug with an old effective one will imply a risk of failures. Fortunately for pharmaceutical companies, a drug is never efficient for everyone because of pharmacogenetic differences, which allows outsiders and new market entrants to capture certain market shares. Due to the high risk of developing a completely new molecular entity in an already competitive market, there was a tendency in the 90's to favor "me too" drugs, i.e. incremental innovation in drugs (using similar molecules, making drug combinations or changing the delivery mode). Moreover, as we stated before, the classical creative destruction of Schumpeter does not apply to medicines: a new drug substitutes rarely to an older one, it just adds a new option to the pharmacopeia. For example, penicillin is still used even if new ATB against gram-positive rods have been developed. With the development of generic drugs, i.e. prescription drugs without patent protection, the competition became even tougher. When a generic exists for a specific indication, it becomes increasingly risky to develop a new drug, as it will be more difficult to prove that the new drug is safer and more effective than the old one. So, as time goes by and R&D costs rise, pharmaceutical companies divert their R&D efforts away from therapeutic areas dominated by a generic reference treatment (e.g. antibiotics, Parkinson's disease, etc.). Ironically, generic drugs can be seen as the perfect example of pharmaceutical Fordism and as an effective way of reducing drug expenditure: mass production and economies of scale.

As long as new drugs are developed for on pathology, it slowly changes the need of the population and the market. In 1971, Abdel Oram proposed a theory called epidemiological transition to describe changing patterns of diseases and causes of death within a population over time. More specifically, it refers to the shift from the prevalence of infectious diseases in the population to that of chronic diseases. This shift is accompanied by a drastic drop in premature mortality, and an increase in life expectancy. This transition typically occurs as societies undergo social, economic, and demographic changes. Originally, Oram described 4 stages: (1) Age of Pestilence and Famine, (2) Age of Receding Pandemics, (3) Age of Degenerative and Man-Made Diseases, and (4) Age of Delayed Degenerative Diseases. It is believed that transition from stage 1 to 2 was mediated by agriculture and improvement of nutrition, the transition, from stage 2 to 3 was due to sanitary measures, vaccination and the discovery of penicillin, and from stage 3 to 4 the priority is the management of chronic diseases, diabetes and cardiovascular diseases and the prevention of risk factors. At the same time, the improvement in health conditions is initially accompanied by demographic growth due to the increase in life expectancy, followed by a slowdown and stabilization of the population due to a drop in the birth rate. It is important to note that the epidemiological transition is not a homogeneous progression. Indeed, different regions or countries may be at different stages of the transition at any given time. Western countries experienced a transition that began in the late eighteenth century and lasted to the post-war era. Other countries like Japan and China have now undergone an accelerated transition, and finally low-income countries are experiencing delayed transition mainly due to slow economic development. It should be noticed that some countries, such as Brazil or India are facing at the same time high prevalence of infectious diseases such as malaria or tuberculosis, and high increase of chronic and degenerative diseases. In addition, the use of antibiotics and antimalarials has evolved over time, and this has been complicated by the emergence of resistance to treatments. (Brives, 2022).

In that context, the pharmaceutical industry has adapted its business model, moving on the one hand towards generic drugs and emerging markets (Ibata-Arens et al., 2026), and on the other towards the development of treatments for chronic diseases such as cardiovascular disease, cancer, diabetes and neurodegenerative disorders. Finally, the pharma industry has adopted the concept of personalized medicine, with the advances in genetics research since the sequencing of the human genome in 2000. By doing so, this industry switches from the blockbuster business model to the "nichebuster" business model, focusing on low prevalence disease, small-patients population or even rare diseases. This move from the industry provides opportunities for the firms to develop high-value therapies with significant market potential. This move was possible because of some changes in drugs' regulation, with the creation of orphan drug designation and several advantages related to it (tax credit in USA; market exclusivity in EU), which makes the investments in small markets profitable, and because the biotechnology, especially genomics, allowed to develop more targeted treatments in a rational drug design (Gorry & Useche, 2019).

This has led to a recent increase in the productivity of pharmaceutical companies: Pammolli et al. (2020) have shown that this recent increase is linked to the development of more targeted treatments, particularly orphan drugs. Digitalization is another strategy to reduce the cost of development of drugs and more generally, to reduce the costs of health services.

3.5 The Promise of Health Innovation as a Cure of the Cost Disease

The healthcare system has been organized during the twentieth century around the delivery of medicines and the socialization of costs. After decades of therapeutic innovation, the pharmaceutical industry is now facing the "Eroom's law". This crisis of innovation is not exogenous, but endometabolic: it is a consequence of longer life expectancy and rising healthcare costs. Today's neo-liberal regimes are looking for new strategies to reduce the costs of healthcare systems. Against this backdrop, the pharmaceutical industry has adapted its business model, moving from the 'blockbuster' model to the 'nichebuster' model.

The digitalization is seen as way to solve several problems of healthcare systems and pharmaceutical R&D and is promoting a new paradigm: reduction of administrative costs, better monitoring and diagnosis of patients, limiting the problems of the rationing of medical professionals, promoting a more efficient drug discovery process, enhancing the participation of patients in their own health, promoting prevention instead of treatment etc… All digital tools are complementary: with more health data from applications or genetic tests, we can develop more prevention, prediction and medicines for personalized therapies: this is the essence of the 'paradigm' of precision and personalized medicine, launched in the United States at the initiative of President Obama, which has given rise to the new paradigm of '4P medicine' (Personalized, Preventive, Predictive, Participative). This paradigm has spread to all OECD countries, and has evolved into the concept of 5P medicine and even 6P medicine, with the addition of 2 complementary dimensions (Pertinence, evidence-base, and Platform, for the use of digital platforms).[7] But this trend, which has spread throughout the rich and developed countries, is being challenged by other promises of innovation, such as the care robot, or the return to natural medicines. We develop in section A to C the expectations and solutions provided and the remaining problems and possible side effects in the section D.

3.5.1 *The Promises of the Digital Health on Management and Cost Reduction*

One strategy for advancing digital health is to develop connected health applications and solutions to circumvent bureaucratic costs and remedy the medical desertification caused by neoliberal reforms. Healthcare systems involve multiple players and require coordination while ensuring traceability of patient treatment without compromising data confidentiality. The costs of coordination, especially bureaucratic costs, are important in healthcare services, which are labor intensive. Moreover, the medical

[7] https://www.forbes.com/councils/forbestechcouncil/2021/03/30/the-six-ps-of-medicine-how-healthcare-technology-will-transform-access-to-care-and-enable-better-patient-outcomes/.

Fordism is not very efficient to differentiate treatment among patients. Digital platforms and applications can reduce bureaucratic costs, guide patient pathways and personalize treatments by continuously collecting health data, unlike traditional intermittent medical visits. Digital platform capitalism is transforming healthcare by creating multilateral markets with strong network effects and cross externalities (Rochet & Tirole, 2006). These platforms are rapidly becoming monopolies, efficiently coordinating transactions and improving the matching process through the massive collection of data (Montalban, 2023). Examples include Doctolib®, which connects patients and doctors and manages appointments, and Vite ma Dose, designed for COVID vaccination appointments. Intersystems offers innovative data solutions such as HealthShare® care community: "InterSystems HealthShare Unified Care Record helps providers, payers, consumers, social care and wellness services, researchers, and solution developers overcome the challenges of decentralized data by creating a shared, comprehensive, and unified care record" (source: website). Digitalization enables continuous patient monitoring, pathology management, and behavior modification through Internet of Things (IoT) devices, apps, and remote consultations. For instance, Biofourmis® offers apps like Care@home® for remote care and data collection to aid clinical care teams in monitoring and managing adult patients in the comfort and convenience of the home" (source: website). During the pandemic, COVID tracking apps in South Korea and Singapore reduced transmission risks by altering behaviors and avoiding strict lockdowns (Kim, 2021; Whitelaw et al., 2020; Zeng et al., 2020; Lee et al., 2021). Similarly, the widespread use of videoconferencing apps like Zoom and Teams facilitated social distancing and improved labor productivity. Experts predict rapid growth in the global digital health market. (Toscano & Zappala, 2021; George et al., 2022). Digitalization should also spur the discovery of new therapies and medicines. Developing health apps is less costly and regulated than creating new drugs, leading companies and researchers to explore various apps for health improvement. For example, specific video games and apps are being used to treat mental health disorders like ADHD. While excessive gaming is linked to ADHD (Kollins et al., 2020), therapeutic games like EndeavorRx®, approved by the FDA, can improve ADHD symptoms. Logically, experts predict a quick growth of the global digital health market (Fig. 3.12) (Rahul & Banyal, 2020).

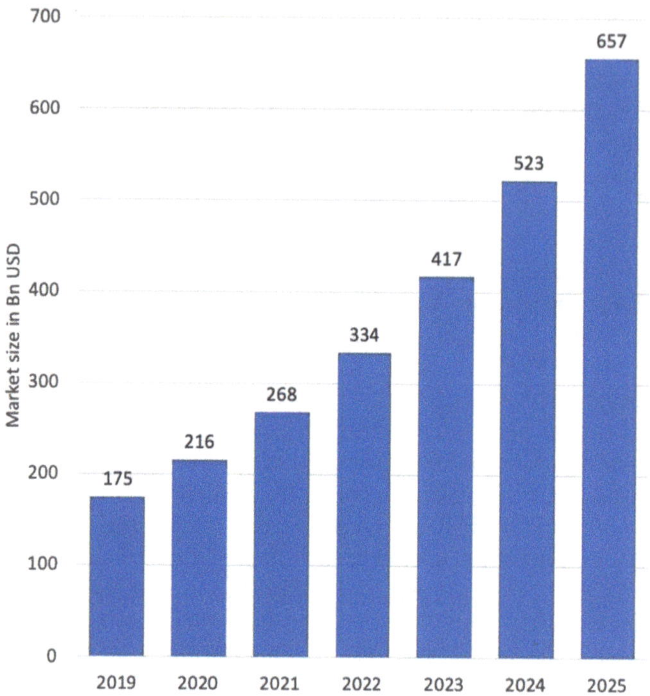

Fig. 3.12 Projected global digital health market size in billions of USD, 2019–2025. *Sources* Authors, Data: Statista

3.5.2 *The Promise of Artificial Intelligence in Medicine: Improving Efficiency*

Over the past 30 years, biomedicines have advanced significantly, including recombinant and RNA vaccines, monoclonal antibodies, and enzyme therapies. This shift from chemical to biopharma treatments has led to personalized medicine, focusing on specific population niches rather than universal drugs. This trend is driven by biological diversity and the need for targeted treatments, such as orphan drugs and phage therapy to combat antibiotic resistance (Brives, 2022). Digitalization helps overcome "Eroom's Law" by improving screening and access to big data, while Moore's Law has dramatically reduced diagnosis costs through advances in computing power. (Fig. 3.13).

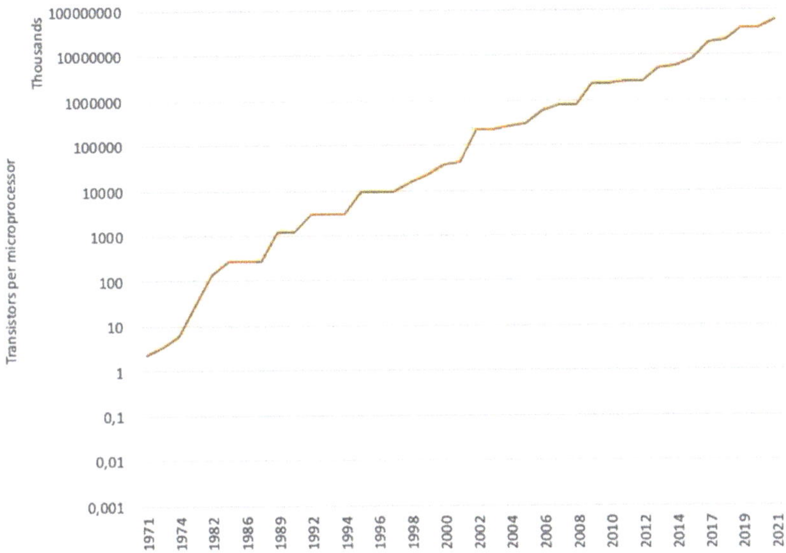

Fig. 3.13 The Moore Law: Computations per second per computer over time, 1971–2021. *Sources* authors; data: OurWorld in data

To counteract the "Eroom's Law" (rising drug development costs) and the limitations of pharmaceutical Fordism, companies are adopting open innovation, drug repurposing, digital and AI technologies, and focusing on niche markets and personalized medicine. Digitalization and AI enhance diagnosis and disease prediction, enabling prevention through genetic testing and imaging analysis, as DNA testing costs have significantly decreased.[8]

New drugs and medical technologies undergo rigorous testing, but not all side effects can be anticipated. Platforms like Biofourmis® offer digital tools for precision medicine and targeted therapies. AI and big data are used to speed up molecule discovery, reduce R&D costs, and improve productivity. Companies like Insilico Medicine®, Schrödinger®, and Exscientia® use AI for efficient molecule screening. Big Pharma companies are investing in AI and partnering with tech giants (Zhavoronkov, 2022; Savage, 2021).

[8] Sources: NCBI, https://www.genome.gov/about-genomics/fact-sheets/DNA-Sequencing-Costs-Data.

For instance, Sanofi® collaborates with Exscientia® and Insilico Medicine®, while Novartis® partners with Microsoft® (Savage, 2021). Alphabet Inc® has Isomorphic Labs® for AI-driven drug discovery and Calico® for aging research. These developments align with transhumanist ideologies endorsed by Silicon Valley leaders, like Sergey Brin, Larry Page, Ray Kurzweil etc. (Damour, 2018). Drawing on Moore's Law, Kurzweil (2005) asserts that the 'Singularity is near', i.e. the moment when a strong A.I. will emerge, solving major human problems, including longer life expectancy or even immortality.

3.5.3 The Promises of Care Robots and Caregivers Labor Productivity

Care robots are another form of digitalization. A care robot is an autonomous or semi-autonomous machine designed to help with various aspects of care, in particular for the elderly, people with disabilities or those who need medical or personal assistance. Care robots can help people maintain their independence by assisting them with everyday tasks and providing the support they need. But these robots remain expensive and limited when faced with complex tasks in unforeseen situations (Kodate et al., 2021).

It is not yet very well developed, but given the rising cost of healthcare services due to Baumol's cost disease, it would be perfectly logical and classic solution for capital/labor substitution that could become widespread in countries suffering from a very ageing population and a severe shortage of care workers. The cost of acquiring a care robot is very high, as is the case with most machines, but it could be profitable if it were to provide a real substitution.

Japan is at the forefront of care robot development due to its aging population and a shortage of caregivers. The Japanese government has invested heavily in robotics research and development to address these challenges (Kodate et al., 2021). Japan is at the forefront of the development of care robots because of its ageing population and shortage of care staff. The Japanese government has invested heavily in robotics research and development to meet these challenges. Car manufacturers such as Toyota and Honda are leading the way, with the first care robots being launched on the market. Japanese car manufacturers are making a parallel with automation in the automotive industry by leveraging their expertise in robotics, quality control, and innovation.

While care robots have the potential to mitigate some of the cost increases associated with Baumol's disease in the healthcare system, they are not a complete solution. They can improve efficiency, provide consistent care and reduce labor costs, but they also come with high upfront costs, technological limitations and ethical considerations.

3.5.4 *The Side Effects of Digital Innovation in Health*

If this new digital paradigm in health is full of interesting promises, it does not mean that it will be necessarily efficient enough to solve the Medical Fordism and the pharmaceutical innovation crisis, reduce the costs of health expenditures and the secular stagnation of advanced economies.

There is a risk of overestimating the potential of AI and digital technologies in healthcare, similar to past biotechnology overestimates in reducing R&D costs. (Scannell et al., 2012). The digital and AI paradigm in pharmaceutical industry is not a radical innovation: it's just an extension of 'rational drug design', using scientific knowledge of the biological properties of a 'target' to find the right molecule (chemical or biological). Using AI to solve these drugs developments problems suppose that health data are well recorded and that scientific literature is accurate. However, science, and especially medical science, is facing several challenges, including issues related to reproducibility, publication biases, conflicts of interest, and the pressure to produce positive and impactful results. For example, Ioannidis et al. (2001) and Ioannidis (2005) showed that a large number of articles in medical science, especially the first estimations of one effect in genetic or neurosciences, tend to overestimate the odds ratios and have a low statistical power. In the same way, Dumas-Mallet et al. (2016, 2017) has shown poor replication validity, especially in studies covered in newspapers. These challenges can impact the reliability and validity of scientific research, including in the development of new treatments. Recent studies show that papers and patents become less and less disruptive (Park et al., 2023). Therefore, even if AI is an interesting innovation, there is no guarantee that AI will solve the crisis of pharmaceutical innovation.

In healthcare, new treatments and technologies can change the way services are organized and delivered. However, an overemphasis on technology risks dehumanizing care by neglecting human interaction, empathy and personalized attention. Neoliberal reforms aim to reduce costs and increase efficiency, but the main expense remains the cost of labor for nurses and doctors. Some reforms are criticized for reducing human interaction and the time devoted to care. In France, for example, nursing and care tasks are increasingly standardized, with a time limit per patient. While mobile applications aim to reduce bureaucracy and reallocate savings to patient care, there is no guarantee that governments will not use digitization to further reduce labor costs and time spent on care, especially given high public deficits.

There is concern that new medical innovations could create opportunities for rent-seeking and inequality, when certain players (pharmaceutical companies, medical specialties) exploit these innovations to make excessive profits through the control or ownership of valuable medical innovations. While digitalization and competition could reduce these rents, current observations show more collaborations between start-ups, Big Tech and those "old" actors.

Finally, the more the targeted therapies, personalized medicine and transhumanist dreams come true, by exploiting small niches of patients, the more the prices of certain treatments resulting from the paradigm of personalized medicine (orphan drugs and anti-cancer drugs, for example) are skyrocketing, leading to new cost-containment policies or restrictions on access. This could well spell the end of the medical Fordism, both because of the personalization of therapies and because of the potential inequalities it could generate in healthcare provision.

3.6 Conclusion

In this chapter, we address the so-called "crises" of pharmaceutical innovation and the Welfare State, showing that it would be more accurate to talk about a crisis of medical Fordism paradoxically linked to its great achievements, namely a longer life of better quality. This is the result of past growth and the innovations that made access to healthcare possible.

As Schumpeter (1942) argued, the success of capitalism through innovation and growth is the source of its own destabilization, through the cultural transformations it generates. In the case of health sectors, crises take the forms of "disease of costs": there are still interesting innovations, but they are increasingly costly; healthcare expenditures have improved patients' lives but its growth is considered too costly, because productivity gains in services are low. Neoliberalism in healthcare was a first, but inefficient, "cure" of those cost diseases, especially in the USA, and now digitalization is the expected new "cure" for these pathologies, leading to the paradigm shift in medicine. This raises many questions on the possibility to implement a version of anthropogenetic mode of development as the so-called society 5.0 (Lechevalier, 2026).

This case in the healthcare sector and pharmaceutical industry also reveals wider problems for mature economies. Indeed, if we consider that there is a lot of innovation in digital and that the slowdown of productivity was one of the main sources of Fordist crisis and that neoliberalism did not solve it and created new problems for healthcare, it is logical to expect that the salvation of mature capitalist economies will come from technical change, i.e. techno-solutionism (Morozov, 2013). Digital technology can help solve certain productivity and coordination problems, but the "techno-neoliberalism" can create new ones by increasing inequalities and rationing some services. While the promises of digitalization are real, the diffusion of digital technologies in healthcare is partly the results of the combination of tighter regulations due to growing risk aversion, low fertility rate and neoliberal rationing of care. There is little chance that digital would reverse those trends ... Without rejecting digital and technological innovation, this chapter raises the question of alternative models such as the development of frugal innovations (Gaudillière & Madhavan, 2026), care-led innovation (Lechevalier, 2026) improving the access to traditional medicines (Ibata-Arens et al., 2026).

Of course, these very global trends are not exactly the same from one country or healthcare system to another. The BRICS countries, such as India and China, are experiencing all these phases of evolution at the same time (or at an accelerated pace), because of the size of their populations and their strong growth: they still have a certain form of medical Fordism (from generic drugs to traditional medicine), but must also manage the consequences of an aging population and adopt "modern" treatments and norms. Similarly, the acceptance of care robots, for example, may be very different from one country to another, due to different cultural norms. Comparative studies are useful in this respect, and the other chapters give several insights into these differences.

References

Abrams, M. T., & Wolfe, S. M. (2024). *Thirty-one years of pharmaceutical industry criminal and civil penalities: 1991–2021*. Public Citizen report.

Aghion, P., Cohen, E., David, B., & Gigout-Magiorani, T. (2021). Pour une nouvelle politique industrielle après le Covid19. *Le Grand Continent*, https://legrandcontinent.eu/fr/2021/06/04/pour-une-nouvelle-politique-industrielle-apres-le-covid-19/

Aglietta, M. (1976). *Régulation et crises du capitalisme: L'expérience américaine*. Calmann-Lévy.

Andersen, T. M., & Kreiner, C. T. (2017). Baumol's cost disease and the sustainability of the welfare state. *Economica*, *84*(335), 417–429.

Atanda, A., Menclova, A. K., & Reed, W. R. (2018). Is health care infected by B aumol's cost disease? Test of a new model. *Health Economics, 27*(5), 832–849.

Bailey, S. J., Anttiroiko, A. V., & Valkama, P. (2016). Application of Baumol's cost disease to public sector services: Conceptual, theoretical and empirical falsities. *Public Management Review, 18*(1), 91–109.

Batifoulier, P. (2015). Aux origines de la privatisation du financement du soin: quand la théorie de l'aléa moral rencontre le capitalisme sanitaire. *Revue de la régulation. Capitalisme, institutions, pouvoirs*, (17).

Baumol, W. J. (1993). Health care, education and the cost disease: A looming crisis for public choice. In *The next twenty-five years of public choice* (pp. 17–28). Springer Netherlands.

Baumol, W. J. (2012). *The cost disease: Why computers get cheaper and health care doesn't*. Yale university press.

Baumol, W. J., & Bowen, W. G. (1965). On the performing arts: The anatomy of their economic problems. *The American Economic Review, 55*(1/2), 495–502.

Bélis-Bergouignan, M. C., Montalban, M., Sakinç, M. E., & Smith, A. (2014). *L'industrie pharmaceutique: Règles, acteurs et pouvoir*. La documentation française.

Boyer, R. (2000). Is a finance-led growth regime a viable alternative to Fordism? A preliminary analysis. *Economy and Society, 29*(1), 111–145.

Boyer, R. (2009). Feu le régime d'accumulation tiré par la finance. La crise des subprimes en perspective historique. *Revue de la Régulation. Capitalisme, Institutions, Pouvoirs*, (5).

Boyer, R. (2015). "L'essor du secteur de la santé annonce-t-il un modèle de développement anthropogénétique?", *Revue de la Régulation. Capitalisme, Institutions, Pouvoirs*, (17).

Boyer, R. (2022). Platform capitalism: A socio-economic analysis. *Socio-Economic Review, 20*(4), 1857–1879.

Boyer, R., & Boylaud, O. (2026). Anthropogenetic development: Long unnoticed and already in crisis. In S. Lechevalier, J.-P. Gaudillière, K. Ibata-Arens, & K. Takuma (Eds.), *Capitalism, innovations, and health after Covid-19. An Asian perspective*. Palgrave MacMillan.

Boyer, R., & Freyssenet, M. (2000). *Les modèles productifs*. La découverte.

Breschi, S., Malerba, F., & Orsenigo, L. (2000). Technological regimes and Schumpeterian patterns of innovation. *The Economic Journal, 110*(463), 388–410.

Brives, C. (2022). *Face à l'antibiorésistance. Une écologie politique des mircobes*. Amsterdam éditions.

Cabannes, M. (2012). *La trajectoire néolibérale. Histoire d'un dérèglement sans fin*. Le Bord de l'eau.

Cabannes, M. (2015). *La gauche à l'épreuve du néolibéralisme*. Le Bord de l'eau.

Chauveau, S. (1999). *L'invention pharmaceutique: La pharmacie française entre l'état et la société au XXe siècle*. Les empêcheurs de penser en rond.

Clévenot, M. (2008). Les difficultés à nommer le nouveau régime de croissance. *Revue de la Régulation. Capitalisme, Institutions, Pouvoirs*, (3/4).

Colombier, C. (2017). Drivers of health-care expenditure: What role does Baumol's cost disease play? *Social Science Quarterly*, *98*(5), 1603–1621.

Coris, M., Piveteau, A., Gorry, P., & Montalban, M. (2021). Sécurité sanitaire sous dépendance. Une construction politique à repenser. *Revue de la Régulation. Capitalisme, Institutions, Pouvoirs*, (29).

Damour, F. (2018). Le mouvement transhumaniste: Approches historiques d'une utopie technologique contemporaine. *Vingtième Siècle*, (2), 143–156.

Di Masi, J. A., & Grabowski, H. G. (2007). The cost of biopharmaceutical R&D: Is biotech different? *Managerial and Decision Economics*, *28*(4–5), 469–479.

Di Masi, J. A., & Grabowski, H. G. (2012). R&D costs and returns to new drug development: A review of the evidence. *The Oxford handbook of the economics of the biopharmaceutical industry* (pp. 21–46).

Di Masi, J. A., Grabowski, H. G., & Hansen, R. W. (2016). Innovation in the pharmaceutical industry: New estimates of R&D costs. *Journal of Health Economics*, *47*, 20–33.

Di Masi, J. A., Hansen, R. W., & Grabowski, H. G. (2002). The price of innovation: New estimates of drug development costs. *Journal of Health Economics*, *22*(2), 151–185.

Dumas-Mallet, E., Button, K., Boraud, T., Munafo, M., & Gonon, F. (2016). Replication validity of initial association studies: A comparison between psychiatry, neurology and four somatic diseases. *PLoS One*, *11*(6), e0158064.

Dumas-Mallet, E., Smith, A., Boraud, T., & Gonon, F. (2017). Poor replication validity of biomedical association studies reported by newspapers. *PloS One*, *12* (2), e0172650.

Duménil, G., & Lévy, D. (2014). *La grande bifurcation: En finir avec le néolibéralisme*. La Découverte.

Esping-Andersen, G. (1990). *The three worlds of welfare capitalism*. Princeton university press.

Gagnon, M. A. (2021). Ghost management as a central feature of accumulation in corporate capitalism: The case of the global pharmaceutical sector. In *Marlène Benquet and Théo Bourgeon, Accumulating capital today: Contemporary strategies of profit and dispossessive policies* (pp. 163–177). Routledge.

Gaudillière, J.-P. (2008). How pharmaceuticals became patentable: The production and appropriation of drugs in the twentieth century. *History and Technology*, *24*(2), 99–106.

Gaudillière, J.-P. (2021). Pharmaceutical innovation and its crisis: Drug markets, screening, and the dialectics of value. *BioSocieties*, *16*(3), 411–432.

Gaudillière, J.-P., & Madhavan, H. (2026). A case for frugal innovation? Local and community-based responses to Covid 19 in India. In S. Lechevalier, J.-P. Gaudillière, K. Ibata-Arens, & K. Takuma (Eds.), *Capitalism, innovations, and health after Covid-19. An Asian perspective*. Palgrave MacMillan.

George, T. J., Atwater, L. E., Maneethai, D., & Madera, J. M. (2022). Supporting the productivity and wellbeing of remote workers: Lessons from COVID-19. *Organizational Dynamics, 51*(2), 100869.

Gordon, R. J. (2012). Is US economic growth over? Faltering innovation confronts the six headwinds (No. w18315) *National Bureau of Economic Research*.

Gordon, R. J. (2018). Declining American economic growth despite ongoing innovation. *Explorations in Economic History, 69*(C), 1–12.

Gorry, P. (2015). Medical literature imprinting by pharma ghost writing: A scientometric evaluation. *Proceedings of International Society of Scientometric and Infometrics* (pp. 650–651).

Gorry, P. (2023). Pharma supply chain and globalization in face of the COVID pandemic: A review. In C. Chatterjee, A. B. Deolalikar, & A. Chakrabarti (Eds.), *Flattening the curve: Covid-19 & grand challenges for global health*. Innovation & Economics, World Scientific.

Gorry, P., & Useche, D. (2019). Orphan drug designations as valuable intangible assets for IPO investors in pharma-biotech companies. In E. Berndt, D. Goldman, & J. Rowe (Eds.), *Economic dimensions of personalized and precision medicine*. University of Chicago Press.

Grabowki, H. G., & Vernon, J. M. (1977). Consumer protection regulation in ethical drugs. *The American Economic Review, 67*(1), 359–364.

Hillhouse, T. M., & Porter, J. H. (2015). A brief history of the development of antidepressant drugs: From monoamines to glutamate. *Experimental and Clinical Psychopharmacology, 23*(1), 1.

Ibata-Arens, K., Gaudillière, J-P., Madhavan, H., & Nouguez, E. (2026). The moral economy of access: Generics, neotraditional formulations and the dominant intellectual property regime. In S. Lechevalier, J.-P. Gaudillière, K. Ibata-Arens, & K. Takuma (Eds.), *Capitalism, innovations, and health after Covid-19. An Asian perspective*. Palgrave MacMillan.

Ioannidis, J., Ntzani, E. E., Trikalinos, T. A., & Contopoulos-Ioannidis, D. G. (2001). Replication validity of genetic association studies. *Nature Genetics, 29*(3), 306–309.

Ioannidis, J. P. (2005). Why most published research findings are false. *PLoS Medicine, 2*(8), e124.

Kim, H. (2021). COVID-19 apps as a digital intervention policy: A longitudinal panel data analysis in South Korea. *Health Policy, 125*(11), 1430–1440.

Kodate, N., Donnelly, S., Cheung, M., Maeda, Y., Mannan, H., Chan, W. H., & O'Shea, D. (2021). Can care robots assist older people and long-term care systems? Key stakeholders' perceptions in HOng-Kong SAR, China and Ireland. *Age and Ageing*, *50*(Supplement_3), 9–41.

Kollins, S. H., DeLoss, D. J., Cañadas, E., Lutz, J., Findling, R. L., Keefe, R. S. … & Faraone, S. V. (2020). A novel digital intervention for actively reducing severity of paediatric ADHD (STARS-ADHD): A randomised controlled trial. *The Lancet Digital Health*, *2*(4), e168–e178.

Kurzweil, R. (2005). *The singularity is near. When humans transcend biology*. Viking.

Lazonick, W. (2009). The new economy business model and the crisis of US capitalism. *Capitalism and Society*, *4*(2).

Lechevalier, S. (2026). Care-led innovation, a new paradigm and an application in the Japanese context of Society 5.0. In S. Lechevalier, J.-P. Gaudillière, K. Ibata-Arens, & K. Takuma (Eds.), *Capitalism, innovations, and health after Covid-19. An Asian perspective*. Palgrave MacMillan.

Lee, B., Ibrahim, S. A., & Zhang, T. (2021). Mobile apps leveraged in the COVID-19 pandemic in East and South-East Asia: Review and content analysis. *JMIR mHealth and uHealth*, *9*(11), e32093.

Marx, K. (2008). *Le capital, Livre I à III*. Folio.

Montalban, M. (2007). *Financiarization, dynamique des industries et modèles productifs. Une analyse institutionnaliste de l'industrie pharmaceutique*. Thèse de doctorat ès sciences économiques, université Montesquieu Bordeaux IV.

Montalban, M. (2023). Economie numérique et organization industrielle: Enjeux du capitalisme de plateformes. In R. Boyer, J.-P. Chanteau, & T. Lamarche *Théorie de la regulation: Le nouvel état des savoirs* (Vol. 64. pp. 530–537). Dunod.

Montalban, M., Frigant, V., & Jullien, B. (2019). Platform economy as a new form of capitalism: A Régulationist research programme. *Cambridge Journal of Economics*, *43*(4), 805–824.

Montalban, M., & Sakinç, M. E. (2013). Financialization and productive models in the pharmaceutical industry. *Industrial and Corporate Change*, *22*(3), 981–1030.

Morozov, E. (2013). *To save everything, click here: Technology, solutionism, and the urge to fix problems that don't exist*. Allen Lane.

Nelson, R. R., & Winter, S. G. (1982). The Schumpeterian tradeoff revisited. *The American Economic Review*, *72*(1), 114–132.

Nordhaus, W. D. (2008). Baumol's diseases: A macroeconomic perspective. *The BE Journal of Macroeconomics*, *8*(1).

OECD (2024), *Fiscal sustainability of health systems: How to finance more resilient health systems when money is tight?* https://doi.org/10.1787/880f3195-en

Pammolli, F., Righetto, L., Abrignani, S., Pani, L., Pelicci, P. G., & Rabosio, E. (2020). The endless frontier? The recent increase of R&D productivity in pharmaceuticals. *Journal of Translational Medicine*, *18*, 1–14.

Park, M., Leahey, E., & Funk, R. J. (2023). Papers and patents are becoming less disruptive over time. *Nature*, *613*(7942), 138–144.

Pierru, F. (2008). La santé au régime néolibéral. *Savoir/agir*, *5*(3), 13–14.

Pignarre, P. (2003). *Le grand secret de l'industrie pharmaceutique*. La découverte.

Rahul, K., & Banyal, R. K. (2020). Data life cycle management in big data analytics. *Procedia Computer Science*, *173*, 364–371.

Rai, M., & Goyal, R. (2017). Chapter 33: Pharmacoeconomics in healthcare. In D. Vohora & G. Singh (Eds.), *Pharmaceutical medecine and translational clinical research* (pp. 465–472). Academic Press.

Ramachandraiah, C. T., Subramaniam, N., & Tancer, M. (2009). The story of antipsychotics: Past and present. *Indian Journal of Psychiatry*, *51*(4), 324.

Ricardo, D. (1819). *Principes de l'économie politique et de l'impôt*. Librairie J.P. Aillaud.

Rochet, J. C., & Tirole, J. (2006). Two-sided markets: A progress report. *The RAND Journal of Economics*, *37*(3), 645–667.

Rosanvallon, P. (2015). *La crise de l'État-providence*. Média Diffusion.

Savage, N. (2021). Tapping into the drug discovery potential of AI. *Nature Biopharma Dealmakers*, B37–B39.

Scannell, J. W., Blanckley, A., Boldon, H., & Warrington, B. (2012). Diagnosing the decline in pharmaceutical R&D efficiency. *Nature Reviews Drug Discovery*, *11*(3), 191–200.

Schlander, M., Hernandez-Villafuerte, K., Cheng, C. Y., Mestre-Ferrandiz, J., & Baumann, M. (2021). How much does it cost to research and develop a new drug? A systematic review and assessment. *PharmacoEconomics*, *39*, 1243–1269.

Schuhmacher, A., Gassmann, O., Kwisda, S., Kremer, M., Hinder, M., & Hartl, D. (2025). The R&D productivity challenge: Transforming the pharmaceutical ecosystem. *Drug Discovery Today*, *30*(11), 104494.

Schumpeter, J. A. (1934). *The theory of economic development*. Cambridge MA.

Schumpeter, J. A. (1942). *Capitalism, socialism and democracy*. George Allen & Unwin.

Solow, R. M. (1956). A contribution to the theory of economic growth. *The Quarterly Journal of Economics*, *70*(1), 65–94.

Srnicek, N. (2017). *Platform capitalism*. John Wiley & Sons.

Streeck, W. (2014). *Buying time: The delayed crisis of democratic capitalism*. Verso Books.

Tabarrok, A. (2022). Baumol and the cost disease. In L. Fiorito, S. Scheall, & C. E. Suprinyak (Eds.), *Research in the history of economic thought and methodology:*

Including a symposium on the work of William J. Baumol: Heterodox inspirations and neoclassical models (pp. 1–26). Emerald Publishing Limited.
Toscano, F., & Zappalà, S. (2021). Overall job performance, remote work engagement, living with children, and remote work productivity during the COVID-19 pandemic. *European Journal of Psychology Open.*
Van Zon, A., & Muysken, J. (2001). Health and endogenous growth. *Journal of Health Economics, 20*(2), 169–185.
Van Zon, A., Muysken, J., López-Casanovas, G., Rivera, B., & Currais, L. (2005). Health as determinant of economic growth. In *Health and economic growth: Findings and policy implications* (Vol. 41, pp. 41–65).
Velte, F., Sotrz, C., & Lee, K. (2026). The Covid-19 crisis and the vaccine development in Asia and Europe: Comparative lessons for innovation successes and failures. In S. Lechevalier, J.-P. Gaudillière, K. Ibata-Arens, & K. Takuma (Eds.), *Capitalism, innovations, and health after Covid-19. An Asian perspective.* Palgrave MacMillan.
Whitelaw, S., Mamas, M. A., Topol, E., & Van Spall, H. G. (2020). Applications of digital technology in COVID-19 pandemic planning and response. *The Lancet Digital Health, 2*(8), e435–e440.
Zeng, K., Bernardo, S. N., & Havins, W. E. (2020). The use of digital tools to mitigate the COVID-19 pandemic: Comparative retrospective study of six countries. *JMIR Public Health and Surveillance, 6*(4), e24598.
Zhavoronkov, A. (2022, August 22). When will AI beat the Eroom's law in the pharmaceutical industry? *Forbes.*

CHAPTER 4

The Mission-Oriented Science, Technology and Innovation (STI) Policies in Japan and Korea with a Focus on Health

Hideaki Shiroyama, Jeehoon Ki, Makiko Matsuo, and Hyeonoh Kim

Abstract Mission-oriented innovation policy (MOIP) is one form of transformative innovation policy addressing specific social issues, with a package of policy instruments and multiple actors. In Japan, the turn of science and technology policy began advancing around 2009. The administration changed from one centered on the Liberal Democratic Party to one centered on the Democratic Party in 2009, and amid that the social issues of health and the environment became emphasized in science and technology policy. Thereafter, at the end of 2012, the administration changed again to an administration centered on the

H. Shiroyama (✉) · M. Matsuo
The University of Tokyo, Tokyo, Japan
e-mail: siroyama@j.u-tokyo.ac.jp

J. Ki · H. Kim
KISTEP, Eumseong-gun, South Korea

S. Lechevalier et al. (eds.), *Capitalism, Innovations, and Health after Covid-19*,
https://doi.org/10.1007/978-3-032-24479-6_4

Liberal Democratic Party, but the approach to social issues continued. The 5th Science and Technology Basic Plan in 2016 presented Society 5.0 as a social vision to aim for and positioned technology as a tool to achieve the vision of society. Korea's STI policy also emphasized the social contribution of science and technology. Since the First Basic Plan for Science and Technology, released in 2003, the Basic Plan for Science and Technology, the top-level plan for science and technology that is formulated every five years, has continued to include policies for the social role of science and technology. There are several common aspects between the experiences of MOIP in Japan and Korea. The concepts and concrete programs of MOIP have been explicitly discussed and implemented. In Japan, the first phase of the Cross-ministerial Strategic Innovation Promotion Program (SIP) was established in 2014 at the Cabinet level, In Korea, the government established the First Comprehensive Plan for Solving Social Problems Based on Science and Technology, a comprehensive plan in 2013 (CP1). There are also several differences. The first difference is about the program structure. There have been diverse forms of MOIP in Japan. The SIP was established in 2014 at the Cabinet level. Subsequently, the Moonshot Research and Development Program was also established at the Cabinet level in 2020. In Korea, the Comprehensive Plan series was separated from the Science and Technology Basic Plan but integrated as a plan for social issues. The second difference is about historical development. In Japan, the focus of the first phase of the SIPs was on research and development of technology, although they had in mind social issues in a broader sense, But in the third phase of the SIP since 2023, systems, platforms and networks, including institutional, policy and behavioral elements as well as technical elements, have been the main targets. In Korea, the feature of CP1 targeted 10 social problems. But the purpose of CP2 was the creation of a social problem-solving ecosystem including local governments and wider ministries. The third difference is about the structure of governance. In Japan, governance structure at the cabinet level, CSTI (Council for Science, Technology and Innovation Policy), is important in addition to the ministries level. In Korea, the focus is on the role of MSIT (Ministry of Science and ICT) and KISTEP (Korea Institute for S&T Evaluation and Planning) which performs important analytical functions under MSIT.

4.1 Introduction—Asian and European Perspectives on STI Policies

4.1.1 *Trends of Transformative Innovation Policies*

In recent years, there has been much interest in transformative innovation policy from a variety of perspectives, and there are several important elements to transformative innovation policy. The first element is that it addresses specific social issues,[1] the so-called grand challenges. The second element is that, as an extension of addressing social challenges, it targets complex socio-technical systems, rather than specific technical challenges. Therefore, the policy instruments in transformative innovation policy are not a single policy instrument, but a package of several policy instruments, which are used in a multifaceted policy intervention (Borrás & Edler, 2020; Borrás & Schwaag Serger, 2022). The third element is the need for multiple actors to act in concert, rather than a single entity. These multiple actors work together across ministries, sectors, and public-private boundaries (Haddad et al., 2022).

The contemporary version of mission-oriented innovation policy (MOIP) is one form of transformative innovation policy. The OECD, which conducted a comparative study of national policies on MOIP, states that MOIP is "a coordinated package of policy and regulatory measures tailored specifically to mobilize science, technology, and innovation in order to address well-defined objectives related to social challenges" (Larrue, 2021). In this OECD definition, contemporary MOIP is positioned as one specific tool to realize transformative innovation policies in the sense of addressing societal challenges.

4.1.2 *Transformation of STI Policies in the EU*

One of the sites and testing grounds where transformative MOIPs were practiced was the European Union (EU). Already in the Aho Report (EC, 2006) published in 2006, it was pointed out that in science and

[1] This chapter uses the term "social problems" when referring to Korea's policy context, where societal challenges are formally identified and directly linked to R&D interventions. In contrast, we use "social issues" for the Japanese case and general analysis, reflecting the broader framing as policy-relevant concerns that encompass both current and anticipated societal needs.

technology policy, it is necessary to consider not only technology development but also demand creation as a set, specifically, the use of policy instruments such as regulation and procurement and the use of lead users. The need for a high-level coordinator in science and technology policy was also pointed out. In addition, the report on the European Research Area published in 2007 (EC, 2007) indicated that the objective of the European Research Area was to respond to grand challenges.

In response to these concerns, the predecessor to the current Horizon Europe, Horizon 2020, was implemented from 2014 to 2020. Addressing societal challenges was one of the three pillars of Horizon 2020 with specific examples including health, food security, energy, transportation, climate, and inclusion (EC, 2011).

The basics of the current MOIP of the EU, Horizon Europe, took shape during the interim evaluation of Horizon 2020 (EC, 2017a). In this interim evaluation, the lower achievement of social challenges was identified, and factors such as regulations, standards, and financing were cited as contributing factors for the lower achievement. As a future improvement direction, the interim evaluation suggested developing a mission-oriented, impact-focused approach to better implement the Sustainable Development Goals (SDGs). The Lamy report was then published as the report of the political-level committee established in response to this interim report (EC, 2017b). In the Lamy report, a mission-oriented approach for tackling global challenges was explicitly formulated. An important element of this mission-oriented approach is the translation of social challenges into concrete missions and the establishment of measurable impacts related to the missions. The program contents were expected to be both breakthrough and transformational.

Horizon Europe was designed based on the aforementioned studies and has been implemented since 2021. In terms of the institutional framework, the three pillars were reorganized, with "Open Science," "Global Challenges and Industrial Competitiveness," and "Open Innovation" (EC, 2018). Of these, "Global Challenges and Industrial Competitiveness" is the integration of the two former pillars of Horizon 2020, "Industrial Leadership" and "Societal Challenges". This is the primary area of focus for the mission-oriented approach.

The mission was defined as "a portfolio of actions across disciplines intended to achieve a bold and inspirational and measurable goal within a set timeframe" (EC, 2022). Five specific missions were then set

(EC, 2022): Conquering Cancer (Mission Possible), Climate Adaptation (A Climate Resilient Europe—Prepare Europe for climate disasters and accelerate the transformation to a climate resilient and just Europe by 2030), Mission Starfish 2030 (Restore our Ocean and Waters), 100 Climate-Neutral Cities by 2030—by and for the citizens and Caring for Soil is Caring for Life.

The governance of Horizon Europe has several interesting operational features. First, each mission has a board of outsiders, with a politically prominent person serving as chair. This committee is particularly important in the mission setting process, and extensive efforts have been made to involve the public in the setting process. However, the strategic involvement of this committee in day-to-day management does not necessarily seem to be the case, and its role is mainly limited to communication, monitoring, and evaluation functions.

Second, inter-sectoral coordination is important in mission-oriented programs. The mission manager who plays an important role for this coordination is an employee of the European Commission. Specifically, the mission managers are deputy Director-Generals in charge of sectors (e.g., energy, medicine, health, etc.), who are supported by the directors of the Research and Innovation DG as the deputy mission managers. In other words, the sector managers and R&D managers work in close cooperation, within the European Commission.

In addition, as a mechanism to facilitate inter-sectoral coordination, a high-level Steering Board (in which all DGs participate) and a Mission Owners Group (at the section head level) have been established. The DG Research and Innovation has also established a Common Policy Center, which is organizationally located in the DG Research and Innovation but reports to all DGs involved in R&D, not just to the DG Research and Innovation.

Third, as individual activities, the importance of evaluation and exit strategy is emphasized in Horizon Europe. The importance of these activities is understandable, given that an important element of the mission is the setting of measurable goals, and that in terms of responding to social challenges, it is important how to promote transitions in the socio-technical system triggered by individual science and technology innovation programs.

Fourth, it can be confirmed that a variety of programs exist in the EU MOIPs. For example, while missions such as the conquest of cancer have a strong classical research and development aspect, missions such as climate-neutral cities target a wide range of issues and involve a wide range of actors and industries. However, even in the case of conquering cancer, it can be said to be dealing with a certain range of social issues in that it also targets quality of life and work-life balance of caregivers in cancer treatment.

4.1.3 Transformation of STI Policies in Japan

The relation between science and technology policy and society was recognized in Japan from a relatively early time. For example, the 2nd Science and Technology Basic Plan implemented from 2001 stressed building new relations between science and technology and society and emphasized communication between science and technology and society and the return of the fruits of science and technology to society through industry as means to those ends. As a specific research and development program in response to such policy concerns, the Japan Science and Technology Agency (JST) and the Japan Atomic Energy Research Institute (JAERI) under the initiative of the Ministry of Education, Culture, Sports, Science and Technology (MEXT) established the "System for Research in Science and Technology for Society" in 2001. This was a research and development program to promote technology to construct new social systems integrating knowledge from multiple fields of the natural sciences and the humanities and social sciences, that is, science and technology for society. This program subsequently underwent operating structure reviews leading to the present Research Institute of Science and Technology for Society (RISTEX), JST in 2005.

The turn of science and technology policy began advancing around 2009. In Japan, the administration changed from one centered on the Liberal Democratic Party to one centered on the Democratic Party in 2009, and amid that the social issues of health and the environment became emphasized in science and technology policy. Moreover, the Great East Japan Earthquake and tsunami occurred in 2011, and the 4th Science and Technology Basic Plan which was set in 2011 amid big issues on securing trust in science became a framework that prioritized social issues as a major direction (Shiroyama, 2018).

Thereafter, at the end of 2012, the administration changed again to an administration centered on the Liberal Democratic Party, but the approach to social issues was continued to some extent. For example, the 5th Science and Technology Basic Plan in 2016 presented Society

5.0[2] and a super smart society as a social vision to aim for and positioned technology as a tool to achieve the vision of society. It defined Society 5.0 as "a human-centered society that upholds both economic development and the solution of social issues through systems with a high degree of integration between cyberspace and physical space." Certainly, it gave substantial focus to technological means, but it continued the direction of science and technology policy that addresses social issues. In the 6th Science, Technology and Innovation Basic Plan, drafted in 2021, Society 5.0 was made slightly more concrete as a social vision with the contribution of science and technology. Specifically, it describes Society 5.0 as "a society that is sustainable and resilient that secures the safety and security of the people and that enables each and every one of them to realize diverse happiness (well-being)" (Cabinet Office, 2021).

Amid the above change in the overall direction of science and technology policy, various innovation policies and programs that may be called mission-oriented were established as individual programs at cabinet level and ministry level.

For example, the first phase of the Cross-ministerial Strategic Innovation Promotion Program (SIP) was established in 2014 at the Cabinet level, followed by the second phase in 2018 and the third phase in 2023. From the beginning, the SIPs have been aimed at promoting top-down research and development efforts from basic research through to implementation in society in an integrated manner for the purpose of responding to social issues and important issues for Japan's economy and industrial competitiveness.

This sort of direction toward emphasizing the response to social issues has brought about revisions in the legal framework. In 2020 the Basic Act on Science and Technology was amended as the Basic Act on Science, Technology and Innovation. "Innovation creation" was specified as a subject of the Basic Act (Article 1), and a provision defining "innovation creation" was newly established. Specifically, the Basic Act prescribes that new value is created through scientific discovery and invention, the development of new products and new services, and other creative activities, and that the dissemination of these generates major changes in the economy and society (Article 2 Paragraph 1). Also, in order to realize science and

[2] For the concept of Society 5. 0 in the 5th Science and Technology Basic Plan in Japan, please refer to Lechevalier (2026).

technology innovation, the humanities and social sciences were included as subjects of the Basic Act (Article 1).

The 6th Science, Technology and Innovation Basic Plan, which was formulated based on this amendment to the Basic Act and has been implemented since 2021, states that the concept of innovation, which was once seen as an act directly connected to product development and production activities in corporate activities, is now seen as an activity by a wide range of actors that creates major changes in the economy and society, and is evolving into the concept of "transformative innovation" which focuses on the creation of new value and the transformation of society itself. In this way, transformative innovation policy became explicitly recognized in innovation policy (Cabinet Office, 2021).

4.1.4 Transformation of STI Policies in Korea[3]

Korea's STI policy also emphasizes the social contribution of science and technology. This can be seen as a relatively new policy area. Traditionally, the contribution to economic and industrial development and the advancement of knowledge have been the main areas of S&T policy and R&D investment in Korea. This shift means that S&T in Korea is recognized as more than a tool for academic research or industrial development, but also as a tool to address social issues and contribute to improving the quality of life of the people.

Since the First Basic Plan for Science and Technology (2003–2007), released in 2003, the Basic Plan for Science and Technology, the top-level plan for science and technology that is formulated every five years, has continued to include policies for the social role of science and technology. In 2013, the government established the First Comprehensive Plan for Solving Social Problems Based on Science and Technology, a comprehensive plan to utilize science and technology to solve social problems such as chronic diseases and cybercrime. The Comprehensive Plan for Solving Social Problems Based on Science and Technology (hereafter "Comprehensive Plan" or "CP") is a five-year plan implemented by the Ministry of Science and ICT (MSIT) in collaboration with related ministries. Three iterations have been established: CP1 (2013–2017), CP2 (2018–2022), and CP3 (2023–2027). Each plan is jointly prepared by

[3] This subsection adapts content from Ki et al. (2024b).

the relevant ministries, and—starting with CP2—involves local as well as central governments. Local-government participation and the number of participating ministries grew further under CP3, indicating that social-problem-solving STI policy is becoming increasingly widespread across the public sector.

The institutionalization process of Korea's social problem-solving STI policy represented by CP is quite significant. This is because it has been legally established in the Basic Act on Science and Technology, the highest law in the field of science and technology. In 2014, during CP1 period (2013–2017), the Basic Act on Science and Technology was amended to specify social problem-solving as the purpose of utilizing science and technology. Meanwhile, in November of the same year, the relevant enforcement decree was amended to specify the establishment of a five-year CP.

What is noteworthy here is that it specifically presents social contributions as 'solving social problems' and improving the quality of life through science and technology. On the one hand, it can be seen as a clarification of social contribution, which can be abstract. However, on the other hand, it also reveals that the perspective on how science and technology can contribute to society is limited to problem-solving, even though there are various ways in which science and technology can contribute to society.

The main content of CP consists of a vision, goals, strategies, and actions. The main contents are usually presented in a single, easy-to-read figure.

Along with the establishment and implementation of CP, national R&D projects aimed at solving social problems gradually expanded in scale. From KRW 1.2 trillion in 2018 to KRW 1.6 trillion in 2021 and KRW 1.8 trillion in 2023, the amount has steadily increased. In terms of the proportion of the total government R&D budget, it has remained at about 6% level from 2018 to 2023, maintaining a certain level of status as an area of national R&D investment.

4.1.5 *Structure of the Chapter*

The concept of transformative innovation policy and its specific form, contemporary MOIP, has been explicitly discussed on the basis of practices in the EU and European countries, etc. However, even in the different cultural and institutional contexts of Asian countries, programs that are substantially equivalent to these have been implemented in countries such as Japan and Korea. This chapter therefore provides a comparative analysis of programs for mission-oriented innovation policies to address social challenges in Japan and Korea, with European examples for references. European practices and Asian practices might have some common elements and different elements. In addition, both Japan and Korea have a history as developmental states that utilized industrial policies in the second half of the twentieth century. A comparative study of Japan and Korea is meaningful in examining what the experience as developmental states means for the current transformative innovation policy and contemporary MOIPs.

When making comparisons, three perspectives will be considered. First, the focus will be on the development of the programs. Specifically, the focus will be on the Strategic Innovation Program (SIP) launched in Japan in 2014, the Moonshot R&D system launched in 2020, etc., and the Comprehensive Plan launched in South Korea in 2013. Second, this chapter focuses on the cross-sectoral governance structures that manage such programs. In Japan, the focus will be on the role of the Council for Science, Technology Policy (CSTP), established in the Cabinet Office, and its successor organization, the Council for Science, Technology and Innovation Policy (CSTI). In Korea, the focus will be on the role of MSIT (Ministry of Science and ICT) and the Korea Institute of S&P Evaluation and Planning (KISTEP) which performs important analytical functions under MSIT. Third, the current operation and limitations of the MOIPs are analyzed focusing on the use of ELSI (Ethical Legal and Social Issues), SSH (Social Sciences and Humanities) and performance impact assessment. Then the concrete applications of MOIPs in the health sector are examined.

4.2 Mission-Oriented STI Policies in Japan

4.2.1 Development

4.2.1.1 Diverse Forms of MOIPs

Looking from the perspectives of technology-driven or social-issues-driven, there are diverse variations within the SIPs. As the fact that social implementation is emphasized in the third phase of SIPs shows, the social-issues-driven aspect seems to be becoming stronger. This type of change can be confirmed by looking at how SIPs with similar subjects transformed during the first, second, and third phases. For example, in the first phase SIP, with autonomous driving systems as the theme, the issues of reducing traffic accidents and realizing and spreading autonomous driving systems which have a large technological aspect were set as social goals, and specifically the mapping data (dynamic mapping) required for autonomous driving was set as a technological goal. Thereafter, in the second phase of SIPs, with autonomous driving (expansion of systems and services) as the theme, the social goals set were not only reducing traffic accidents but also improving the shortage of drivers in logistics and transportation services, which was becoming a major social issue in Japan. In addition, in the third phase of SIPs, constructing a smart mobility platform was set as a theme which seeks a new concept of mobility that is not limited to autonomous driving as narrowly defined. Initially, the SIPs set the solutions and then sought out the social issues, but in recent years the SIPs focus on the issues and then seek a broad range of solutions including non-technological options.

Subsequently, the Moonshot Research and Development Program was proposed at the Council for Science, Technology, and Innovation in 2018 and established at the Cabinet level in 2020. The use of the name "moonshot" seems to have in mind a classic mission highlighting technology, but at the same time this also has in mind the setting of long-term goals looking ahead to the grand challenge of 2050. Because high-risk, high-return research and development must be conducted to achieve such long-term goals and because it is important to combine various types of projects to conduct high-risk, high-return research, the Moonshot Research and Development Program emphasizes adopting a "portfolio approach". Specifically, it sets nine Moonshot Goals, and these include both goals focused on research and development and goals focused on social aspects (Shiroyama, 2024).

Aside from the programs set at the Cabinet level, the programs set at each ministry level include programs with an MOIP nature. For example, Green Technologies of Excellence (GteX) presently being advanced by the Japan Science and Technology Agency (JST) of the Ministry of Education, Culture, Sports, Science and Technology (MEXT) can be cited as an example. GteX sets three technology areas that facilitate CO2 reduction for green innovation (biomanufacturing, hydrogen, and storage batteries), and it aims at realizing goals by combining these entirely different sectors. For that purpose, in achieving missions, close coordination is sought between GteX, which is mostly under the jurisdiction of the MEXT, and the Ministry of Economy, Trade and Industry (METI), which is in charge of the areas linked to implementation in society (Matsuo, 2024).

In addition, historically, in the area of the development and diffusion of welfare technology, there was collaboration between the former Ministry of Welfare and the former Ministry of International Trade and Industry with similar spirit.[4]

4.2.1.2 Changing Nature of SIPs—From First to Third SIPs

Among the Japanese MOIPs, the first phase of SIPs has been implemented since 2014, the second phase SIP since 2019 and the third phase SIPs since 2023. Specifically, as can be seen in Tables 4.1, 4.2 and 4.3 programs have been implemented as the first phase SIPs, 11 programs as the second phase SIPs and 14 programs as the third phase SIPs'. As there is a certain historical accumulation of SIP cases, the development of the content is analyzed in order.

In terms of budget, for example, in the FY2023 budget, 55.5 billion yen was allocated as the Cabinet Office's own budget for the Science and Technology Innovation Promotion Fund, of which 24.556 billion was allocated to SIP programs as its initial budget

From Table 4.1, it can be seen that the focus of the first phase of the SIPs was on research and development of technology, although they had in mind social issues in a broader sense, such as strengthening competitiveness, addressing environmental issues such as CO2 reduction, and ensuring safety and security. For example, as can be seen from the themes of the programs in the first phase of the SIPs, these included innovative combustion technology, next-generation power electronics, innovative structural materials, energy carriers, next-generation marine resource survey technology, infrastructure maintenance, renewal and management technology, next-generation agriculture, forestry and fisheries creation technology and innovative design and production technology. The focus was on the development of technology.

As can be seen from Table 4.2, the second phase of SIPs focused on fundamental technologies that bridge cyberspace and physical space, as seen in the following themes: cyberspace infrastructure technology utilizing big data and AI, physical space digital data processing infrastructure, cyber and physical security for IoT society, and technology to realize Society 5.0 utilizing optical and quantum technology. The focus was on fundamental technologies bridging cyberspace and physical space. This is

[4] Please refer to chapter 8 Kodate et al. (2026) for the development and diffusion of care robots in Japan from comparative perspective.

Table 4.1 SIP Program 1st phase (2014 ~ 2018)

	Theme	*Affiliation of Program Director*	*Budget (total: million yen)*	*Summary of Program*
1	Innovative combustion technology	Industry	9,423	To realize innovative combustion technology that improves the maximum thermal efficiency of internal combustion engines for passenger cars to 50% by establishing a sustainable industry-academia collaboration. Contribute to the development of world-class internal combustion engine researchers, energy savings, CO2 reduction and industrial competitiveness.
2	Next generation power electronics	Industry	11,431	Next-generation materials will significantly improve the performance of current power electronics and contribute to energy savings and the increased introduction of renewable energy. At the same time, a large market will be created and global market share will be increased.
3	Innovative structural materials	Academia	18,690	Accelerate the development of innovative materials that are lightweight and have excellent heat and environmental resistance, and their application in aircraft and other applications, thereby contributing to energy conservation and CO2 emissions reduction. At the same time, maintain and strengthen the competitiveness of Japan's materials industry.
4	Energy Carrier	Industry	16,576	Build a clean, efficient society with a high level of security by utilizing hydrogen and hydrogen energy carriers originating from renewable energy sources, etc., and present the innovation to the world.

(continued)

Table 4.1 (continued)

	Theme	*Affiliation of Program Director*	*Budget (total: million yen)*	*Summary of Program*
5	Next generation marine resource survey technology	Academia	25,150	Establish a world-leading technology for highly efficient survey of marine resources such as seabed hydrothermal deposits, including copper, zinc and rare metals, to create a marine resource survey industry.
6	Automated driving systems	Industry	13,776	Promote research and development on technological issues (cooperation areas) that should be addressed jointly by industry, academia and government to realize advanced automated driving systems.
7	Infrastructure maintenance, renewal and management technologies	Academia	16,041	To improve the level of maintenance management through preventive maintenance at low cost, amid concerns about the emergence of serious accident risks and lack of maintenance costs due to the ageing of infrastructure. At the same time, create a stable maintenance and management market and promote overseas business.
8	Strengthen resilient disaster prevention and mitigation functions	Academia	12,316	To prepare for natural disasters such as major earthquakes and tsunamis, torrential rains and tornadoes, volcanoes and other natural disasters, the public and private sectors will establish a system for sharing disaster information in real time to improve prevention and strengthen response capabilities.
9	Ensuring cyber security in critical infrastructure, etc.	Academia	(8,060 + 1,840 in 2019)	In order to protect critical infrastructure, etc. from cyber-attacks, research and development of technologies for determining the authenticity of control and communication equipment, operation monitoring and analysis technologies and defense technologies will be carried out to strengthen the international competitiveness of the critical infrastructure industry and contribute to the stable operation of the 2020 Tokyo Olympics.

(continued)

Table 4.1 (continued)

	Theme	*Affiliation of Program Director*	*Budget (total: million yen)*	*Summary of Program*
10	Next generation agriculture, forestry and fisheries creation technology	Academia	14,955	In conjunction with agricultural policy reform, realize technological innovations to make agriculture smarter and add value to agricultural, forestry and fisheries products, thereby contributing to increased incomes for new farmers, agriculture and rural areas. At the same time, it will contribute to improving the quality of life and expanding related industries.
11	Innovative design and production technology	Industry	9,110	Strengthen the competitiveness of industries and regions by establishing a system that facilitates the creation of high value-added products by increasing the options available to companies and individuals when designing them.

Source https://www8.cao.go.jp/cstp/gaiyo/sip/sipkenkyukaihatu11kadai.pdf

Table 4.2 SIP Program 2nd phase (2019 ~ 2022)

	Theme	*Affiliation of Program Director*	*Budget (total: million yen)*	*Summary of Program*
1	Cyberspace infrastructure technology using big data and AI	Academia	6,833	The highly sophisticated 'human interaction infrastructure technology' that contributes to collaboration between humans and AI, the 'inter-disciplinary data collaboration infrastructure' and 'inter-AI collaboration infrastructure technology' will be established within the 'cyberspace infrastructure technology', and cyber-physical systems utilizing big data and AI will be implemented in society.
2	Physical space digital data processing infrastructure	Industry	5,900	In the advanced cyber-physical system (CPS), which is the key to realizing Society 5.0, the following technologies are important: technology to control the physical space within the required time; ultra-low power consumption technology to significantly reduce power consumption; innovative sensor technology; and social implementation technology necessary for building a CPS. This program aims to solve these technological issues and build a platform that enables the creation of advanced IoT solutions easily without the need for specialized IT personnel.
3	Cyber and physical security for the IoT society	Academia	8,004	Develop and demonstrate a 'cyber-physical security countermeasure infrastructure' that can be used to protect IoT systems and services and the entire large-scale supply chain, including SMEs. Promote social implementation in various industrial sectors, such as manufacturing, distribution and buildings, which have diverse social infrastructures and services and a wide range of supply chains.

(continued)

Table 4.2 (continued)

	Theme	*Affiliation of Program Director*	*Budget (total: million yen)*	*Summary of Program*
4	Automated driving (extension of systems and services)	Industry	12,145	By extending the practical application of automated driving from motorways to ordinary roads, and by putting logistics and mobility services that utilize automated driving technology to practical use, the program will contribute to reducing traffic accidents, reducing traffic congestion, securing means of transport in depopulated areas, etc. and solving social problems such as driver shortages in the logistics industry, with the aim of creating a safe and secure society in which all citizens can move around.
5	Material revolution through integrated materials development systems	Academia	7,920	By utilizing Materials Integration (MI), which has been undertaken by industry, academia and government, to innovate materials development methods through the fusion of materials engineering and information engineering, develop the world's first 'Inverse Problem MI', which designs materials and processes based on desired performance, deploy it in advanced materials and processes, and accelerate its implementation in society.
6	Technology for realizing Society 5.0 through the use of optical and quantum	Industry	8,893	The key to realizing Society 5.0 is the construction of cyber-physical systems (CPS) that highly integrate cyberspace and physical space, but there are bottlenecks preventing investment. By utilizing Japan's strengths in optical and quantum technologies, and carefully selecting and developing key technologies in processing, information processing and communications that can resolve these bottlenecks, we will achieve the commercialization of core technologies originating in Japan to regain a share of the laser processing market and the optimization of manufacturing design and production processes.

(continued)

Table 4.2 (continued)

	Theme	*Affiliation of Program Director*	*Budget (total: million yen)*	*Summary of Program*
7	Smart bio-industrial and agricultural infrastructure technology	Industry	7,994	With the sustainability of the global environment and resources sustainability becoming an issue, implement a "system" of mechanisms that not only contributes to "sustainability" of "agriculture", "food products" and "food-related resources/environment" independently, but also generates added value by linking and chaining data and information from each stage, and comprehensively reduces the global environmental burden.
8	Energy systems in an IoE society	Academia	3,858	The design of energy systems for a society in which renewable energy is the main source of power is examined, and research and development is carried out to build energy systems that contribute to optimizing energy use and to achieve innovation in energy conversion and transmission systems for social implementation.
9	Strengthening national resilience (disaster prevention and mitigation)	Academia	8,888	It is necessary to implement the Government Program on Disaster Management for Nankai Trough Earthquakes and Other Disasters. This program aims to research and develop new technologies for strengthening national resilience using satellites, AI, big data, etc., and implement them in the government and municipalities, thereby contributing to the achievement of government goals and realizing Society 5.0 in times of disaster.
10	Advanced diagnosis and treatment systems by AI Hospitals	Academia	11,760	Develop, build and implement an 'AI Hospital System' using AI, IoT and Big Data technologies to provide advanced and advanced medical services, improve efficiency in medical institutions and drastically reduce the burden on doctors, nurses and other healthcare professionals.

(continued)

Table 4.2 (continued)

	Theme	*Affiliation of Program Director*	*Budget (total: million yen)*	*Summary of Program*
11	Smart logistics service	Industry	2,780	Optimize the entire supply chain, create new industries and added value by utilizing data in the logistics and commercial distribution sector, and solve the problems of labor shortages and low productivity in the logistics and retail industry. Visualize logistics and commercial flow data held by various players in the supply chain and build an open and security-secured data infrastructure that can be shared and utilized.
12	Innovative deep-sea resource survey technology	Industry	11,305	Establish and demonstrate world-leading deep-sea resource survey and recovery technologies at depths of 2000 m and deeper by utilizing the results of the first phase of the SIP, which mainly targeted depths of 2000 m and deeper, and by developing and applying these technologies step by step, with prospects for social implementation.

Sources https://www8.cao.go.jp/cstp/gaiyo/sip/sip2nd_list.html, https://www8.cao.go.jp/cstp/gaiyo/sip/96kai/siryo2-2.pdf, https://www8.cao.go.jp/cstp/gaiyo/sip/200227/siryo2-2.pdf, https://www8.cao.go.jp/cstp/gaiyo/sip/210225/siryo7.pdf, https://www8.cao.go.jp/cstp/gaiyo/sip/220303/siryo4.pdf

Table 4.3 SIP Program 3rd phase (2023 ~)

	Theme	*Affiliation of Program Director*	*Budget (total: million yen)*	*Summary of Program*
1	Creating a sustainable food chain where abundant meals are provided	Industry	2,030	Use of cyber-physical systems to revitalize domestic industry and rebuild domestic food chains.
2	Building an integrated healthcare system	Academia	2,300	Develop a 'medical digital twin' that standardizes and projects on-site medical and healthcare data into digital space.
3	Building an inclusive community platform	Academia	791	To build and provide a platform for projects and services that can be selected and adopted by residents, local authorities and businesses to form inclusive communities.
4	Building a platform for learning and working in the post-Corona era	Academia	695	Build a 'platform' to develop human resources who can design the 'new learning' required for people living in Society 5.0, think independently about their own way of life throughout their lives, recognize the different values of others, collaborate with others and make the most of themselves within society. Develop an environment where anyone can choose the way they want to learn and work, regardless of time and place.
5	Building a maritime security platform	Industry	2,700	Aim to establish a rare earths mining and production system, as well as to upgrade marine environmental monitoring technology. In addition, basic research and conceptual design of marine basalt CCS will be carried out for large-scale CO2 storage technology.

(continued)

Table 4.3 (continued)

	Theme	*Affiliation of Program Director*	*Budget (total: million yen)*	*Summary of Program*
6	Building a smart energy management system	Academia	1,720	Establish a next-generation social infrastructure by building a cross-border, cross-sectoral Energy Management System that also encompasses heat, hydrogen and synthetic fuels, in order to make renewable energy the main energy source.
7	Building a Circular Economy System	Academia	1,200	Arterial companies work together to build a plastic CE value chain through circulation-friendly initiatives by players in materials, products, collection, sorting and recycling.
8	Building a smart disaster prevention network	Academia	2,430	Work on 'further sophistication of information collection and understanding to support disaster response' and 'enhancement of disaster response capabilities by individuals, local governments and businesses based on the results of information analysis' by highly integrating real and cyber space and utilizing advanced ICT, AI, etc.
9	Building a smart infrastructure management system	Academia	2,030	Works on technology development and research and development that contributes to the construction of 'cities of the future', 'infrastructure of the future' and 'construction technology of the future', aiming at the realization of Society 5.0.
10	Building a smart mobility platform	Academia	1,850	In addition to promoting the redefinition of mobility services and the formulation of strategies for social implementation, research and development for infrastructure re-design will develop safe, comfortable and vibrant transport infrastructure technologies and build a data infrastructure to support mobility services. Furthermore, to support the implementation of smart mobility services, comprehensive promotion of the use of digital sandboxes, community formation, human resource development, start-up support, etc. will be undertaken.

(continued)

Table 4.3 (continued)

	Theme	*Affiliation of Program Director*	*Budget (total: million yen)*	*Summary of Program*
11	Developing basic technologies and rules for the expansion of human-collaborative robotics	Academia	1,260	Develop basic technologies for HCPS ('human' + 'cyber-physical space') coordinated robotics and social implementation technologies. At the same time, promote social implementation by integrally linking the development of rules for promoting introduction.
12	Developing the basic technologies and rules for the expansion of the virtual economy	Academia	1,410	Take advantage of our country's strengths in industries such as automobiles, consumer electronics and sensor devices, and promote interverse development and rules to take a different touchpoint from other countries that are ahead of us in the virtual economy sphere.
13	Promoting the application of advanced quantum technology platforms to social issues	Industry	2,650	In order to attract long-term investment and human resources for quantum technology, which includes basic research stages, "concrete examples of solutions to real social and industrial problems" will be created through the development of the utilization environment and the development and demonstration of use cases.
14	Building an ecosystem for fostering innovation in materials commercialization	Industry	1,490	Form an ecosystem with a platform to realize Society 5.0 at its core, which will generate a series of new businesses (from start-ups, etc. to unicorns) in the materials sector that will lead to the resolution of social issues in 20–30 years' time.

Sources https://www8.cao.go.jp/cstp/gaiyo/sip/sip_3/230324gaiyo.pdf, https://www8.cao.go.jp/cstp/gaiyo/sip/230316/shiryo8.pdf

related to the presentation of Society 5.0, which utilizes instruments integrating cyberspace and physical space, as the social vision to be pursued in the Fifth Science and Technology Basic Plan, which was implemented from 2016. In these programs, while there has been a specific focus on individual technological developments, the emphasis has also been on their contribution to the realization of Society 5.0.

But Table 4.3 shows that systems, platforms and networks, including institutional, policy and behavioral elements as well as technical elements, have been the main targets in the third phase of SIPs. It is clear from themes of each program: building a sustainable food chain where abundant food is provided; building an integrated healthcare system; building an inclusive community platform; building a platform for learning and working in the post-Corona era; building a maritime security platform; building a smart energy management system; building a circular economy system; building a smart disaster prevention network; building a smart infrastructure management system; building a smart mobility platform; and building an ecosystem for fostering innovation in material commercialization. The program themes also indicate that, with regard to human-coordinated robotics and the virtual economy, the emphasis will be on the development of the rules as well as the fundamental technologies.

Such institutional, policy and behavioral elements were also found in the first and second phases of SIPs, but to a limited extent. Strengthening resilient disaster prevention and mitigation functions in the first phase of SIPs, strengthening national resilience (disaster prevention and mitigation) and smart logistics services in the second phase of SIP were such examples.

This change in the nature of the programs was also associated with a change in the origin of the program directors (PDs). In the first phase of SIPs, the ratio of PDs from industry to PDs from academia was 5:6, while in the second phase of SIPs the ratio of PDs from industry to academia was 6:6. The ratio was almost equal in between the two SIPs. In the third phase of SIPs, on the other hand, the ratio of people from industry to people from academia was 4:10, with a much higher ratio of people from academia. This seems to be due to the fact that in the third phase of SIPs, the aspect of responding to social challenges by combining technical and institutional policy and behavioral elements has become stronger, requiring more coordination with wider stakeholders. However, the difficulty for those from academia to receive informal support from their home organizations has also led to implementation challenges.

4.2.2 *Governance of Japan's STI Policies*

4.2.2.1 Roles of the Council for Science and Technology Policy (CSTP)

As a result of the reorganization of the central government ministries and agencies in 2001, the Ministry of Education, Science, Sports and Culture and the Science and Technology Agency were combined as the Ministry of Education, Culture, Sports, Science and Technology (MEXT). Also, the newly established Cabinet Office was given the roles of assisting the Cabinet Secretariat and contributing to strengthening Cabinet functions, and the Council for Science and Technology Policy (CSTP) was established to support those roles in the field of science and technology policy. Then in formulating the Science and Technology Basic Plan, it first had to pass through discussions at the CSTP.

The CSTP was established as a council for overall coordination through the means of budgets, plans, and assessments. However, the role of the CSTP was limited in the point that while the Ministry of Finance permitted "multi-stage assessments," it did not permit the "externalization of assessments". Also, systematically, because "the planning, formulation, and promotion of basic policies concerning science and technology" remained at MEXT as affairs carried over from the former Science and Technology Agency, preparatory works for the Science and Technology Basic Plan were also carried out at MEXT in parallel (Ito, 2006).

The Council for Science and Technology Policy comprised the prime minister, the chief cabinet secretary, the minister of state for science and technology policy, the minister of internal affairs and communications, the minister of finance, the minister of education, culture, sports, science and technology, the minister of economy, trade and industry, and private-sector members. Because an increase of members including those from the humanities and social sciences was sought in the process of examining the reorganization of central government agencies and ministries, in fact humanities and social sciences members were added (Ito, 2006).

4.2.2.2 Reorganization into the Council for Science, Technology and Innovation (CSTI) and Use of MOIP for Centralization and Its Limits

Subsequently, the bill to revise the Act for Establishment of the Cabinet Office was passed in 2014. As a result, matters concerning comprehensive preparation of an environment to promote innovation creation through commercialization of research and development results were added to the affairs under the jurisdiction of the Cabinet Office and the name of the CSTP was changed to the CSTI (Council for Science, Technology and Innovation). Also, works concerning the formulation and promotion of the Science and Technology Basic Plan were transferred from MEXT to the Cabinet Office and the overlapping works of the Cabinet Office and MEXT in preparing the formulation of the Science and Technology Basic Plan were consolidated (Shiroyama, 2018).

Under the basic conditions stated above, SIP and the Moonshot Research and Development Program were established as research and development programs under the direct management at the Cabinet level. Because the coordination capacities of the CSTI as a control center were insufficient, there was a desire to supplement the centralization power of CSTI using direct program operation at the Cabinet level.

Regarding SIP, a top-down governance structure was established. A governing board regarding SIP overall was set up within the CSTI. Under this board, program directors (PDs), program managers (PMs), and promotion committees with the participation of concerned ministries and agencies were established for each issue. In particular, implementation in society was emphasized in the third phase of the SIP which started in 2023 specifically with emphasis on the five perspectives: technology, commercialization, systems, social acceptance, and human resources. Also, while the primary role of the PMs was set as research and development management, the main role of the PDs was set as implementation in society (Cabinet Office, 2022).

The governance structure of the Moonshot Research and Development Program is somewhat decentralized. Goals are set by the CSTI and the Headquarters for Healthcare Policy at the Cabinet level, day-to-day management is conducted by the individual ministries, agencies, etc., and the Strategy Promotion Council comprising experts and concerned ministries and agencies makes overall advice in collaboration with the Visionary Council. Then, a program director (PD) and multiple program managers (PMs) are set for each goal. Compared with SIP, the Moonshot Research and Development Program has a strong aspect of long-term research and development, so while its framework is top-down, it permits some level of autonomous responses by the researchers. Also, while the response to the grand challenge is a future goal, the Strategy Promotion Council gives support regarding social implementation and coordination, and the research promotion agency responsible for research and development management gives support regarding ethical, legal, and social issues (ELSI).

Such MOIP at the Cabinet level in Japan has various characteristics compared, for example, with MOIP in the EU (Shiroyama, 2024). First, in MOIP in the EU, efforts were made on how to link the existing research and development programs of the Directorate-General for Research and Innovation and other Directorate-Generals for sectors utilizing the mission cross-sectional framework, while in Japan's case a framework was established at the Cabinet level separated from the research and development programs of each ministry and agency, and the SIP and Moonshot Research and Development Program were separately established at the Cabinet level. For that reason, in MOIP at the Cabinet level in Japan, the issue remained of how to link the SIP and Moonshot Research and Development Program in the Cabinet Office with the research and development programs of each ministry and agency. Also, the issue remained of how to link the multiple MOIPs of SIP and the Moonshot Research and Development Program. Second, in the EU's Horizon Europe, European Commission employees are responsible for coordination among sectors as mission managers (Deputy DGs for sectors as mission managers and Directors of DG of Research and Innovation as deputy mission managers), while in Japan the PDs and PMs are sourced externally from industry and academia.

The overall changing structure of science, technology innovation governance in Japan is shown in Fig. 4.1.

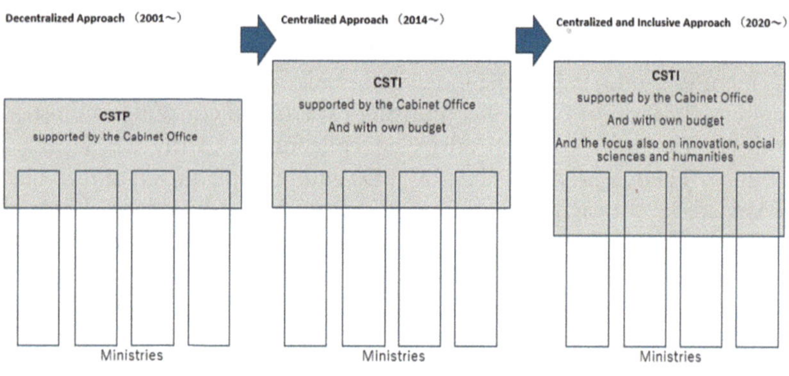

Fig. 4.1 Changing structure of science, technology innovation governance in Japan. *Source* Authors

Since the administrative reorganization in 2001, the Council of Science, Technology Policy (CSTP) was established for strengthening the coordination function for science, technology policy supported by the Cabinet Office. But the autonomy of ministries was relatively strong, and the approach taken can be characterized as a decentralized approach. After the reorganization from the CSTP to the CSTI (Council for Science, Technology and Innovation Policy) and establishment of its own budget for SIP program and others in 2014, the CSTI and the Cabinet Office was strengthened. The approach taken can be characterized as a centralized approach. Then after the revision of the Basic Law of Science and Technology into the Basic Law of Science, technology and Innovation in 2020, the target was explicitly focused on innovation including social dimensions, and the scope was expanded into social sciences and humanities for strengthening social implementation. The approach taken can be characterized as a centralized and inclusive approach.

4.2.3 Operation of Japan's STI Policies

4.2.3.1 Incorporation of Ethical, Legal and Social Issues (ELSI) Perspectives

When trying to implement a MOIP, which is a mix of diverse policy and technological options, it is necessary to consider issues and risks in relation to the mission to be achieved. In this context, the ELSI perspective becomes more important than ever in analyzing the contribution to solving social problems (Matsuo, 2024). In Japan, the need to address ELSI has been explicitly discussed in policy documents from the Third Science and Technology Basic Plan to the current Sixth Science and Technology Innovation Plan. As a result, the JST CRDS has worked and published many reports on ELSI, and JST RISTEX has conducted various research programs related to ELSI (for example, Responsible Innovation with Conscience and Agility (RInCA)) (Shiroyama & Matsuo, 2024). On the other hand, ELSI has yet to permeate in every research program and projects. Under such circumstances, it is noteworthy that the Moonshot R&D system recognizes the need to consider ELSI in research promotion and has established an ELSI subcommittee to support activities across moonshot programs (however, since the ELSI subcommittee is established by JST, it mainly support for JST funded Moonshot goals—goal 1, goal 2, goal 3, goal 6, goal 8, Goal 9).

In addition to the incorporation of ELSI perspectives into MOIP program, wider concept of "convergence of knowledge" was introduced to incorporate elements of social science and humanities into STI policies, following the previously mentioned amendment of Science and Technology Basic Law in 2020 focusing on innovation and including humanities and social sciences as subjects of the Basic Act. Concretely, the 6th Science, Technology and Innovation Basic Plan implemented from 2021 mentions the importance of the "convergence of knowledge" from the fusion of "knowledge" in the humanities and social sciences that creates social value and "knowledge" in the natural sciences (Cabinet Office, 2021, p. 10).

Specifically, the Basic Plan presumes four potential roles for the humanities and social sciences which contribute to the convergence of knowledge. First is the role of the humanities and social sciences as a provider of checklists concerning ELSI. "In order to respond to ELSI that arise when new technologies are used in society at the time of the transition to Society 5.0, it is necessary to look at things from a holistic perspective. It is necessary to construct a system that can utilize convergence of knowledge not only in natural science but also in humanities and social science" (Cabinet Office, 2021, p. 14). Second is the role of the humanities and social sciences such as behavioral economics as a tool to encourage changes in the behavior of citizens, etc. For example, "The government will promote the creation of a public understanding of the importance of individual efforts to realize carbon neutrality and the transformation of behavior to decarbonizing by utilizing the convergence of knowledge through the fusion of humanities, social sciences, and natural sciences" (Cabinet Office, 2021, p. 28). Third is the role of the humanities and social sciences as a foundation for systems reform for social implementation. "With regard to issues that are important for Japan's economic and industrial competitiveness and are related to multiple ministries and agencies, a large-scale industry-academia-government collaboration system will continue to be established, and comprehensive R&D will be promoted, including institutional reforms, to realize social implementation" (Cabinet Office, 2021, p. 45). Fourth is the role of the humanities and social sciences as presenting various pathways and showing multiple values relating to the choice of the pathways. "When embodying the vision of a future society and formulating and promoting policies, it is necessary to utilize the convergence of knowledge based on the fusion of the humanities, social sciences, and natural sciences. Instead of deciding on a single direction, it is necessary to have options for double-line scenarios and new technologies and advance while continuously conducting verification" (Cabinet Office, 2021, p. 44). Also, "In order to solve social issues, it is necessary to present new values and to take a systematic approach, in addition to the approaches that are an extension of conventional approaches" (Cabinet Office, 2021, p. 82).

As with ELSI above, portions of the convergence of knowledge are being implemented fragmentarily. However, at the current time, this is limited to calling for the utilization of the convergence of knowledge including the humanities and the social sciences, and there is a gap between the expected functions and the current implementations.

4.2.3.2 *Evaluation of Social Impacts*

One major issue for science, technology, and innovation programs responding to social issues is the method of evaluating such social aspects and impacts. Factors that can be cited as for why evaluation of social performance and value creation are difficult include (1) quantification is difficult because evaluation concerning many social impacts contain many qualitative factors, (2) evaluation of cause-effect relationships between policies and results are difficult because many factors complexly contribute to the results, and (3) it is difficult to set the scope. After recognizing such issues, some efforts have been made to make the path of social performance visible using narratives, etc.

There are interesting attempts to measure the potential impact of the MOIP (Matsuo, 2024). As an indicator of the potential social impact of R&D, the extended concept of the Technology Readiness Level (TRL) has already been used to examine many technology development research projects. Whilst technology is one of the major factors that bring about social change, technology alone cannot bring about social change. In the third phase of the SIP program, four additional "X-readiness levels" were introduced alongside TRL: Business (BRL), Governance (GRL), Social/Community [S(C)RL], and Human-Resource (HRL). Based on the nine levels used in TRL (basic research → hypothesis → verification → initial testing at laboratory level → testing in assumed use environment → verification (system) → production planning → scale (pilot line) → stable supply), nine levels were considered for each X readiness levels taking into account the characteristics of each perspective. For each SIP project the readiness levels above are set to visualize which level to aim for from which level. However, as this is the first time such an attempt has been introduced, this will be an exercise of trial and error as to how to put the evaluation of each level into practice.

According to Reed et al. (2021), who reviewed the evaluation of impact of research, there are already several methods for evaluating the impact of research, including experimental and statistical methods, systems analysis methods, textual, oral and arts-based methods, indicator-based approaches, evidence synthesis approaches, etc. But the problem of how to design an appropriate evaluation and implement it with appropriate methods remains.

4.2.4 Japan's STI Policies in Health Area

4.2.4.1 Portfolio Development in SIP Focusing on Health Area

Corresponding to this change in the nature of the programs of SIPs in Japan, there has also been a shift in the content of the programs. For example, programs in the field of medicine and health care, where institutional and people's behavioral factors are of greater importance, are now also being implemented. For example, in the second phase of the SIPs, the 'Advanced Diagnostic and Treatment Systems with AI Hospitals' program was set up and implemented. The program aims to develop, build and socially implement an 'AI Hospital System' using AI, IoT and Big Data technologies to provide advanced and advanced medical services, improve efficiency in medical institutions and drastically reduce the burden on doctors, nurses and other healthcare professionals.

In the third phase of the SIPs, the "Establishment of an Integrated Healthcare System" and "Establishment of an Inclusive Community Platform" programs were also implemented. In the 'Establishment of an Integrated Healthcare System' program, in addition to the 'technology development' required for the medical digital twin, 'business development' of solutions to medical and healthcare issues using the medical digital twin, promotion of standardization of the medical information system infrastructure and 'institutional building' such as legislation on the use of medical data, promoting 'social acceptance' and developing 'human resources' are included. Furthermore, in the "Construction of Inclusive Community Platforms", the promotion of social mechanisms and values were also targeted, together with science-based social technologies, to improve social tolerance, individual autonomy, the well-being of child-rearing generations and women, and the fulfilment of life for the disabled and the elderly. Furthermore, inclusive community platforms were expected to contribute to other related SIPs programs, such as the construction of circular economy systems and smart mobility platforms.

4.2.4.2 Case of Health Program in the Moonshot Research and Development Program—Possibilities and Limitations

There are 9 goals for the Moonshot research and development program and two goals among them focus on health issues. For example, Moonshot goal 7 is titled "Living without health concerns until age 100".

Japan is heading toward a rapidly aging society. By 2040, there will be 300,000 people over the age of 100. Especially in terms of the Quality of Life (QOL), extending healthy life expectancy and also being free from chronic diseases without any physical restriction (i.e., reducing unhealthy time or need for care to as close to zero as possible) is in need. Against this backdrop, Moonshot goal 7 was launched with the goal of "achieving a sustainable health and care system to prevent and overcome major diseases and enjoy life without health concerns until age 100 by 2040".

In the Moonshot Goal 7, chronic inflammation is considered to be the cause of various diseases, including cancer, and aging. It is hoped that by understanding the mechanism of chronic inflammation and measuring the indicators related to this chronic inflammation, it is possible to build a network that will enable medical intervention for prevention and treatment, leading to the maintenance of a healthy state. To achieve this goal, three targets are set: (1) to realize a society where prevention is a part of daily life, (2) to realize a medical network that allows access to necessary medical care anywhere in the world, and (3) to realize dramatic improvement in QOL without feeling the burden (realization of an inclusionary society that eliminates health disparities). Moonshot's goal 7 began calling for application in FY2020, and eight projects are currently being developed. Goal of the Moonshot 7 focuses on the "health and care system" which can include social and institutional elements. But most of the current research projects under Moonshot 7 still seem to focus first on the elucidation of medical mechanisms and the realization of technological research and development, such as the understanding of the mechanisms of intestinal bacteria and the elimination of inflammation-inducing cells. In order to actually realize the goal of living a healthy life until 100 years of age, various social changes are required that go beyond the mere elucidation of medical mechanisms and technological research and development. For example, changing peoples' behavior to achieve healthy status before they fall illness cannot simply be achieved by merely understanding the mechanisms of illness and their biological markers and indicators. In addition to the development of methods and devices to measure indicators, to overcome the institutional challenges to introduce them into society, it is necessary to make the public aware and accept such measurements (e.g., understanding that data is constantly collected and accepting the cost of introducing such machines into daily life). One of the projects, for example, aims to "bring the hospital into the home," which requires deployment of various technologies into their home, but it cannot be achieved without people understanding the meaning and necessity of the measurements to change their everyday behavior. Another issue to be considered is whether the cost of medical intervention before the stage of illness is covered by the public insurance and whether the coverage scheme for prevention at an earlier stage is acceptable to society as a whole. Furthermore, even if the physical health of the elderly is achieved, it will not be possible to improve their wellbeing if the society is not ready for such elderly people to play an active role. The Cabinet Office's Goal 7 website states, "Due to the decline in quality of life associated with aging and physical factors in life stages, elderly people may give up social participation. There is a growing need to build a social system that enables the elderly to participate in society" (Moonshot 7 website).

In achieving these elements, further adjustments beyond items stipulated under the current Goal 7 program will be required in terms of both policy and research and development. In terms of policy coordination, the Cabinet Office will need to collaborate more with related ministries (MEXT, MHLW, METI) based on the strategy led by the Cabinet's Health and Medical Care Strategy Headquarters, and also with local governments. In terms of collaboration relating to R&D projects, the role of AMED as a funding agency that handles all aspects of healthcare will be important and coordination between the Moonshot goal 7 program and other AMED R&D programs will be necessary.

4.3 Mission-Oriented STI Policies in Korea[5]

We now turn to the Korean experience. While Korea shares Japan's developmental-state legacy, it has pursued a distinct pathway through its Comprehensive Plan (CP) series, which explicitly targets social problems as the organizing principle for STI investment.

4.3.1 Development

4.3.1.1 Mission Orientation of the Comprehensive Plans

Using the OECD's twelve-element MOIP lens (Larrue, 2021), Ki et al. (2024b) revealed that Korea's three Comprehensive Plans (CP1 2013–2017, CP2 2018–2022, CP3 2023–2027) gradually deepened their mission orientation.[6] For example, CP1 clarified policy *direction* by selecting target social problems and secured *legitimacy* through a legal basis. CP2 strengthened *legitimacy* and *horizontality* by establishing a public-private council, while its new online "Social Problem-Solving Platform" (further upgraded in CP3) reinforced *directionality*. CP3, for the first time, designated the creation of a performance-evaluation system as one of ten strategic policy initiatives, laying the groundwork for stronger *evaluability*.

4.3.1.2 Changing Nature of Comprehensive Plans

CP1 (2013–2017): Centralized Problem Selection

CP1 identified 30 social problems across 10 domains, including health, environment, and public safety. From these, 10 key problems were selected—for example, cybercrime, food safety, and water pollution—and for each, a strategic policy action was formulated. Each action included problem definition, intervention rationale, policy response approach,

[5] This section adapts content from Ki et al. (2024b). The views expressed in Section 3 are solely those of its authors—Jeehoon Ki and Hyeonoh Kim—and do not necessarily reflect the official positions of their employer, the Korea Institute of S&T Evaluation and Planning (KISTEP), nor those of the Ministry of Science and ICT, the lead ministry for mission-oriented STI policy in Korea.

[6] The twelve elements include legitimacy, directionality, intentionality, flexibility, horizontality, verticality, intensity, novelty, policy mix, fundability, evaluability, and reflexivity.

solution goals, and science-and-technology-based implementation tasks with corresponding R&D projects.

The most significant features of CP1 were: (1) providing legal foundation for five-year CP cycles through statutory establishment, and (2) officially selecting social problems as targets for science and technology policy.

CP2 (2018–2022): Ecosystem Building

CP2 adopted three strategic focuses. First, inter-ministerial cooperation and policy alignment, including establishment of a public-private council for social problem-solving and coordination mechanisms across ministries. Second, creation of a social problem-solving ecosystem through initiatives such as the "Social Problem-Solving Platform" for information sharing and citizen participation, and the "Social Problem Science and Technology Policy Center" for systematic support. Third, integration of science and technology innovation with social innovation to address the complex, systemic nature of social problems.

Unlike CP1, CP2 did not prioritize specific social problems for government R&D investment, instead emphasizing ecosystem creation where stakeholders could autonomously identify and address social problems. The scope expanded from 30 to 40 social problems, with participation from eight local governments.

CP3 (2023–2027): Hybrid Approach

CP3 combines the focused prioritization of CP1 with the ecosystem-building approach of CP2. It selects five core social problems from an expanded list of 43 and establishes mission-oriented programs while continuing ecosystem development initiatives. For the first time, CP3 introduces quantitative targets and designates performance evaluation as a strategic policy initiative, strengthening the evaluability dimension of mission orientation. Text-mining analysis of the plans' implementation tasks independently confirms this trajectory, showing mission-oriented R&D investment emerging as a distinct new strategic direction in CP3 (ki et al. 2024a).

Participation expanded to 16 central ministries and 10 local governments, indicating broader consensus on the importance of STI for social problem-solving.

Table 4.4 Evolution of governance approaches across Korea's comprehensive plans (2013–2027)

Dimension	*CP1 (2013–2017)*	*CP2 (2018–2022)*	*CP3 (2023–2027)*
Governance logic	Centralized, state-led pilot	Ecosystem-building, participatory	Selective-focus hybrid
Problem selection	Government-led prioritization (10 key problems)	No government prioritization; stakeholder-driven	Hybrid: 5 core problems selected + ecosystem support
Implementation focus	Detailed roadmaps with high specificity	Ecosystem creation for autonomous problem-solving	Mission-oriented programs + ecosystem development
Participation scope	Limited stakeholder involvement	Broad participation (8 local governments)	Expanded (16 ministries, 10 local governments)
Performance orientation	Qualitative targets	Qualitative targets	Quantitative targets; evaluation as strategic initiative
Key trade-off	Specificity vs. participation	Participation vs. demonstrable short-term results	Balancing ecosystem logic with outcome accountability

4.3.2 Governance Evolution and Policy Design Logic

The evolution of Korea's social problem-solving STI policies exhibits three distinct governance approaches corresponding to each CP phase. Table 4.4 summarizes the key characteristics of each approach.

This evolutionary trajectory reveals an adaptive governance pattern responding to both policy learning and institutional pressures for performance demonstration. The shift toward quantitative performance management in CP3 reflects the challenge of securing continued policy support while maintaining the systemic, long-term nature of social problem-solving STI (Fig. 4.2).

Centralized, State-Led Pilot (CP1)

CP1 reflected a top-down approach where the government selected and prioritized social problems, concentrating policy resources on 10 key social problems with detailed implementation roadmaps. This approach ensured high implementation specificity but limited stakeholder participation.

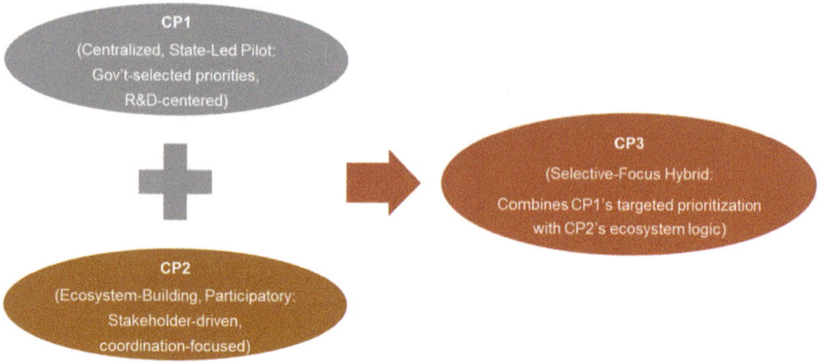

Fig. 4.2 Evolution of Korea's comprehensive plans: From pilot and ecosystem to hybrid model

Ecosystem-Building, Participatory (CP2)
CP2 shifted to a bottom-up approach, refraining from government-led prioritization and instead emphasizing creation of a social problem-solving ecosystem where diverse actors could autonomously define and address problems. This approach promoted broader participation but made it difficult to demonstrate short-term tangible results.

Selective-Focus Hybrid (CP3)
CP3 exhibits a hybrid approach, combining CP2's ecosystem-building logic with CP1's focused prioritization strategy. This reflects the need to balance ecosystem development with demonstrable policy outcomes within budget and evaluation cycles.

The evolution reveals an adaptive governance pattern responding to both policy learning and institutional pressures for performance demonstration. The shift toward quantitative performance management in CP3 reflects the challenge of securing continued policy support while maintaining the systemic, long-term nature of social problem-solving STI.

4.3.3 Operation of Korea's STI Policies

4.3.3.1 Incorporation of ELSI Perspectives
The introduction of Ethical, Legal, and Social Implications (ELSI) perspectives in Korean science and technology innovation policy began in the early

2000s, primarily through health sector research programs. In June 2001, the Ministry of Science and Technology (now the Ministry of Science and ICT) initiated an ELSI program as part of the "Human Genome Function Research Project" under the twenty-first Century Frontier Program (Yoon, 2001). This project aimed to develop early diagnostic technologies for intractable diseases and identify therapeutic target genes (MSIT and KISTEP, Ministry of Science and ICT and Korea Institute of S&T Evaluation and Planning, 2010, p. 16).

Subsequently, ELSI research expanded into various advanced scientific fields, including precision medicine, nanoscience, and neuroscience. Key ELSI research programs include studies on the human genome and humanities in 2002, cell applications in 2004, the establishment of ELSI centers for next-generation genomics in 2012, and multi-ministry post-genome genomics initiatives in 2015 (Lee & Yang, 2022).

At the systemic level, the Technology Impact Assessment (TIA) program, initiated in 2003, represents a significant ELSI-related initiative. This program evaluates the potential economic, social, ethical, cultural, and environmental impacts of emerging technologies (Lee et al., 2023, p. 35). The Ministry of Science and ICT annually selects specific technologies for future impact assessment, with KISTEP conducting these assessments.

While TIA and ELSI research differ in approach, both signify a systematic consideration of ELSI perspectives in Korea's STI policy. The design of the TIA program drew upon international ELSI research trends from the United States, United Kingdom, and Japan. However, TIA focuses primarily on predictive analysis, whereas ELSI research engages with the entire process of scientific and technological development (Lee & Yang, 2022).

ELSI perspectives are also partially reflected in the performance management system of national R&D projects. The "Act on the Performance Evaluation and Management of National Research and Development Projects" requires the establishment and regular updating of strategic plans for each national R&D project. These plans must address potential risks, mitigation strategies, and expected policy, scientific, technological, and socioeconomic impacts, indirectly incorporating ELSI considerations.

Recent years have seen an increasing demand for ELSI research. For instance, a 2022 TIA on synthetic biology recommended allocating 3% of research funding to gendered ELSI studies (Lee et al., 2023, p. 23). Additionally, the "Advanced Bio Initiative" of 2024 emphasized the importance of ELSI and regulatory science research in evaluating the social impact of new technologies (Joint Ministries, 2024, p. 26).

CP series, one of Korea's key MOIP initiatives, does not explicitly mention ELSI. However, CP3 incorporates several elements aligned with ELSI principles. These include citizen-based problem identification, multi-stakeholder participation, citizen-led problem-solving approaches, emphasis on social outcomes and impact measurement, and the promotion of networks for information sharing among problem-solving entities.

While CP3 lacks explicit consideration of ethical and legal aspects and may underemphasize potential technological side effects or ethical dilemmas, it provides a foundation for future integration of ELSI perspectives. The emphasis on citizen participation, multi-stakeholder collaboration, and social value suggests potential for expanded application of ELSI approaches.

In conclusion, although CP3 does not explicitly address ELSI, it reflects core ELSI principles in various aspects, particularly in its social dimensions. Future iterations of the plan could benefit from more explicit incorporation of ELSI considerations, especially in ethical and legal domains. Such integration could enhance the balanced approach to social problems, potentially improving the field applicability and acceptability of solutions, thereby increasing the likelihood of achieving the plan's ultimate goal of solving social problems.

4.3.3.2 Program Performance Management—Changes in Mission Orientation

National R&D programs in Korea generate five types of outcomes: scientific, technological, economic, social, and infrastructure (MSIT and KISTEP, 2020). While social problem-solving programs naturally produce all five outcome types, social outcomes best reflect their core mission orientation, as these programs fundamentally aim to solve social problems rather than advance knowledge or technology for their own sake.

To analyze changes in the mission orientation of the national R&D programs, we examined changes in the types of performance indicators (PIs) used in three program types—basic research, industrial technology development, and social problem-solving. In addition, we analyzed the types of outcomes highlighted as exemplary achievements in the social problem-solving program group, in order to assess which categories of performance (e.g., scientific, technological, economic, social, or infrastructural) were emphasized as representative. This analysis of performance management of national R&D programs covers the period 2018–2022 for which data is available.

The total number of R&D programs included in the analysis is categorized into three types: basic research, industrial technology development, and social problem-solving. The total number of PIs collected also follows this classification. On average, the number of PIs per program is highest in the social problem-solving category (7.8), followed by basic research (6.2) and industrial technology development (4.6).

Among the five types of PIs, PIs for social outcome[7] are the most frequently set by social problem-solving programs on average (Fig. 4.3).

An analysis of program performance indicators from 2018 to 2022 shows that while basic research and industrial technology development programs allocate only about 12% and 7% of their PIs, respectively, to social outcomes, social problem-solving programs allocate 22%—two to three times higher than the other groups. This shows that social problem-solving programs are using more PIs for social outcome that reveal their ultimate mission orientation.

However, when analyzing the year-to-year changes in this outcome over the five years combined, an interesting pattern emerged. The use of social PIs in social problem-solving programs increased in 2018 and 2019, but then decreased for three consecutive years starting in 2020 (Fig. 4.4).

During the five-year period analyzed (2018–2022), the policy area continued to support STI policies for solving social problems, and the budget for national R&D programs for solving social problems increased. In other words, while the importance of solving social problems using S&T was maintained or expanded in the policy and budget allocation areas, the proportion of programs that demonstrate social outcomes (or

[7] The main types of PIs for social outcome include the following examples: (1) Workforce training and job-related figures (e.g., number of graduates in the field at the university, number of jobs, etc.), (2) Social values such as safety, health, welfare, environment, etc. (e.g., customer satisfaction with safety technology, laboratory safety management implementation or awareness rate), (3) Track record of popularizing and promoting science (e.g., scale of events for the public or the students, number of media outreach such as newspaper and broadcast), (4) International exchange track record (e.g., level of people exchange through international exchange, performance in attracting overseas research centers), (5) Policy effectiveness (e.g., free technology transfer and dissemination, effectiveness of energy reduction, effectiveness of damage prevention), (6) Level of public services (e.g., number of people served or service satisfaction, on-site activities such as on-site technical guidance or consulting) (MSIT and KISTEP, 2020).

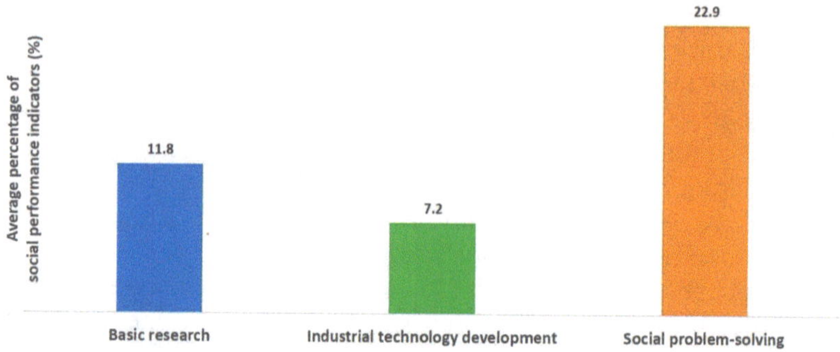

Fig. 4.3 Average percentage of programs with at least one social performance indicator (2018–2022), by R&D program group. *Source* Translated from Figure 5–1 in Ki, et al. (2024b)

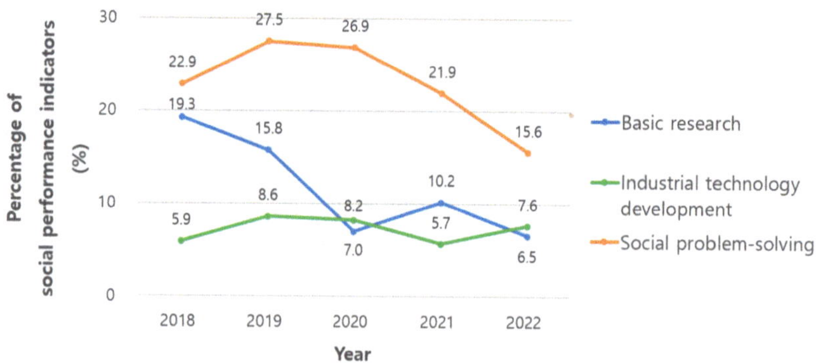

Fig. 4.4 Yearly Changes in the Percentage of Programs with at Least One Social Performance Indicator (2018–2022), by R&D Program Group. *Source* Translated from Figure 5–2 in Ki et al. (2024b)

more precisely, the proportion that set social PIs) began to decline, and this trend has continued in the latter three years of the analysis period (2020–2022).

So, what types of performance indicators have social problem-solving programs increased their use of at the expense of social PIs? The proportion of technical PIs tended to move in the opposite direction to the trend of social PIs (Fig. 4.5).

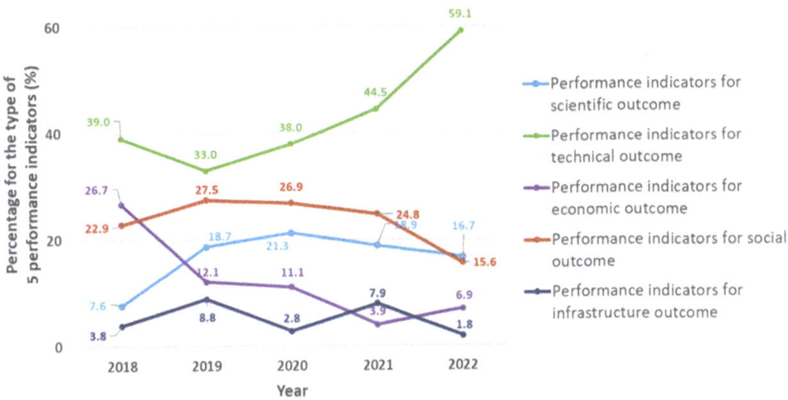

Fig. 4.5 Changes in the Proportion of Five Performance Indicator Types (2018–2022) in the Social Problem-Solving R&D Program Group. *Source* Translated and Adapted from Figure 5–3 in Ki et al. (2024b)

Specifically, the proportion of technical PIs decreased in social problem-solving programs from 2018 to 2019, but increased for three consecutive years starting in 2020. This suggests that social problem-solving organizations have increased their use of technical PIs at the expense of decreasing their use of social PIs.

Building on the previous analysis of the types of PIs initially set by each program, we next examine the characteristics of actual outcomes highlighted as representative achievements in program evaluations. This analysis focuses on 36 social problem-solving programs whose self-evaluation reports were available between 2018 and 2022 (Fig. 4.6).

First, the cross-sectional analysis shows that the type with the highest average percentage above 90% (92.5%) over the five-year period (2018–2022) was technical performance. The 90% means that 90% of the 36 programs included technical achievements in their representation. This likely reflects the fact that technical achievements are in line with the nature of technology development and that there is an easily quantifiable technical achievement, for example patents. The next largest performance type is social performance (75.7%). This means that 75.7% of the 36 programs included social outcomes in their representative performance. This is followed by scientific, economic, and infrastructure outcomes, with five-year (2018–2022) average percentages of 67.6%, 49.0%, and 4.9%, respectively.

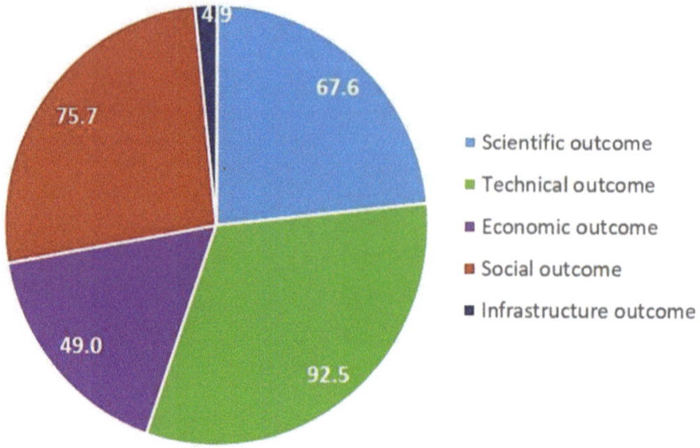

Fig. 4.6 Average Share of Programs Including Each Outcome Type in Representative Performance (2018–2022), Social Problem-Solving R&D Group (Unit: Percentage (%)). *Source* Translated from Figure 5–4 in Ki, et al. (2024b) *Note* A program is counted as including an outcome type if at least one of its representative achievements corresponds to that type. For example, the 75.7% for social outcomes means that 75.7% of programs included at least one social achievement in their representative performance over the 2018–2022 period. Totals exceed 100% because multiple outcome types can be reported per program

An analysis of the time-series trend in representative performance outcomes—those submitted by programs as key results during midterm evaluations—reveals a substantial decline in the proportion of social outcomes presented by social problem-solving programs between 2018 and 2022 (Fig. 4.7).

This proportion peaked in 2018, showed rebounds in 2020 and 2022, but the overall trend remained downward throughout the five-year period.

Interestingly, this trajectory mirrors the trend in the proportion of social PIs initially set in each program's Strategic Plan, which has consistently declined since 2020. In other words, despite continued policy emphasis on using science and technology to address social problems—and increased budget allocations for social problem-solving R&D—the actual performance outcomes emphasized by programs in both planning and evaluation have become less socially oriented.

This suggests a growing gap between policy rhetoric and program-level implementation, in which technical performance increasingly dominates

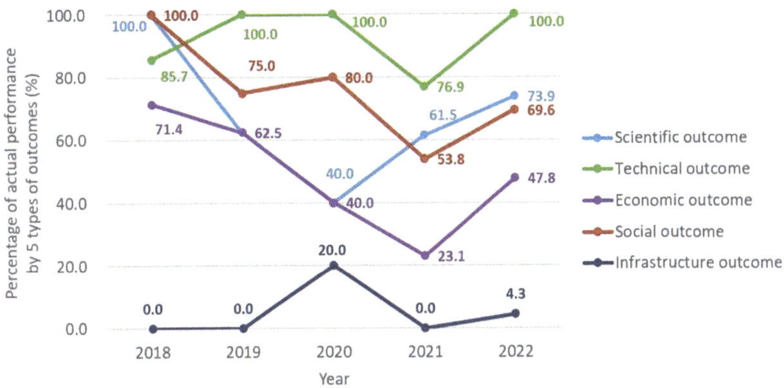

Fig. 4.7 Yearly Share of Programs Including Each Outcome Type in Their Representative Performance (2018–2022), Social Problem-Solving R&D Group. *Source* Translated from Figure 5–5 in Ki et al. (2024b) *Note* A program is counted as including a given outcome type if at least one of its representative achievements submitted at midterm evaluation falls under that type. Since each program can present multiple representative achievements, the total across outcome types may exceed 100%. For example, in 2020, 80% for social outcomes means that 80% of social problem-solving programs included at least one social outcome among their representative performance results

the narrative of success, potentially at the expense of the programs' original social missions.

In conclusion, among the three types of R&D program groups, social problem-solving R&D program group was the most likely to set PIs for social outcome. However, over time, the PIs that best reflect the mission orientation of social problem-solving, i.e., the tendency to include social performance in performance plans and the tendency to present social performance as actual performance, tended to decrease. This void has been largely filled by technical performance.

A key difference between social and technical outcomes lies in their demonstrability within a relatively short timeframe. Technical outcomes, such as patents, can often be explicitly demonstrated relatively quickly. In contrast, social outcomes are much harder to present within a short period and are often difficult to objectify and quantify—for example, participants' satisfaction in a demonstration project. However, it is often necessary to present program results or performance in order to secure budgets or launch follow-up programs, etc. In this case, technical achievements can be more useful for presentation and persuasion than social achievements. The analysis shows that, despite growing demand for PIs related to social outcomes, identifying and operationalizing appropriate indicators remains a significant challenge. In response, Korea has recently initiated efforts to develop a measurement framework for the social value of problem-solving R&D. A recent study (Ki et al., 2025) proposed an initial framework and conducted pilot applications across selected programs, complemented by stakeholder consultations to explore institutionalization strategies.

4.3.4 Korea's STI Policies in the Health Area

This section examines how CP3 formulated two missions on ageing. This case study shows how policy-makers progressed systematically from problem diagnosis, to mission setting, to cross-ministerial Research-and-Solution-Development (R&SD) road-mapping, and finally to the design of a multi-ministry mission program.

First, CP3 re-classified 40 social problems from CP2 into 43, merging "older-adult marginalization" and "suicide" into the broader social problem of "ageing" and adding several emerging issues identified through public/expert surveys, big-data analytics, and foresight exercises.

CP3 then prioritized five core social problems—aging, cybercrime, fine dust, microplastics, and household waste—and prescribed phased roll-outs of mission-oriented programs for each. For ageing, CP3 issued two mission statements—each accompanied by a cross-sectoral R&SD roadmap with quantitative targets and integrated technology–policy mixes:

- Mission 1—Enhancing safety for older adults
- Mission 2—Closing the digital divide for older adults

The STI Office in the Ministry of Science and ICT (MSIT) led the preparation of both roadmaps. It (i) analyzed the causes and impacts of ageing across health, social, and economic dimensions; (ii) built an issue tree (logic tree) to visualize twelve sub-issues—from mental-health deterioration to rising social-burden costs; (iii) benchmarked global megatrends and domestic/international R&D; and (iv) distilled older-adult needs into key issues, solution directions, and priority R&D areas. Vision, goals, and implementation strategies were derived for each mission.

Mission 1—Enhancing safety for older adults

Its R&SD roadmap proposes, as strategic technologies, accident-prediction systems, age-friendly road-improvement technologies, public-transport upgrades, and smart mobility tailored to older adults. It also calls for wearable walking-assist robots and fall-prevention devices. Key performance indicators (KPIs) include pedestrian accident rates, walking-safety indices, and fall incidences. Complementary non-R&D interventions include:

- Revised road-design standards reflecting older adults' physical and cognitive traits
- Workforce training for the age-friendly industry
- Public-opinion channels to feed user insights into policy
- Age-friendly transport-infrastructure retrofits
- Awareness campaigns that foster empathy toward older adults

The visualized roadmap for this mission is presented in Fig. 4.8.

Mission 2—Closing the digital divide for older adults

Strategic technologies encompass customized ICT assistive devices, older-adult-friendly kiosks, cognitive- and sensory-augmentation systems, and digital-literacy content tailored to older adults. Supporting policy instruments include:

- Guidelines for digital use by older adults
- Regulatory reforms to prevent harm from digital exclusion
- Training of digital-education instructors

Figure 4.9 illustrates the roadmap developed for this mission.

In CP3's first implementation year (2023), the STI Office provided funding and facilitated coordination for an R&D program planning study targeting Mission 2, encouraging the Ministry of Health and Welfare (lead) and MSIT (participant) to take joint leadership. While the two ministries led the study, the STI Office established and operated a planning committee to offer strategic feedback and support inter-ministerial dialogue.

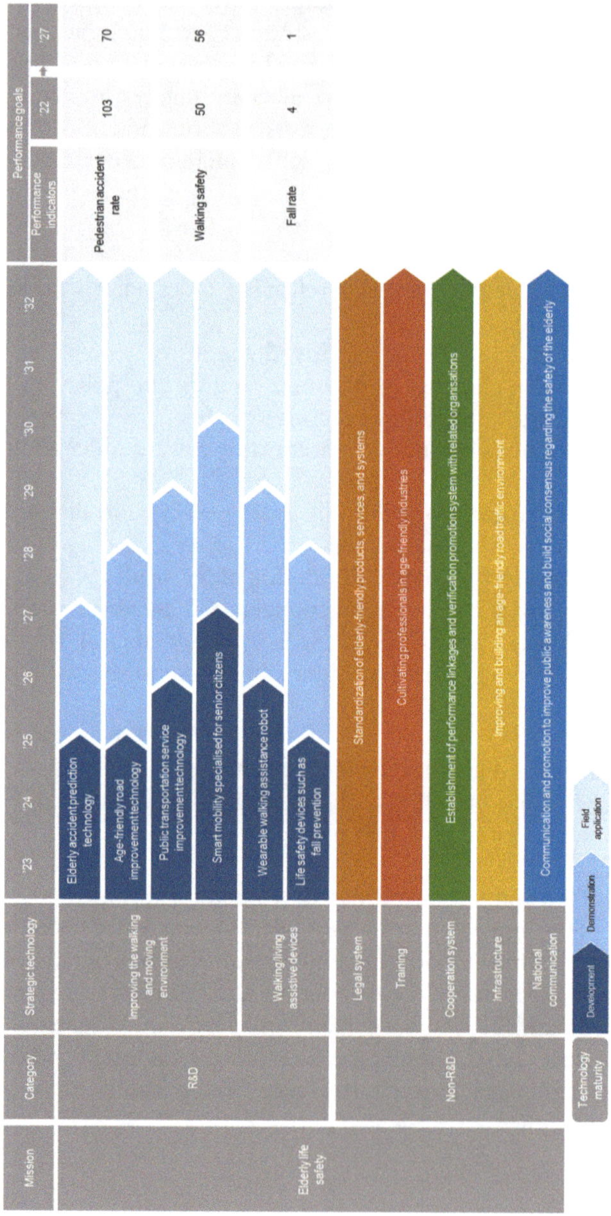

Fig. 4.8 Mission 1 Roadmap: Enhancing Safety for Older Adults. *Source* OECD (2025, p. 25)

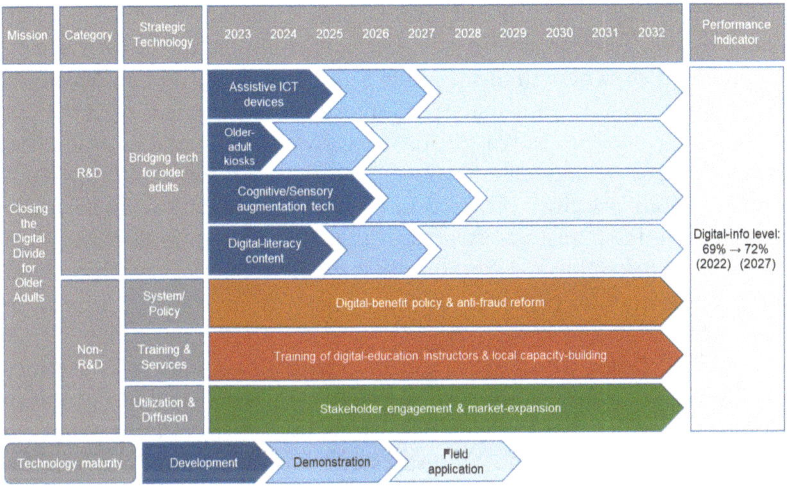

Fig. 4.9 Mission 2 Roadmap: Closing the Digital Divide for Older Adults. *Source* Translated and adapted from the figure on p. 55 in Joint Ministries (2023)

CP3's ageing initiative thus demonstrates three policy strengths:

1. Demand-side intelligence drawn from user needs and big-data analysis
2. Tight inter-ministerial coordination through dedicated multi-ministry planning bodies
3. Balanced tool mixes that blend R&D with institutional, human-resource, and cultural measures

The prioritization of aging as a core mission area in CP3 may be situated within the broader structural challenges facing health systems in advanced economies. As Boyer and Boylau (2026) argues, the aging of OECD populations poses fundamental challenges to the "anthropogenetic development" model, in which health and education expenditures serve as central drivers of growth. Gorry and Montalban (2026) further suggest that the healthcare sector faces an endogenous productivity crisis—characterized by declining marginal returns on pharmaceutical innovation and the limited effectiveness of neoliberal cost-containment strategies. Korea's turn toward mission-oriented approaches in the health domain, as documented in this section, can thus be understood as an institutional response to these structural pressures, seeking to mobilize STI policy where market-based frameworks alone have proven insufficient.

The emphasis on cross-ministerial coordination in CP3's health missions also resonates with the challenges of pandemic governance documented elsewhere in this volume. Storz et al. (2026) examine vaccine development as a sectoral system of innovation under crisis, with the case of SK BioScience in Korea illustrating how government coordination, advance purchase agreements, and technology transfer arrangements enabled rapid vaccine production. These coordination mechanisms parallel the inter-ministerial structures that Korea's Comprehensive Plans have sought to establish, suggesting that the institutional capacities developed through social problem-solving STI policy may also contribute to crisis preparedness.

Looking ahead, Korea's STI policy has identified aging as a critical social problem and is responding through a mission-oriented innovation approach. CP3 establishes ageing missions that require cooperation and coordination across relevant ministries and has planned a multi-ministry mission program accordingly. Effective monitoring and evaluation will be essential to ensure that the coordinated policy mix is implemented as intended and that progress toward mission goals is sustained over time.

4.4 Conclusion—Comparison Between Japan and Korea

In this concluding section, the experiences of MOIP in Japan and Korea are compared. There are several common aspects between the experiences of MOIP in Japan and Korea.

The first common aspect is that the concept of transformative innovation policy and its specific form, MOIP, has been explicitly discussed and implemented in Japan and Korea. The 2nd Science and Technology Basic Plan implemented from 2001 in Japan stressed building new relations between science, technology and society and emphasized the return of the fruits of science and technology to society through industry as means. As a specific research and development program in response to such policy concerns, the "System for Research in Science and Technology for Society" was established in 2001. The change of science and technology policy was advanced from around 2009, when the administration changed from one centered on the Liberal Democratic Party to one centered on the Democratic Party and the social issues of health and the environment became emphasized in the 4th Science and Technology Basic Plan which was set in 2011. Even after the change of administration again to one centered on the Liberal Democratic Party in 2012, the basic trend continued. The 5th Science and Technology Basic Plan formulated in 2016 presented Society 5.0 and a super smart society as a social vision to aim for and positioned technology as a tool to achieve the vision of society. In Korea, since the First Basic Plan for Science and Technology, released in 2003, the Basic Plan for Science and Technology, that is formulated every five years, has continued to include policies for the social role of science and technology. Those developments roughly correspond to the development of STI policy in the EU—Aho report and European Research Area. And as backgrounds for the adoption of MOIP in Japan and Korea, there were the experiences of industrial policy of the Developmental State in the second half of the twentieth century.

The second common aspect is that concrete programs of MOIP were designed and implemented in Japan and Korea since around 2013. In Japan, the first phase of the Cross-ministerial Strategic Innovation Promotion Program (SIP) was established in 2014 at the Cabinet level, followed by the second phase in 2018 and the third phase in 2023. From the beginning, the SIPs have been aimed at promoting top-down research and development efforts from basic research through to implementation in society in an integrated manner for the purpose of responding to social issues and important issues for Japan's economy and industrial competitiveness. In Korea, the government established the "First Comprehensive Plan for Solving Social Problems Based on Science and Technology," a comprehensive plan in 2013 to utilize science and technology to solve social problems such as chronic diseases and cybercrime. Those developments also roughly correspond to the development of STI policy in the EU—Horizon 2020 and Horizon Europe.

The third common aspect is that there were discussions and experiments of evaluation of social impacts of programs as the social impacts were the focus in the MOIP. In Japan, factors identified for why evaluation of social performance are difficult include (1) quantification is difficult because evaluation concerning many social impacts contain many qualitative factors, (2) evaluation of cause-effect relationships between policies and results are difficult because many factors complexly contribute to the results, and (3) it is difficult to set the scope. There are some interesting attempts to measure the potential impact of the MOIP. As an indicator of the potential social impact of R&D, the extended concept of the Technology Readiness Level (TRL) has been used to examine many technology development research projects. As noted earlier, the third-phase SIP also adopted four "X-readiness" measures—BRL, GRL, S(C)

RL, and HRL—alongside TRL. In Korea, CP3 marks a significant shift by emphasizing performance management through the introduction of quantitative targets—departing from the qualitative targets that characterized CP1 and CP2. The use of social performance indicators for social problem-solving national R&D programs increased in 2018 and 2019, but then decreased for three consecutive years starting in 2020. While the importance of solving social problems using S&T was expanded in the policy, the proportion of projects that demonstrate social outcomes began to decline. On the other hand, the proportion of technical metrics tended to move in the opposite direction. The analysis also showed that, despite growing demand for performance indicators (PIs) related to social outcomes, appropriate criteria for such evaluation remain difficult to define and operationalize—an issue also observed in Japan, as noted above. In Korea, this challenge has begun to receive institutional attention. Recent efforts have been made to develop a framework for assessing the social impact of problem-solving R&D, including pilot applications and stakeholder engagement (Ki et al., 2025), signaling a shift toward more systematic approaches to performance evaluation.

The fourth common aspect is that health became one of the priority areas of the MOIP in Japan and Korea. Corresponding to this change in the nature of the programs of SIPs in Japan, programs in the field of medicine and health care, where institutional and people's behavioral factors are of greater importance, are now implemented. For example, in the second phase of the SIPs, the 'Advanced Diagnostic and Treatment Systems with AI Hospitals' program was set up. In the third phase of the SIPs, the "Establishment of an Integrated Healthcare System" and "Establishment of an Inclusive Community Platform" programs were also implemented. In addition, Goal of the Moonshot 7 focuses on the "health and care system" which can include social and institutional elements. But most of the current research projects under Moonshot 7 still seem to focus first on the elucidation of medical mechanisms and the realization of technological research and development. In order to actually realize the goal of living a healthy life until 100 years of age, various social changes are required that go beyond the mere elucidation of medical mechanisms and technological research and development. In Korea, CP3 adjusted and reorganized the target social problem areas into 43 problem areas in 10 domains. Among the adjusted and reorganized problem areas, older-adult marginalization and suicide of CP2 were newly reorganized into the area of aging from an integrated perspective. Through this process, roadmaps for two missions in response to aging are proposed: enhancing safety for older adults and closing the digital divide for older adults. Based on this roadmap, in 2023, the STI Office supported the planning study of a mission-oriented flagship program. Flagship program planning committee for aging response was organized and operated to coordinate differences and consultations among related ministries and strengthen mission orientation.

There are also several differences between the experiences of MOIP in Japan and Korea.

The first difference is about the program structure. There have been diverse forms of MOIP in Japan. The Cross-ministerial Strategic Innovation Promotion Program (SIP) was established in 2014 at the Cabinet level, which is different from the pattern of Korea and the EU. Subsequently, the Moonshot Research and Development Program was proposed at the Council for Science, Technology, and Innovation in 2018 and established also at the Cabinet level in 2020. Aside from the programs set at the Cabinet level, the programs set at each ministry level include programs with an MOIP nature such as the Green Technologies of Excellence (GteX) presently being advanced by the Japan Science and Technology Agency (JST) of the Ministry of Education, Culture, Sports, Science and Technology (MEXT). In Korea, the government established CP1 in 2013. CP1 sought to utilize science and technology to solve social problems such as chronic diseases and cybercrime. The Comprehensive Plan series was separated from the Science and Technology Basic Plan but integrated as a plan for social issues.

The second difference is about the historical development since around 2013 in concrete programs. In Japan, the focus of the first phase of the SIPs since 2014 was on research and development of technology, although they had in mind social issues in a broader sense, such as strengthening competitiveness, addressing environmental issues such as CO2 reduction, and ensuring safety and security. But in the third phase of the SIP since 2023, systems, platforms and networks, including institutional, policy and behavioral elements as well as technical elements, have been the main targets. This change in the nature of the programs was also associated with a change in the origin of the program directors (PDs). In the first phase of SIPs, the ratio of PDs from industry to PDs from academia was 5:6, while in the second phase of SIPs the ratio of PDs from industry to academia was 6:6. The ratio was almost equal in between the two SIPs. In the third phase of SIPs, on the other hand, the ratio of people from industry to people from academia was 4:10, with a much higher ratio of people from academia. This seems to be due to the fact that in the third phase of SIPs, the aspect of responding to social challenges by combining technical and institutional policy and behavioral elements has become stronger, requiring more coordination with wider stakeholders. In Korea, the feature of CP1 was that it defined social problems. Then 10 social problems were prioritized out of the 30 selected social problems. For each of these 10 social problems, specific policy actions based on cross-sectoral cooperation were proposed. CP2 focused on three strategic priorities: establishing inter-ministerial cooperation, creating a public-private council for social problem-solving, and strengthening coordination between social problem-solving-related policies across ministries. The purpose of CP2 was the creation of a social problem-solving ecosystem including local governments and wider ministries. CP2 did not prioritize social problems for government R&D. CP3 is a hybrid of CP1 and CP2. This is because it contains both the upgrading of the social problem-solving ecosystem proposed in CP2 and the strategy of focusing capabilities on specific social problems proposed in CP1.

The third difference is about the structure of governance. In Japan, governance structure at the cabinet level is important in addition to the ministries level. In Japan, the Council for Science, Technology Policy (CSTP) was established in the Cabinet Office in 2001 after administrative reform, and its successor organization, the Council for Science, Technology and Innovation Policy (CSTI) was established in 2014. SIP and the Moonshot Research and Development Program were established as research and development programs under the direct management at the Cabinet level. Because the coordination capacities of the CSTI as a control center were insufficient, there was a desire to supplement the centralization power of CSTI using direct program operation at the Cabinet level. In Korea, the focus will be on the role of MSIT (Ministry of Science and ICT) and KISTEP (Korea Institute for S&T Evaluation and Planning) which performs important analytical functions under MSIT. The trajectory from CP1 to CP3 illustrates a clear transformation in policy design logic—moving from centralized, state-led problem selection, to ecosystem formation, and eventually arriving at a hybrid model that integrates both strategic orientations.

The fourth difference is about the use and the development of the ELSI and SSH (social science and humanities) in STI policy. In Japan, the need to address ELSI has been explicitly discussed in policy documents from the Third Science and Technology Basic Plan in 2006 to the current Sixth Science and Technology Innovation Plan in 2021. As a result, the JST

CRDS has worked and published many reports on ELSI, and JST RISTEX has conducted various research programs related to ELSI. On the other hand, ELSI has yet to permeate in every research program and projects. Under such circumstances, it is noteworthy that the Moonshot R&D system recognizes the need to consider ELSI in research promotion and has established an ELSI subcommittee to support activities across moonshot programs. This sort of direction toward emphasizing the response to social issues has brought about revisions in the legal framework. In 2020 the Basic Act on Science and Technology was amended as the Basic Act on Science, Technology and Innovation. In order to realize science and technology innovation, the humanities and social sciences were included as subjects of the Basic Act (Article 1). In addition to the incorporation of ELSI perspectives into MOIP program, wider concept of "convergence of knowledge" was introduced to incorporate elements of social science and humanities into STI policies, following the amendment of Science and Technology Basic Law in 2020, the 6th Science, Technology and Innovation Basic Plan implemented from 2021 mentioned the importance of the "convergence of knowledge" from the fusion of "knowledge" in the humanities and social sciences that creates social value and "knowledge" in the natural sciences. Specifically, the Basic Plan presumes four potential roles for the humanities and social sciences, including a provider of inputs around issues concerning ELSI; a function to encourage changes in the behavior of citizens; a foundation for systems reform for social implementation, a presenter of various pathways and showing multiple values. In Korea, the introduction of Ethical, Legal, and Social Implications (ELSI) perspectives began in the early 2000s, primarily through health sector research programs. In June 2001, the Ministry of Science and Technology (now the Ministry of Science and ICT) initiated an ELSI program as part of the "Human Genome Function Research Project" under the twenty-first Century Frontier Program. Subsequently, ELSI research expanded into various advanced scientific fields, including precision medicine, nanoscience, and neuroscience. At the systemic level, the Technology Impact Assessment (TIA) program, initiated in 2003, represents a significant ELSI-related initiative. This program evaluates the potential economic, social, ethical, cultural, and environmental impacts of emerging technologies. The Ministry of Science and ICT (MSIT) annually selects specific technologies for future impact assessment, with the Korea Institute of S&T Evaluation and Planning (KISTEP) conducting these assessments. Recent years have seen an increasing demand for ELSI research. For instance, a 2022 TIA on synthetic biology recommended allocating 3% of research funding to ELSI studies. CP series does not explicitly mention ELSI. However, CP3 incorporates several elements aligned with ELSI principles.

For countries planning their first MOIP, the Japanese and Korean trajectories show the various possible options for their MOIP either in fragmented structure under the executive office or comprehensive structure under the relevant ministry. The trajectories also show that starting with a tightly scoped pilot, then deliberately expanding toward participatory ecosystem-building, and finally combining both with strong evaluation rules can shorten the learning curve. Established coordination assets inherited from developmental-state traditions are helpful, but only if new mechanisms for cross-sectoral learning and social-impact measurement are added.

References

Borrás, S., & Edler, J. (2020). The roles of the state in the governance of socio-technical systems' transformation. *Research Policy, 49–5.*

Borrás, S., & Schwaag Serger, S. (2022). The design of transformative research and innovation policy instruments for grand challenges: The policy-nesting perspective. *Science and Public Policy, 49*(5), 659–672.

Boyer, R., & Boylau, O. (2026). Anthropogenetic development: Long unnoticed and already in crisis. In S. Lechevalier, J.-P. Gaudillière, K. Ibata-Arens, & K. Takuma (Eds.), *Capitalism, innovations, and health after Covid-19: An Asian perspective.* Palgrave MacMillan.

Cabinet Office (2021). *6th science, technology and innovation basic plan.* Cabinet Office (In Japanese) https://www8.cao.go.jp/cstp/kihonkeikaku/index6.html

Cabinet Office (2022). *Regarding the strengthening of the system of social implementation in the next phase SIP.* Cabinet Office (In Japanese) https://www8.cao.go.jp/cstp/gaiyo/sip/220929/siryo1-1.pdf

EC (European Commission). (2006). *Creating an innovative Europe: Report of the independent expert group on R&D and innovation.* European Commission.

EC (European Commission). (2007). *Challenging Europe's research: Rationales for the European research area (ERA).* European Commission.

EC (European Commission). (2011). *Communication from the commission to the European parliament, the council, the European economic and social committee and the committee of the regions horizon 2020—the framework programme for research and innovation (COM/2011/0808 final).* European Commission.

EC (European Commission). (2017a). *Interim evaluation of horizon 2020.* European Commission.

EC (European Commission). (2017b). *LAB—FAB—APP—Investing in the European future we want.* European Commission.

EC (European Commission). (2018). *Proposal for a regulation of the European parliament and of the council establishing horizon Europe (COM(2018) 435 final).* European Commission.

EC (European Commission). (2022). *Horizon Europe.* https://research-and-innovation.ec.europa.eu/system/files/2022-06/ec_rtd_he-investing-to-shape-our-future_0.pdf

Gorry, P., & Montalban, M. (2026). The crisis of capitalism and health innovation: Symptoms of a crisis or of success?". In S. Lechevalier, J.-P. Gaudillière, K. Ibata-Arens, & K. Takuma (Eds.), *Capitalism, innovations, and health after Covid-19: An Asian perspective.* Palgrave MacMillan.

Haddad, C. R., Nakić, V., Bergek, A., & Hellsmark, H. (2022). Transformative innovation policy: A systematic review. *Environmental Innovation and Societal Transitions, 43*, 14–40.

Ito, M. (2006). Council for science and technology policy as a 'specific general coordination organ'—Regarding 'coordination by Budget' and 'Coordination by Plan', *Public Policy Studies*, Vol. *6* (In Japanese).

Joint Ministries. (2023). *3rd comprehensive plan for solving social problems based on science and technology (2023–2027)* (In Korean). https://www.pacst.go.kr/jsp/council/councilArchiveView.jsp?archive_id=1070&cpage=3

Joint Ministries. (2024). *Advanced bio initiative (draft)—toward becoming a global bio powerhouse by 2035* (In Korean). https://www.pacst.go.kr/jsp/council/councilArchiveView.jsp?archive_id=1147&archive_nm_text=%EB%B0%94%EC%9D%B4%EC%98%A4

Ki, J., Kim, H., & Cho, S. (2024a). Evolving strategies in science and technology policy for social problem-solving: Insights from text mining of comprehensive plans. *Journal of Korea Technology Innovation Society*, 27–6. (In Korean).

Ki, J., Kim, H., & Kim, H. (2024b). *Changes in the mission orientation of social problem-solving science and technology policy and of national R&D programs in Korea* (Research Report No. 2023-057). Korea Institute of S&T Evaluation and Planning (KISTEP). (In Korean) https://www.kistep.re.kr/reportDetail.es?mid=a10305030000&rpt_tp=831-002&rpt_no=RES0220240083

Ki, J., Kim, J., Kim, H., & Lee, S. (2025). *Developing and institutionalizing a framework for evaluating the social value of problem-solving R&D: Focusing on pilot application cases* (Research Report No. 2024–047). Korea Institute of S&T Evaluation and Planning (KISTEP). (In Korean) https://www.kistep.re.kr/reportDetail.es?mid=a10305030000&rpt_tp=831-002&rpt_no=RES0220250075

Kodate, N., Cheung, M. C., Yumoto, A., Donnelly, S., Maeda, Y., Tsujimura, M., Mannan, H., Yu, W., Suwa, S., Obayashi, K., Masuyama, S., Chan, W. C. H., Hauray, B., & O'Shea, D. (2026). Care systems in crisis and innovative welfare technologies: Stakeholders' views regarding care robots in Hong Kong SAR (China), Ireland and Japan. In S. Lechevalier, J.-P. Gaudillière, K. Ibata-Arens, & K. Takuma (Eds.), *Capitalism, innovations, and health after Covid-19: An Asian perspective*. Palgrave MacMillan.

Larrue, P. (2021). The design and implementation of mission-oriented innovation policies: A new systemic policy approach to address societal challenges. In *OECD science, technology and industry policy papers, No. 100*. OECD Publishing. https://doi.org/10.1787/3f6c76a4-en

Lechevalier, S. (2026). Care-led innovation: A new paradigm and an application in the Japanese context of society 5.0. In S. Lechevalier, J.-P. Gaudillière, K. Ibata-Arens, & K. Takuma (Eds.), *Capitalism, innovations, and health after Covid-19: An Asian perspective*. Palgrave MacMillan.

Lee, D., Park, C., Choi, M., & Ji, S. (2023). *2022 technology impact assessment report—Synthetic biology* (Institutional Report No. 2022–038). Korea Institute of S&T Evaluation and Planning (KISTEP). (In Korean) https://www.kistep.re.kr/reportDetail.es?mid=a10305020000&rpt_tp=831-006&rpt_no=RES0220230033

Lee, I., & Yang, J. H. (2022). Ethical, legal, and social implications research in South Korea. *Korean Journal of Medical Ethics, 25-2.* (In Korean).

Matsuo, M. (2024). *Transformative mission-oriented science and technology innovation (STI) policy process design and implications for existing STI Policy*. Policy Studies, Tokyo Foundation for Policy Research (In Japanese).

Ministry of Science and ICT and Korea Institute of S&T Evaluation and Planning (2010). *Interim report—twenty-first Century frontier research and development program* (In Korean).

Ministry of Science and ICT and Korea Institute of S&T Evaluation and Planning. (2020). Standard performance indicators for national R&D programs (5th). *Ministry of Science and ICT*. (In Korean).

OECD. (2025). Challenges and opportunities of mission-oriented innovation policy in Korea. In *OECD science, technology and industry policy papers, No. 172*. OECD Publishing. https://doi.org/10.1787/d725304c-en

Reed, M. S., Ferré, M., Martin-Ortega, J., Blanche, R., Lawford-Rolfe, R., Dallimer, M., & Holden, J. (2021). Evaluating impact from research: A methodological framework. *Research Policy, 50*(4), 104147.

Shiroyama, H. (2018). *Science and Technology and Politics*, Minerva Shobō (In Japanese).

Shiroyama, H. (2024). *Transformative science and technology innovation policy—system design and operation of mission-oriented innovation policy*. Policy Studies, Tokyo Foundation for Policy Research (In Japanese).

Shiroyama, H., & Matsuo, M. (2024). Technology assessment and technology assessment like activities in Japan. In A. Grunwald (Ed.), *International Handbook of Technology Assessment*. Edward Elgar.

Storz, C., Lee, K., Kuo, W.-H., & Velte, F. D. (2026). Innovation systems under crisis: Vaccine development in Asia and Europe". In S. Lechevalier, J.-P. Gaudillière, K. Ibata-Arens, & K. Takuma (Eds.), *Capitalism, innovations, and health after Covid-19: An Asian perspective*. Palgrave MacMillan.

Yoon, J. R. (2001). Human genome research and ELSI program. *Journal of Science & Technology Studies, 1–2*.

PART II

A Critical Moment and Its Openings: Covid Responses

CHAPTER 5

Innovation Systems Under Crisis: Vaccine Development in Asia and Europe

Cornelia Storz, Keun Lee, Wen-Hua Kuo, and Franziska Dorothea Velte

Abstract The COVID-19 pandemic triggered unprecedented efforts in vaccine development, manufacturing, and distribution, revealing both the strengths and weaknesses of contemporary health-related innovation systems in many countries around the world. This chapter examines the conditions under which vaccines could be developed rapidly and made available in a timely manner, drawing comparative lessons from Europe and East Asia. Conceptualizing vaccines as part of a highly complex sectoral system of innovation, we define success as the speedy development and manufacturing of safe and effective vaccines and their timely availability to populations. Building on an analysis of vaccine technologies and the vaccine value chain,

C. Storz (✉) · F. D. Velte
Goethe University, Frankfurt, Germany
e-mail: storz@wiwi.uni-frankfurt.de

K. Lee
Chung-Ang University and Seoul National University, Seoul, South Korea

W.-H. Kuo
National Yang Ming Chiao Tung University, Hsinchu, Taiwan

S. Lechevalier et al. (eds.), *Capitalism, Innovations, and Health after Covid-19*,
https://doi.org/10.1007/978-3-032-24479-6_5

the chapter identifies key trade-offs between safety and efficacy, time-to-market, and global availability. We conduct comparative case studies of four prominent vaccine development efforts: BioNTech–Pfizer (Germany–USA), Oxford–AstraZeneca (UK), SK BioScience (South Korea), and Medigen Vaccine Biologics Corporation (Taiwan). These cases allow us to examine how firms, governments, international organizations, universities, and philanthropic actors interacted to overcome coordination, market, and regulatory failures under crisis conditions. Empirically, the chapter highlights the partially successful role of (international) innovation ecosystems, access to substantial public and private funding—including advance purchase agreements—and new regulatory arrangements such as rolling reviews and emergency use authorizations. These mechanisms enabled firms to compress development timelines, scale up manufacturing at risk, and navigate regulatory uncertainty. At the same time, the analysis reveals important limitations of these "success cases," notably the constrained global availability of high-end vaccines and the exclusion of low- and middle-income countries, raising questions about vaccines as global public goods. The chapter contributes to the sectoral system of innovation literature by extending the notion of success beyond technological performance to include distribution and availability. It argues that in health-related sectors, innovation outcomes must be assessed not only from firm-level or national perspectives, but also in terms of global welfare. The findings offer lessons for future industrial and innovation policy aimed at building resilient, equitable vaccine ecosystems beyond the COVID-19 crisis.

5.1 Introduction

This chapter fills an empirical and conceptual gap in the social science literature on COVID-19 vaccines by analyzing vaccine development as a *sectoral system of innovation under crisis*, rather than focusing narrowly on scientific speed, firm-level innovation, or procurement and intellectual property in isolation (Malerba, 2002, 2005; Sampat & Shadlen, 2021). Its unique contribution lies in extending the notion of innovation "success" beyond technological performance to include manufacturing scale-up, regulatory acceleration, and timely availability, and in assessing these outcomes from a comparative Europe–East Asia perspective. By drawing on detailed case studies, the chapter shows how innovation ecosystems, advance purchase agreements, and emergency regulatory arrangements jointly addressed coordination, market, and regulatory failures, while simultaneously producing new tensions around global access and public value creation (Bustamante et al., 2023; Da Fonseca et al., 2023; Teece, 1986; Wouters et al., 2021).

SARS-Cov-2 (commonly referred to as COVID-19) resulted in diverse responses by actors around the world. Based on these experiences, this chapter derives conditions for successful vaccine development from European and Asian case studies (Tiberghien, 2021)—success conceived as the (speedy) development and manufacturing and the (timely) availability of vaccines. Given the importance of regulation and related governmental roles in developing vaccines and making them available to the public, COVID-19 can be assessed as a successful case of industrial and innovation policy in the health sector. In this chapter, we spell out how national governments, international governmental organizations, pharmaceutical firms and non-market actors such as universities or private donors contributed to overcoming regulatory, coordination, and market failures, so that, as a result, effective vaccines have been timely available. Thus, our chapter—complementing others in this volume (Gorry & Montalban, 2026; Lechevalier, 2026; Kuo & Takuma, 2026)—analyses a case where the "traditional" model of Schumpeterian innovation has been successful. At the same time, though, it also identifies weaknesses of our "success cases", such as the possible non-availability of high-end vaccines through APA schemes (Advance Purchase Agreements) in developing countries, linking back to discussions of the moral economy and to vaccines as a common pool resource (see our discussion section; Bustamante et al., 2023; Ibata-Arens et al., 2026).

In the following, Sect. 5.2 discusses the nature of vaccines, along with vaccine technologies and the vaccine value chain. Section 5.3 provides the theoretical framework from a sectoral system of innovation perspective and the success factors for vaccine development. Section 5.4 elaborates on the details of the four cases in Europe and Asia. Section 5.5 provides a discussion and concludes the chapter.

5.2 Understanding Vaccine Technologies and the Vaccine Value Chain

5.2.1 Vaccine Safety and Efficacy

In response to the global pandemic evoked by the virus COVID-19, a wide range of vaccines has been developed. In response to the spreading virus, during the first stage of the pandemic (Tiberghien, 2021), vaccines were quickly developed in China and Russia. These vaccines, which did not have adequate clinical trials before being applied to mass vaccination, are not the concern of this chapter. Neither do we cover some locally produced and used vaccines that appeared in the third stage of the pandemic, as defined by Tiberghien 2021). By speaking of innovation, our focuses in this chapter are the mainstream pharmaceutical companies and two from East Asian states, which attempted to join the race in terms of public health.

In retrospect, the most prominent ones are in common parlance referred to as inactivated vaccines, recombinant vaccines, and mRNA vaccines. More precisely, inactivated vaccines constitute a subcategory of *virus vaccines*, whereas mRNA vaccines pertain to the category of *nucleic acid vaccines*. Among the recombinant COVID-19 vaccines, it can mainly be differentiated between *protein vaccines* and *viral vector vaccines*.[1] Based on the underlying manufacturing technologies, the vaccines are either categorized as conventional or novel vaccines (WIPO, 2023).[2]

To determine the suitability of these vaccines to counter the pandemic, in a first step, vaccines need to be evaluated in terms of their *safety* and *efficacy* (Ashby et al., 2021; Dellepiane & Wood, 2015; Li et al., 2022). A vaccine is safe in case the virus cannot replicate plus the risks and side effects of the vaccine are negligible. Meanwhile, a vaccine is effective if it (i) elicits strong long-term memory immune responses after a minimal number of immunizations/ booster doses, and (ii) robust adaptive immune responses leading to long-term protection against several strains (i.e. variants) of the pathogen (Kyriakidis et al., 2021).

Regarding *vaccine safety and efficacy,* novel vaccines in general and mRNA vaccines in specific take the lead towards conventional vaccines, as they induce protective immunity without triggering side effects (Hansson et al., 2000), and don't convey the potential risk of insertional mutagenesis. With mRNA degrading by normal cellular processes and its half-life in the human body being regulable, mRNA vaccines are the safest option (WIPO, 2023). Novel vaccines are also more effective than

[1] With patents indicating research intensity, between January and September 2022 ca. 41.2% of the vaccine patent dataset was related to protein subunit vaccines, ca.18.7% to viral vector vaccines, ca. 15.9% to nucleic acid vaccines and ca. 7.6% to inactivated vaccines. The remainder (ca. 16.6%) is spread across a range of other vaccines.

[2] For details see Table 1A. Accessible in our online appendix (https://hessenbox-a10.rz.uni-frankfurt.de/getlink/fiDhPUToNezzxG6YUuLbNf/).

conventional vaccines, and again, mRNA vaccines are taking the lead. For example, Pfizer-BioNTech's mRNA vaccine leads by eliciting immune response in 95% (Ahmed et al., 2021), and Oxford-AZ's adenovirus vector vaccine in 70.4% of the vaccinations (Poland & Hung, 2021). Among novel vaccines, mRNA vaccines appear to provide better protection against several strains of the pathogen (Li et al., 2021, 2022; Poland & Hung, 2021; Shin et al., 2020).

Table 5.1 summarizes the *safety* and *efficacy* of common COVID-19 vaccines, with I indicating the highest *vaccine safety and efficacy.*

Table 5.1 Vaccine safety and efficacy of common COVID-19 vaccines

Vaccine	*Conventional vaccines*		*Novel vaccines*	
Category	*Virus vaccine*	*Protein vaccine*	*Viral Vector vaccine*	*Nucleic Acid vaccine*
Subcategory	*Inactivated*	*Protein subunit*	*Adenovirus vector*	*mRNA*
Case studies	-	Medigen (Taiwan) SKYCovione (South Korea)	Oxford–AstraZeneca[a] (UK-Sweden)	BioNTech–Pfizer (Germany-USA)[b]
Safety	+	+	++	+++
Efficacy	+	++	++	+++
Evaluation	*IV*	*III*	*II*	*I*

[a]Yielding a pooled efficacy of around 70% pursuant to the interim report, the interval of efficacy is quite large (ranging between 62% and 90%) (Poland & Hung, 2021; Voysey et al., 2021). Analysis suggested that the gains in efficacy of the 90% co-hort may be attributable to the exclusion of the elderly (i.e. 56-years-old individuals) (Ahmed et al., 2021). The vaccine did not prove to be effective against mutations of the COVID-19 virus. Though considered safe insofar as it does not al-low for replication, the vaccine conveyed non-negligible risks and side-effects: vaccine recipients developed unusual thrombosis (Dal-Ré, 2023; Kelland, 2021; McCarthy, 2021; Schultz et al., 2021).

[b]Measured from 7 days after the second dose, the vaccine has an efficacy rate of 95% at $p < 0.0001$ (Lewis et al., 2023; Pfizer, 2020a). Inducing strong COVID-19 spike protein-specific immune responses (both humoral and cellular) and exhibiting a high breadth of T cell responses, it elicits a strong long term memory immune response (Ahmed et al., 2021; EMA, 2022; Li et al., 2021; Sahin et al., 2021) The vaccine also proved to be efficient against mutations of the COVID-19 spike protein. Besides, the vaccine has a strong safety profile. No serious risks and side effects were detected. Most systemic side effects (e.g. headache, fatigue) were of mild/ moderate severity and resolved shortly after vaccination (Lamb, 2021; Polack, et al., 2020).

Note The number of (+) signs indicates the extent, to which the criteria is satisfied. Own representation based on publications in leading medical journals (see Table 1A)

Furthermore, in times of a pandemic, speedy development/ manufacturing and (timely) availability are crucial. Both are shaped by the vaccine value chain which will be outlined next.

5.2.2 *Vaccine Value Chain: Time-to-market and Availability*

5.2.2.1 Framework

The vaccine value chain consists of the dimensions of *Research & Development* (R&D), *Manufacturing* and *Distribution* (Fig. 5.1).

A peculiarity of the vaccine value chain is that R&D, Manufacturing and Distribution do not occur in chronological order but rather are horizontally and vertically intertwined, making the vaccines' innovation system highly complex, interrelated, and uncertain.

To start with *R&D* and *Manufacturing*, the approval for the conduction of clinical trials is contingent on the approval of the manufacturing technology, and the vaccine approval on the approval of the manufacturing process. Whenever approval is denied, *R&D* and *Manufacturing* have to restart from scratch (i.e. steps 1 and 2a, respectively). Pfizer for instance allocates a timeframe of 16 to 24 years for these phases (Pfizer, 2023). Thus, substantial funding is required; and the risk is substantial that the new product is entering the market too late.

Fig. 5.1 Vaccine value chain. *Source* Own representation

Subsequently, we briefly describe the full vaccine value chain. Throughout *research & discovery* (step 1), the idea for a potential vaccine is developed and the efficacy of a vaccine candidate is explored (*Proof of Concept*). In case a vaccine candidate shows promising results, its efficacy is to be scrutinized in vivo through pre-clinical trials (step 4); then, *manufacturing development* (step 2a) is initiated. Differing from regular new product development, the presence of manufacturing capabilities meeting high safety and efficacy standards thus constitute a precedent for actual trials (Abrahamsen et al., 2011). Step 2a entails the choice of manufacturing technology and facility, as well as the selection of suppliers for key ingredients and the sourcing of primary packaging. Vaccine manufacturing requires specialized running utilities and equipment (Ashby et al., 2021); such as up to 9000 materials sourced from 300 suppliers across 30 countries. Thus, highly specialized complementary assets and sophisticated capabilities are needed (Teece, 1986). Thus, trade dependencies -and hence potential shortages- are contingent on the vaccine properties.[3] Concurrent with *manufacturing development*, *storage* (step 2b) requirements need to be fathomed and respective equipment (e.g. freezers, dry ice) secured. Once all prerequisites for vaccine manufacturing and storage are met, manufacturing (step 3a) can be initiated. To actually make the manufactured vaccines available and usable at the (pre-) clinical trial sites, access to secondary packaging (e.g. cold boxes) and a multitude of ancillary goods (e.g. syringes, needles) need to be secured for vaccine distribution and administration (step 3b).[4]

Once steps (2a) to (3b) have successfully been accomplished, *pre-clinical trials* (step 4) can be initiated, first using laboratory animals. In the absence of safety concerns and provided that the vaccine candidate shows promising results plus regulators grant *manufacturing technology approval* (step 5) and *approval for clinical trials* (step 6). Conducted in pre-/post-vaccine-approval phases (steps 7/8/10/12), the safety and efficacy of the vaccine candidate is prudentially fathomed via administration to volunteers, and the manufacturer needs further to ensure reliable and consistent *large-scale manufacturing* (step 9). Most vaccines (70%) pass the early phase, while the rate drops later to 25–30%

[3] See potential shortages in Table 2A (https://hessenbox-a10.rz.uni-frankfurt.de/getlink/fiDhPUToNezzxG6YUuLbNf/).

[4] Packaging and mode of administration determine to which extent further ancillary supplies are (Ashby et al., 2021).

(Cern Foundation, 2023; LUPUS Research Alliance, 2023). In case of successful completion, *manufacturing process & facility approval and vaccine approval* for commercial use are granted (steps 10–12) (FDA, 2020, 2021).

Only afterward, *commercial manufacturing* and *distribution* (steps 13,14) start. An important challenge is often the *last mile delivery* (step 15); for example, up to 20% of temperature-sensitive pharmaceutical products are already damaged at arrival, among others, due to the disruption of the cold chain during transport (Andrenelli et al., 2021; IATA, 2015; OECD, 2019). In the pandemic, vaccines were often approved for commercial use under *Emergency Use Authorization* (EUA; Step 16)[5] (FDA, 2023).

Summing up, the complexity and interrelatedness within and across the dimensions of R&D, manufacturing, and distribution differentiate vaccines from non-pharmaceutical products. The analysis also shows, what has been often overseen (e.g. in the case of Sanofi) that manufacturing plays a core role already within the R&D dimension. Uncertainty for pharmaceuticals is in general very high; however, in the case of the pandemic, this uncertainty was to a certain extent reduced, given that there has been a large demand for vaccines.

5.2.2.2 Comparison of COVID-19 Vaccines

As the pandemic evinced that "we are only as healthy as our neighbors are" (Torreele et al., 2021: 2), *time-to-market* and *availability* are core criteria to evaluate the effectiveness of vaccines. *Time-to-market* approximates the speed for completing *R&D* and *Manufacturing* (i.e. time), and *availability* is the suitability of a vaccine for straightforward *Distribution* (i.e. scope).

In terms of *time-to-market*, mRNA vaccines perform best. Based on a comprehensive literature review, Table 5.2 summarizes the *time-to-market* of common COVID-19 vaccines, with I indicating the vaccines most suited for speedy completion of *R&D* and *Manufacturing*.

Regarding the criteria *availability*, mRNA vaccines are inferior to other vaccines as they require ultra-cold temperatures between – 20 °C

[5] In case certain criteria are met, "the EUA authority allows FDA to help strengthen the nation's public health protections against chemical, biological, radiological, and nuclear threats including infectious diseases, by facilitating the availability and use of medical counter-measures needed during public health emergencies" (EUA, 2024).

Table 5.2 Time-to-market of common COVID-19 vaccines

Vaccine	*Conventional Vaccines*		*Novel Vaccines*	
Category	*Virus Vaccine*	*Protein Vaccine*	*Viral Vector Vaccine*	*Nucleic Acid Vaccine*
Subcategory	*Inactivated*	*Protein Subunit*	*Adenovirus Vector*	*mRNA*
Case studies	-	Medigen (Taiwan) SKYCovione (South Korea)	Oxford–AstraZeneca (UK-Sweden)	BioNTech–Pfizer (Germany-USA)
Time-to-market	+	++	+++	++++
Evaluation	*IV*	*III*	*II*	*I*

Note The number of (+) signs indicates the extent, to which the criteria is satisfied. Own representation based on publications in leading medical journals (see Table 1A.)

(Moderna's vaccine) and − 70 °C (BioNTech-Pfizer's vaccine) for long-term storage. Thus, the distribution of mRNA vaccines was contingent on appropriate distribution mechanisms (Kyriakidis et al., 2021). This limited the availability in particular for *low-and middle-income countries* (LMICs) characterized by often weak transport capacity and supply of electricity (Ashby et al., 2021; Nwagwu et al., 2022; WIPO, 2023). Again based on a comprehensive review of the specialized literature, Table 5.3 summarizes the *availability* of common COVID-19 vaccines, with I indicating the ease of global *Distribution*.

In sum, while in terms of *vaccine safety and efficacy* and speedy development/ manufacturing (i.e. *time-to-market*), mRNA vaccines perform the best, they lag in terms of global distribution (i.e. *availability*). Thus, there is a trade-off between the criteria *safety* and *efficacy, time-to-market,* and *availability* (Ashby et al., 2021; Songane, 2018). This trade-off implies that even if a vaccine is successful in teams of *safety, efficacy,* and *time-to-market* such as mRNA vaccines, the success is "bounded", given that, at least at the beginning of the crisis, global *availability* was not achieved.

Table 5.3 Availability of common COVID-19 vaccines

Vaccine	*Conventional Vaccines*		*Novel Vaccines*	
Category	*Virus Vaccine*	*Protein Vaccine*	*Viral Vector Vaccine*	*Nucleic Acid Vaccine*
Subcategory	*Inactivated*	*Protein Subunit*	*Adenovirus Vector*	*mRNA*
Case studies	-	Medigen (Taiwan) SKYCovione (South Korea)	Oxford–AstraZeneca (UK-Sweden)	BioNTech–Pfizer (Germany-USA)
Availability	++	++	++	+
Evaluation	*I*	*I*	*I*	*II*

Note The number of (+) signs indicates the extent of ease of global distribution. Own representation based on publications in leading medical journals (see Table 1A)

5.3 Case Studies and Comparative Analyses

5.3.1 The Framework of Sectoral System of Innovation

Learning and capability building at the firm level are necessary conditions for firms to develop successful products and are strongly affected by the context in which they operate. This context, composed of a range of actors and institutions, is typically referred to as "innovation systems" (Fagerberg et al., 2017; Freeman, 1987). The systemic dimension is attributable to the notion that throughout the innovation process, a firm's behavior and strategies are shaped by and co-evolved with various actors (e.g. suppliers, users/ consumers, financial organizations, universities, public research laboratories, government) and institutions.[6] These relationships and interactions determine the innovation and economic performance of firms and

[6] Universities and public research organizations also play a key role because they conduct basic and applied research plus supply advanced human capital (Mazzoleni & Nelson, 2007). Financial organizations (such as banks, stock markets as well as internal funding) constitute major sources of support for technology diffusion and innovation. Vertical linkages with suppliers are also instrumental (Lundvall, 1988; Von Hippel, 1988). The government and public policy may foster the diffusion of knowledge and direct the efforts of private firms in a systemic and forward looking way (Fransman, 1985; Freeman, 1987).

ultimately countries. Innovation systems can hereby be considered at several levels, such as nations, sectors, regions and firms (Lee, 2013). Subsequently, we focus on sectoral innovation systems.

The *Sectoral System of Innovation* (SSI) approach focuses on certain sectors of the economy (e.g. vaccine sector) and considers the respective sector to constitute a system, focussing on firms' learning and capabilities, as well as the knowledge underpinning and the non-firm actors/ institutions involved in sectoral innovation and manufacturing (Malerba, 2002, 2005). In the SSI approach, institutions thus play a major role in shaping the relationships and interactions within the system, and national institutions affect the sectors differently. For instance, regulations such as *intellectual property* (IP) rights and patenting rules may favor one sector (e.g. vaccine sector) but hamper others (e.g. food sector). Effects may moreover vary across countries, with European pharmaceutical companies often benefiting more from the *Trade Related Aspects of Intellectual Property Rights* (TRIPS) regime than Indian generic drug manufacturers. As implied by the Pavitt taxonomy, there are major differences in the patterns of learning and innovative activities across sectors and sectoral systems (Pavitt, 1984). There is ample evidence that the sectoral system dimension hereby constitutes a crucial explanatory factor for the inter-country differences in innovative and economic performance.[7] Subsequently, we focus on the SSI of vaccines in the context of four case studies across four countries. Naturally, as we start from a SSI approach, institutions established on the global level play a key role. We start with describing them, and then enter into the national-level case studies.

5.3.2 Case Studies: Benefiting From an Institutional Infrastructure of International Governmental Collaborations

During the pandemic, both the scope and the degree of often international cooperation were enhanced, giving rise to greater cooperation across stakeholders and nations; in particular the NIH, the *Coalition for Epidemic Preparedness Innovations* (CEPI), and the *World Health Organization* (WHO). The steps taken by NIH to coordinate global efforts of public and private researchers contributed to avoid duplicative research and focus on promising candidates (NIH, 2020). CEPI contributed to speeding up

[7] See Lee, 2013; Malerba, 2005; Malerba and Mani, 2009; Malerba and Nelson, 2012; Mowery and Nelson, 1999.

development and manufacturing by "matchmaking" competent global manufacturers to different types of vaccines (CEPI, 2021). Transparency about the potential of vaccine candidates was enhanced by the WHO's establishment of a clinical trial registry (i.e. *International Clinical Trials Registry Platform*) comprising a searchable database to provide access to information about ongoing and completed clinical trials (Mayer, 2020). Besides, the WHO established the *COVID-19 Technology Access Pool* (C-TAP) to promote the sharing of knowledge, technology, and data (Kumraj et al., 2022). The contribution of private actors to these endeavors was often instrumental (Excler et al., 2023); for instance, the success of WHO's clinical trial registry was contingent on the participation of private actors (i.e. AZ, BioNTech, Moderna, J&J, Pfizer) making their study protocols available for public scrutiny (Ashby et al., 2021; Mahase, 2020).

5.3.3 Cases in Europe

5.3.3.1 Germany: BioNTech–Pfizer

The COVID-19 vaccine Comirnaty® (technically: BNT162b2) was developed by the German biotechnology firm BioNTech and the US pharma group Pfizer. Constituting a mRNA vaccine, this COVID-19 vaccine ranks highest in terms of *vaccine safety and efficacy* and *time-to-market* yet falls behind the other vaccines in terms of *availability* (see Tables 5.1, 5.2 and 5.3). In December 2020, it became the first COVID-19 vaccine to be granted EUA/ approval and the first mRNA-based vaccine altogether to obtain approval.[8] Moreover, it was the first to receive emergency validation via the *WHO Emergency Use Listing Procedure* (Lamb, 2021; WHO, 2020a). Pfizer assumes worldwide commercialization rights, excluding Germany and Turkey (covered by BioNTech) as well as China, Hong Kong, Macau, and Taiwan (covered by Fosun Pharma) (Druedahl et al., 2021). For the present case study, we focus on the collaboration between BioNTech and Pfizer.

Ecosystems. Largely due to (international) collaborations, the vaccine completed the value chain within nine months (Lamb, 2021). Building upon an existing R&D collaboration regarding a mRNA-based influenza

[8] Thus far, mRNA vaccines had only entered the (pre-) clinical trials for various infectious diseases, such as rabies, influenza, Ebola, Zika, and dengue virus (Fang et al., 2022; Pardi et al. 2019; Schnee et al., 2016).

vaccine and respective mRNA-related learnings and capabilities, in mid-March 2020 BioNTech and Pfizer signed a letter of intent to mobilize their collective assets and capabilities for the co-development and global distribution of a potential mRNA-based COVID-19 vaccine (BioNTech., 2020a; Lewis et al., 2023; Pfizer, 2020c). BioNTech's and Pfizer's contribution hereby reflect the typical distribution of assets between biotechnology SMEs (innovative capacity) and large incumbents (financial means, network). BioNTech provided multiple mRNA vaccine candidates from its Good Manufacturing Practice (GMP)-certified manufacturing facilities for clinical trials, and Pfizer contributed its global infrastructure concerning clinical R&D, manufacturing, distribution and regulatory (Druedahl et al., 2021; Lamb, 2021; Pfizer, 2020b; SEC, 2020).

R&D. Shortly after the release of the genetic sequence of SARS-CoV-2 in mid-January 2020, BioNTech initiated *Project Lightspeed* to develop a mRNA-based COVID-19 vaccine. In line with prior research indicating the mobilization of a broader range of immune responses, BioNTech/ Pfizer encapsulated a nucleoside-modified mRNA encoding the viral COVID-19 spike protein in a lipid nanoparticle delivery system (EMA, 2022; Lamb, 2021). The vaccine was mainstreamed as a platform, with platform technologies constituting a radical medical invention (Anderson, 2023; FDA, 2020a). In the absence of capacity constraints, BioNTech/ Pfizer could pursue four vaccine candidates, each representing different mRNA formats and target antigens in parallel, hereby diversifying risk.

Manufacturing. Given its novelty, large-scale manufacturing capabilities of mRNA-based vaccines did not exist at the onset of the pandemic. To ensure timely ***availability***, Pfizer made preparations in parallel with R&D, i.e. even before the lead candidate was identified (Lewis et al., 2023). Hereby, Pfizer's prior experience in manufacturing plasmid DNA for gene therapy was conducive. Though the pandemic constituted an exogenous demand shock for all COVID-19 related goods, the lipids needed to synthesize the lipid nanoparticles were particularly difficult to source as they had previously not been used at scale in other vaccines (Bourla, 2022). In response to the supply shortages arising during Phase III clinical trials, BioNTech/ Pfizer implemented several countermeasures such as the establishment of co-operations with further contract development and manufacturing organizations besides Polymun (AUT), scale-out of the lipid nanoparticle manufacturing process, usage of multi-dose vials allowing for six doses Hence, Phase III clinical trials were completed and the foundation for continuous large-scale manufacturing was laid (Lewis et al., 2023).

Distribution. As the vaccine has an ultra-cold chain requirement at −70 °C for long-term storage, the maintenance of the temperatures conveys substantial logistical exigencies, making the vaccine, together with other specific requirements, to one of the most expensive COVID-19 vaccines (WIPO, 2023).

Funding. Pre-pandemic, at least US$337 m were invested in mRNA related research (1985–2019), with substantial investments from the NIH, BARDA and the *Department of Defense* (Lalani et al., 2023). Further, NIH licensed several COVID-19 technologies arising from NIH intramural research to the *Medicines Patent Pool* for access through the WHO's C-TAP (Griffin et al., 2020; NIH, 2022). Similarly, throughout the pandemic, funding of public actors was pivotal. In September 2020 BioNTech received €375 m from the *European Fund for Strategic Investments* (aimed to expand BioNTech's manufacturing; EIB, 2020b), and the *German Federal Ministry of Education and Research* (BioNTech., 2021c).

Further, APAs were heavily used as a means to secure vaccines. In July 2020, BioNTech/ Pfizer agreed to provide the US government's *Operation Warp Speed* with 100 m vaccine doses. With the option to acquire as many as 500 m more upon clearance, the US government paid BioNTech/ Pfizer US$1.95bn for the initial doses (BioNTech., 2020a; Gross, 2020; Pfizer, 2020d). As of November 2020, BioNTech/ Pfizer announced further APAs including the EU, UK, Canada, and Japan. The amount covered by these agreements amounts to more than 570 m doses (BioNTech., 2020b; Lamb, 2021; Titan, 2020).

New Regulatory Arrangements. Effective collaboration across multiple actors was essential for the timely ***availability*** of the vaccine. To overcome practical challenges to regulatory compliance instantly and address them appropriately throughout the trials and the development/ refinement of the manufacturing process, BioNTech/ Pfizer established a continuous dialogue between its development teams, on-site vaccine providers, and various global regulatory agencies. This dialogue likely contributed to the impediment of regulatory roadblocks for vaccine deployment (Lewis et al., 2023). Besides, the BioNTech/ Pfizer vaccine was subject to a rolling submission review of EMA's human medicines committee. Respective procedures were initiated 6th October 2020 (EMA, 2020).

5.3.3.2 United Kingdom: Oxford–AstraZeneca

The COVID-19 vaccine AZD1222 (technically: ChAdOx1 nCoV-19) was developed by the British *University of Oxford* and the British-Swedish biopharmaceutical firm *AstraZeneca* (AZ) (Ahmed et al., 2021; Cross et al., 2021). Constituting an adenovirus vector vaccine, this COVID-19 vaccine ranks second in terms of *vaccine safety and efficacy* and *time-to-market*, yet is superior to mRNA vaccines in terms of *availability* (see Tables 5.1 5.2 and 5.3). The vaccine obtained its first EUA from the *UK Medicines and Healthcare Products Regulatory Agency* (Holder, 2023). EMA granted conditional marketing authorization for Europe upon approval by the European Commission on 29th January 2021.

Ecosystems. Also in this case, international collaborations have been core to the vaccine's *time-to-market* and *availability*.

R&D. The *University of Oxford* could build upon prior basic and applied research related to COVID-19 (vaccines), in particular its capabilities developed in the course of two decades of R&D conducted by the *Oxford Vaccine Group* at the Jenner Institute on behalf of the technology underlying the COVID-19 vaccine (i.e. *chimpanzee adenovirus vector* (ChAdOx) vaccine platform technology). Utilizing an invariant platform base, the *Oxford Vaccine Group* could simply "copy and paste" the genetic code for the coronavirus spike protein into the priorly developed proprietary vaccine platform technology ChAdOx platform to create the COVID-19 vaccine (Akpan, 2020; Torreele et al., 2021; UKRI, 2021).

Manufacturing. To achieve speedy large-scale manufacturing of the vaccine, AZ set up a global manufacturing network comprising 25 GMP-certified manufacturing sites in 15 countries, including advanced and emerging economies, reaching from Europe, North, Central, and South America, to Asia, and Australia. AZ engaged in technology transfer to build up respectively required manufacturing capacities and capabilities, also called the "franchise model of technology transfer" or "distributed manufacturing". Pre-pandemic capabilities and complementary assets have been important for the choice of manufacturing sites, as well as for the technology transfer process. An interesting example is the collaboration between AZ and the Brazilian *Institute of Technology on Immunobiologicals* (hereinafter: Bio-Manguinhos), a public laboratory linked to the Brazilian Ministry of Health. Prior to entering the collaboration with AZ, Bio-Manguinhos had engaged in various technology transfer agreements for vaccine manufacturing with other firms, thus acquiring capabilities to manufacture a range of vaccines using different technological approaches. The complementarity of Bio-Manguinhos' capabilities in working with cells in bioreactors and the viral vector technology leveraged by the vaccine forged the collaboration between Bio-Manguinhos and AZ. The technology transfer comprised two stages, from initially importing the vaccine substance, to complete manufacturing. During these stages, Bio-Manguinhos learned to locally manufacture the full vaccine. Within this process, the support of private sector actors and philanthropists was again important; for instance, the largest Brazilian bank (Itau Bank) and brewing firm (Ambev/ Inbev) donated US$20 m for Bio-Manguinhos's manufacturing facilities and provided assistance with logistics. This technology transfer allowed Bio-Manguinhos to develop new capabilities for the post-pandemic development of vaccines, gene therapies, and other biologics (Da Fonseca et al., 2023; Defendi & Santiago, 2021; Flynn, 2008; Shadlen & da Fonseca, 2013).

Distribution. As the vaccine can harness established distributional mechanisms, it is suited for straightforward global distribution, being important for the *availability* of the vaccine in resource-limited settings (Cross et al., 2021; Jimenez, 2021; Wouters et al., 2021).

Funding. Provided that the vaccine builds up on two decades of R&D by the *Oxford Vaccine Group* at the *University of Oxford*'s Jenner Institute, pre-pandemic funding substantially facilitated the timely *availability* of the vaccine. The majority of funding came from public and charitable institutions such as the European Commission (34.0%), the Wellcome Trust (20.4%) and CEPI (17.5%). Its application for the COVID-19 vaccine was mainly funded by the UK government, with the *Department of Health and Social Care* funding hereof the majority (Cross et al., 2021). Besides, APA schemes played a core role to fund downstream activities, inter alia with the UK government and the US government. Again, such APA schemes were highly attractive for AZ but became a barrier to provide vaccines as a common pool resource (Bustamante et al., 2023).

New Regulatory Arrangements. Last, but not least, new regulatory arrangements were conducive to speedy development/ manufacturing and (timely) availability, i.e. the *time-to-market* and *availability* of the vaccine. An example hereof is the manufacturing collaboration between AZ and Bio-Manguinhos: Brazil's initial investments to prepare for manufacturing of the vaccine were made at a high risk, i.e. while clinical trials were ongoing, partly because local vaccine manufacturing was expected to reduce external vulnerability (Defendi & Santiago, 2021;

Flynn, 2008; Shadlen & da Fonseca, 2013). To allow the public institution Bio-Manguinhos to procure development contracts for technological products requiring regulatory approval even when such approval is still outstanding, the Brazilian Ministry of Health made exceptional use of a legal instrument, the *Encomenda Tecnológica*. Further, the Brazilian health regulatory agency, ANVISA engaged in rolling submission and made officials available for constant communication and unscheduled meetings with Bio-Manguinhos (Da Fonseca et al., 2023).

5.3.4 *Cases in East Asia*

5.3.4.1 South Korea: SK BioScience

The first COVID-19 vaccine in Korea was developed by *SK BioScience* (SKBS hereafter) in collaboration with the Institute for Protein Design of the University of Washington. SKYCovione® is a vaccine that uses *GlaxoSmithKline*'s (GSK) adjuvant AS03 to enhance the immune response and induce high levels of neutralizing antibodies.[9] In addition, unlike Moderna, Pfizer, and AZ's corona vaccines, it is made using a synthetic antigen method. The synthetic antigen method has been used for a long time in other vaccines, such as influenza and hepatitis B, and has proven efficacy. It is a kind of recombinatory, protein-based, vaccine.

On the other hand, unlike the Pfizer and Moderna vaccines, SKYCoviOne Multi is made by synthetic antigen method and can be stored and distributed at room temperature of + 2 °C to + 8 °C, and it is expected to be effective in supplying developing countries that do not have ultra-cold temperature facilities. When SKYCovioneMulti was administered twice at 4-week intervals, the neutralizing antibodies that neutralize the virus were about twice better than those of the AZ vaccine (3.14 times more neutralizing antibodies were formed after 2 days).

Ecosystems. The *Institute for Protein Design* (IPD) at the University of Washington, USA, collaborated on R&D. In particular, it was supported by the *Bill & Melinda Gates Foundation* (BMGF) and CEPI from the early stages of development.[10] SKBS's SKYCoviOne Multiju, the country's No. 1 corona vaccine, is produced domestically from raw materials to

[9] Source: https://m.terms.naver.com/entry.naver?cid=42107&docId=6627110&categoryId=42107.

[10] See https://www.enewstoday.co.kr/news/articleView.html?idxno=1579773.

finished products. In this process, the SKBS' experience in manufacturing vaccines of AZ and Novavax must have helped this company to be able to develop its own vaccines in short period of time or within 28 months.

One important factor in this Korean case is the importance of effective governance enabling international collaboration or networking to solve the problem of lacking complementary assets in the development process. Actually, during the meeting, President Ahn of SKBS constantly mentioned the so-called "One Team" spirit.[11] The naming of the vaccine as SKYCovione reflects this idea of an international team by using the word of "One". At the same time, it is also to reflect the fact that it was the first vaccine in Korea and the only vaccine that led the global vaccine market.

Specifically, he repeatedly emphasized that the development of a vaccine would have been impossible without the support of various sources, such as the antigen candidate from the IPD at the *University of Washington*, the adjuvant 'AS19' from GSK, and the control vaccine from AZ. There was coordinated collaboration among international actors, such as BMGF, CEPI, and the *Inter-national Vaccine Institute* (IVI), as well as domestic actors, such as the *Ministry of Health and Wel-fare*, the *Ministry of Food and Drug Safety*, and the Korean *Disease Control and Prevention Agency*.

Funding. The initial financial support from the BMGF was possible because the BMGF wanted to supply these vaccines to low-and middle-income countries although it is bargained by SKBS to be able to supply the Korean market on a priority basis if such supply is in critical need. In a sense, it can be said that without the financial commitment by the BMGF and CEPI, the SK would have not started this project. Actually, while the Korean government allocated less than 300 billion (or 257.5 billion) won for financial support for vaccine development by four or 5 different companies, they (these two organizations) provided about 2450bn Won to SKBS.[12] Considering that CEPI is closely related to Bill Gates, it can be said that SK bioscience's SKYCovione vaccine is a vaccine created by Bill Gates. Such cooperation and commitment seem to have been possible owing the ongoing cooperation between SK and BMGF. It was as early as around 2013 that the BMGF began to directly or indirectly support SKBS's development of vaccines against typhoid fever and rotavirus, and

[11] See a newspaper article available at https://n.news.naver.com/article/277/0005117447.

[12] See http://www.fntoday.co.kr/news/articleView.html?idxno=276525.

at that time, SKBS was about to license the world's first quadrivalent cell culture influenza vaccine.

The critical importance of this financial support from the international actors can also be discussed in terms of the timing issue. That seems to be one of the reasons that the Korean effort to develop the vaccines started somewhat late or in early 2021. Actually, Mr Ahn of SKBS said that the most difficult moment was the first time he made a decision to develop. He said, "There were at least three reasons why we shouldn't participate in vaccine development." In a situation where it was difficult to be sure of the success of the development, there were only uncertain factors such as financial resources, the expected timing of the end of COVID-19, and competition from other global Big Pharma companies. Nevertheless, he explained the reason for his decision, saying, "In the end, I had a great sense of mission that I had to do as a representative vaccine company in Korea." Also, Liu Ji-hwa, director of the *Office of Clinical Authorization Development*, recalled speed as the most difficult factor. "The biggest pain point is that what was developed for 19 years was completed in two years," Liu said, emphasizing that "it was not that we skipped or omitted what we had to do, but that we condensed the whole process and did it in a short period of time." The fact that the development of COVID-19 vaccines and treatments has progressed at a much faster pace than the existing clinical process is a rebuttal to the fact that it is used as a basis for vaccine distrust.

There are also limitations associated with this vaccine by SKBS. First of all,, it is more for the early-stage variation of the COVID-19 virus but is weaker in terms of adaptability to develop updated variety of vaccines suitable to Omicron or later stage variation of COVID-19, compared to mRNA vaccines which is better equipped to develop updated variety for Omicron. In other words, when this SKYCovione vaccine is approved by the Korean authority, it was already the second stage of the vaccine wave or time of Omicron. So, demand for this vaccine was not much from the Korean population. Thus, although the government had a contract with this SKBS via a kind of APA to pre-procurement of 10 million doses, its manufacturing was stopped after the initial volume of 400,000 doses as there was no further demand. This also meant the waste of the government budget set as pre-procurement in the amount of 220 billion Won, whereas some of the volumes were shipped to Africa to be available as complementary basis.

Actually, in Korea, there were other companies which tried to develop mRNA vaccines but it did not go for the 2nd or 3rd clinical trial due to the lack of the financial resources, which was too big compared to any subsidy budget allocated by the government (less than 300bn Won total). For SKBS, they have no concrete plan to develop mRNA vaccine, which seems to be a technological challenge that cannot be solved alone. So, one can say that if the Korean government had an idea of industry policy in vaccine development, it should have opted again a leapfrogging strategy by targeting mRNA vaccine and by allocating enough subsidies for critical trials by several companies which was on this track of developing mRNA vaccine.

In the meantime, taking advantage of its international recognition (e.g. by UK and WHO) of its vaccine platform, SKBS has been trying to target international markets in not only COVID-19 but other vaccines.

New Regulatory Arrangements. The *Ministry of Food and Drug Safety* in Korea had taken just two months in reviewing the application by SKBS of the new Covid-19 vaccines and finally approving its production and distribution. As a member of ICH, the ministry stated that it took all the necessary three stepsfor giving approval, following the same international safety and efficacy standards and safety requirements for vaccines.[13] To reduce the time for submission and approval, the ministry also implemented the so-called rolling submission and review in which reviews were going for the first submitted documents even before all the necessary documents were not ready and submitted.[14] There was also a role by the Institute for Evaluation of Food & Drug Safety, as it helped to arrange a special process for trials and approval in which this vaccine was compared with other vaccines in their post-shot reactions by patients, rather than applying the normal process of examining the post-shot response in two groups of patients, treated vs. reference group.[15] The application was submitted in April 29, 2022, and on 29th June 2022, the company formally obtained the item approval from the *Ministry*. It has then obtained its first overseas approval in the UK at the end of April 2023, and, finally in mid June, 2023, it was also added to the WHO's *Emergency Use List*.

[13] See https://www.enewstoday.co.kr/news/articleView.html?idxno=1579773.

[14] See https://www.whosaeng.com/sub_read.html?uid=137126&section=sc5.

[15] See https://www.whosaeng.com/sub_read.html?uid=137126&section=sc5.

5.3.4.2 Taiwan: Medigen Vaccine Biologics Corporation

The MVC COVID-19 vaccine (高端新冠肺炎疫苗), designated MVC-COV1901 and also known as the Medigen vaccine, is a protein subunit COVID-19 vaccine developed by *Medigen Vaccine Biologics Corporation* (高端疫苗) in Taiwan in collaboration with the American company *Dynavax Technologies* and the NIH. Made by the recombinant S-2P spike protein secured from the NIH, the Medigen vaccine was one of the candidates when Taiwan's *Center for Disease Control* (CDC) announced its vaccine policy in March 2020. It was granted an EUA by Taiwan FDA in May, 2021 and was listed as one the four vaccines for mass vaccination. In order to have the access to international market, the developer of Medigen vaccine, *Medigen Vaccine Biologics Corporation* (renamed in 2017, hereafter the MVC), made several attempts for the phase III trials on its vaccine.[16] It filed phase III trial IND with the regulatory authority Paraguay (one of few countries in the world that have an official relationship with Taiwan) in July 2021 and received EUA from Paraguay in February 2022. In October 2021, Medigen vaccine was able to be selected by the WHO as one of its *Solidarity Trial Vaccines*.[17]

Ecosystem. MVC is a company that reflects Taiwan's biotechnology policy in the past two decades. Founded in 2012 for developing biologics, the origin of the MVC can be found in its parent organization, Medigen Biotechnology Corporation (基亞生物科技, the MBC) in 1999, shortly before Taiwan proposed a national plan for biotechnology and pharmaceuticals in 2000. Working with the government in several projects, the MVC build up its strength in vaccine development and manufacturing (facilities that are PIC/S GMP certified), in particular vaccines for enterovirus A71 and Dengue before working on COVID-19.

[16] For the clinical studies reported by Medigen, see Covid-19 vaccine tracker website at https://covid19.trackvaccines.org/vaccines/24/?fbclid=IwAR0wvzfC4Jog1sG7gGjTFub_WZr-1nTTVsSfVU9tn4FnumW8RUllMCp88IE#trial-isrctn15779782 (last date updated on December 2, 2022).

[17] For the detail of this WHO facilitated study, see https://www.isrctn.com/ISRCTN15779782?fbclid=IwAR2tVw4mvYeVWRjFP1WGNf5v7OSrPajbcBZF1MwjP7bonhS6N_41c7aSjk0. https://www.isrctn.com/ISRCTN15779782?fbclid=IwAR2tVw4mvYeVWRjFP1WGNf5v7OSrPajbcBZF1MwjP7bonhS6N_41c7aSjk0.

Meanwhile, we cannot overlook the transformation of the Taiwanese government's efforts put in vaccine development. Shortly before the end of the SARS epidemic, in June 2003, Taiwan launched its vaccine industry plan and established a vaccine development center, which merged with the research group on infectious disease in 2011, under the *National Health Research Institute* (NHRI). Aiming to streamline all research resources for vaccine development and supply, since 2009 the NHRI has worked with the MBC on H1N1 and H5N1 vaccines. It also provided technology support to the domestic companies for COVID-19 vaccine development.

Another organizational move took place in infectious disease governance is Taiwan's CDC. In response to the international threats of infectious diseases, Taiwan established its CDC in 1999, which centralizes the government's authority in disease control. Based on its long relationship with US CDC, Taiwan's CDC also played to some extent an active role in assisting the MVC to secure the recombinant S-2P spike protein needed for vaccine development from the NIH in March 2020.

Funding. Despite its long-term collaboration through vaccine projects, financially the MVC as a private company does not have the government's involvement. It should also be clear that the government's sponsorship is project-based, which means that the MVC has to compete with other domestic companies and its performance has to be regularly evaluated. Since 2018, nearly twenty years after its establishment, the MVC has been listed on Taiwan OTC/TaiSDAQ market (since 2018).

The project-based sponsorship can be also seen in emergent cases such as COVID-19. In order to secure more vaccines, Taiwan CDC formulated a sponsorship scheme by the stages of development in March 2020: when granting approval, the product sponsors will receive subsidies to initiate clinical trials. The results of each phase of these studies have to be reviewed by an ad-hoc committee, which decided which product can be granted support to proceed to the next phase of caliceal trial. With the one that withdrew at the very early stage of this policy, three candidate products finished the phase I study by October 2020. The product developed by Adimmune Cooperation, the company chosen for domestically made vaccine for H1N1 back to 2009, failed in the review, making only two vaccines of MVC COVID-19 and UB-612 2019 (a peptide subunit vaccine developed by United Biomedical Asia and Vaxxinity, Inc) entered to the phase II studies. In the end, the MAC COVID-19 was chosen to proceed into a pre-order exclusive deal of five million doses (single shot 29.3 US dollar/shot; multiple shots 27 US dollar/shot) with Taiwan CDC in May 2021.

New Regulatory Arrangements. The 2021 May became a tricky period of time in terms of vaccine policy. There was a second-wave outbreak of COVID-19, which quickly accumulated hundreds of confirmed cases and made mass vaccination an emergent issue. Meanwhile, it was the time when the results of the Phase II clinical trials, which used surrogate makers instead of testing on real patients (the so-called "immune-bridging trial"), were about to be released. While the government showed confidence in the Medigen vaccine even before the release of its interim analysis, the interpretation of the results read controversial. As a result, on 19 July the Taiwanese government granted EUA to the Medigen vaccine.

Under the EUA without efficient data of the Phase III clinical trial (especially data of efficacy), Medigen vaccine faced difficulties in the market. Despite it was used along with major vaccines (e.g. AZ and Moderna) in Taiwan and acuminated about 1.5 m shots on human beings (5% of total shots on the Taiwanese population, not including those as boosters), no adequate design was made for these "real world" experience. In addition to Taiwan, it was recognized as a recommended vaccine in only three counties—Eswatini, Paraguay, and Somaliland—to which Taiwan had stable diplomatic relationship (for an analysis of health diplomacy during the COVID-19 pandemic, see the chapter by Kuo and Takuma in this book), and it failed to reach out lobal markets in the world as Medigen promoted during the development of vaccine. As the pandemic was about to move toward its end, there was no much policy benefit or justification for the Taiwanese government to sponsor a single product.

The MVC COVID-19 vaccine was not the only vaccine product that suffered from this fate. Without robust policy support or planning for innovation, the tempo of vaccine development in Taiwan generally dropped. For instance, UB-612, Medigen's competing product, continued its phase III studies with the recognition of the CEPI, targeting COVID-19 variants as boosters. Some positive results were claimed by the company but so far (as of April 2024), this product has not been granted any approval for market.[18]

[18] For a clinical trial of UB-612, see https://www.ubiasia.com/products_detail/UB-612-covid-vaccine.

5.4 Success Factors for Vaccine Development and Development of Propositions

With our analysis of the vaccine value chain, we documented a highly complex, interrelated and uncertain process of vaccines, and our case studies demonstrate how countries and organizations in these countries addressed the inherent challenges and potential failures arising from it. In the following, we interpret our findings against the sectoral innovation system approach. Our basic argument is that the "success cases" have been able to overcome coordination, market and regulatory failures through ecosystems, funding, and new regulatory arrangements. However, also important tensions emerged.

5.4.1 Overcoming Failures: Ecosystems, Funding and New Regulatory Arrangements

Ecosystems. Access to highly specialized complementary assets and sophisticated capabilities is pivotal for the completion of the vaccine value chain, and (international) collaborations are key for safeguarding respective access (Moscicki, 2021; Mukherjee, 2021); in particular, public-private collaborations of ventures in biotech with academic labs and large pharmaceutical firms (Gaviria & Kilic, 2021; Lane, 2020). As our case studies illustrated, such collaborations also induced substantial knowledge transfer.

During the pandemic, a firm's capability to leverage (international) collaborations was critical for securing constant supply and meeting the criteria for a robust and stable manufac-turing process (Ashby et al., 2021; Bourla, 2022; Plotkin et al., 2017). Meanwhile, trade restrictions crucially influenced the success of collaborations, and, in the end, the *time-to-market* and *availability* of vaccines (OECD, 2020, 2020a; WTO, 2020). It is important to note that previous studies already highlighted the important role of collaborations in particular in the biotechnology sector (Owen-Smith & Powell, 2004; Powell et al., 2005); what seems to be distinct in the case of COVID-19 vaccines, though, is that these collaborations obtained a truly global dimension.

Funding. Given the long timeframe and substantial costs for the completion of the value chain, funding is imperative. To start with, throughout COVID-19, the focus of innovation policy (or: *industrial policy*) in the bio-medical industry shifted from providing financial stimulus for basic research towards downstream activities such as late-stage development and manufacturing (including the support of clinical trials) (Department of Justice, 2020). Besides governmental funding, donations from philanthropists such as Bill Gates and Carlos Slim played a core role (Ashby et al., 2021; Sampat & Shadlen, 2021; Warfield, 2016).

The biggest and most influential global actor is the *US National Institutes of Health* (NIH). Between 2000 and 2019, NIH funded over US$17.2bn in research on vaccine technologies, providing the foundation for the COVID-19 vaccines (Cross et al., 2021; UK Government, 2021). During the pandemic, NIH's focus shifted from providing grants to universities and medical schools towards funding trials of specific treatments. Similarly targeting downstream activities, the *U.S. Biomedical Advanced Research and Development Authority* (BARDA) funded clinical trials and at-risk manufacturing of "antibody" cocktails developed by Regeneron and AZ. In Europe, the *European Union Vaccine Program*—funded by the *European Investment Bank* (EIB) and several EU member states—was aligned with the U.S. approach. Altogether, over US$12bn was invested into vaccine R&D and at-risk manufacturing of the leading vaccine candidates[19] (Gross, 2020; Médecins Sans Frontières, 2020; Torreele et al., 2021).

Another important and novel tool has been *Advance Purchase Agreements* (APAs). While patents are a well-known and well-studied innovation incentive for the pharmaceutical industry (Levin et al., 1987), in the pandemic, patents would have failed to incentivize innovation, given the augmented probability of overlapping patent claims and the lengthy time of patent approval (Department of Commerce, 2020; USPTO). Hence, patents have been "replaced" with APAs. APAs essentially constituted procurement agreements, whereby actors entered into APAs by committing to purchase large volumes upon vaccine approval (like in other cases of public procurement; Zou et al., 2022). By sharing the financial burden and risk of failure among multiple stakeholders, APAs provided financial security for vaccine development and manufacturing (Lassi et al., 2021; Roberts, 2021; Saville et al., 2022)—keeping in mind that though in general the burden and risk of failure of vaccine development is

[19] Namely Oxford/AZ (US$1.7bn), J&J/ BiologicalE (US$1.5bn), BioNTech/Pfizer (US$2.5bn), Glaxo Smith Kline/Sanofi Pasteur (US$2.1bn), Novavax/Serum Institute of India (US$2bn), and Moderna/NIH/Lonza (US$2.48bn).

high, up-front investments are de-risked in a pandemic situation as there is a foreseeably large-scale demand. Pharmaceutical companies thus began to scale-up manufacturing prior to obtaining respective regulatory approval (Excler et al., 2023). At the same time, APAs were used to secure vaccines for their own population, and thus constituted a barrier to vaccines becoming a common pool resource (Bustamante et al., 2023).

New Regulatory Arrangements. Several new regulatory arrangements were put in place to streamline the value chain. To start with, regulators prioritized reviews of COVID-19-related vaccine approval applications over other health-related products (Heinrich & Jangho, 2022; WIPO, 2023) (which caused other issues for important diseases, though). Owing to the *European Medicines Agency* (EMA)'s rolling review process, COVID-19 vaccines could thus be approved in record times (i.e. 17 to 36 days). Similarly, the FDA activated the EMA mechanisms to promote rapid access to COVID-19 vaccines (Kumraj et al., 2022). Timeframes were streamlined via early and iterative guidance consultations of regulators with vaccine developers and manufacturers; for example, open regulatory forums for dialogues were set up (Excler et al., 2023; Marinus et al., 2022). Given the importance of trade for the value chain, regulators facilitated trade (Evenett et al., 2020; OECD, 2020, 2020a); e.g. import and export declaration forms were simplified, electronic submission of documents for pre-arrival processing was introduced, business hours at specific border posts were extended, and cooperations between customs and other relevant agencies were enhanced (Andrenelli et al., 2021).

5.4.2 *Propositions for the Conditions for Success*

The COVID-19 pandemic itself created "favorable" conditions for the vaccines' *time-to-market* and *availability*, such as the sustained large-scale demand that de-risked up-front investments, and facilitated the search of volunteers for clinical trials, or shortened time frames. Besides, previous exposure to pandemic threats as well as previous conduction of COVID-19-related research enhances the speedy development of vaccines as prior learnings and capabilities can be leveraged. However, based on the preceding discussion, we identify distinct properties of the sectoral system of vaccines which are key conditions for being successful (or not) in the development and manufacturing of vaccines, and develop the following propositions—reminding our readers that we refer with success to a (speedy) development and manufacturing and a (timely) availability of vaccines.

Overall, besides the prevalence of an effective regulatory system, domestic and international collaborations and coordination for arranging access to funding and managing the availability of complementary assets and capabilities were crucial for the successful develop-ment and manufacturing of vaccines. Specifically, the following three factors can be identified.

- **Proposition 1** on **overcoming coordination failure**: Domestic and international collaborations and coordination are some of the most important success conditions, which are needed to enhance knowledge and technology transfer and, in turn, to address the global vaccine manufacturing capacity bottleneck. Close cooperations between diverse stakeholders and across nations expedite the availability of vaccines.
- **Proposition 2** on **overcoming market failure**: Given the exceptionally long and risky vaccine development process, sharing financial burden and risk of failure among multiple stakeholders (e.g. via APAs) constitutes a core condition for the success and failure of vaccine development and manufacturing.
- **Proposition 3** on **overcoming regulatory failure**: New regulatory arrangements, the expansion of regulatory capacities and cross-country regulatory harmonization increase the timely availability of COVID-19 vaccines.

5.5 Discussion and Conclusion

Our chapter is dedicated to the exploration of success factors for the (speedy) development and manufacturing and (timely) availability of vaccines. To account for the unique framework of the SSI of vaccines, we established criteria for vaccine evaluation—namely *safety*, *efficacy*, *time-to-market*, and *availability*—and provided an overview of the vaccine value chain. We subsequently focused on determining the success factors of speedy development and manufacturing in order to allow for a (timely) availability of vaccines (i.e. *time-to-market* and *availability*). As indicated by the summary of the main results of the comparative analysis of

European and East Asian cases (see Table 5.4), building up ecosystems, access to funding, and new regulatory arrangements were at the core of overcoming coordination, market and regulatory failures; building up on an international institutional infrastructure, and pre-existing firm-level capabilities. As a side note, we find that success has different meanings across our cases; for instance, in Taiwan, successful commercialization of the Medigen vaccine was not achieved, reflecting the fragile infrastructure of the Taiwanese pharma sector.

At the same time, our study makes important contributions to the SSI approach. To start with, firm capabilities considered necessary for firms to succeed are usually linked to technological capabilities. As illustrated by the Taiwanese case, however, marketing capabilities may need to be added to the set of critical capabilities.

Second, the sectoral system of innovation approach implicitly assumes that firm-level strengths are related to high-quality products. However, the definition of quality is not an easy one—what "good" means in the case of health products is open to discourse. Though the safest and most effective vaccines (i.e. mRNA vaccines) were successfully developed and manufactured, at the beginning of the crisis they were not available in the developing world. Hence, while for instance the BioNTech-Pfizer case was depicted as a success case, it may rather be considered to constitute a success from a firm-level perspective and from the point of view of those with access to the vaccine—but less from a global welfare point of view (see Gorry & Montalban, 2026; Shiroyama et al., 2026). Consequently, it may even be conceived as a failure—given that the better vaccines could not be globally provided. This implies that when it comes to the analysis of health-related products, the SSI approach may need to consider distribution—and thus availability—stronger. Put differently, while this chapter has focused on identifying the conditions under which rapid vaccine development and manufacturing were possible, it also highlights important limitations of these so-called success cases. From a firm-level and national innovation system perspective, vaccine development—most notably in the case of BioNTech–Pfizer—was extraordinarily successful, enabled by public funding, advance purchase agreements, emergency regulatory arrangements, and the protection of intellectual property rights under the global TRIPS regime. At the same time, these arrangements allowed private firms to appropriate substantial rents from publicly de-risked innovation processes, reinforcing a neo-Schumpeterian innovation system that rewards rapid techno-innovation and maybe even monopolies, while falling short in

Table 5.4 Summary of the cases

Category	*Germany: BioNTech-Pfizer*	*UK: Oxford-AstraZeneca*	*Korea: SK bioscience*	*Taiwan: Medigen vaccine biologics corporation*	*Success Factors*
Type of vaccines	• nucleic acid-based mRNA vaccine • requires – 70 °C for long-term storage	• viral vector-based vaccine • stable at + 2 °C to + 8 °C for 6 months	• recombinatory, protein-based, vaccine; • made by synthetic antigen method; • can be stored and distributed at room temperature	• protein subunit vaccine that contains recombinant spike protein of SARS-CoV-2 virus	
Institutional Infrastructure of international governmental collaborations	Throughout COVID-19 there were supportive structures in place enhancing the timely availability of vaccines. These initiatives were mainly provided by international organizations (e.g. WHO) though, the contributions of private actors were crucial for the success of these initiatives (e.g. COVID-19 Technology Access Pool, International Clinical Trials Registry Platform). Also, new cooperation within nations and state actors can be observed across countries (e.g. Ministry of Health and Welfare, the Ministry of Food and Drug Safety, and the Korean Disease Control and Prevention Agency in Korea				Important collective institutional infrastructure as a necessary condition
Capabilities	• BioNTech: innovative capacity • Pfizer: global network & money	• University of Oxford: innovative capacity • AstraZeneca: global network	• Since 2013 the BMGF has supported SKBS's development of vaccines	• Founded in 2012 for developing biologics and renamed in 2017, MCV has focused on vaccines of enterovirus A71 and Dengue before working on Covid-19	Firm-level capabilities as a necessary condition

(continued)

Table 5.4 (continued)

Category	*Germany: BioNTech-Pfizer*	*UK: Oxford-AstraZeneca*	*Korea: SK bioscience*	*Taiwan: Medigen vaccine biologics corporation*	*Success Factors*
Ecosystems	• Manufacturing: contract development and manufacturing organizations • Distribution: software provider	• Manufacturing: franchise model of technology transfer featuring distributed manufacturing • Distribution: Itau Bank, Ambev/ Inbev (brewing firm)	• Initial support in R&D: *University of Washington*, GSK, AZ • R&D collaboration: BMGF, CEPI, and the *International Vaccine Institute* (IVI), as well as domestic actors • Manufacturing: SKBS	• R&D: Signed a license agreement with US NIH for COVID-19 vaccine • Manufacturing: in-house facilities (PIC/S GMP certified)	Strategies to overcome **coordination failures**
Funding	• Pre-Pandemic: US governmental institutions (i.e. NIH, BARDA, US DoD) • Pandemic: German & European institutions (i.e. BMBF, EIB) • APAs: EU, the UK, Canada, and Japan	• Pre-pandemic: public & charitable institutions (i.e. European Commission Wellcome Trust, CEPI) • Pandemic: UK governmental institution (i.e. DHSC)	• Main: BMGF & CEPI; • Minor: Korean gov't	• Main: MVC listed on Taiwan OTC/ TaiSDAQ market (since 2018); Medigen Biotechnology Corp.; partly sponsored by contracts with the Taiwanese gov't	Strategies to overcome **market failure**

(continued)

Table 5.4 (continued)

Category	*Germany: BioNTech-Pfizer*	*UK: Oxford-AstraZeneca*	*Korea: SK bioscience*	*Taiwan: Medigen vaccine biologics corporation*	*Success Factors*
		• APAs: esp. with the UK and the USA			
New Regulatory arrangements	New regulatory arrangements such as continuous dialogue	New regulatory arrangements such as rolling submission, continuous dialogue	Quick approval (2 mos.) applying rolling submission and review process by *Ministry of Food & Drug Safety*	In May 2021 MVC COVID-19 Vaccine obtained Taiwan EUA approval	Strategies to overcome **regulatory failure**

delivering vaccines as global public goods and in ensuring equitable access, particularly for low- and middle-income countries (Bustamante et al., 2023; Sampat & Shadlen, 2021; Torreele et al., 2021; Wouters et al., 2021). This tension points to a broader implication for the sectoral system of innovation and STI literature: in health-related sectors, innovation "success" cannot be assessed solely in terms of speed, technological sophistication, or firm profitability, but must also incorporate distribution, availability, and global welfare outcomes as core dimensions of performance (Malerba, 2002, 2005; Da Fonseca et al., 2023). Chapter 6 builds up on these arguments and elaborates the unequal access to COVID-19 vaccines more in detail (Kuo & Takuma, 2026).

Finally, our comparative analyses imply that advance purchase agreements (APAs) were beneficial for funding and for achieving rapid vaccine development and manufacturing, thereby improving timeliness and early availability (distributional feasibility, storage requirements, last-mile delivery) for firms and for high-income countries able to secure supply through these agreements. When assessed against this availability criterion, however, these gains were unevenly distributed, as APAs prioritized access for sponsoring governments and constrained early availability for low- and middle-income countries (LMICs), despite later vaccine donations once domestic demand had largely been met. At the same time, the inclusion of LMICs in international innovation networks, the enhancement of knowledge and technology transfer (as illustrated by the technology transfer model in the Oxford–AstraZeneca case), and broader efforts to build an institutional infrastructure of international governmental and public-private collaboration point to potential pathways for strengthening end-to-end vaccine ecosystems and improving availability in future crises.

References

Abrahamsen, M., Acar, O., Bahar, D., Brinded, B. & Rainisch, V. (2011). *The Belgian pharmaceutical cluster*. Retrieved from Institute for Strategy and Competitiveness Harvard Business School https://www.isc.hbs.edu/Documents/resources/courses/moc-course-at-harvard/pdf/student-projects/Belgium_Pharmaceuticals_2011.pdf

Ahmed, S., Khan, S., Imran, I., Al Mughairbi, F., Sheikh, F. S., Hussain, J., Khan, A., & Al-Harrasi, A. (2021). Vaccine development against covid-19: Study from pre-clinical phases to clinical trials and global use. *Vaccines, 9*(8), Article 836.

Akpan, N. (2020). *Moderna's mRNA vaccine reaches its final phase: Here's how it works.* Retrieved from National Geographic https://www.nationalgeographic.com/science/2020/05/moderna-coronavirus-vaccine-how-it-works-cvd/

Anderson, S. (2023, March 2). *U.S. government invested $31.9 billion in mRNA vaccine research and procurement.* Retrieved from Health Policy Watch https://healthpolicy-watch.news/u-s-government-invested-31-9-billion-in-mrna-vaccine-research-and-procurement/

Andrenelli, A., Lopez Gonzalez, J. & Sorescu, S. (2021, February 11). *Using trade to fight COVID-19: Manufacturing and distributing vaccines.* Retrieved from OECD https://www.oecd.org/coronavirus/policy-responses/using-trade-to-fight-covid-19-manufacturing-and-distributing-vaccines-dc0d37fc/

Ashby, E., Anupindi, R., Jefferson, K.M.P. & Yadav, P. (2021). *Globally resilient supply chains for seasonal and pandemic influenza vaccines.* National Academies Press (US).

BioNTech. (2020a). *Pfizer and BioNTech to Co-develop Potential COVID-19 Vaccine.* Retrieved from BioNTech https://investors.biontech.de/news-releases/news-release-details/pfizer-and-biontech-co-develop-potential-covid-19-vaccine

BioNTech. (2020b). *BioNTech and fosun pharma to supply China with mRNA-based COVID-19 vaccine.* Retrieved from BioNTech https://investors.biontech.de/news-releases/news-release-details/biontech-and-fosun-pharma-supply-china-mrna-based-covid-19

BioNTech. (2021c). *BioNTech to receive up to €375M in funding from German federal ministry of education and research to support COVID-19 vaccine program BNT162.* Retrieved from BioNTech https://investors.biontech.de/news-releases/news-release-details/biontech-receive-eu375m-funding-german-federal-ministry

BioNTech. (2024, May 29). *BioNTech and CEPI expand partnership to strengthen Africa's mRNA vaccine ecosystem.* Retrieved from BioNTech https://investors.biontech.de/news-releases/news-release-details/biontech-and-cepi-expand-partnership-strengthen-africas-mrna

Bourla, A. (2022). *Moonshot: Inside Pfizer's nine-month race to make the impossible possible.* HarperCollins Publishers.

Bustamante, J., Oughton, C., Pesque-Cela, V., & Tobin, D. (2023). Resolving the patents paradox in the era of COVID-19 and climate change: Towards a patents taxonomy. *Research Policy, 52*(9), 104850.

CEPI. (2021, January 26). *Enabling equitable access to COVID-19 vaccines: Summary of equitable access provisions in CEPI's COVID-19 vaccine development agreement.* Retrieved from CEPI https://cepi.net/wp-content/uploads/2020/12/Enabling-equitable-access-to-COVID19-vaccines-v1-17Dec2020.pdf

Cern Foundation. (2023, November 4). *Clinical trial phases.* Retrieved from Cern Foundation https://www.cern-foundation.org/education/clinical-trials/clinical-trial-phases

Cross, S., Rho, Y., Reddy, H., Pepperrell, T., Rodgers, F., Osborne, R., Eni-Olotu, A., Banerjee, R., Wimmer, S. & Keestra, S. (2021, December). Who funded the research behind the Oxford-AstraZeneca COVID-19 vaccine? *BMJ Global Health*, *6*(12), 1–11.

Da Fonseca, E. M., Shadlen, K. C., & De Moraes Achcar, H. (2023). Vaccine technology transfer in a global health crisis: Actors, capabilities, and institutions. *Research Policy*, *52*(4), 104739.

Dal-Ré, R. (2023). The winding 12-month journey of the AstraZeneca COVID-19 vaccine since its first administration to humans. *Therapie*, *78*(3), 293–302. https://doi.org/10.1016/j.therap.2022.07.003

Defendi, H., & Santiago, L. (2021). *Speeding up technology transfe—A case study of an emerging country on the pursuit of a COVID-19 vaccine.* 2021 IEEE Technology & Engineering Management Conference - Europe (TEMSCON-EUR), 1–6.

Dellepiane, N., & Wood, D. (2015). Twenty-five years of the WHO vaccines prequalification programme (1987–2012): Lessons learned and future perspectives. *Vaccine*, *33*(1), 52–61.

Department of Commerce. (2020). *COVID-19 prioritized examination pilot program: Fed Regist*, *85*(94), 28932–28935. United States Patent and Trademark Office.

Department of Justice. (2020). *Department of justice issues business review letter to monoclonal antibody manufacturers to expedite and increase the production of Covid-19.* Mab Treatment.

Druedahl, L. C., Minssen, T., & Price, W. N. (2021, October 8). Collaboration in times of crisis: A study on COVID-19 vaccine R&D partnerships. *Vaccine*, *39*(42), 6291–6295.

EIB. (2020b). *How we helped BioNTech develop the first COVID-19 vaccine.* Retrieved from EIB https://www.eib.org/en/projects/all/20200325

EMA. (2020). *EMA starts second rolling review of a COVID-19 vaccine.* Retrieved from EMA https://www.ema.europa.eu/en/news/ema-starts-second-rolling-review-covid-19-vaccine

EMA. (2022). *Annex I—Summary of product characteristics.* Retrieved from EMA https://www.ema.europa.eu/en/documents/product-information/comirnaty-epar-product-information_en.pdf

EUA. (2024, April 3). Retrieved from FDA https://www.fda.gov/emergency-preparedness-and-response/mcm-legal-regulatory-and-policy-framework/emergency-use-authorization

Evenett, S., Fiorini, M., Fritz, J., Hoekman, B., Lukaszuk, P., Rocha, N., Ruta, M., Santi, F. & Shingal, A. (2020). *Trade policy responses to the COVID-19 pandemic: Evidence from a new dataset*. Retrieved from https://voxeu.org/article/trade-policy-responses-covid-19-pandemic-new-dataset

Excler, J.-L., Saville, M.m Privor-Dumm, L., Gilbert, S., Hotez, P.J., Thompson, D., Abdool-Karim, S. & Kim, J.H. (2023, March 18). *Factors, enablers and challenges for COVID-19*. BMJ Glob Health, 1–6.

Fagerberg, J., Lundvall, B.-Å., & Srholec, M. (2017). Global value chains, national innovation systems and economic development. In *Papers in Innovation Studies 2017/15*. Lund University, CIRCLE-Centre for Innovation Research.

Fang, E., Liu, X., Li, M., Zhang, Z., Song, L., Zhu, B., Wu, X., Liu, J., Zhao, D. & Li, Y. (2022, de March de 23). Advances in COVID-19 mRNA vaccine development. *Signal Transduction and Targeted Therapy*, *7*(94), 1–31.

FDA. (2020). *Vaccine development—101*. Retrieved from U.S. Food & Drug Administration https://www.fda.gov/vaccines-blood-biologics/development-approval-process-cber/vaccine-development-101

FDA. (2020a). *BNT162b2 vaccine candidate against COVID-19*. Retrieved from FDA https://www.fda.gov/media/144325/download

FDA. (2021, August 28). *FDA*. Retrieved from mutual recognition agreements https://www.fda.gov/international-programs/international-arrangements/mutual-recognition-agreement-mra

FDA. (2023, June 15). *Emergency Use authorization*. Retrieved from FDA https://www.fda.gov/emergency-preparedness-and-response/mcm-legal-regulatory-and-policy-framework/emergency-use-authorization

Flynn, M. (2008, October 6). Public production of anti-retroviral medicines in Brazil, 1990–2007. *Development and Change*, *39*(4), 513–536.

Fransman, M. (1985). Conceptualising technical change in the third world in the 1980s: An interpretive survey. *The Journal of Development Studies*, *21*(4), 572–652.

Freeman, C. (1987). *Technology policy and economic performance: Lesson from Japan*. Pinter Publishers.

Gaviria, M., & Kilic, B. (2021). A network analysis of COVID-19 mRNA vaccine patents. *Nature Biotechnology*, *39*(5), 546–549.

Gorry, P., & Montalban, M. (2026). The crisis of capitalism and health innovation: Symptoms of a crisis or of success? In S. Lechevalier, J.-P. Gaudillière, K. Ibata-Arens, & K. Takuma (Eds.), *Capitalism, innovations, and health after Covid-19. An Asian perspective*. Palgrave MacMillan.

Griffin, R., Armstrong, D., & Bloomberg. (2020, November 10). *Germany funded the development of Pfizer's COVID vaccine—not U.S.'s Operation Warp Speed*. Retrieved from Fortune https://fortune.com/2020/11/09/pfizer-vaccine-funding-warp-speed-germany/

Gross, A. (2020, November 12). *Covid vaccine presents pharma with shot at redemption and profits*. Retrieved from Financial Times https://www.ft.com/content/0b18aac0-50a3-4694-9d28-ccbc44debcb2

Hansson, M., Nygren, P. A., & Ståhl, S. (2000). Review: Design and production of recombinant subunit vaccines. *Biotechnology and Applied Biochemistry, 32*, 95–107.

Heinrich, T., & Jangho, Y. (2022, December 29). *Innovation in times of Covid-19.* MPRA Paper, No. 115809, 1–23.

Holder, J. (2023, March 13). *Tracking coronavirus vaccinations around the world.* Retrieved from New York Times https://www.nytimes.com/interactive/2021/world/covid-vaccinations-tracker.html

IATA. (2015). *IATA CEIV certification.* Retrieved from IATA https://www.iata.org/contentassets/494bc14afd934b0193735e9a47091d72/iata_ceiv-pharma_how20to20become20ceiv20pharma20certified.pdf

Ibata Arens, K., Gaudillière, J.-P., Madhavan, H., & Nouguez, E. (2026). Commons and the political economy of access: Generics, neo traditional formulations and the dominant intellectual property regime of "medicine. In S. Lechevalier, J.-P. Gaudillière, K. Ibata-Arens, & K. Takuma (Eds.), *Capitalism, innovations, and health after Covid-19. An Asian perspective.* Palgrave MacMillan.

Jimenez, D. (2021, October 26). *Covid-19: vaccine pricing varies wildly by country and company.* Retrieved from Pharmaceutical Technology https://www.pharmaceutical-technology.com/features/covid-19-vaccine-pricing-varies-country-company/

Kelland, K. (2021, March 22). European trust in AstraZeneca COVID-19 vaccine plunges, poll shows, *Reuters*, https://www.reuters.com/business/healthcare-pharmaceuticals/european-trust-astrazeneca-covid-19-vaccine-plunges-poll-shows-2021-03-22/

Kumraj, G., Pathak, S., Shah, S., Majumder, P., Jain, J., Bhati, D., Hanif, S., Mukherjee, S. & Ahmed, S. (2022). Capacity building for vaccine manufacturing across developing countries: The way forward. *Human Vaccines & Immunotherapeutics, 18*(1), 1–17.

Kyriakidis, N. C., López-Cortés, A., Vásconez González, E., Barreto Grimaldos, A. & Ortiz Prado, E. (2021). SARS-CoV-2 vaccines strategies: A comprehensive review of phase 3 candidates. *Npj Vaccines, 6*(28), 1–17.

Kuo, W.-H., & Takuma, K. (2026). Glocal Health Governance: Organizational Innovations in the Era of COVID-19. In S. Lechevalier, J.-P. Gaudillière, K. Ibata-Arens, & K. Takuma (Eds.), *Capitalism, innovations, and health after Covid-19. An Asian perspective.* Palgrave MacMillan.

Lalani, H. S., Nagar, S., Sarpatwari, A., Barenie, R.E., Avorn, J., Rome, B.N. & Kesselheim, A.S. (2023, March 14). *US public investment in development of mRNA covid-19 vaccines: Retrospective cohort study.* BMJ.

Lamb, Y. N. (2021, March 8). BNT162b2 mRNA COVID-19 Vaccine: First Approval. *Drugs, 81*(4), 495–501.

Lane, R. (2020). Sarah Gilbert: Carving a path towards a COVID-19. *Lancet, 395.*

Lassi, Z. S., Naseem, R., Salam, R.A., Siddiqui, F. & Das, J.K. The impact of the COVID-19 pandemic on immunization campaigns and programs: A systematic review. *Ijerph, 18.*

Lechevalier, S. (2026). Care-led innovation. A new paradigm and an application in the Japanese context of Society 5.0. In S. Lechevalier, J.-P. Gaudillière, K. Ibata-Arens, & K. Takuma (Eds.), *Capitalism, innovations, and health after Covid-19. An Asian perspective.* Palgrave MacMillan.

Lee, K. (2013) *Capability failure and industrial policy to move beyond the middle-income trap: From trade-based to technology-based specialization.* The industrial policy revolution I: The role of government beyond ideology: 244–272.

Levin, R. C., Klevorick, A.K., Nelson, R.R. & Winter, S.G. (1987). Appropriating the returns from industrial research and development. *Brookings Papers on Economic Activity, 3,* 783–831.

Lewis, L. M., Badkar, A.V., Cirelli, D., Combs, R. & Lerch, T.F. (2023, March). The race to develop the Pfizer-BioNTech COVID-19 Vaccine. *Pharmaceutical Scientists' Perspective.*

Li, M., Lou, F., & Fan, H. (2021). SARS-CoV-2 variants of concern Delta: A great challenge to prevention and control of COVID-19. *Signal Transduction and Targeted Therapy, 6,* 349.

Li, M., Wang, H., Tian, L., Pang, Z, Yang, Q., Huang, T., Fan, J., Song, L., Tong, Y. & Fan, H. (2022, May 3). COVID-19 vaccine development: Milestones, lessons and prospects. *Signal Transduction and Targeted Therapy, 7*(146), 1–32.

Lundvall, B.-Å. (1988). Innovation as an interactive process. In G. Dosi, et al. (Ed.), *Technical Change and Economic Theory.* Frances Pinter.

LUPUS Research Alliance. (2023, November 4). *Phases of a Clinical Trial.* Retrieved from LUPUS Research Alliance https://lupustrials.org/about-trials/phases-of-a-trial/

Mahase, E. (2020). COVID-19: Vaccine trials need more transparency to enable scrutiny and earn public trust, say experts. *British Medical Journal, 371.*

Malerba, F. (2002). Sectoral systems of innovation and production. *Research Policy, 31*(2), 247–264.

Malerba, F. (2005). *Sectoral systems of innovation: Concepts, issues and analyses of six major sectors in Europe.* Cambridge University Press.

Malerba, F., & Mani, S. (2009). Sectoral systems of innovation and production in developing countries: An introduction. In F. Malerba & S. Mani (Eds.), *Sectoral systems of innovation and production in developing Countries, chapter 1.* Edward Elgar Publishing.

Malerba, F., & Nelson, R. (2012). *Economic Development as a Learning Process: Variation Across Sectoral Systems.* Edward Elgar Publishing.

Marinus, R., Mofid, S., Mpandzou, M., & Kühler, T. (2022). Rolling reviews during COVID-19: The European Union experience in a global context. *Clinical Therapeutics, 44*, 352–363.

Mayer, C. S. (2020). Computerized monitoring of COVID-19 trials, studies and registries in clinicaltrials.gov registry. *PeerJ, 8*, e10261.

Mazzoleni, R., & Nelson, R. R. (2007). Public research institutions and economic catch-up. *Research Policy, 36*(10), 1512–1528.

McCarthy, N. (2021, March 16). Which countries have stopped using the AstraZeneca Vaccine? *Statista*, https://www.statista.com/chart/24420/astrazeneca-vaccine-suspensions/

Médecins Sans Frontières. (2020). *Governments must demand pharma make all COVID-19 vaccine deals public.* Retrieved from https://www.msf.org/governments-must-demand-all-coronavirus-covid-19-vaccine-deals-are-made-public

Moscicki, R. (2021 de August de 28). *How industry collaboration and partnerships are supporting COVID-19 vaccine manufacturing*. Retrieved from https://catalyst.phrma.org/how-industry-collaboration-andpartnerships-are-supporting-covid-19-vaccine-manufacturing

Mowery, D. C., & Nelson, R. R. (1999). Explaining industrial leadership. In D. C. Mowery & R. R. Nelson (Eds.), *Sources of industrial leadership* (pp. 359–382). Cambridge University Press.

Mukherjee, S. (2021, August 28). *Fortune.* Retrieved from The companies making COVID vaccines aren't household names, but they're increasingly important https://fortune.com/2021/04/14/covid-vaccinemanufacturers-coronavirus-vaccines-who-makes-them

NIH. (2020, September 9). *Testimony on vaccines: Saving lives, ensuring confidence, and protecting public health.* Retrieved from National Institutes of Health https://www.nih.gov/about-nih/who-we-are/nih-director/testimony-vaccines-saving-lives-ensuring-confidence-protecting-public-health

NIH. (2022, May 12). *NIH contributions to WHO COVID-19 technology access pool and Q&As.* Retrieved from NIH Technology Transfer https://www.techtransfer.nih.gov/policy/ctap

Nwagwu, C. S., Ugwu, C.N., Nwabueze Ogbonna, J.D., Onugwu, A.L., Agbo, C.P., Echezona, A.C., Ezeibe, E.N., Uzondu, S., Kenechukwu, F.C., Akpa, P. A., Momoh, M.A., Nnamani, P.O., Tarirai, C., Ofokansi, K.C. & Attama, A.A. (2022). Recent and advanced nano-technological strategies for COVID-19 vaccine development. In V. G. Charles & S. Pavia, *Methods in microbiology* (pp. 151–188). Academic Press, Volume 50.

OECD. (2019). *OECD analytical database on individual multinationals and affiliates.* Retrieved from OECD https://www.oecd.org/sdd/its/statistical-insights-the-adima-database-on-multinational-enterprises.htm

OECD. (2020). *Getting goods across borders in times of COVID-19.* Retrieved from OECD https://read.oecd-ilibrary.org/view/?ref=436_436393-3urd6d5n5i&title=Getting-goods-across-borders-in-times-of-COVID-19

OECD. (2020a). *Trade interdependencies in COVID-19 goods.* Retrieved from OECD https://www.oecd.org/coronavirus/policy-responses/trade-interdependencies-in-covid-19-goods-79aaa1d6/

Owen-Smith, J., & Powell, W. W. (2004). Knowledge networks as channels and conduits: The effects of spillovers in the boston biotechnology community. *Organization Science, 51*, 5–21.

Pardi, N., LaBranche, C.C., Ferrari, G., Cain, D.W., Tombácz, I., Pars, R.J., Muramatsu, H., Mui, B.L., Tam, Y.K., Karikó, K., Polacino, P., Barbosa, C. J., Madden, T.D., Hope, M.J., Haynes, B.F., Montefiori, D.C., Hu, S.-L- & Weissman, D. (2019). *Characterization of HIV-1 nucleoside-modified mRNA vaccines in rabbits and rhesus macaques.* Mol. Ther. *Nucleic Acids Research, 15*, 36–47.

Pavitt, K. (1984). Sectoral patterns of technical change: Towards a taxonomy and a theory. *Research Policy, 13*(6), 343–373.

Pfizer (2020b). *Pfizer and BioNTech announce further details on collaboration to accelerate global COVID-19 vaccine development.* Retrieved from Pfizer https://www.pfizer.com/news/press-release/press-release-detail/pfizer-and-biontech-announce-further-details-collaboration

Pfizer (2020c). *Pfizer and BioNTech to Co-develop potential COVID-19 vaccine.* Retrieved from Pfizer https://investors.biontech.de/news-releases/news-release-details/pfizer-and-biontech-co-develop-potential-covid-19-vaccine

Pfizer (2020d). *Pfizer update On Our U.S. COVID-19 vaccine candidate distribution preparedness.* Retrieved from Pfizer https://www.pfizer.com/news/press-release/press-release-detail/pfizer-update-our-us-covid-19-vaccine-candidate

Pfizer (2023). *How are vaccines developed?* Retrieved from Pfizer https://www.pfizer.com/news/articles/how_are_vaccines_developed

Plotkin, S., Robinson, J.M., Cunningham, G., Iqbal, R. & Larsen, S. (2017). The complexity and cost of vaccine manufacturing–an overview. *Vaccine, 35*(33), 4064–4071.

Polack, F. P., Thomas, S. J., Kitchin, N., Absalon, J., Gurtman, A., Lockhart, S., Perez, J. L., Pérez Marc, G., Moreira, E. D., Zerbini, C., Bailey, R., Swanson, K. A., Roychoudhury, S., Koury, K., Li, P., Kalina, W. V., Cooper, D., Frenck, R. W., Jr., Hammitt, L. L., ... Gruber, W. C. (2020, December 10). Safety and efficacy of the BNT162b2 mRNA Covid-19 vaccine. *New England Journal of Medicine, 383*(27), 2603–2615. https://doi.org/10.1056/NEJMoa2034577

Poland, G. A., & Hung, I. F. N. (2021, March 6). Single-dose Oxford–AstraZeneca COVID-19 vaccine followed by a 12-week booster. *Lancet, 397* (10277), P854–855.

Powell, W. W., White, D. R., Koput, K. W., & Owen-Smith, J. (2005). Network dynamics and field evolution: The growth of inter-organizational collaboration in the life sciences. *American Journal of Sociology, 1104*, 1132–1205.

Roberts, L. (2021). How COVID hurt the fight against other dangerous diseases. *Nature, 592*, 502–504.

Sahin, U., Muik, A., Vogler, I., Derhovanessian, E., Kranz, L. M., Vormehr, M., Quandt, J., Bidmon, N., Ulges, A., Baum, A., Pascal, K., Maurus, D., Brachtendorf, S., Lörks, V., Sikorski, J., Koch, P., Hilker, R., Becker, D., Eller, A.-K., … Türeci, Ö. (2021). BNT162b2 vaccine induces neutralizing antibodies and poly-specific T cells in humans. *Nature, 595*(7868), 572–577. https://doi.org/10.1038/s41586-021-03653-6

Sampat, B. N., & Shadlen, K. C. (2021, March). The COVID-19 innovation system. *Health Affairs, 40*(3), 400–409.

Saville, M., Cramer, J.P., Downham, M., Hacker, A., Lurie, N., Van der Veken, L., Whelan, M. & Hatchett, R. (2022). Delivering pandemic vaccines in 100 days—what will it take. *New England Journal of Medicine, 387*(2).

Schnee, M., Vogel, A.B., Voss, D., Petsch, B., Baumhof, P., Kramps, T. & Stitz, L. (2016) An mRNA vaccine encoding rabies virus glycoprotein induces protection against lethal infection in mice and correlates of protection in adult and newborn pigs. *PLOS Neglected Tropical Diseases, 10*

Schultz, N. H., Sørvoll, I. H., Michelsen, A. E., Munthe, L. A., Lund-Johansen, F., Ahlen, M. T., Wiedmann, M., Aamodt, A.-H., Skattør, T. H., Tjønnfjord, G. E., Holme, P. A. (2021, April 9) Thrombosis and Thrombocytopenia after ChAdOx1 nCoV-19 vaccination. *New England Journal of Medicine, 384*(22), 2124-2130. https://doi.org/10.1056/NEJMoa2104882

Shiroyama, H., Ki, J., & Matsuo, M. (2026). The mission oriented science, innovation and technology (STI) policies in Japan and Korea with a focus on health. In S. Lechevalier, J.-P. Gaudillière, K. Ibata-Arens, & K. Takuma (Eds.), *Capitalism, innovations, and health after Covid-19. An Asian perspective*. Palgrave MacMillan.

SEC. (2020, July 21). *U.S. Securities and Exchange Commission (SEC). FormF-1registration*. Retrieved from SEC. https://www.sec.gov/Archives/edgar/data/1776985/000119312520195911/d939702df1.htm

Shadlen, K. C., & da Fonseca, E. M. (2013). Health policy as industrial policy: Brazil in comparative perspective. *Politics & Society, 41*, 560–586.

Shin, M. D., Shukla, S., Chung, Y. H. Beiss, V., Chan S.K., Ortega-Rivera, O.A., Wirth. D.M., Chen, A., Sack, M., Pokorski, J.K. & Steinmetz, N.F. (2020). COVID-19 vaccine development and a potential nanomaterial path forward. *Nature Nanotechnology, 15*, 646–655.

Songane, M. (2018). Challenges for nationwide vaccine delivery in African countries. *International Journal of Health Economics and Management, 18*(2), 197–219.

Titan, S. (2020, October 11). *BioNTech announces third quarter 2020 financial results and corporate progress*. Retrieved from Stock Titan https://www.stocktitan.net/news/BNTX/bio-n-tech-announces-third-quarter-2020-financial-results-and-373hnojhvho4.html

Teece, D. J. (1986, December). Profiting from technological innovation: Implications for integration, collaboration, licensing and public policy. *Research Policy, 15*(6), 285–305.

Tiberghien, Y. (2021). *The East Asian Covid-19 Paradox (elements in politics and society in East Asia)*. Cambridge University Press.

Torreele, E., Mazzucato, M., & Li, H. L. (2021, Janury). *Delivering the people's vaccine: Challenges and Proposals for the biopharmaceutical innovation system*. UCL Institute for Innovation and Public Purpose. Policy Brief series (IIPP PB 12).

UK Government. (2021, September 9). *Medicines & healthcare products regulatory agency: conditions of authorisation for COVID-19 vaccine AstraZeneca*. Retrieved from UK Government https://www.gov.uk/government/publications/regulatory-approval-of-covid-19-vaccine-astrazeneca/conditions-of-authorisation-for-covid-19-vaccine-astrazeneca

UKRI. (2021, November 30). *The story behind the Oxford-AstraZeneca*. Retrieved from UKRI https://www.ukri.org/news-and-events/tackling-the-impact-of-covid-19/vaccines-and-treatments/the-story-behind-the-oxford-astrazeneca-covid-19%E2%80%A6

USPTO. (s.f.). *USPTO's prioritized patent examination program*. Retrieved from United States Patent and Trademark Office https://www.uspto.gov/patent/initiatives/usptos-prioritized-patent-examination-program

Von Hippel, E. (1988). *The Sources of Innovation*. Oxford University Press.

Voysey, M., Clemens, S. A. C., Madhi, S. A., Weckx, L. Y., Folegatti, P. M., Aley, P. K., Angus, B., Baillie, V. L., Barnabas, S. L., Bhorat, Q. E., Bibi, S., Briner, C., Cicconi, P., Collins, A. M., Colin-Jones, R., Cutland, C. L., Darton, T. C., Dheda, K., Duncan, C. J. A., … Pollard, A. J. (2021, January 9). Safety and efficacy of the ChAdOx1 nCoV-19 vaccine (AZD1222) against SARS-CoV-2: An interim analysis of four randomised controlled trials in Brazil, South Africa, and the UK. *The Lancet, 397*(10269), 99–111. https://doi.org/10.1016/S0140-6736(20)32661-1

Warfield, K. L. (2016). Role of small biotechnology companies in the fledgling biodefense vaccine industry. *Expert Review of Vaccines, 15*(9), 1079–1082.

WHO. (2020a). *WHO issues its first emergency use validation for a COVID-19 vaccine and emphasizes need for equitable global access*. Retrieved from WHO https://www.who.int/news/item/31-12-2020-who-issues-its-first-emergency-use-validation-for-a-covid-19-vaccine-and-emphasizes-need-for-equitable-global-access

WIPO. (2023). *COVID-19 vaccines and therapeutics: Insights into related patenting activity throughout the pandemic*. Patent Landscape Report.

Wouters, O., Shadlen, K. C., Salcher-Konrad, M., Pollard, A. J., Larson, H. J., Teerawattananon, Y., & Jit, M. (2021). Challenges in ensuring global access to COVID-19 vaccines: Production, affordability, allocation, and deployment. *The Lancet, 397*(10278), 1023–1034.

WTO. (2020). *Developing and delivering COVID-19 vaccines around the world*. Retrieved from WTO https://www.wto.org/english/tratop_e/covid19_e/vaccine_report_e.pdf

Zou, N., ten Brink, T., & Storz, C. (2022). Innovation in emerging economies: How do university-industry linkages and public procurement matter for small businesses? *Asia Pacific Journal of Management, 39*, 1439–1480.

CHAPTER 6

Glocal Health Governance: Organizational Innovations in the Era of COVID-19

Wen-Hua Kuo and Kayo Takuma

Abstract The COVID-19 Pandemic offers a critical opportunity to reassess global health governance. This chapter examines the vulnerabilities of existing governance frameworks during the initial outbreak and early responses, and analyzes how local and regional networks joined the global efforts and generated novel organizational innovations. Moving beyond narratives that focus primarily on the World Health Organization's (WHO) shortcomings or geopolitical failure, the chapter introduces the concept of "glocal health governance" to capture the dynamic, multilayered interactions among global, regional, national, and non-state actors during the pandemic. Drawing on global health security scholarship and institutional analysis, the authors argue that COVID-19 revealed both the limits of centralized global coordination and the growing importance of regional and local capacities. The chapter conceptualizes the pandemic as a governance "tabletop exercise" unfolding across three stages: initial

W.-H. Kuo (✉)
National Yang Ming Chiao Tung University, Taipei, Taiwan
e-mail: whkuo@ym.edu.tw

K. Takuma
Keio University, Tokyo, Japan

S. Lechevalier et al. (eds.), *Capitalism, Innovations, and Health after Covid-19*,
https://doi.org/10.1007/978-3-032-24479-6_6

outbreak and early responses; vaccine development and distribution; and post-crisis institutional stabilization. In the first stage, delayed WHO action—constrained by political pressures and the International Health Regulations (IHR)—coincided with more proactive responses by regions and individual states, signaling a shift away from a single global gatekeeper model. The second stage examines vaccine governance as a central arena of health diplomacy, where initiatives such as COVAX demonstrated both unprecedented collaboration and deep inequities shaped by vaccine nationalism and geopolitical rivalry. The third stage analyzes efforts to stabilize pandemic governance through institutional reforms, including the revision of the IHR, negotiations over the Pandemic Agreement, and the strengthening of regional health infrastructures in Europe, Africa, and Asia. Through comparative regional analysis, the chapter shows that organizational innovations—such as the European Health Union, Africa CDC–led procurement mechanisms, vaccine manufacturing partnerships, and biomanufacturing training hubs in Asia—played a critical role in addressing governance gaps at the global level. The chapter concludes that glocal health governance provides a more realistic and flexible framework for understanding pandemic response and for building more resilient health governance systems in an increasingly unstable world.

6.1 Introduction

It has been six years since the world encountered the SARS-CoV-2 virus and its variants. Thanks to the innovation that featured the fast development of a vaccine and prompt vaccination on the global scale, millions of people were lucky to survive the first ever pandemic in the twentieth-first century. Nonetheless, from the perspective of health governance, we believe that this is the right time for assessment. In this chapter, we aim to reveal the lessons of the coronavirus disease 19 (COVID-19) in terms of a dynamic, nuanced framework in which diverse actors work together to address global health challenges.

Among the numerous publications focusing on COVID-19 and its social impact, two are relevant to this chapter. The first is by physician and historian of medicine Jacalyn Duffin (Duffin, 2022). In *Covid-19: A History,* Duffin craftily shows how the public comprehended this pandemic—from a local issue to the global one, from pinning down the pathogen and finding treatments to the development of vaccines, and from how individual misfortunes are presented as collective phenomena of global health to how vaccines became both a sought-after resource and a target of international politics. As a historian, Duffin does not make decisive suggestions to prepare for the next pandemic; however, she rightly points out that epidemics

> always follow a series of stages, a dramaturgic form ... A new infectious disease begins with fear, panic, blaming, and scapegoating, often driven by xenophobia. It moves on to acceptance and hard work of management. It closes with resolution, new knowledge, and, alas, eventual forgetting. The new knowledge is what shapes the public-health barriers of the after time—barriers that will break with the next new challenge, and the cycle begins again Duffin (2022, p. 202).

Guided by the wider concept of global health security, in his book *Global Health Security: A Blueprint for the Future,* Lawrence O. Gostin reviews the lessons learned from infectious pandemics, pointing out that weak governance and ineffective health systems are key sources of risk. Like Duffin, Gostin reminds readers what would happen in the wake of the COVID-19 Pandemic:

> That new habits of personal hygiene will wane. Chronic health inequalities can continue as before. In other words, returning to normal means that we can prepare for the next pandemic in the future. Perhaps we will act surprised again when the next biological threat strikes. It seems unlikely that we will take that path, but it is possible (Gostin, 2021, p. 216).

Having written that, he nevertheless proposes some solutions, such as robust international institutions, research programs targeting global health, and resilient societies.

Benefiting from the above narratives, this chapter focuses on organizational infrastructure in response to the COVID-19 Pandemic. It examines institutional changes in health governance during the pandemic, aiming to draw upon their policy implications, which we call organizational innovations. David Fidler defines global health governance as "the use of formal and informal institutions, rules, and processes by states, intergovernmental organizations, and non-state actors to deal with challenges to health that require cross-border collective action to address effectively." Youde offers an overview of organizational actors, such as the WHO, World Bank, UNAIDS, Global Fund, and private foundations—notably the William

J. Clinton Foundation and Bill and Melinda Gates Foundation—and civil society organizations (Youde, 2012). Youde also identifies three key issues: the surveillance of global infectious diseases, framing of health security, and access to pharmaceuticals. As in the case of the COVID-19 Pandemic, when these issues occur together in various governing contexts and in a rather unexpected order and pace, how can these organizations respond to them and what are their actions?

Let us briefly review the recent organizational changes in health governance. In July 2000, the UN Security Council first addressed the global impact of HIV/AIDS. The terrorist attacks and SARS that followed sparked concerns about the impact of the threat of biological and bacteriological weapon terrorism and the spread of new infectious diseases. Several public-private partnerships (PPPs) were created on specific issues, such as eradicating HIV/AIDS, developing new drugs and vaccines, and expanding access to treatment. Moreover, an increasing number of engagements in recent years have aimed to improve health systems through foreign affairs ministries, foreign aid, and development agencies in individual countries. In many cases, this has been accompanied by an expansion of the country's political influence or purpose.

To understand these trends, the analytical focus is placed on the state. As political scientist Michael R. Reich depicts, modern states at the turn of this century were simultaneously reshaped by multiple forces (Reich, 2002). They were influenced by international agencies through multinational corporations, from within by the increasing marketization and corruption problems, and from below by nongovernmental organizations. Reconceptualizing the state in global health, Reich investigates the shaping processes these organizations were bringing, pointing out "the discontinuity between the relatively stable boundaries of states and the ever-shifting boundaries of problems." (Reich, 2002, p. 1673).

Meanwhile, an increasing number of scholars have addressed the history and development of the WHO. Among the studies on the pollution characteristics of the WHO and its operating challenges in the first half of the century (Chorev, 2012; Packard, 2016; Cueto et al., 2019). *Global Health for All: Knowledge, Politics, and Practices* presents a constructive approach to setting this aging organization free from taking unrealistic responsibilities in global health (Gaudillière et al., 2022). Arguing against a narrative that casts the WHO as an institution to realize health universalism, the authors of this book provide an infrastructural analysis of how it manages—financially, politically, and technically—to address real public health tasks in the changing world. Knowing that the WHO is both "inadequate and indispensable" (Gaudillière et al., 2022, p. 195), the insight they offer is of "provincializing the WHO." It is also in this light that they make their preliminary comments on the COVID-19 Pandemic as a reminder to "highlight the necessity of a reconceived international and decidedly more social an ecological approach to health" (Gaudillière et al., 2022, p. 201). As indicated by the authors, this new framework requires more flexible and responsive institutions.

To follow these organizational trends with a reflection about the meaning and limit of global health, our take in this chapter is an analysis of the innovations of health governance in the COVID-19 Pandemic, which is aptly called "glocal health governance." The meaning of glocal health governance is twofold. First, from an organizational viewpoint, we find nuances that move beyond "horizontal" and "vertical" programs—the metaphor Michael Reich uses for thinking about the forces in pushing large scale public health (Reich, 2002). Specifically, we focus on the strengthening of regional networks and international connections triggered by the spread of the disease. The second, and more important, meaning of global health governance is organizational dynamics. As shown in this chapter, various policy efforts have been made in terms of health governance, such as revising the International Health Regulations (IHR), along with policies to strengthen existing organizations or frames for disease control. Therefore, we hope to provide a preliminary assessment of these organizational innovations. As geopolitical turmoil increases, what direction will health governance take in the future?

The main body of this chapter, inspired by the notion of Gostin, is a "tabletop exercise" on governance during the COVID-19 Pandemic (Gostin, 2021). It generally follows the three stages of Yves Tiberghien's analytical frame (Tiberghien, 2022): the outbreak of COVID-19 and initial policy reactions (stage one), the development and distribution of COVID-19 vaccines (stage two), and institutional prospects for future pandemics (stage three). Looking from hindsight, this analytical frame shows the ways in which the three-year-long COVID-19 Pandemic should be conceived. Echoing the issues concerning the access to medicine, which is addressed in Chaps. 5 and 11, this chapter highlights the innovative dynamics in terms of health governance: the interactions between the global and the regional, and between public health and geopolitics. As previously mentioned, COVID-19 is not the first global threat of an infectious disease, and the concept of health governance is not new. Nonetheless, in terms of health policy on a global scale, a close examination of the public health infrastructure at each stage of the COVID-19 Pandemic is necessary. The transformations in global health governance discussed in this chapter can be seen as part of a response to the broader crisis of contemporary innovation systems and capitalist regulation, the main theme of this book.

6.2 From Local Issues to Global Threats: Initial Responses to COVID-19 and Organizational Innovations

This section deals with the outbreaks of COVID-19, some governing policies and actions taken before it, and the changing conception of this infectious disease from local issues to global threat as the WHO declared on March 11. At first glance, the "default" scenario of health governance seemed to be similar to those of infectious diseases in the past, which featured several local outbreaks, on-site investigation, and subsequent alerts and measures on the potential to and consequences of developing into a pandemic. In such scenarios, the WHO was undoubtedly the major actor; however, as criticized, it had grown too old and lost its energy in leading coordination among actors in global health governance.

This situation was reflected in the WHO's initial reactions to the COVID-19 outbreak, which had quietly been spreading in the People's Republic of China (hereafter PRC, China) since the last months of 2019. Although the first official notice reporting cases of "viral pneumonia" detected by the Wuhan Municipal Health Commission was released on the website of its PRC country office as early as the end of 2019, in the following months, the WHO did not take aggressive measures of evaluation, treating it as a local epidemic event.

In hindsight, the reference of governance at this stage was SARS, a viral respiratory disease that spread to some parts of the world in 2003. After receiving a notification from Wuhan, the WHO published a package of guidance documents for countries in January. On 22nd and 23rd January 2020, the WHO Director-General convened the IHR Emergency Committee (EC) to examine whether the outbreak constituted a public health emergency of international concern (PHEIC). However, no conclusions were drawn until January 30, when the EC recognized the coronavirus outbreak to be a PHEIC. This was done after the WHO Director-General visited the PRC and met President Xi Jinping to collaborate on containment measures and overall responses. By that time, four countries outside China (Germany, Japan, the United States, and Vietnam) had evidence of human-to-human transmission.

In addition to the opaque information about this "pneumonia with unknown cause," geopolitics played a critical role in the WHO's delayed declaration. In fact, at the first EC meeting, the PRC opposed the declaration of a state of emergency, while some criticized the WHO's hesitation by citing IHR regulations.[1] As in the SARS epidemic, in the months that followed, the WHO issued various recommendations regarding travel restrictions and public health measures, such as wearing masks, most of which were unfortunately not followed; advice was provided but seldom put into action. As the virus quickly spread, the WHO lost its credibility as the gatekeeper of global health. A petition campaign calling for the dismissal of its Director-General was launched on the Internet, along with harsh attacks from President Donald J. Trump of the United States (US), another world leader.

While the WHO adjusted its pace to deal with the challenges brought by COVID-19, regional networks and individual states implemented anti-pandemic measures, deviating from the "default" scenario of health governance. Historically, the WHO has been divided into six regional offices, each of which retains, to some extent, policy autonomy within its territory. Bureaucratically speaking, as subordinate organizations of the WHO, these regional offices facilitate information sharing and mutual assistance with neighboring countries as well as cooperation among concerned countries, and they provide a platform for jointly addressing regional challenges. Nonetheless, the independence of each regional secretariat has increased dramatically in recent years (Cueto et al., 2019). In response to the outbreak of COVID-19, actions were taken in some regions.

As early as 16th January 2020, the Pan American Health Organization (PAHO) Regional Office for the Americas (AMRO) issued its first epidemiological alert on the novel coronavirus, followed by PAHO's urge to prepare to detect, isolate, and care for infected patients. On 25th January 2020, the WHO Regional Director for Europe issued a public statement outlining the importance of readiness to fight outbreaks at the

[1] A PHEIC is considered if at least two of the following four conditions are met: (1) it has a serious public health impact; (2) is an unusual or unexpected event; (3) has a significant risk of international spread; and (4) carries a significant risk of travel or trade restrictions. According to the Independent Panel for Pandemic Preparedness and Response (PPPR), which submitted its report in 2021, the outbreak in Wuhan was likely to have met the criteria to be declared a PHEIC by the first meeting of the Emergency Committee in January 2020. The PPPR concluded that the alert system did not operate at sufficient speed when faced with a fast-moving respiratory pathogen.

local and national levels. Within a week, the WHO Regional Directors for South-East Asia and Africa issued anti-epidemic statements. Although none of the regional bureaus has strong authority over member countries, they have attempted to improve their response capabilities within the region and contain as much damage to it as possible.

The actions of individual states were notable during the early stages of the pandemic. Until 20th January 2020, many countries were trying to determine whether this infectious disease could spread beyond China, as had been the case with SARS in 2003. However, when public transportation in Wuhan stopped on 23rd January 2020, countries began evacuating their people despite the WHO's recommendation that travel restrictions were not necessary. An extreme case was Taiwan (Republic of China), which has not been a WHO member state since 1972. The disease outbreak created a difficult situation for its Ministry of Health and Welfare (MHW) due to Taiwan's close business relationship with the PRC and to having been the epicenter of SARS and this time of COVID-19. As soon as the WHO released its first notice on 31st December 2019, Taiwan implemented a border control procedure for flights from Wuhan on 7th January and conducted an on-site investigation on 12th January 2020. Reporting its findings via IHR on 21st January, Taiwan did not follow the WHO's recommendations and went ahead to announce a travel warning for Wuhan and prohibited PRC citizens from entering. Tourism between Taiwan and the PRC was forced to cease on 25th January, a week earlier than the WHO's declaration.

However, this does not mean that Taiwan was wiser than the WHO or that it had better information to make such decisions. At the domestic level, serious policy disputes arose over travel restrictions and quarantine measures. One of the concerns in pushing the timing of decision-making was the Lunar New Year holidays, which started around late January that year. Aware that over one million Taiwanese people might return from China then, the MHW could not make ambiguous policies. As a historian of global health, Wayne Soon points out that Taiwan's anti-COVID response had to be a reflection of the historical context in which it had learned, on the one hand, how to access the health information needed after losing its seat at the WHO, and on the other hand, how to interpret the WHO's advice that usually overlooked political specificities—in Taiwan's case, those with the PRC (Soon, 2020). Taiwan's success, in this sense, could be understood as how the "locals," such as regions and individual states, had to take actions to prevent the

COVID-19 when the WHO failed to provide adequate evaluation and advice for its member states.

A larger problem for the WHO, in its encounter of COVID-19, was the emergent need for further reforms in health governance. One regulatory framework, as we have discussed in this section, was the IHR, a legally binding agreement in 2005 to build the capability to detect and report potential public health emergencies worldwide. Although the IHR did function during the H1N1, MERS, and Ebola outbreaks, the COVID-19 revealed the complexity of the responses of different specialized areas to infectious diseases, not to mention the consideration of "one health" that took into account the health of humans, animals, and the environment as one. Knowing the problems it had had in terms of health governance, in November 2021, the WHO agreed to formulate a pandemic convention and revise the IHR. Nevertheless, it would inevitably step onto international politics—a boundary that the WHO hesitated to cross.

However, political concerns complicated this discussion. For example, the European Union (EU) originally proposed a new pandemic treaty, while China and Russia showed the same interest in proposing their own versions. Even after Ukraine's invasion in February 2022, Russia proposed amendments to the IHR at the World Health Assembly. The PRC also had its own agenda that hindered global cooperation; as noted, "[t]he great test for the international community will be to judge when to compete and when to cooperate: preventing the next pandemic means confronting and correcting old prejudices while better integrating China into the global health landscape"(Horton, 2023).

The following section shows that, upon their availability, vaccines as a critical resource for health governance intensified the tensions between the global and local in terms of their production and distribution. Health diplomacy refers to this.

6.3 Health Diplomacy and Governance: Policy Landscape of COVID-19 Vaccines

Following the outbreak of COVID-19 and its global spread, as well as the initial response by the WHO and regional networks, this section focuses on the geopolitical dynamics shaping the policy landscape of COVID-19 governance that featured vaccines, particularly their distribution.

We have discussed the "default" scenario concerning COVID-19 outbreak, in which the PRC pressured the WHO to delay the declaration of a health emergency by defining this disease a local problem. As COVID-19 was widely recognized as a global threat, the confrontation between the US and China intensified, and its spreading implications not only affected the WHO's response to COVID-19 but also the distribution of vaccines.

Let us consider the politics of naming first. In his introduction to *Framing Disease: Studies in Cultural History* (1992), Charles Rosenberg sets that the processional phases of the public's reaction to disease start with naming, which can be also applied to the case of COVID-19 (Rosenberg, 1992). The WHO carefully gave the pathogen that caused this outbreak the name "severe acute respiratory syndrome 2" (or "SARS-CoV-2") on 12th February 2020, stating that this official naming would not be attached with any specific people, places, or animals—a policy that had been in place since 2015. Nevertheless, disputes arose, in particular between the US and China, over how to properly call this pandemic to set sound prevention policies.

Taking an anti-PRC standpoint, the then US President Donald Trump provocatively called the coronavirus "the Chinese virus" at a news briefing on 18th March 2020, sparking China's anger, which used to use "Wuhan virus" to indicate its locality before an official name was settled (Ullah & Ferdous, 2022, Chap. 3). Although Trump explained that the naming had nothing to do with politics but indicated that "the disease comes from China," this stance should be considered a political action with two immediate policy implications. First, by risking domestic criticism of racism and anti-Asian sentiment in the US presidential campaign, Trump redefined the COVID-19 Pandemic as an issue of global politics and accused the PRC of being responsible for it. Second, unlike the WHO's ambiguous attitude that COVID-19 was a local problem and could be under control, Trump intentionally made it a signal favoring his geopolitical view that cast China as the major threat to the US.

The naming of the COVID-19 Pandemic, in this sense, became an indicator of the polarization of global politics. On the one hand, China changed the Chinese name of COVID-19 into "*Shin Guan Fei Yen*" ("pneumonia caused by novel coronavirus") to obey the WHO's naming policy; on the other hand, it avoided using "Wuhan pneumonia" in international occasions that used Mandarin. Meanwhile, by using "Wuhan virus" or "China virus," the US became increasingly critical of the WHO. In April 2020, Trump openly criticized the WHO for being too "China-centric" and stated that he would suspend US funding to it. In early July, the Trump administration formally notified the UN of its withdrawal from the WHO, a violent political gesture showing distrust toward this organization (Cohen et al., 2020). The PRC, in response, commented that "some figures insisted on politicizing the outbreak and defaming the World Health Organization," implicitly referring to the US (Kabakci, 2020). In the following months, states took sides in the US–China conflict over health governance. The confrontation between North Korea, Iran, and Western countries was also reflected in their response to COVID-19 (Ullah & Ferdous, 2022).

The subsequent phase was what Charles Rosenberg would call the phase of "negotiating disease"(Rosenberg, 1992). The divided nature of global politics, as seen in the development and distribution of COVID-19 vaccines, had an impact on international organizations and multilateral cooperation. The pharmaceutical industry declared that it would be achieved at an astonishing rate within a year; however, geopolitical conflicts cast a significant shadow over the production and distribution of these vaccines.

COVAX, launched in April 2020, was an attempt of extraordinary and unique global collaboration. Led by Gavi, the Vaccine Alliance, the Coalition for Epidemic Preparedness Innovations (CEPI), UNICEF, and the WHO, COVAX was part of the global initiative Access to COVID-19 Tools (ACT) Accelerator, an ambitious effort to accelerate the development and manufacture of vaccines and guarantee fair and equitable access for every country in the world (GAVI, 2022). ACT linked the most profit-driven pharmaceutical sector with the politically driven entity of governments, and COVAX was its technical platform on which the research, development, and manufacturing of a wide range of COVID-19 vaccine candidates would be supported and their pricing negotiated.

The WHO participated in COVAX, providing guidance on vaccine policy, regulations, safety, research and development (R&D), allocation, and country readiness and delivery. One of the early efforts of COVAX was to facilitate vaccine R&D. Over a two-year period starting in 2020, CEPI has spent almost $2 billion in mostly public funding to support more than a dozen promising COVID-19 vaccine candidates (Usher, 2022). COVAX was also involved in fixing disparities in vaccine access, aiming to supply one billion doses of vaccines via advance market commitment (AMC) by September 2021 and another two billion doses by mid-2022.

Although with good intentions, the operation was significantly behind schedule. While COVAX supplied one billion doses of vaccines to 144 countries by the end of 2021 (GAVI, 2022), the delay had a political impact on some states. More importantly, although the delay had to do with institutional issues, such as negotiating major developers of vaccines and streamlining efforts, different democracies had different concerns in deviating the WHO's advice.

In such an uncertain situation, health diplomacy emerged in line with geopolitics. It took shape as soon as Russia produced its own COVID-19 vaccine "Sputnik V" in August 2020, followed by the PRC's "Sinopharm BBIBP" in December that year. Even before Sinopharm-BBIBP was granted Emergency Use Authorization (EUA), Chinese Premier Li Keqiang had pledged in August 2020 to prioritize supplying Chinese vaccines to five Southeast Asian countries as a gesture of friendship to its neighboring states (South China Morning Post, 2020). By this time, China had prioritized supplies to Brazil, Indonesia, and the Philippines (Wall Street Journal, 2020).

Before the COVID-19 vaccines, anti-pandemic tools such as surgical masks were exchanged as gifts between states that were less affected by the outbreak and those that had been damaged by it. Nonetheless, vaccines had a higher scarcity value than masks and could function as a diplomatic tool; the supply lag of vaccines from global institutions such as COVAX created vacuums for political maneuvers, which ran on a bilateral basis or through a framework of like-minded countries. For example, the PRC's gift to southeast countries, as *The Wall Street Journal* commented, was not free; it was used to gain support for actions in the South China Sea in exchange for supply (Wall Street Journal, 2020).

At the end of 2020, less than a year after the pandemic was declared, vaccines were on their way. As of February 2021, there were 289 COVID-19 vaccines in development, of which 66 were in clinical trials, of which 20 were in the final stage of clinical trials (Ahmed et al., 2021). Even so, the gap in global vaccine supply widened, as seen in mid-2021, when major pharmaceutical companies such as Pfizer-Biotech, AstraZeneca, and Moderna successfully developed their products. While over 20 COVID-19 vaccines were granted EUA by the regulatory authorities of the states in which they were intended to sell, only six of them were included in the WHO's Emergency Use

Listing (EUL). The dilemma between accessing vaccines in a timely fashion and jeopardizing people's lives with insufficiently regulated products complicated the policy landscape of COVID-19 governance. For example, in June 2021, after signing an agreement with the PRC on local manufacturing of Sinovac vaccines, Egypt stated at the UN Human Rights Council that "Hong Kong, Xinjiang Uyghur, and Tibet issues are China's internal affairs and should not be interfered with by other countries" (South China Morning Post, 2021). In fact, on the PRC's map of health diplomacy, vaccines were distributed to middle-income countries in Asia and Central and South America. In addition to Egypt, China also cooperated in the local production of vaccines in Morocco and Indonesia.

In the US, the prospect of vaccination was clear only around April 2021. Through donations to COVAX, India, Japan, the United States, and Australia also added vaccine diplomacy to their joint diplomatic and security policy framework "Quad," stating that they had been "working on expanding support for vaccine donation, vaccine manufacturing capacity, and cold chain support." These strategic considerations were conspicuous in such vaccine diplomacy. Notably, in June 2021, when Taiwan was eventually overtaken by COVID-19 and suffered from the shortage of vaccines allocated by COVAX, Japan and the US spared their vaccines and shipped them to Taiwan to back up its anti-PRC government.

Due to geopolitics, the distribution of vaccines in response to the COVID-19 Pandemic was uneven. In Europe, more than 34 million vaccine doses were administered by March 2021, less than a year after the pandemic began, and the number increased rapidly to 840 million shots per year. However, as in previous pandemics, vaccine supply remained a serious problem for some areas that required help. According to the US Council on Foreign Relations (Council on Foreign Relations, 2021), at the end of 2021, the vaccine diplomacy exercised by the US, Europe, China, Japan, and Australia went to the Asia-Pacific region, where the US and China confronted each other with diplomatic means. However, sub-Saharan Africa, which had the lowest vaccination rate in the world and needed vaccines the most, failed to gain adequate support.

Facing the reality of geopolitics, the WHO could not escape the criticism that was summarized in an independent investigative report released in May 2021. Some suggestions for short-term reforms included actions to accelerate the operation of COVAX and the quick transfer of vaccine manufacturing technology and licensed production via the WHO; nevertheless, recommendations for long-term issues, that is, a clear vision and roadmap for pandemic governance, were more important (Independent Panel for Pandemic Preparedness and Response, 2021).[2]

Complementing this report, we offer a view of the WHO and COVAX performances in terms of health governance. Considering the policies of COVID-19 vaccines, we found that they had a positive start in the production of certified vaccines. In contrast to regular practices that took more than 10 years to develop new vaccine products, the development of COVID-19 vaccines proceeded swiftly. The forces pushing this success, in addition to the extraordinary investment by the US and Germany, were the regulatory authorities, which gave approval to these products under the EUA scheme and made them available in the markets. Further regulatory innovations, such as the use of real-world evidence, were introduced in September 2021 to facilitate faster vaccine development.

Nonetheless, vaccine regulations constituted the policy bottleneck in the case of COVID-19 vaccine distribution. On the one hand, the emergence of variants complicated the regulatory process; on the other hand, disputes arose over the protective power of multiple shots and whether reliable herd immunity could be achieved with them. For example, as of October 2022, developed countries were administering the third and fourth booster doses, whereas some developing countries

[2] The recommendations include the followings: first, to launch a global health threats council, formulate a pandemic treaty, and discuss pandemic preparedness and response politically at an UN-sponsored summit. Second, to establish a financially and administratively independent WHO, which, in turn, should strengthen its discipline, especially its guidance function for strengthening preparedness. Third, to enhance preparedness of pandemic governance at the global, national, and regional levels. The WHO should institutionalize a system of mutual evaluation of preparedness among countries on a regular basis. Fourth, to call for a more responsive surveillance and alert system which should be empowered to release urgent information that could lead to a pandemic without the consent of member states, and conduct investigations into pandemic-prone pathogens in all countries. Fifth, to facilitate a framework on the discussion of financial and manufacturing sources for pandemic preparedness and response. Although COVAX was considered a leap for the WHO, it also demonstrated the fact that there was hardly any coordinated action centered on this aging organization.

had barely made progress in administering even the first dose (NIKKEI ASIA, 2022).[3] This was partly the result of "vaccine nationalism," where each country secured and administered COVID-19 vaccines to its people with the highest priority. As argued, this distorted landscape of vaccines nurtured channels for diplomatic action using vaccines that were either on the EUL or not yet endorsed by COVAX.

Health diplomacy, in this sense, placed a global institution such as COVAX in a difficult position. Although the WHO made reforms to increase its capacity in coping with the health emergency, it did not and could not please all. As revealed below, political entities, regions and individual states were embarking on new endeavors to fight COVID-19. Working along the fragile lines of geopolitics, they chose to cooperate diplomatically with the states they trusted, and organizational innovations were made apparent as a way of seeking survival during the pandemic.

6.4 Toward Glocal Health Governance? Stabilizing COVID-19 Policies

We take a closer look at the dynamics between the global/WHO and the local/regional after fall 2021, focusing on the stabilizing policies, that is, to resume international travels to some extent by lowering quarantine requirements. While the WHO was on the way to organizational reforms, attempts were made to strengthen regional response capabilities to improve health governance.

Let us first consider the WHO's legal reform. One pillar of such effort was the revision of the IHR and the adoption of the new Pandemic Agreement. The third edition of the IHR, released in 2005, included considerations of regional efforts in stipulating public health emergency response. Article 57(3), for example, established relationships with other international agreements, stating, "Without prejudice to their obligations under these Regulations, States Parties that are members of a regional economic integration organization shall apply in their mutual relationship

[3] Reportedly, the percentage of people who had received the required dose was 78.8% in France, 76.3% in Germany, and 80.4% in Japan, and the number of booster doses per 100 population was 95.2 in Belgium, 79.5 in South Korea, and 74.5 in Italy. On the other hand, in developing countries, as of October 2022, the number of people vaccinated with at least one dose was 3.2% in Haiti, 6.1% in Cameroon, and 17.9% in Algeria, and the number of booster doses per 100 people was 1.5 in Jamaica and 0.2 in Cameroon.

the common rules in force in that regional economic integration organization." In other words, global and regional agreements complemented each other. Article 44 also stated, "Collaboration under this Article may be implemented through multiple channels, including bilaterally, through regional networks and the WHO regional offices, and through intergovernmental organizations and international bodies" (IHR, 2005).

> As for the Pandemic Agreement, which was adopted in May 2025, it boldly recognized that the international spread of disease is a global threat with serious consequences for lives, livelihoods, societies and economies that calls for the widest possible international and regional collaboration, cooperation and solidarity with all people and countries, especially developing countries, and notably least developed countries and small island developing States, in order to ensure an effective, coordinated, appropriate, comprehensive and equitable international response, while reaffirming the principle of the sovereignty of States in addressing public health matters, (Preface) (WHO, 2025)

Meanwhile, efforts were made to eliminate regional and national disparities through international cooperation.

The remainder of this section discusses the efforts in Europe, Africa, and Asia. With respect to the individuality of epidemics depending on the region, such as climate characteristics and the state of the sanitation system, we argue that because infectious diseases can spread easily through the movement of people and goods from countries that are physically close to each other, regional cooperation has historically developed ahead of the global level.

The first is Europe, where the WHO European Regional Office is located. Since Russia's invasion of Ukraine, it has become difficult for the regional secretariat to respond effectively to infectious diseases. In 2023, following the criticism against Russia at the regional secretariat meeting in 2022, a majority voted in favor of moving the WHO's office on non-communicable diseases, currently in Moscow, outside of Russia (Politico, 2023). This was followed by a debate at the World Health Assembly, where Russia was criticized for its invasion and the impact on public health and replied that "This is not the Security Council in New York." Deep geopolitical divisions have cast a shadow over international health cooperation, and the regional departments for Europe cannot escape from it.

Under such circumstances, progress is being promoted by states cooperation rather than by the WHO Regional Office. In the fall of 2020, the EU agreed to establish the European Health Union, a new institution that aimed to strengthen local preparedness and response to public health crises by monitoring the supply of medicines and medical devices in the region, coordinating information and research on vaccine clinical trials, developing a surveillance system at the EU level, and sharing data on hospital bed occupancy rates and the number of medical workers within member countries (European Commission, 2020). The core of the European Health Union came from the rebuilding of existing frameworks for serious cross-border health crises, the upgrading of selected EU institutions in response to crises—in particular, the European Center for Preventive Control (ECDC) and the European Medicines Agency (EMA)—and the establishment of new EU authorities for emergency response.

Despite its good intentions, whether this organizational innovation succeeded remains unclear (De Rujiter, 2020). The main anti-COVID efforts were made by individual states instead of regional responses, which were significantly delayed. Furthermore, member states reached no consensus on the type of COVID-19 vaccine to be used. Hungary, for example, was the first EU country to approve a Chinese vaccine in early 2021, while many member states used Western-made mRNA vaccines (Politico, 2021), and it was further agreed to produce the Sinopharm vaccine in Hungary. Member states did not undertake joint actions on travel restrictions, among other matters. When the US, Japan, and neighboring countries strengthened their border control measures as the PRC finally ended its COVID-zero policy at the end of 2022, some EU states were urged to make their own decisions. Only countries such as Spain and Italy took strict border measures against China.

Meanwhile, regional health cooperation went along with such efforts at the global level. The WHO Lyon Office, for example, was jointly established with the French government and functioned as part of the WHO Health Emergencies Programme (Takuma, 2020). During the pandemic, this office contributed to regional and global cooperation by providing an interlaboratory collaboration platform and working with the ACT-A. France and WHO are also establishing the WHO Academy in Lyon, which will be a WHO hub providing training on pandemics and in collaboration with local digital affiliates.

The COVID-19 Pandemic reaffirmed the importance of Africa, known for its fragile public health, in regional cooperation and as a venue for organizational innovations. The African CDC, launched in 2017, has taken the lead in surveillance, testing, and procurement of necessary supplies. Specific departments were also established. For example, the Africa Medical Supplies Platform was established in 2020 as a regional framework for the procurement of medicines and medical supplies within the continent in response to COVID-19. A partnership between regional organizations such as the African Union (AU), the African CDC, and the United Nations Economic Commission for Africa (ECA) was established (The Africa Report, 2021). This platform played a major role in the procurement of medical supplies from outside Africa.

As part of Africa's COVID-19 vaccination strategy, in August 2020, the AU established The African Vaccine Acquisition Task (AVAT) for effective vaccine distribution and uptake in the region, with the aim of vaccinating at least 60% of the African population. It acted as a central purchasing agent on behalf of AU member states and formed partnerships with the African CDC, African Export-Import Bank, ECA, and others to move toward its goals (Afreximbank, 2022). It did not mean, however, that the procurement of sufficient vaccines for Africa would be easy. When Europe and the United States reached a vaccination rate of 50% of the population by the end of 2021, Africa had reached 11%, and it would take another 18 months to reach 45.6% by February 2023 (Chirinda & Machingaidze, 2023).

One of the problems for such a task was the public health infrastructure, such as the lack of locally produced vaccines. Africa's strategy was organizational. In April 2021, the AU and the African CDC established Partnerships for African Vaccine Manufacturing (PAVM) to reduce the vaccine import rate by increasing local production capacity (Reuters, 2021). At the end of 2021, the treaty for the establishment of the African Medicines Agency (AMA) came into effect to improve the regulatory environment for medicines on the continent (Sidibé et al., 2023). However, during the pandemic, the perception was of a global vaccine supply shortage in Africa, and more frustratingly, the global distributor COVAX could not provide the necessary vaccines in a timely fashion (Cullinan, 2021).

Regional cooperation in Africa also met the limitations of connecting at the global level. On the one hand, the WHO set up a WHO mRNA vaccine technology transfer hub in South Africa in November 2021;

on the other hand, South Africa's Afrigen challenged to develop its own mRNA COVID vaccines, one of the most difficult to produce and to distribute, using only publicly available information (Nature, 2022). Pharmaceutical companies would also increase their involvement in Africa (BioNTech, 2023),[4] and a new WHO mRNA vaccine hub would be established in Cape Town in April 2023 (Reuters, 2023).

Having a history of regional cooperation even before the birth of the WHO (Takuma, 2023), Asia presented different characteristics in terms of organizational innovations during the COVID-19 Pandemic. Despite the regional office of West-Pacific being in place, no specific cooperation framework on public health was established, which allowed for geopolitical interventions. For example, Japan, China, and South Korea have held health ministers' meetings every year since 2007 except 2012, when tensions rose between Japan and China over the dispute over the Senkaku/Diaoyutai Islands. In May 2020, a special meeting of the Japan-China-Korea Health Ministers' Meeting was held to deal with COVID-19. However, no further progress was made on cooperation as distrust of China's response grew and Japan–Korea relations became strained due to trade issues, among others.

The dynamics among East Asian states can also be observed in their regional strategies. In 2020, ASEAN (the Association of Southeast Asian Nations) leaders announced to establish the ASEAN Centre for Public Health Emergencies and Emerging Diseases (ACPHEED) to strengthen ASEAN's preparedness and response capabilities to emerging infectious diseases. With Japan's deep involvement since its establishment, ACPHEED can be read as a crucial step, via infectious disease control, toward regional health security; in addition, from a geopolitical perspective, this center may become a base for cooperation that favors Japan's strategic plan in this region, such as conducting clinical trials for Japan-made pharmaceuticals.[5]

[4] Reportedly, since June 2022, BioNTech has established an mRNA vaccine manufacturing plant in Rwanda, aiming to start operation by 2024 and contribute to job creation.

[5] For example, in 2021, Japan's National Center for Global Health and Medicine (On April 1 2025, NCGM merged with the National Institute of Infectious Diseases (NIID) to form a new organization named the Japan Institute for Health Security, JIHS) began collaborating with multiple research institutes in Asian countries to launch the ARO Alliance for ASEAN and East Asia (ARISE), a clinical trial platform for the Asian region. ARISE aims to lead clinical research in Asia and the world by conducting international joint clinical trials aiming for pharmaceutical approval. They will work on international

South Korea has its own strategies to promote health governance in Asia. In February 2022, Korea and the WHO established the WHO Biomanufacturing Training Hub, similar to the vaccine technology transfer hub in South Africa, to serve low- and middle-income countries wishing to produce biologics such as vaccines (WHO, 2022). Korean companies, such as SK Bioscience, are said to have been key, and the center has been conducted in close cooperation with these companies. Even with a strong presence of Korea, Bangladesh, Indonesia, Pakistan, Serbia, and Vietnam, among others, have announced their participation. As an organizational innovation, this hub will extend its coverage beyond Asia, welcoming a wide range of middle- and low-income countries (Cullinan, 2022).

As part of the Cold War legacy, cooperation between the US and Asian countries strengthened during the pandemic. The U.S. Department of Health and Human Services established a country office in Vietnam in 1998 and has continued health cooperation with Vietnam ever since. As part of the Global Health Security Agenda (GHSA) launched by the US in 2014, Vietnam's Ministry of Health (MOH) signed a new five-year cooperation agreement to build a stronger foundation for Vietnam to prevent, detect, and respond to disease outbreaks. In November 2022, the two countries reaffirmed their partnerships during the pandemic (US Embassy and Consulate in Vietnam, 2022).

The US has also established connections with East Asian states. In addition to the information channel on epidemics set up with Taiwan during and after SARS, as well as expert exchanges on pharmaceutical regulations with the FDAs of Taiwan and the PRC, the East Asia and Pacific (EAP) regional office of the US CDC was launched in February 2024 in Tokyo (U.S. Embassy and Consulate in Japan, 2024). Even under Trump 2.0, this regional office continues to function as a hub for regional health cooperation between the US and Japan, and between the US and Asia. Cooperation among Quad countries—the US, India, Japan, and Australia—has also shown progress. As part of this foreign and security policy framework, they jointly provided vaccines manufactured in India to Southeast

collaborative clinical trials not only for emerging, re-emerging, and tropical infectious diseases prevalent in Asia, but also for chronic diseases. Japan Institute for Health Security, ARISE (ARO Alliance for ASEAN & East Asia) website (https://arise.jihs.go.jp).

Asian countries, supported the expansion of vaccine manufacturing capacity, and provided cold-chain support (Ministry of Foreign Affairs of Japan, 2022).

In summary, this section described the characteristics of what we term "glocal health governance." Despite the legal innovations pushed by the WHO using a top-down approach, fragmentation of the international community and geopolitical trends have led to a multilayered structure of health governance. The cooperative framework introduced at the global level was normative and sparked responses from regional and individual states for cooperation. In contrast, organizational innovations were initiated within regions, reflecting geopolitics to some extent yet being more realistic. Further, the cooperation within each region could widen the disparities among regions; even worse, closely tied with geopolitics, the colonial past, and the Cold War logic, they could also create tensions among individual states in a region.

6.5 Organizational Innovations Revisited in the Era of COVID-19

The COVID-19 Pandemic, as shown in this chapter, is the latest recurrent pandemic that featured the involvement of multiple species, a fragile global system of health governance, and post-Cold War international relations. While the vision of "Health for All" was presented as an ideal and the reason for cooperation at the global level, current international politics and geopolitical divisions are strongly reflected in the response during a pandemic.

Even so, our task is not to repeat the criticisms on the WHO, its structure, or its leadership, asking to strengthen its function to cope with emergent health threats in the changing world. Neither do we want to criticize the reality of geopolitics, which continues to play out in the attempts to contain and mitigate the impact brought by COVID-19 Pandemic. The nuance we hope to convey in this chapter is the positive side of coping with the pandemic, which can be understood as organizational innovation. From this perspective, we point out innovative initiatives that connect or span multiple levels; these, to some extent, complicate the analytical grid of global health offered by Michael R. Reich, who envisioned this new approach by indicating

> Conflicts are likely to continue to grow between the political boundaries of states and the cross-national nature of today's problems, creating continuing challenges for states and for other international actors (Reich, 2002, p. 1673).

Reich's view was also shared by political scientist Andrew F. Cooper and his colleagues, who remind us that "[t]he central challenge for global public health is not only to add more, but above all to determine in disciplined fashion which ones work under different circumstances to generate the health all deserve" (Cooper et al., 2008, Chap. 1). The initiatives we introduced in this chapter should go beyond simply repeating the approach of partnership. As we argue, these attempts show novelty and potential with concrete results that could solve individual problems, such as improving surveillance or eliminating disparities in vaccine access.

The term "glocal health governance," which refers to the local and the global efforts in response to COVID-19 and to further pandemic threats, was coined to better capture these innovative initiatives. Departing from the WHO definition that simply states a new or improved solution to accelerate positive health impact, we consider health innovation in policy terms, which, as Jeremy Youde put it, is "willingness within the international community to create new types of global health governance organizations to address new problems and concerns" (Youde, 2012). Health innovation is not a novel concept. In the case of COVID-19, we aim to further contextualize these institutional innovations in the analytical scheme of glocal health governance.

To conclude this chapter, we would like to raise three points, connected to other chapters of this book, that the scheme of glocal health governance can offer in making discussions on global health more constructive and realistic. The first is the changing meaning of global health and the strategies to identify and prioritize health tasks. In the introduction to *Global Health and the New World Order*, Gaudillière et al. point to a historical and conceptual shift from international health to global health (Gaudillière et al., 2022). One of the reasons to introduce this shift is to better address the scope of the problems that need to be solved; therefore, the approach to see how the political infrastructure of health governance must be revised. The scheme of glocal health governance, in this light, reflects the discussions of this thread and can be applied in the cases introduced in this book.

The second point has to do with the testability of the glocal health governance scheme. As shown in this chapter, the COVID-19 Pandemic is a "tabletop exercise" in which, according to Lawrence Gostin,

> key actors will gain a deeper understanding of the most pressing health threats (Gostin, 2021). They will learn about the twists and turns requiring advance preparation. They will understand the art of global health diplomacy and working as a team (Gostin, 2021, pp. 227–28).

Thus, we adopt Yves Tiberghien's analytical frame of staging to make the COVID-19 Pandemic a scenario to test the glocal health governance scheme as the disease gradually unfolds. In addition, we follow the evolution of health governance conducted by various actors, which their actions or capacities might have led.

One thing that we do not mention in this chapter but that is critical in testing glocal health governance scheme is the "back to normal" policy as the pandemic (Omicron variant, among other less fatal COVID-19-related threats) has gradually blended with seasonal flu governance. We have discussed the policy differences in Asia that can be clustered into more fractious politics in some countries (Korea, Australia, and partially Taiwan over vaccines, also discussed in this book) and less in others with reassertion of the state (Japan, Vietnam, and Singapore), highlighting the unique case of the PRC. Similarly, for individual states, the timing to further lower quarantine bars to resume international travel and to remove overly strict custom requirements for people generate policy concerns. While our argument aligns with that of Yves Tiberghien in addressing the long-term impact of the COVID-19 Pandemic, we also indicate factors from the perspective of glocal health governance. Against the general background of global political economy, each state chose a different timing to open its door to selected people for various reasons. Again, the WHO failed to give clear advice, but upon their domestic anti-pandemic situations (such as the vaccination coverage rate populations in residence) and geopolitical relations regions (notably EU and Latin America), states made their own policy decisions. We believe that the glocal health governance scheme can better accommodate these factors and non-public health-related occasions during the pandemic, such as the war between Russia and Ukraine that erupted in 2022 and the tensions in Palestine–Israel relations, as well as the cases of other politically fragile and sensitive areas in the world.

The third and final point is clarification. While introducing a holistic approach to health governance, we do not intend to overlook the WHO's leading role or downplay global initiatives. In this chapter, we discuss organizational innovations made as part of the WHO's anti-pandemic strategies, such as COVAX, the Global Training Hub for Biomanufacturing, the WHO Academy, and the WHO Hub for Pandemic and Epidemic Intelligence. The COVID-19 Pandemic also triggered legal and regulatory innovations, such as the revision of the IHR or the creation of the Pandemic Agreement. The analytical problem in global health governance is the pace and agenda of such reforms. Madhavan and Gaudillière argue the significance in incorporating traditional medicine into the anti-pandemic repertory; nonetheless, while the WHO has created strategies for the use of traditional medicines, it has not assigned any active positions in its reform to deal with future pandemics (Madhavan & Gaudilliere, 2026).

Glocal health governance, in this sense, could be a better frame. Not only does it "provincialize" the global, but it also creates a vision of future global health that is flexible, multicentered, and diverse. It is also a scheme in which these organizational innovations in public health can be properly placed and geopolitical dynamics well situated. Echoing John Law's proactive notion to consider the world as small and non-coherent (Law, 2004), we may be free from mainstream questions on global health ourselves and start asking the following questions: how can regional and national government-led initiatives overcome geopolitical dynamics? How can China and North Korea be incorporated into initiatives led by Japan and South Korea?

By increasing the complexity and diversity of the anti-pandemic repertoire, we believe that the glocal health governance scheme will lead to realistic, innovative solutions. As Michael Reich rightly states, "Complex social problems usually demand complex solutions—along with analytical tools that can explore how single solutions and packages of multi-solutions might be adopted and implemented in network environments"(Reich, 2002, p. 1674). With a more appropriate frame and perspective, the answer to whether we can make health governance more resilient depends on our innovation and political leadership.

References

Afreximbank. (2022). AVAT establishes a no-fault compensation scheme to support widespread COVID-19 vaccine delivery. https://www.afreximbank.com/avat-establishes-a-no-fault-compensation-scheme-to-support-widespread-covid-19-vaccine-delivery/

Ahmed, S., Khan, S., Imran, I., Al Mughairbi, F., Sheikh, F. S., Hussain, J., Khan, A., & Al-Harrasi, A. (2021). Vaccine development against COVID-19: Study from pre-clinical phases to clinical trials and global use. *Vaccines (Basel)*, *9*(8).

ARISE (ARO Alliance for ASEAN & East Asia) website. https://arise.jihs.go.jp

BioNTech. (2023). BioNTech achieves milestone at mRNA-based vaccine manufacturing site in Rwanda. https://investors.biontech.de/news-releases/news-release-details/biontech-achieves-milestone-mrna-based-vaccine-manufacturing-0/

Chirinda, G., & Machingaidze, S.(2023). Africa is better prepared for future pandemics. https://www.devex.com/news/opinion-africa-is-better-prepared-for-future-pandemics-104935

Chorev, N. (2012). *The World Health Organization between North and South.* Cornell University Press.

Cohen, Z., Hansler, J., Atwood, K., Salama, V., & Murray, S. (2020). *Trump administration begins formal withdrawal from World Health Organization.* CNN.

Cooper, A. F., Kirton, J., & Stevenson, M. (2008). Critical cases in global health innovation. In A. F. Cooper & J. J. Kirton, *Innovation in global health governance: Critical cases, chapter 1.* Ashgate Publishing Company.

Council on Foreign Relations. (2021). Visualizing: Trends to watch. https://www.cfr.org/article/visualizing-2022-trends-watch?utm_medium=social_share&utm_source=tw. Last updated December 6, 2021 3:00 pm EST.

Cueto, M., Brown, T., & Fee, E. (2019). *The World Health Organization: A history.* Cambridge University Press.

Cullinan, K. (2021). African Union special envoy slams COVAX as COVID deaths spike on the continent, urges donors to 'pay up' on vaccine pledges. *Health Policy Watch.* https://healthpolicy-watch.news/african-union-special-envoy-slams-covax-as-covid-deaths-spike-on-the-continent-urges-donors-to-pay-up-on-vaccine-pledges/

Cullinan, K.(2022). Republic of Korea named as WHO-supported global training hub for manufacturing vaccines and biologicals. *Health Policy Watch.* https://healthpolicy-watch.news/republic-of-korea-named-as-global-training-hub-for-biological-manufacturing/

De Rujiter, A. (2020). What do we actually mean by the 'European Health Union'? *Eurohealth*, *26*(3), 30–31.

Duffin, J. (2022). *Covid-19: A history.* McGill-Queen's University Press.

European Commission. (2020). *Building a European Health Union: Stronger crisis preparedness and response for Europe*. Press release.

Gaudillière, J.-P., McDowell, A., Lang, C., & Beaudevin, C. (Eds.) (2022). *Global health for all: Knowledge, politics, and practices*, Rutgers University Press.

GAVI. (2022, January 17). COVAX has so far shipped over 1 billion COVID-19 vaccines to 144 participants. https://www.gavi.org/covax-vaccine-roll-out

Gostin, L. O. (2021). *Global health security: A blueprint for the future*. Harvard University Press.

Horton, R. (2023). Offline: Why we must make peace with China. *The Lancet*, *401* (10375), 421.

IHR. (2005). *International Health Regulations* (3rd ed.). World Health Organization.

Independent Panel for Pandemic Preparedness and Response. (2021). *COVID-19: Make it the last pandemic*. https://theindependentpanel.org/wp-content/uploads/2021/05/COVID-19-Make-it-the-Last-Pandemic_final.pdf

Kabakci, F. (2020, May 15). *China: COVID-19 outbreak under control*. Anadolu Agency.

Law, J. (2004). And if the global were small and non-coherent? Method, complexity and the baroque. *Environment and Planning D: Society and Space*, *22*, 13–26.

Madhavan, H., & Gaudilliere, J. (2026). Frugal innovations and health system resilience. The conceptualization, policy support and forms of frugality during Covid-19 in South India. In S. Lechevalier, J.-P. Gaudillière, K. Ibata-Arens, & K. Takuma (Eds.), *Capitalism, innovations, and health after Covid-19. An Asian perspective*. Palgrave MacMillan.

Ministry of Foreign Affairs of Japan. (2022). Provision of vaccines to Thailand by Japan, the United States, Australia and India. https://www.mofa.go.jp/mofaj/press/release/press1_000837.html

Nature. (2022). First African-made mRNA vaccine, a test platform for the future. https://www.nature.com/articles/d44148-022-00151-3

NIKKEI ASIA. (2022). Charting coronavirus vaccinations around the world. https://vdata.nikkei.com/en/newsgraphics/coronavirus-vaccine-status/. Last updated on October 28, 2022.

Packard, R. M. (2016). *A history of global health: Interventions into the lives of other peoples*. Johns Hopkins University Press.

Politico (2021). Hungary becomes first EU country to authorize Chinese coronavirus vaccine. https://www.politico.eu/article/hungary-becomes-first-eu-country-to-authorize-chinese-coronavirus-vaccine/

Politico. (2023). European countries succeed in yearlong push to relocate WHO Moscow office: The WHO's non-communicable diseases office will move to Copenhagen. https://www.politico.eu/article/europe-succeed-year-long-push-relocate-who-moscow-office-non-communicable-diseases-copenhagen/

Reich, M. R. (2002). Reshaping the state from above, from within, from below: Implications for public health. *Social Science & Medicine*, *54*(11), 1669–1675.
Reuters. (2021). Africa must expand vaccine production, leaders say. https://www.reuters.com/world/africa/africa-must-expand-medical-manufacturing-capacity-south-africas-president-2021-04-12/
Reuters. (2023, April 21). WHO launches mRNA vaccine hub in Cape Town. https://www.reuters.com/business/healthcare-pharmaceuticals/who-officially-launches-mrna-vaccine-hub-cape-town-2023-04-20/
Rosenberg, C. (1992). *Framing disease: Studies in cultural history.* Rutgers University Press.
Sidibé, M., Dieng, A., & Buse, K. (2023). Advance the African medicines agency to benefit health and economic development. *Bmj*, *380*, 386.
Soon, W. (2020). From SARS to COVID-19: Rethinking global health lessons from Taiwan. *East Asian Science, Technology, and Society: An International Journal*, *14*(4), 647–655.
South China Morning Post. (2020). China promises its Mekong neighbors priority access to a coronavirus vaccine developed in China. https://www.scmp.com/news/china/diplomacy/article/3098610/china-promises-its-mekong-neighbours-priority-access
South China Morning Post. (2021). Sinovac set to start making Covid-19 jabs in Egypt as China expands vaccine push. https://www.scmp.com/news/china/diplomacy/article/3139036/sinovac-set-start-making-covid-19-jabs-egypt-china-expands?utm_source=Twitter&utm_medium=share_widget&utm_campaign=3139036
Takuma, K. (2020). Health diplomacy of the developed countries—Focusing on collaboration between France and the WHO (in Japanese). In H. Shiroyama (Ed.), *Global health governance.* Toshindo, chapter 7.
Takuma, K. (2023). The Far-Eastern Bureau of the League of Nations: Linking the regional and international orders through health work. In R. H. Christopher & H. Shinohara (Eds.), *East Asians in the League of Nations: Actors, empires and regions in early global politics* (pp. 61–79). Springer.
The Africa Report. (2021). Africa: Regional cooperation is crucial for the continent's growth. https://www.theafricareport.com/107923/africa-regional-cooperation-is-crucial-for-the-continents-growth/
Tiberghien, Y. (2022). The East Asian Covid-19 Paradox (Elements in Politics and Society in East Asia). Cambridge University Press.
Ullah, A., & Ferdous, J. (2022). *The post-pandemic world and global politics.* Springer.
US Embassy and Consulate in Japan. (2024). CDC opens new East Asia and Pacific regional office in Japan. https://jp.usembassy.gov/cdc-opens-new-eap-office-in-japan/

US Embassy and Consulate in Vietnam. (2022). U.S. Department of Health and Human Services deputy secretary Andrea Palm visits Vietnam and meets with government of Vietnam partners. https://vn.usembassy.gov/u-s-department-of-health-and-human-services-deputy-secretary-andrea-palm-visits-vietnam-and-meets-with-government-of-vietnam-partners/

Usher, A. (2022). CEPI launches 100-day vaccine 'moonshot'. *The Lancet, 399* (10330), 1107–1108.

Wall Street Journal. (2020). China seeks to use access to Covid-19 vaccines for diplomacy. https://www.wsj.com/articles/china-seeks-to-use-access-to-covid-19-vaccines-for-diplomacy-11597690215

WHO. (2022). Moving forward on goal to boost local pharmaceutical production, WHO establishes global biomanufacturing training hub in Republic of Korea. https://www.who.int/news/item/23-02-2022-moving-forward-on-goal-to-boost-local-pharmaceutical-production-who-establishes-global-biomanufacturing-training-hub-in-republic-of-korea

WHO. (2025). *WHO pandemic agreement.* WHA78.1.

Youde, J. (2012). *Global health governance.* Polity.

CHAPTER 7

Frugal Innovations and Health System Resilience. The Conceptualization, Policy Support and Forms of Frugality During Covid-19 in South India

Harilal Madhavan and Jean-Paul Gaudilliere

Abstract This chapter discusses the conceptualization of frugal innovations in the healthcare sector and offers empirical evidences of frugality and its success in the context of Covid-19 pandemic in India. It attempts to elaborate on the following arguments: (i) The concept of frugal innovations goes beyond simple cost-effectiveness argument for business models in developing societies, it offers multiple forms of affordable, adaptive and sustainable possibilities as evidenced during the pandemic. (ii) The spatiotemporal context is important, but the success and effectiveness of frugality also depends on the social, political and cultural fabric of innovations (innovation ecosystem) (iii) Frugal innovations are part of a regional innovation system in health that provide for local solutions, which can't

H. Madhavan (✉)
CHRIST University, Bengaluru, India
e-mail: harilalms@gmail.com

J.-P. Gaudilliere
Inserm & EHESS, Paris, France

S. Lechevalier et al. (eds.), *Capitalism, Innovations, and Health after Covid-19*,
https://doi.org/10.1007/978-3-032-24479-6_7

simply be standardized and reproduced in different contexts or for other healthcare systems. The chapter presents three types of frugal innovations from south of India, especially in the state of Kerala during the Covid-19 time to explain the relevance of this alternative, which confines not to health sector alone but applies to allied sectors too: (i) community mutual aid systems and decentralized delivery ('break the chain' campaign, community kitchen); (ii) use of low-cost alternative medical systems (rapid deployment in 'Ayur Raksha' clinics, repurposed Ayurveda preventive medicines and formation of a repository of traditional medical innovations in the Covid-19 treatment); (iii) complementary livelihood innovations ('chekkutty dolls' and women self-help groups that manufactured masks). In the context of Kerala, one can trace the reasons why these frugal innovations could be developed and easily adopted to an *innovation culture* that the state has nurtured through a decentralized governance and people's participation; a strong co-existence of biomedical and indigenous health system; the mobilization of community women groups and neighbourhood entrepreneurship in association with a strategy for the common pooling of resources.

7.1 Introduction—The Multiple Shades of Frugality

The positive effects of technology on the expansion of healthcare services and quality are undeniable; however, the burden of diseases and the deep inequalities in access to care remain very high, especially outside Europe and North America. The long-awaited decline of infectious diseases in the global South has not materialized partly due to emerging diseases like HIV/AIDS while urbanization, changes in ways of living, access to cheap processed food, or exposure to pollutants have dramatically increased the incidence of non-transmissible disorders like obesity, diabetes, hypertension or cancer. Most innovation processes considered in international health policies and initiatives usually focus on the necessity of providing access to pharmaceuticals and other biomedical devices like vaccines targeting infectious diseases.

While access to technological goods is valuable, they are therefore barely sufficient. Since the 1970s, analysts of health policies and public health experts have argued that health technology innovations developed by large firms oriented to rich markets in the global North rarely fulfil their promises and respond to the needs of populations living in low and middle-income countries (LMICs).[1] Such inadaptation is not only due to the inequal and inefficient allocations of resources to cover costs, but also due to the framing of the technology, i.e. inappropriate targets, difficulties of operation, complex and demanding maintenance, centralized nature, social or cultural non-acceptability.[2] This issue is all the more important to consider that various prevalent diseases in low and middle-income countries such as child malnourishment, measles, maternal deaths, HIV and different types of chronic non-communicable diseases are repeatedly claimed to be preventable through an early access to more adapted and more acceptable technologies and care practices (COHRED, 2012).

In the health sector, where the relations between stakeholders are quite complex as it is expert based and where information asymmetries are inflicted with moral hazard issues, the concept of innovation does not always refer to major technological breakthroughs as highlighted by Schumpeter (1934) and later by the analysts of the pharmaceutical sector, but often focus on the improvements and adaptation of existing technologies. These have for instance received close attention from development economists such as Sanjaya Lall, Nathan Rosenberg and evolutionary economists such as Richard Nelson. Within the health literature, examples of more adequate—if not alternative—innovations are numerous. They are usually discussed either in terms of ability to lower costs or in terms of simplicity and adaptation to the local needs. For instance, General Electric's successful introduction of lullaby warmers in India (with the sales of 1500 units during the first 12 months of offer) is attributed to the classical practice of differential pricing: the lullaby warmer costs 3000 $ in India while it costs 12,000 $ in the US (Arshad, 2021). At the opposite end of the spectrum, MSF's efficient promotion of innovative Oral Rehydration Solution (ORS) to treat cases of diarrhoea or cholera in Liberia and Costa Rica has been interpreted in terms of simplicity and social adaptation. These solutions, which contain glucose and electrolytes, are given to patients to replace fluids lost. They are easy to prepare and administer, eventually with local materials.

This closely relates to the main theme of this book—as one key aspect of health systems is the tension between policies of access to products and

[1] For recent analysis see (Grover et al., 2014), (WHO, 2010), (Chataway et al., 2010), (Kumar & Bhaduri, 2014).

[2] On the history legacy of debates on these criteria of appropriateness see Gaudilliere and Madhavan (2026).

policies of healthcare organizations. If innovations are considered as interactive processes in which different actors exchange knowledge and resources, complementing each other in a sort of positive sum game; the outcome is an emergent property of systemic interactions rather than the sum of the individual actions. This vision sees innovation as a social process in the first place relying on the ability of different agents—and not only the experts or the innovators—to interact, address, and eventually solve health problems following a cumulative path (Nelson & Winter, 1982). According to the Schumpeterian model, the value of innovation is achieved with and reflected in a peculiar combination of product, process, market, and organization etc. Since constructing such a combination implies evaluative action as well as coordination, a specific stakeholder, agent or institution is required to define the degree of novelty and usefulness. In the Schumpeterian structure, the market is the main evaluative institution. In contrast to this optimistic gaze, we contend that what appears profitable to the market, might not always respond to health needs or fulfil social requirements. Lundvall's concept of 'unsatisfactory innovations' reflects those cases, where a new solution—even when being technologically suitable—is applied without considering the specific needs of users, thus producing an unsatisfactory—i.e. a not fully useful- solution to problems. Hence the idea that satisfactoriness may be a more accurate criterion than usefulness (Bianchi et al., 2017). Similar notions have been discussed under the motto of the 'socially acceptable" in the recent history of health governance.

By focusing on the concept of frugality, this chapter is an attempt to approach the very same questions with a notion, which has attracted great attention in Asian countries, especially those classified as "low and middle income", in relations to development policies and their priorities, i.e. the production of (export) goods and/or the provision of (public) services. The conceptualization of frugality owes part of its extension to its varied usage in the context of countries like India, where innovation often happens outside both the formal organisation of and the institutional structure of incentives. The terms 'Jugaad' or grassroot innovations are used to represent innovations, which do get much attention from mainstream market or institutions. The term "grassroot" has gained considerable attraction since the early 1990s, while the term 'jugaad' is ancient and familiar in the context of India. Frequently, the so-called grassroot innovations do not aim at markets, but respond to the gaps that markets have created: they are neither motivated by aiming at the creation of, or the accumulation of private property, or the retribution of financial capital.

The frugal innovation concept has indeed roots in the "appropriate technology" movement (Kaplinsky, 2011; Schumacher, 1973) which called for the employment of "technologies which are appropriate for low-income countries in that they are labour-intensive, simple to operate and repair, producing products for low-income consumers" (Kaplinsky, 2011).[3]

Frugality has since then acquired other meanings, linking it to the notion of affordability. The new frugal conceptualization takes multiple meanings of affordability in order to soften the opposition between 'low cost' and 'socially adapted', as Agarwal et al. (2020) and Ahuja and Chan (2020) have suggested:

(a) *financial tenability*: taking into account the overall cost of use and/or ownership spread over the entire product lifecycle, including costs of purchase, usage, maintenance and governance, that determines financial tenability of an innovative product, which would be much less in frugal innovations than the alternate solution.
(b) *Social justifiability*: Innovative solutions that are based on frugality must be justifiable/acceptable in a given social context (Banerjee and Duflo, 2007, Karnani, 2007). For example, the state promotes or positively incentivise diffusion of products/services that cater to larger societal good.
(c) *Infrastructural reasonability*: Technologies, products, services that are created as frugal solutions must be careful not to make 'unreasonable' demands on the infrastructural prerequisites for their use. If suggested infrastructural necessities are prohibitively expensive in a given use-context, then the solution cannot be considered affordable for those users.
(d) *Environmental sustainability*: Frugal solutions must be responsible in the use of natural resources, and should not threaten ecological systems and endanger social welfare (Herstatt & Tiwari, 2020)

In other words, affordability in the context of frugal innovation must be transformed into something more wide-ranging and inclusive to ensure its own longevity (sustainability) and broader acceptance (Tiwari and Herstatt, 2012). Weyrouch and Herstatt (2017) for instance label an innovation as frugal if three criteria are met: substantial cost reduction, concentration on core functionalities, and optimised

[3] See Gaudilliere and Madhavan (2026).

performance level. Most frugal innovations in healthcare encompass a wide range of solutions, which are consistently low-cost, and of an adequate performance level to serve the underserved and subaltern populations.

Through this paper, we attempt to analyse experiences of frugal innovation keeping efficiency in line in the health sector, especially in low-resource setting contexts. The significance of such theorization from the South is however of general interest. If health emergencies like the Covid-19 may be considered as resource-limiting situations in Europe and North America as well, many of the existing health system infrastructure and delivery frameworks of high-income countries proved insufficient in—and poorly prepared to—dealing with the massive requirements of the pandemic. If the pertinence of frugality goes beyond the low- and middle- income contexts, our discussion is nonetheless focused on the relevance of frugal innovations in the context of the Covid-19 pandemic in India, where local developments have contrasted the central government's failure at providing adequate responses. It points to the larger possibility of this framework for dealing with inequities of capitalism in healthcare developed "from below" and enabling health system strengthening.

7.2 Frugality in Global Health Institutions

International organizations working on health have accepted frugal innovations as a desirable complement if not a radical alternative to the technological market-oriented innovation system. In the context of global health, frugality is very often equated with low cost and market-based innovations. In WHO, UNICEF and other UN organizations, however, frugality in cost of production and frugality in affordability are often approached as two different things—their conceptualization makes the meaning of the latter close to the idea of sustainable social solutions through affordable and accessible products and services. The following section explores these tensions.

In line with a decades-long tradition of priority settings (Cueto et al., 2019), WHO recent documents on innovation consider the importance of low-cost innovations in varied contexts of highly unequal resource availability. One issue is the concentration of medical devices in high-income countries, with just 13% of the global population using 76% of global medical devices. This situation raises major concerns over the access to care in low and middle -income economies, especially in sub-Saharan Africa, where—for instance—blood donations in many countries fail to meet the demand for transfusions and where clinics, particularly those in remote rural areas, are underequipped. In the absence of blood and equipment, patients in need of transfusion—such as women haemorrhaging as a result of a ruptured ectopic pregnancy—are forced to fall back on a crude form of auto-transfusion using kitchen equipment—it certainly saves some lives—but can create much higher risks (Arasaratnam & Humphreys, 2013). A second issue is the non-suitability of medical tools. Again, in sub-Saharan Africa, up to 70% of medical equipment stands idle, according to the WHO's Guidelines for healthcare equipment donations (Webber et al., 2020). Moreover, devices that are not designed to cope with heat, humidity and dust or to be used intensively are quickly out of order. High electricity consuming devices and lack of refrigeration facilities are also referred to as problems again and again.

Examples of frugal innovations emerging as responses to increasing demand for effective and robust low-cost medical devices are often highlighted as coming from India or China. The latter is indeed spending around 45 billion US $ per annum in the health sector. According to WHO, the development of emerging markets brings new reasons to create appropriate, affordable and accessible medical innovations for low-income markets. It is no longer just something that 'well intended' people do to reduce health-care disparities. It is also hoped to be a profitable activity. WHO supports and emphasizes the local development and design of low-cost medical devices, their clinical efficacy and robustness, and suggests that such devices could be more reliable and widespread. It claims that low-cost medical devices have enormous potential to reduce the gap between the developed and developing worlds, and to reach the 'last mile' of people in the most innovative ways.

For its part, UNICEF has adopted a more cautious approach of frugal innovation and its effectiveness. The organization defines it as, "frugal innovations are simple products or services that are dramatically lower in cost, outperform alternatives and can be scaled up through adoption by people, who do not need special expertise or equipment." This statement resonates with the discussion of appropriate technologies in the 1970s when UNICEF partnered with WHO to support the Primary Healthcare strategy (Gaudilliere & Madhavan, 2026).

In the 1980s however under the leadership of J. Grant, UNICEF shifted perspective, criticized the broadness of the strategy and started to advocate interventions focusing on one problem and the mobilization of one technology at a time, for instance oral rehydration in new-borns. During the 1990s, UNICEF operationalized this selective care approach joining efforts with the Rockefeller Foundation, the World Bank and the Gates Foundation to support vaccines R&D, and access to extended vaccination in children.

The return to more integrative perspectives took place in the late 2000s under the influence of the mobilizations against HIV/AIDS and their critique of "enclaves" providing access to antiretrovirals without strengthening health systems and without adjusting treatment to patients' living conditions. This now means that, for UNICEF, frugal innovation is not only defined by cost effectiveness, but equally that the solution should be able to be adopted and adapted to local needs. The organization insists on a human re-centering of innovation strategies explaining that: "Human-centered design is a problem-solving process that begins with understanding the 'human factors' and context surrounding a challenge and works directly with users—the intended clients or consumers of services—to develop solutions that are viable and appropriate in a given context. Designing for people and their everyday interactions helps uncover and solve the right problems using local capacities and resources. No expert has more knowledge than a caregiver, nurse, or a community health worker about how to solve their most pressing problems." (UNICEF, 2018, p. 3)

UNICEF considers that international organizations can make useful contributions by using their larger geographical networks to connect communities and solvers to each other and to relevant ideas and efforts. Many of the frugal innovations that UNICEF has contributed to (in partnership with local stakeholders) can be found across geographies and programs areas for this reason. For example, in Tanzania UNICEF has been spearheading the 'Kangaroo Mother Care (KMC) initiative' to address the lack of incubators for preterm babies in rural areas. KMC uses skin-to-skin contact to help premature babies by wrapping them with a cloth close to their mother's skin, mimicking a Kangaroo pouch. This method raises survival rates. Skin-to- skin contact helps the babies gain warmth, it calms them and helps regulate their heartbeat, enhances bonding, and helps establish good breastfeeding practices. Moreover, KMC can be practiced by any caretaker, anywhere.[4]

UNDP sparsely uses frugality, usually as meaning 'user-led innovation solution'. It concentrates on higher overall quality, use value, feasibility, and social impact. And unlike the solutions that emerged from the mainstream innovation paths, these user-led innovations are considered allow for continuous improvement, and usually bring along novel approaches specially to deal with the challenges of sustainability (Gustilo Ong & Gustale, 2020).

Most global health organizations recognize the importance of frugal innovation as a means to ensure the provision of both low-cost and adapted medical technologies. The one big exception is the Bill and Melinda Gates Foundation, which does not use the category since its operations foster entrepreneurial biomedical innovations and access to these. UN institutions however have different understandings of what frugality means, while for some the most important feature is cost effectiveness, for others it is the social validation or the user-driven initiative. In international health, frugality has thus moved beyond just being a cost-cutting concept, to a more comprehensive one, that aims to strip out unnecessary features to focus on what is essential, i.e. to provide customers and patients with an affordable, accessible, and simpler solution than what is made available through markets and big corporations.

7.3 The Ambivalent Indian Health System: From Technological to Frugal Solutions

The Indian healthcare system is a diverse and complex network of public and private sectors that provide a wide range of medical services to India's 1.4 billion inhabitants. It is characterized with high out-of-pocket dependent expenditures (47.1% of the total in 2019–20) and low government spending (1.35% of GDP in 2019–20), and with a large population (82% of the employed (Ministry of Finance, 2022) working outside the organised sector with no or minimal health benefits.

Despite progress in the control of mortality, India still faces major challenges in controlling communicable diseases like tuberculosis, malaria, and HIV/AIDS, which continue to pose significant problems of morbidity. Non-communicable diseases, such as diabetes, cardiovascular diseases, and

[4] https://www.unicef.org/tanzania/stories/kangaroo-mother-care.

cancer, have been on the rise in India, putting additional strain on the healthcare system. Epidemiological changes contrasting the expected transition from infectious to chronic has led public health experts to insist on the double burden of both infectious diseases and NCDs the Indian people face (Dyson, 2004).

Even if various efforts towards universal healthcare—both at centre and state levels—have taken place the model does not cover much: only 41–50% of the households have at least one person insured, while a large section of the middle class is uninsured (Kumar & Sarwal, 2021). For instance, the expansion of ABPMJAY (*Ayushman Bharat Prime Minister's Jan Arogya Yojana*—Prime Minister Health Scheme) in parallel with state health extension schemes officially ensure that hospitalization is covered for the bottom 50% of the population, the ambulatory care of chronic disorders in contrast remains poorly addressed. Around 20% of the population is covered through a form of social health insurance, and private voluntary health insurance is primarily designed for high-income groups. The remaining 30% of the population (around 400 millions), devoid of health coverage, is designated as the "missing middle." This missing middle includes multiple groups across all expenditure quintiles and is spread across both urban and rural areas (Kumar & Sarwal, 2021). The accessibility and affordability remain pressing issues along with the availability of healthcare professionals.

There is a high disparity among the regional states in terms of the public health facilities and also in achievement index (for example the difference between Kerala's health indicators and Bihar's indicators is quite extreme). Digitalization of health and new technologies in healthcare are considered to have a significant impact on the overall cost of healthcare services in India: by reducing the need for hospitalization and enabling early detection of diseases some new technologies have helped in reducing the overall cost of healthcare services (Awad et al., 2021). In response to the emerging need for digitization of healthcare in India, the Ayushman Bharat Digital Mission (ABDM) was launched in September 2021 with the official aim of enhancing availability, accessibility, affordability and acceptability of healthcare through different building blocks (Sharma et al., 2023). Many Indian states like Kerala, Tamil Nadu, and Rajasthan have also made significant leaps towards launching digital health initiatives. Tamil Nadu was one of the first states in the country to implement a digital health program.

Technological rather than frugal innovations seem therefore to be the favoured means for achieving widespread access and affordability.

Health institutions have indeed been witnessing the recreation or regeneration of a robust supply chain and international companies are now rapidly leveraging India's affordable innovation platform (availability of high-quality doctors and engineers at relatively cheaper cost) through outsourcing, risk-sharing, and co-development partnerships (Mazumdar-Shaw, 2018). For instance, General Electric's Research Centre in India has developed a number of cheaper bio-medical equipment from scanners to portable electrocardiograms. Bristol-Myers Squibb developed a number of promising novel drugs at its partnered with medical research centres in Bangalore. Biocon company has developed insulins in India indigenously through a proprietary technology[5] in the early 2000s. Narayana Hridayalaya[6] (Bangalore based hospital network) offers so-called low-cost open-heart surgeries, etc. According to the dominant scenario, the major inequities in accessing healthcare will be managed not only with less expensive technological innovations, but also with a more cost-effective raw material supply chain.

Although prevailing, the low-cost imperative is not always aligned with an absence of frugality's other dimensions. Digitisation in the Indian health landscape began with the government's proclaimed intent and vision of providing quality healthcare using accessible and affordable technology through the National Health Policy in 2017 (Govt. of India, 2017). In 2018, NITI Aayog (the public policy think tank the Government of India established in place of the earlier Planning commission) released the National Health Stack that envisaged the creation of common public goods for healthcare. The National Innovation Council report on the sector (Ministry of Health, 2013) also considers frugality as integral to healthcare innovation. It emphasizes that its aim is not to understand what constitutes "novelty" but what constitutes overcoming

[5] Biocon's innovation strategy involves the development of affordable follow-on versions of biologic drugs, or biosimilars, to provide cost-effective alternatives to expensive reference biologics, which impose a tremendous strain on healthcare budgets for patients and the government. For example, the introduction of Biocon's recombinant human insulin, Insugen, at a fraction of the price of imported insulins, compelled MNC brands to drop prices, which hugely benefitted diabetes patients (Mazumdar Shaw, 2018).

[6] Cardiac surgeon Dr. Devi Shetty's hospital in Bangalore offers heart surgeries at a fraction of what it costs in developed countries, and caters to patients from Africa, South & South East Asia, and the Middle East. The hospital charges an average of USD 2000 for open-heart surgery, compared with USD 20,000–100,000 in America, but its success rates are as good as in the best American hospitals (Jayakumar et al., 2024).

an existing constraint or barrier or fulfilling a need. This may include innovations related to service delivery that could be a comprehensive business model, or could involve select elements in the implementation chain. It adds that an innovation need not be altogether a new idea, it is possible to have some elements which are combined with existing elements, or a different configuration of existing elements (Ministry of Health, 2013).

These initiatives not only claim to provide digital and other technological innovations but to offer affordable public health services. Whether this move means better access, better services and better outcomes remains an open issue. Whatever its overall consequences, digitalization has been strongly reinforced during the Covid-19 pandemic in resonance with—and this all the more paradoxical—the institutionalization of low-cost technologies and public provision of the same as important ingredients of successful responses. Moreover, in many states and regional settings, it was realized in the aftermath of the pandemic, that strong community participation and local-level resilience strategies that can complement or even replace technological responses to handling emerging diseases, played an important role in containing the Covid-19 spread. In the next section we analyse some examples of frugal experiences from India during the pandemic.

7.4 Frugal Experiences in Indian Healthcare During Covid-19

The success of frugal innovations depends on metrics that must be defined more broadly than just looking at profitability or market success in order to include social and ecological impacts. The Covid-19 experiences in India provide a few good examples. Their description serves two purposes: one, beyond the romanticized versions of frugal innovations, to show how things worked (and didn't work) at the ground level, how frugal innovation can create more lasting benefits to the communities, and two, help clarify and redefine frugality beyond the dominant idiom of low-cost.

In the examples below, the reference to frugality emanated from various stakeholders: state institutions, community and voluntary organizations, alternative health system providers, women self-help organizations. Not all these innovations deemed frugal are strongly connected to health interventions, but all of them catered to the health crisis and definitely contributed to the systemic response. There were instances of other successful "frugal" innovations in India's health-related industrial sector, for instance associated with the development of vaccines, drugs and medical devices of various types (Mani, 2020), but our effort here is to point towards other and more social types of frugality, which were closely knit, economically feasible, and community-oriented.

7.4.1 Frugality in Community: The Civil Society Aid Networks

7.4.1.1 Community Kitchen and Party Based Voluntary Participation

One of the very upfront innovative behaviour of the Kerala state was visible in ensuring the food safety of the people during the 2020 lockdown. This was critical in 2020 since dozens of thousands migrant workers, the vast majority in the informal sector, couldn't leave the state to return home due to the national lockdown and were left without any revenues. The government of Kerala set up community kitchens across the state in all panchayats (local governance areas) to provide affordable food products along with the free distribution of food kits to all those considered in need The state government towards the end of 2020 decided to extend the distribution of free grocery kits through the Public Distribution Systems (PDS) for all ration card holders in the state for several months as part of a 100-day programme.[7] Over 87.14 lakh (8.7 million) ration card owners in the state were given these free kits ensuring food security during the lockdown. Each kit contained 1 kg sunflower oil, ½ kg coconut oil, 1 kg salt, 1 kg semolina, 1 kg green gram, 1 kg black *chana*, 1/4 kg *tur dal*, 100 gm mustard, 100 gm fenugreek, 100 gm coriander, 1 kg *urad dal*, 100 gm chilli powder, 1 kg sugar, 250 gm tea powder and 2 soaps.

The 4.3 million women volunteers involved in the *Kudumbashree*[8] self-help groups joined hands with other voluntary organisations, youth associations as well as new formations like the Rapid Response Team (RRT)

[7] Kerala Chief Minister announced a 100-day action plan to advance the achievements of health, education and social security amid the Covid-19 (from Sep 19). Economic stimulus and job creation schemes were included in the 100-day programme to address the Covid impact and the emphasis will be on policies and schemes to advance the achievements of health, education and social security.

[8] *Kudumbashree* is a poverty eradication mission and one of the most successful women empowerment models of the state government.

(formed by the state government) at the ward level, to provide around 280.000 food packets every day. The 'Janakeeya hotels' (popular hotels), they set up sprung up across the state providing an average of 70,000 meals sold daily at the rate of Rs. 20 (0,2 euros) each. The standard meal includes rice, *sambar/dal*, *upperi* (stir-fried vegetables), pickle and *papad*. Fish, beef, eggs and pork are also served at reasonable rates. The meal packets, sold by the *Kudumbashree* volunteers through these budget kitchens or hotels have been a big hit among commoners during the time of lockdown.

Community kitchens were continued even after the Covid-19 pandemic, as they offer regular income for certain communities. Meals are prepared under family supervision, which ensures a certain affordability and quality of the food. The kitchens equipped with *vermi composting* (an organic manure made by earthworms feeding on biological waste and plant residues) unit, are not only budget-friendly but also time-efficient (The earthworms speed up the process, aerate the organic material, and add nutrients and enzymes from their digestive tracts to the compost).[9]

7.4.1.2 Break the Chain Campaign and Covid Literacy Mission

'Break the chain' campaign is used as a public health education strategy and has the official goal of achieving "social good". In the context of public health, it promotes general health, raises awareness and seeks to induce changes in people's behaviour for the benefit of individuals and society. Kerala thus organized a 'washing the hands' mass drive to 'break the chain' of Covid-19 infection during the first months of 2020. The government used prosocial assertion to value public and personal cleanliness and their importance in the fight against the new coronavirus. Local self-government successfully used local science education campaigns like the Corona Literacy Mission to increase peoples' health awareness and ability to face the pandemic (Stalin & Kenoth, 2022). The Kerala government used such communication strategies to influence citizens' behaviour without restricting freedom of choice or imposing mandatory obligations. On the other hand, it reduced the heavy responsibilities of the central and the state governments as it devolved activities and responsibility of

[9] News click report (11 Nov 2020) "With Community Kitchens and Food Kits, Kerala Progresses towards Hunger-Free Status amid Pandemic". Available online: https://www.newsclick.in/With-Community-Kitchens-Food-Kits-Kerala-Progresses-Hunger-Free-Status-Pandemic (accessed on January 20, 2024).

coordination at more local level. The Corona safe network[10] was for instance an open-source public utility developed to provide a single stop location for citizens to access ambulance, medical networks and track the COVID-19 local situation.

7.4.2 *Frugality in Medical Systems and Care*

7.4.2.1 Identifying and Repurposing Classical Drugs

In 2020, based on the recommendations of an interdisciplinary committee, the ministry of AYUSH[11] promoted the repurposing of existing Ayurveda interventions based on their scientific evaluation through preclinical studies, safety and toxicity studies, clinical trials, and observational studies in large cohorts. Initially four interventions were proposed beside Yoga interventions: AYUSH-64, Guduchi, Ashwagandha and Pippali preparations were recommended both for their prophylactic role and as add-on intervention complementing biomedical treatment.

AYUSH-64 is a polyherbal Ayurveda formulation developed in compliance with the standards of the Central Council for Research in Ayurvedic Sciences (CCRAS), the apex body for research in Ayurveda under the Ministry of AYUSH. It was found effective and safe in various infective febrile conditions like malaria, microfilaremia, chikungunya, and influenza (Manohar et al., 2022). AYUSH-64, was repurposed for the management of asymptomatic and mild to moderate Covid-19 based on its ingredients having notable antiviral, immune-modulating and antipyretic properties observed in clinical outcomes indicating potential benefits and safety in influenza-like illness. An in-vitro study was done on AYUSH-64, which confirmed this potential as it showed that about 35 of its

[10] *Coronasafe Network*, is a pioneering open-source organization dedicated to enhancing healthcare delivery and management. At the core of OHC's innovation is its flagship Electronic Medical Record (EMR) system, recognized as the 50th Digital Public Good by the United Nations. Originally a volunteer-driven initiative during the Covid-19 pandemic (developed by a few college students), OHC has continually addressed citizen-level healthcare problems. Its CARE software, adopted by several Indian states, played a crucial role in optimizing healthcare resource management during the pandemic.

[11] The Ministry of AYUSH, a ministry of the Government of India, is responsible for developing education, research and propagation of traditional medicine and alternative medicine systems in India. AYUSH is a name devised from the names of the alternative healthcare systems covered by the ministry: Ayurveda, yoga & naturopathy, Unani, Siddha, Sowa Rigpa, and homeopathy.

phyto-constituents have high binding affinity to the COVID 19 virus. The Government of India then recommended the use of AYUSH-64 to manage the asymptomatic and mild Covid-19 cases.

The plant Guduchi (*Tinospora cordifolia*) has also been considered effective in viral fevers, as anti-inflammatory, antipyretic and immuno-modulatory agent. There are three in-vitro studies, which show high binding efficacy against SARS-CoV-2 targets involved in the attachment and replication of the virus—the same targets as the antivirals Favipiravir, Lopinavir/ Ritonavir and Remdesivir. About seven studies are also being done under the Ministry of AYUSH on Guduchi in prophylactic care on about 133 thousand people and with good results in preventing COVID 19 and in management of mild to moderate cases of COVID 19 (Shukla et al., 2020). Ayurveda prescribes the decoction of Guduchi and Pippali (*Piper longum*) for management of a humoral disease (*Vata Kaphaja Sannipatik Jvara*) that has manifestations akin to the symptoms of infection in COVID-19. These two herbs are very common in clinical practice of Ayurveda and are used for various respiratory diseases. There have been extensive studies on both the herbs and their phytoconstituents to establish their safety profile, and confirm their immuno-modulatory, antipyretic, antiviral and anti-inflammatory potency (Ganguly & Bakhshi, 2020; Niraj & Varsha, 2020). In-vitro studies on Pippli and Guduchi have shown high affinity to potential targets of SARS-COV 2 (COVID 19 causing virus. Ashwagandha (*Withania somnifera*) has also been selected due to its recognized immune-modulatory, anti-stress and antiviral properties.

Besides these proposals from the central government, many states have promoted the use of indigenous medicines as part of their Covid-management protocols. The south Indian state of Tamil Nadu reveals a coherent strategy on the part of their governments to harness traditional medicines practices in public health delivery to address various ailments like dengue, chikungunya and SARS in the past decade. Here are examples of how this approach was implemented in the management of Covid-19.

Kabasura kudineer is a siddha[12] preparation, prominently used in South India among Siddha physicians, for managing the effects of fever related ailments. Well into the twentieth century, Siddha physicians have been developing ways of correlating epidemic fevers with their classification of

[12] Another Indian system of medicine mostly used in Tamil Nadu, India.

fevers based on functional, seasonal and pathological characteristics—including fevers which biomedicine regards as new from the viewpoint of the microorganisms involved.[13] Siddha doctors thus correlated the WHO definitions of dengue, SARS1 and Covid-19 symptoms with the Siddha classification of diseases to identify those akin to these infections using Siddha texts like '*Kudineer nooru*' (literally, 'hundred types of decoctions') by the renowned Siddha physician, Theraiyar of the fourteenth to fifteenth centuries. This compendium contains instructions for the preparation of 100 herbal decoctions among which 48 are for the treatment of various fevers. Covid-19 symptoms like mild fever, lack of appetite and diminished sense of smell, cough, cold and breathing difficulty, thus match with the Siddha classification of *Kabasuram* disorder (Sujatha & Payyapallimana, 2022)

Based on its experience of using *Kabasura kudineer* for swine flu in 2009, the Tamil Nadu government released a Siddha protocol for Covid-19 on 24, April 2020, promoting the preparation only as an immunity booster to be taken along with other precautions, and starting the distribution of such KSK packets to 100.000 families in the containment zones of Chennai under the *Arogyam scheme* (health access scheme). Later huge amounts of KSK in the form of powder and readymade packs were made available for police persons, health personnel and—occasionally—to the public.

7.4.2.2 Ayurvedic Public Health Intervention Programs in Kerala

Similarly, the Government of Kerala (GOK) constituted a seven-member Task Force to prepare the blueprint of an Ayurvedic strategy for prevention and mitigation of Covid-19 in the early phases of the pandemic.[14] Ayurvedic management of infectious diseases in Kerala is generally well-accepted and provided through public and private Ayurvedic dispensaries and hospitals.[15] There are 947 public Ayurvedic healthcare facilities in Kerala managed by about 1500 Ayurvedic doctors. Inpatient services are

[13] For instance, the majority of WHO listed symptoms (National Health Policy, 2017) for dengue were correlated with symptoms mentioned in Siddha texts.

[14] Department of AYUSH, Government of Kerala. *Ayurvedic Strategies for the Prevention, Mitigation and Rehabilitation of COVID-19 in Kerala*—Action plan. (2020). Available online at: https://www.ayurveda.kerala.gov.in/images/pdf/pdf2021/actionplan_ayurveda_covid19.pdf.

[15] On this, see Gaudilliere and Madhavan (2026).

provided through 130 public Ayurvedic hospitals, with a bed strength of 3154, which is significantly lower than that of biomedicine (50,000).

In March 2020, the Ministry of AYUSH—Government of India, had recommended various prophylactic measures based on AYUSH systems against the pandemic. The move was followed by National Clinical management protocol for Ayurveda and Yoga based on "Ayurveda treatises, empirical evidence, experience from clinical practice and preliminary results from ongoing clinical studies".[16] Following the success of its call on Indian systems of medicine, the central government took steps to strengthen the public health intervention program named 'ayurswasthya yojana'[17] for the financial year 2021–22. Major objective of this program was the enlarged use of AYUSH in public health interventions (PHI): promotion of AYUSH intervention for community healthcare, support for UN Sustainable Development Goal-2 (SDG2) and Sustainable Development Goal-3 (SDG 3), documentation of the efficacy of AYUSH systems through AYUSH interventions in public health issues in order to select those worth scaling-up in national health programmes, i.e. issues related to communicable diseases, non-communicable diseases, maternal child health, geriatric care, mental health, and sports medicine.

On April 8, 2020, Mr. Pinarayi Vijayan, the Chief Minister of the Kerala state announced the decision to use Ayurveda in mitigating the spread of Covid-19. Initially the people were classified into seven categories based on the possible spread of the virus- and some categories were advised Ayurvedic treatment as per this classification. The major ayurvedic intervention programs established in Kerala included four segments: '*Swasthyam*' (good health) for the population below 60 years, '*Sukhayushyam*' (healthy old age) for the population above 60 years, *Amritham* (nectar) for the quarantined population and *Punarjani* (rejuvenation) intended to ensure a speedy return to normal health for individuals in the post- Covid phase without any lingering Covid sequelae. Further, the government implemented the *Bheshajam*[18] (which means 'free from disease fear') program, providing Ayurvedic treatments to

[16] National Clinical Management Protocol based on Ayurveda and Yoga for management of Covid-19 | Ministry of AYUSH | GOI. Available online at: https://www.ayush.gov.in/docs/ayush-Protocol-covid-19.pdf.

[17] https://ayush.gov.in/images/Schemes/Ayurswasthya.pdf.

[18] https://www.ism.kerala.gov.in/index.php/directorate/projects/district-projects-2/bheshajam.

asymptomatic or mildly symptomatic Covid-19 patients who had given consent for the use of ayurvedic medicines (Joseph et al., 2021). The deployment of AYUSH doctors at the primary healthcare level namely 'Ayur Raksha clinics' or preventive treatment/immunity clinics was part of the strategy. Kerala health ministry and Indian system of medicine directorate started Ayur Raksha clinics (preliminary life-saving clinics) during the pandemic and they functioned in all government Ayurveda institutions in the primary, secondary and tertiary levels: Ayurveda dispensaries, Ayurveda hospitals and Ayurveda Medical Colleges with broad support from local self-government bodies. They provided preventive medicine and other health support.

There were therefore important differences in how Tamil Nadu and Kerala presented the promotion of traditional medicine as a useful response to the pandemic. In Tamil Nadu, the proactive role of the state focused on the promotion of a classical poly-herbal formulation from the pharmacopeia of Siddha medicine for mild and moderate cases of Covid-19 without co-morbidities. Kerala represents a case in which Ayurveda based protocols for the care of Covid-19 were implemented in existing Ayurveda institutions and restricted by the government for use only for prevention and post recovery phase while the official clinical care remained focused on biomedicine.

7.4.2.3 Repositories of Innovative AYUSH Clinical Cases, Innovative Research and Raw Drugs

Under National AYUSH Mission[19] (NAM), from 2020 onwards, the central government initiated various databases to document clinical cases, best practices, regional raw drug availability etc. The novel AYUSH Clinical Case Repository (ACCR) portal was one of them. Conceptualized and developed by the Ministry of AYUSH, this portal aims to portray the strengths of AYUSH systems for the treatment of various conditions. This repository is considered to be a common open

[19] Centrally Sponsored Scheme of National AYUSH Mission (NAM) is a flagship scheme of Ministry of AYUSH approved and notified on 29.09.2014. The basic objective of NAM is to promote AYUSH medical systems through cost effective AYUSH services, strengthening of educational systems, facilitate the enforcement of quality control of Ayurveda, Siddha and Unani & Homoeopathy (ASU &H) drugs and sustainable availability of ASU & H raw-materials. It envisages flexibility of implementation of the programmes with participation of the State Governments/UT.

resource, through which knowledge is circulated freely. 'Creative commons' repository adds value to on-going research and innovation linked to the Indian systems of medicine and the beneficiaries of this cumulative knowledge are encouraged to deposit back into the repository.

The Regional Raw Drug Repository (RRDR) for AYUSH Medicine (Southern Plateau Region) at the National Institute of Siddha is another example of the centrally sponsored schemes of NAM, which plays an important role in the development of medicinal plants use and cultivation. The Ministry of AYUSH, through the National Medicinal Plants Board (NMPB), decided the establishment of a National Raw Drug Repository and of regional raw drug repositories in 2020. The NMPB identified the National Institute of Siddha as a leading institution with the Regional Research Institute of Unani Medicine, Chennai and the Siddha Central Research Institute, Chennai as collaborating institutes in the southern region of the country. The RRDR is expected to play a major role in the collection, documentation, and authentication of raw drugs collected from the agroclimatic region. This RRDR will not only act as a collection centre but will also serve as an accredited reference library for the authentication of raw drugs, establishing standard protocols and keys for authentication of raw drugs used in the herbal drugs industries.

7.4.3 *Frugality, Low-Cost Technologies and Entrepreneurial Resilience*

7.4.3.1 'Breathe of Hope' Initiative (BoH)

The 'Breathe of Hope' (BoH) initiative is the outcome of an interdisciplinary project gathering voluntary IT professionals, doctors, biomedical engineers and social workers to develop innovative medical devices that are made from locally available materials and affordable low-cost technology products to fight the pandemic. The concept of 'creative commons' is utilized in the development of these low-cost technologies, by adopting the open-source model to ensure that innovative low-cost designs are available for anybody around the world to use and modify, while contributing back to the community.

Its 46 members volunteer team have produced seven simpler and affordable versions of existing medical devices, including a non-invasive ventilator. It did not replace full ventilators, but was used when patients on ventilation support were transferred. This ventilator replaces a pre-existing 'ambulance bag' that is manually stimulated. The new version is automated, allows for adjustment of the volume of air, and can work according to breath per minute. Other low cost and simple technologies have been developed along with the respirator apparatus including an oxygen supply system, a portable intubation chamber, personal air filtering protection systems, a portable decontamination chamber, low-cost face covering shields etc.

7.4.3.2 Women Self-Help Groups and Resilience Enterprises

The frugal innovation schemes that hogged headlines in Kerala during the first two years of the pandemic originated in the *Kudumbashree* units—the self-help women groups and production network, which otherwise do entrepreneurial activities—which engaged in mask production, sanitizer production and—unexpectedly—dolls.

The making of 'Chekutty' dolls—literally 'the child who survived the mud', which started in 2018 as traditional weavers made small dolls from the mud-stained handloom sarees of the flood-hit Chendamangalam, an ancient weaving village of Kerala. Local weavers had lost around Rs. 2.3 million in just one shop in that village as flooding destroyed the saris and the dhotis (Indian traditional wear). Traditional shops like this accumulated losses of crores (tens millions) during the floods. These pretty dolls became very famous, symbolising the resilience of the weaving community and beyond that of Kerala itself. The practice continued and became a major livelihood option for weavers during the Covid-19 time. "Chekuttys are made only out of the soiled clothes. Using fresh clothes wouldn't be just to the cause," explained Lakshmi Menon, who spearheaded this initiative, in the early days of the pandemic. "If there is more demand, we will make dolls out of fresh clothes, woven in Chendamangalam (one of the geographical indications in Kerala). But we wouldn't hide it from the buyers. But right-now we have *mundus* (dhotis) enough to make 40,000 Chekuttys."[20] Besides a lot of media attention, this innovation has indeed been met with a very strong demand, not only in Kerala, but also from the Kerala diaspora in many countries.

Masks, sanitizer or doll production turned out to be important livelihood innovations during the Covid-time for women who are otherwise

[20] Details of the story are available at: https://www.edexlive.com/beinspired/2019/sep/04/the-chekutty-story-how-a-doll-became-a-symbol-of-hope-for-keralas-weavers-after-the-floods-7824.html, accessed on 5th January 2024.

involved in small entrepreneurial activities and rural self-employment guarantee jobs.

7.5 Frugality in the Context of the Kerala 'Model of Development'

Many of the examples of innovations presented above pertain to the state of Kerala. For decades, the so-called Kerala 'model of development' has been discussed for its investments in education, healthcare, and social infrastructure (Drèze & Sen, 1995), which yielded improved health outcomes like high life expectancy, low infant mortality and low birth rate (Kutty, 2000) even with a very low growth of income in the state. Investment in the health sector has traditionally remained a priority for governments in Kerala since the formation of the state. Currently it remains around 7.34% of total government expenditure (Ministry of Finance, 2022) compared to a very low expenditure share from the central government (see above). As health is mostly a state subject in India, Kerala's alternative political coalitions were supportive of welfare investments, ensuring a strong continuity in health and education policies. Nonetheless Kerala remains the Indian state with *the highest per capita out-of-pocket expenditures* (OOPE) on health in the country even though it is also one of the states with the highest per capita government health expenditure (GHE). This paradox is caused by the fact that most public investments were made on the supply side-infrastructural improvement rather than on the demand side-support to financial coverage.

As mentioned in Gaudillière and Madhavan (2026), Kerala has also a strong legacy of community involvement for social causes including health, education, calamity resilience etc. initiated through local planning campaigns and decentralized administration since late 90s reforms, which transferred one third of the state's budget to the panchayats, the basic units of government.

The state recently initiated a new wave of health reforms in continuation with the policies started in the early 2000s to counter the recurrent budget crisis of the previous decade (Sadanandan, 2001). These second level of care initiatives, though focused on improvements in the infrastructure, facility services, relocation of personnel, rearrangement of supply of essential medicines as part of the so-called Aardram program—2017, are conducted in parallel with health coverage reforms aiming at more collective financing of expenditure This choice is linked with the idea of channelling the insurance money for public hospitals. The new reforms are closely aligned with the decentralization process of the late 1990s giving more freedom to local panchayats to govern and respond to the needs of the primary health system. They also support the creation of community volunteer groups called *Arogya senas* (literally translated into health armies) mandated by the state health department to assist staff with documenting local health and health related issues, beginning with the surveillance of vector-borne disease and outbreaks in general.

Kerala has witnessed several community-led initiatives in the past five years to control disease outbreaks and disasters. Previous experiences of handling two consecutive floods in 2019 and 2020, plus a Nipah virus outbreak in 2018, have reinforced the involvement of the *gramasabhas* (the village councils) in health crisis management. There has been a fairly high degree of multisector action and coordination to reach the 'vulnerable populations', for instance interstate migrant workers (Jaison et al., 2023). The state thus implemented a free health insurance scheme called *Awaz* for interstate migrant workers, covering Rs. 15,000/ (181.82 USD) for medical treatment per year and an amount Rs. 200,000/ (2424 USD) for accident deaths.

Systemic factors like high health literacy, strong public sector involvement, local level community participation in reducing the democratic deficits through women organizations, youth wings of political parties, voluntary health organizations etc. definitely contribute to the ecosystem of successful and collective implementation of many health programs.

The following table recapitulates the major characteristics of the innovations identified in the previous section focusing on the nature of frugality, the type of stakeholders, the enabling social and political factors, and the sustainability component.

Table 7.1 highlights various properties of health innovations during the Covid-19 crisis in Kerala consistent with how we have discussed and defined frugality in the introductory section of this chapter. For example, the community kitchen campaign is a great example of civil society engagement. The state's women community network called *kudumbashree* (meaning 'prosperity of the family') has initiated many social activities, facilitated government schemes and various forms of capacity building and training for women-led enterprises across Kerala from the late 1990s onward, with the state budget earmarking certain amounts for these activities. As the local self-governments decided to introduce community

Table 7.1 Innovations, stakeholders and frugal components

Innovations	*Major stakeholders*	*Affordability/ simplicity/ accessibility*	*Community Engagement/ Social acceptability*	*Sustainability (continuity and environmental impact)*
Community Kitchen	Women households, *Kudumbashree* workers, youths from different political party cadres	Highly affordable, fast delivery, door-to door delivery	Women enterprises at decentralized level, local government support, and experience of youth cadre of the Marxist party on running this as part of the palliative programs	Continued Post-covid, adaptation by local governments to provide cheap but quality food with the help of *Kudumbashree/* women cooperatives
'Break the chain' and walk in Kiosks	Local municipalities; cartoonists, sportspersons and other public figures, police and social departments	Inexpensive information campaign; Adapting existing kiosks for provisioning handwashing (Reuse); low-cost portable booths for collection all over the state; minimal operating costs	Coordination of workers from various government departments, engagement of voluntary science organizations	Less energy use, existing networks and locally available infrastructure and resources
Reformulation of Indigenous drugs	AYUSH department, traditional healers, Anganwadi workers (decentralised health workers)	Repurposed drugs, relocation of doctors, reformulation practices	Traditionally strong parallel indigenous medical systems, wide network of primary healthcare centres	Incentive for production of reformulated drugs through local proprietary ownerships as an alternative to the patents. Environmental sustainability is a concern due to high consumption and extinction of plants

(continued)

Table 7.1 (continued)

Innovations	*Major stakeholders*	*Affordability/ simplicity/ accessibility*	*Community Engagement/ Social acceptability*	*Sustainability (continuity and environmental impact)*
Bheshajam and Public health interventions	First line treatment centres, health workers, civil society, media and multiple departments	Rapid deployment of personnel, reserving 30% seats in private hospitals by the government, quick decisions	Network of public- private hospitals, efficient referral systems, high health seeking behaviour of Kerala people, significant health literacy, use of media and social media for information devolution, NIPAH experiences	Socially acceptable remedies in existence for many years and the usage of the system previously piloted in cultural and local contingencies
Repository of Practices	Public and private AYUSH practitioners, AYUSH department	Creative commons and open-source innovations, freely available for innovative acts	Widespread innovative experiences in indigenous sector, highly developed research laboratories at the private AYUSH enterprises	Online platform for documentation of experiential knowledge—repository creation
'Breath of Hope'	Team of multidisciplinary volunteers, including IT professionals, biomedical engineers, doctors and social workers	Low cost and simplicity is prominent in these innovations- Uses existing technology complemented with labour intensive methods, low-cost initial investments and portable	Kerala's pre-existing start-up mission which promotes low-cost social innovations, highly educated and skilled professionals, state support for low-cost private ventures	With institutional support (Kerala start-up mission)—and low energy use

(continued)

Table 7.1 (continued)

Innovations	*Major stakeholders*	*Affordability/ simplicity/ accessibility*	*Community Engagement/ Social acceptability*	*Sustainability (continuity and environmental impact)*
Resilient enterprises-dolls manufacturing	Weaving co-operatives, handloom workers, volunteers from civil society	Reuse of weaving materials, creating new markets, lowered costs by local production	Presence of strong social media, innovative behaviour in local entrepreneurial practices, weaving co-operatives and supports	Sustainable market linkage, low wastage as they used soiled clothes

kitchen in every village in rural areas and in every ten wards of urban areas, *Kudumbashree* embraced the plan with an assurance of efficiently utilizing the local vegetables and other food resources. This idea had been mooted even before the pandemic as a way to provide low budget restaurants and low-cost home delivery of food. For some sections of the population listed by the government, food was provided absolutely free of cost, especially in old age homes and hospitals. Another attractive feature of the community kitchen is the cost-effectiveness and high quality of the services. In many places in the north of the state, it was run by women cooperative societies, in which meals are prepared under family supervision. Youth voluntary associations were engaged in the process mostly for getting orders and organizing delivery. The campaign had a strong component of simplicity and affordability, strong community engagement, and strong sustainability as the kitchen mostly consumed locally cultivated vegetables and resources, which are renewable.

The rise of industrial production within Ayurveda and the design of neo-traditional drugs focusing on new diseases has taken place in Kerala for several decades. Two aspects of this major transformation have been much commented upon. The first one is the way in which industrial Ayurveda participates in the search for alternatives to the international patent regime (Banerjee, 2009; Gaudilliere, 2014; Pordiè & Gaudilliere, 2014; Madhavan & Gaudilliere, 2021).[21] The second dimension pertains to the epistemic and technical dimensions of the invention of new plant compositions, preparation processes and therapeutic uses. The reformulation practices in industrial Ayurveda borrow from heterogeneous bodies of knowledge, for instance the biomedical nosology and the ayurvedic knowledge of plant therapeutic properties. Since 2000, the processes of such reformulation have been strongly supported by the federal state and by states like Kerala.

This infrastructure has proved helpful in repurposing the utility of ayurvedic drugs as we have seen in the case of AYUSH-64 and *kabhasura kudineer*. Analysed from the frugal innovation perspective, indigenous drug repurposing chiefly targets the affordability, simplicity and social acceptability dimensions of frugal innovation. The question of sustainability is not directly aimed at, a failure which results in strong tensions regarding the supply of medicinal plants. On the one hand there are

[21] See also Ibata-Arens et al. (2026).

commitments to minimize consumption of raw plants and materials. On the other hand, the rapid growth of the industry, in conjunction with the fact that collection in the wild dominates the supply, has resulted in serious threats of medicinal plants extinction. In other words, the case of indigenous drugs repurposing may be evaluated as having a strong affordability, strong simplicity/accessibility, strong social acceptability/community engagement but low sustainability.

In the case of resilient enterprises, the mini doll manufacturing was a very innovative idea that represented not just a story of alternate manufacturing, but a powerful symbol of collective resilience. In a short span of time, new manufacturing units of this product appeared in nine countries through brand creation. The dimension of social acceptability appears to spring naturally from the desire of the innovators to improve the daily life *of their communities*. The official website of Chekkutty dolls explains the vision behind the innovation: ensure dignity to weavers who are unemployed in the aftermath of the devastating floods. Affordability is achieved not only through scaling up of production to supply new markets, but also of profitability since a batch of dolls worth Rs. 9000 can be made from a single Chendamangalam saree, which costs Rs. 3000. This frugal innovation does provide not only a livelihood option, but creating a new brand product from otherwise famous geographical indication, chendamangalam sarees. The strong sustainability component is due to reuse of soiled clothes.

Collective repositories of resources through various repositories and enhancing and circulating knowledge through open contribution and usage is considered an important mechanism for community-oriented innovation, which obviously counter the valuation of innovations in terms of intellectual properties like patents and other similar market rights. The creative and experiential innovations within the medical systems through cumulative research and use of freely available pool of resources enhances low-cost advances within health systems. The idea of 'creative commons' opens up the possibilities of accessing innovations without much hindrance especially the basic knowledge and clinical results of earlier research that might

If we keenly observe the above presented efforts, we can see that repurposing, reuse and rapid deployment, free access, community work and mutual aid, or use of sustainable resource usage are recurring features. These are precisely the key points that define frugal innovations. The Kerala examples reflects, how far the institutional support systems are important in the creation and maintenance of frugal innovations, in setting boundary conditions while tackling grand challenges like healthcare crisis and livelihood crisis. Identification of endogenous factors that sustain frugal innovations that runs across various sectors can contribute to a 'frugal innovation ecosystem'. For example, the decentralized governance and village councils' participation, presence of different types of voluntary groups, various government start up initiatives, coordination of various political organizations and institutions seem to have played a very pivotal role in many of the innovations we have analysed. This unique mix of institutional networks can form a 'frugal innovation system' that may vary according to sectors under reference.

This innovative 'culture' is not only the outcome of state investments, it is also based on the promotion of the informal sector and the belief that the stakeholders involved in it can be entrusted with innovation capabilities. The informal sector is competitive, not only because of the cheap labour costs, or because it provides the basis for growth through its transformation into a formal sector, but because it is a reservoir of voluntary civil society engagement, which can be the driver of innovations. Here we have accordingly seen that many frugal innovations of the Kerala Covid response stemmed from private individuals, local associations, and voluntary networks, to be later supported by the state/local governance system. We identify this in the case of 'break the chain campaign' and community kitchen campaign, in the state's initial support as in the case of 'breathe of hope', in the redeployment of the AYUSH personnel, or in the collaborative or mutual aid networks as we have seen in the case of women enterprises, 'breathe of hope' and in knowledge repository development. The local panchayat raj (the system of decentralized governance) provides the basis upon which a frugal innovative culture could further develop. If this ecosystem is in place, then frugal innovations will cease to be emergency-dependent!

The state's response itself during the entire Covid-19 pandemic was indeed backed by decentralized governance (Rahim & Chacko, 2020, Solomon et al., 2020). Local self-governments (LSGs) have a controlling stake in primary healthcare and support them with additional human resources, maintenance funds, medicines and consumables. The local Family Health Centres they administer are the core of the recent health policies Kerala has implemented under the label of *Aardram Mission* to adapt the primary care system to new needs, beginning with the chronic disorders. This was the largest investment the state made in recent years to improve healthcare infrastructure, with over 5289 posts of hospital workers created and doubling plan investments in the health sector (Sankar et al., 2023). LSG leadership in Kerala appears to have the capacity and resources to carry out this stewardship role. This capability is the result of the experience accumulated with the already existing robust network of local health centres in the state, and of over twenty-five years of decentralized governance.

7.6 Conclusion: What Frugality Means for Other Health Systems?

This chapter has discussed the conceptualization of frugal innovations in the healthcare sector, elaborating on the following arguments:

(i) The concept of frugal innovations goes beyond the simple cost-effectiveness argument for business models in developing societies, it offers multiple forms of affordable, adaptive and sustainable possibilities as evidenced during the pandemic.
(ii) The spatiotemporal context is important, but the success and effectiveness of frugality first of all depends on the social, political and cultural fabric of innovations (innovation ecosystem).
(iii) Frugal innovations originate in local situations and experiences, displaying a strong community-oriented perspective but they heavily depend on regional and state-wise social and economic policies.

The chapter has revealed three types of frugal innovations that have emerged in South India, especially in the state of Kerala, during the Covid-19 pandemic:

(i) community mutual aid systems and decentralized delivery ('break the chain' campaign, community kitchen).
(ii) use of low-cost alternative medical products and devices (rapid deployment in Ayur Raksha clinics, repurposed Ayurveda preventive medicines and formation of a repository of traditional medical innovations in the Covid-19 treatment);
(iii) complementary livelihood innovations ('chekkutty dolls' and mask manufacturing by women self-help groups).

Our analysis of these innovations highlights the following specific features that fit the perspective of frugality and social embeddedness. They respond to scarce financial and material resources; they tend to recycle existing technology and redefine their uses for emergency purposes; they rely on the adaptation of traditional knowledge, social forms of intervention and experiences of everyday life; they support low-skilled entrepreneurs and actors of informal sector, creating job/livelihood opportunities for women in the rural areas; they utilize existing social networks and forms of governance focusing on local government, trust in civil society organizations, and decentralization. A last, but more uneven and often less successful, feature is that these cases tend to be sustainable uses of resources.

Tracing the reasons why these frugal innovations could emerge and be easily adopted, we have insisted on: the importance of an innovation culture that the state has nurtured through the decentralized governance and people's participation; the strong co-existence of biomedical and indigenous health systems in the Kerala health sector; the mobilization of women network neighbourhood entrepreneurship and strategy of common pooling of resources.

Innovation marked with some sort of frugality thus appear as socially and territorially embedded, meaning their trajectories cannot be divorced from the institutional and cultural context. Often the value of frugality goes under the radar of larger frameworks of innovation incentives since these are using market-based innovation metrics to assess the efficiency of frugal innovations and therefore miss much of its benefits. Incentives such as profits, intellectual property rights, etc. are not aligned with the logic of many frugal innovations, which are about solving specific needs in cost-effective and socially adapted ways.

These experiences of frugal innovations resonate closely with the 'commons framework' (Ibata-Arens et al., 2026), as they functioned as commons-based arrangements, where communities collectively managed the resources through locally evolved rules rather than centralized market or state control alone. The pandemic responses mentioned illustrates how context- specific, self-organized systems can govern health-related commons effectively, reinforcing the idea that frugal innovations are embedded in and enabled by robust local commons institutions.

One interesting additional trait to be noted is that—unlike the usual definition of frugality—the innovations made during the pandemic have spanned beyond the health sector and were not confined to only the bottom of the social pyramid, hence pushing the boundaries of frugality beyond the informal sector and beyond the lower- and middle-class clientele.

References

Agarwal, N., Chung, K., & Brem, A. (2020). New technologies for frugal innovation. In A. J. McMurray & G. De Waal (Eds.), *Frugal innovation: A cross global research companion* (pp. 137–149). Routledge.

Ahuja, S., & Chan, Y. E. (2020). Frugal innovation and digitalisation: A platform ecosystem perspective. In A. J. McMurray & G. De Waal (Eds.), *Frugal innovation: A cross global research companion* (pp. 89–107). Routledge.

Arasaratnam, J., & Humphreys, G. (2013) Emerging economies drive frugal innovation. *Bulletin of the World Health Organization, 91*(1), 6–7. https://doi.org/10.2471/BLT.13.020113

Arshad, H. (2021) *Frugal Innovation in Healthcare: Aligning Systematic Review, Patterns, and Factors for Diffusion in Developing Economies*, PhD dissertation. University of Leipzig.

Awad, A., Trenfield, S. J., Pollard, T. D., Ong, J. J., Elbadawi, M., McCoubrey, L. M., Goyanes, A., Gaisford, S., & Basit, A. W. (2021). Connected healthcare: Improving patient care using digital health technologies. *Advanced Drug Delivery Reviews, 178*, 113958.

Banerjee, A. V., & Duflo, E. (2007). The economic lives of the poor. *Journal of Economic Perspectives, 21*(1), 141–167. https://doi.org/10.1257/089533007780095556

Banerjee, M. (2009). *Power, knowledge, medicine: Ayurvedic pharmaceuticals at home and in the world.* Orient Blackswan.

Bianchi, C., Bianco, M., Ardanche, M., & Schenck, M. (2017). Healthcare frugal innovation: A solving problem rationale under scarcity conditions. *Technology in Society*. https://doi.org/10.1016/j.techsoc.2017.08.001

Chataway, J., Hanlin, R., Mugwagwa, J., & Muraguri, L. (2010). Global health social technologies: Reflections on evolving theories and landscapes. *Research Policy, 39*(10), 1277–1288.

COHRED. (2012). *Annual report.* Council on Health Research for Development.

Cueto, M., Brown, T. M., & Fee, E. (2019). *The World Health Organization: A history* (Global Health Histories). Cambridge University Press.

Drèze, J., & Sen, A. (1995). *India. Economic development and social opportunity.* Clarendon Press.

Dyson, T. (2004). India's population—The future. In T. Dyson, R. Cassen, & L. Visaria (Eds.), Twenty-first century India: Population, economy, human development, and the environment. *Research Papers in Economics* (pp. 74–107).

Ganguly, S., & Bakhshi, S. (2020). Traditional and complementary medicine during COVID-19 pandemic. *Phytotherapeutic Research, 34*(12), 3083–3084.

Gaudilliere, J.-P. (2014). An Indian path to biocapital? The traditional knowledge digital library, drug patents, and the reformulation regime of contemporary Ayurveda. *East Asian Science, Technology and Society: An International Journal, 8*(4), 391–415.

Gaudilliere, J.-P., & Madhavan, H. (2026). Appropriate technologies, primary healthcare and the integration of traditional medicines in India. In S. Lechevalier, J.-P. Gaudillière, K. Ibata-Arens, & K. Takuma (Eds.), *Capitalism, innovations, and health after Covid-19. An Asian perspective*. Palgrave MacMillan.

Government of India. (2017). *National health policy*. https://www.nhp.gov.in/nhpfiles/national_health_policy_2017.pdf. Accessed January 25, 2023.

Grover, P., Caulfield, K., & Roehrich, J. (2014). Frugal innovation in healthcare and its applicability to developed markets. *British Academy of Management*. http://opus.bath.ac.uk/41361/

Gustilo Ong, A., & Gustale, E. (2020). *Frugal Innovations to accelerate sustainable development*, UNDP Accelerator Labs Blog. Accessed online 12th March 2024.https://www.undp.org/acceleratorlabs/blog/frugal-innovations-accelerate-sustainable-development.

Herstatt, C., & Tiwari, R. (2020). Opportunities of frugality in post-corona era. *International Journal of Technology Management, 83*(1–3).

Ibata Arens, K., Gaudillière, J.-P., Madhavan, H., & Nouguez, E. (2026). Commons and the political economy of access: Generics, neo traditional formulations and the dominant intellectual property regime of medicines. In S. Lechevalier, J.-P. Gaudillière, K. Ibata-Arens, & K. Takuma (Eds.), *Capitalism, innovations, and health after Covid-19. An Asian perspective*. Palgrave MacMillan.

Jaison, J., Sankar, H., Benny, G., & Nambiar, D. (2023). Who are the vulnerable, and how do we reach them? Perspectives of health system actors and community leaders in Kerala, India. *BMC Public Health, 23*(748). https://doi.org/10.1186/s12889-023-15632-9

Jayakumar, D., Bansal, A., Albano, J. E., & Mirhan, J. L. G. (2024). Dr. Devi Prasad Shetty: The visionary cardiothoracic surgeon who championed affordable healthcare. *Cureus, 16*(10), e70683. https://doi.org/10.7759/cureus.70683

Joseph, S. M., Iyer, D. S., & Pillai, R. V. (2021). Ayurvedic response to COVID-19 pandemic in Kerala, India and its impact on quarantined individuals—A community case study. *Frontiers in Public Health, 9*, 732523. https://doi.org/10.3389/fpubh.2021.732523

Karnani, A. (2007). Misfortune at the bottom of the pyramid, *Greener Management Journal*, 51, pp. 99–110.

Kaplinsky, R. (2011). Schumacher meets Schumpeter. Appropriate technology below the radar. *Research Policy, 40*(2), 193–203. https://doi.org/10.1016/j.respol.2010.10.003

Kumar, A., & Sarwal, R. (2021). *Health insurance for India's missing middle.* Niti Ayog Report. Government of India. https://doi.org/10.31219/osf.io/s2x8r

Kumar, H., & Bhaduri, S. (2014). Jugaad to grassroot innovations: Understanding the landscape of the informal sector innovations in India. *African Journal of Science, Technology, Innovation and Development, 6*(1), 13–22.

Kutty, V. R. (2000). Historical analysis of the development of healthcare facilities in Kerala State, India. *Health Policy and Planning, 15*(1), 103–109.

Madhavan, H., & Gaudilliere, J.-P. (2021). Reformulation and appropriation of traditional knowledge in industrial Ayurveda: The trajectory of Jeevani. *East Asian Science, Technology and Society: An International Journal, 14*(4), 603–621.

Mani, S. (2020). India's role in frugal innovations in health-related technologies to deal with Covid-19: *Opportunities and constraints.* Commentary on India's Economy and Society Series 13. Centre for Development Studies.

Manohar, S., Gundeti, S., Bhurke, L. W., Mundada, P. S., Murudkar, S., Surve, A., Sharma, R., Mata, S., Rana, R., Singhal, R., Vyas, N., Khanduri, S., Sharma, B. S., Srikanth, N., & Dhiman, K. S. (2022). AYUSH-64, a polyherbal Ayurvedic formulation in influenza-like illness: Results of a pilot study. *Journal of Ayurveda and Integrative Medicine, 13*(1).

Mazumdar-Shaw, K. (2018). Leveraging affordable innovation to tackle India's healthcare challenge. *IIMB Management Review, 30*, 37–50.

Ministry of Finance. (2022). *Economic survey 2021–22.* Government of India. https://www.indiabudget.gov.in/budget2022-23/economicsurvey/index.php

Ministry of Health. (2013). *Sector innovation council for health.* National Health Systems Resource Centre. New Delhi. Government of India.

Nelson, R., & Winter, S. (1982). *An evolutionary theory of economic change.* Harvard University Press.

Niraj, S., & Varsha, S. (2020). A review on scope of immuno-modulatory drugs in Ayurveda for prevention and treatment of Covid-19. *Plant Science Today, 7*(3), 417–423.

Pordié, L., & Gaudilliere, J.-P. (2014). Industrial Ayurveda: Drug discovery, reformulation, and the market. *Asian Medicine, 9*(1–2), 1–11.

Rahim, A. A., & Chacko, T. V. (2020). Replicating the Kerala State's successful COVID-19 containment model: Insights on what worked. *Indian Journal of Community Medicine, 45*(3), 261–265.

Sadanandan, R. (2001). Government health services in Kerala. Who benefits. *Economic and Political Weekly, 36*(32), 3071–3077.

Sankar, D. H., Joseph, J., Benny, G., & Nambiar, D. (2023). Of primary health care reforms and pandemic responses: Understanding perspectives of health system actors in Kerala before and during COVID-19. *BMC Primary Care, 24*(1), 59. https://doi.org/10.1186/s12875-023-02000-0

Schumacher, E. F. (1973). *Small is beautiful: Economics as if people mattered.* Blond & Briggs.

Schumpeter, J. A. (1934). *The theory of economic development: An inquiry into profits, capital, credit, interest, and the business cycle.* Harvard University Press.

Sharma, R. S., Rohatgi, A., Jain, S., & Singh, D. (2023). The Ayushman Bharat Digital Mission (ABDM): Making of India's digital health story. *CSI Transactions on ICT, 11*(1), 3–9. https://doi.org/10.1007/s40012-023-00375-0

Shukla, U., Ujjaliya, N., Gupta, P., Khare, V., Yadav, B., Rai, A. K., Amin, H., Rana, R., Tripathi, A., Khanduri, S., Sharma, B. S., Chandrasekhararao, B., Srikanth, N., & Dhiman, K. S. (2020). Efficacy and safety of *Guduchighana Vati* in asymptomatic and mild-to-moderate cases of coronavirus disease-19: A randomized controlled pilot study. *Ayu, 41*(3), 188–196. https://doi.org/10.4103/ayu.ayu_11_21

Solomon, N. K. A. G., Krishnan, A., Joseph, A. C., & Dhanuraj, D. (2020). *Kerala model of response to COVID-19.* Centre for Public Policy Research (CPPR), Kochi.

Sujatha, V., & Payyapallimana, U. (2022). Public health and the politics of knowledge: The role of traditional medicine in the management of COVID-19 in two South Indian states. *Journal of Health Management, 25*(2), 340–350. https://doi.org/10.1177/09720634221121998

Stalin, A., & Kenoth, R. (2022). Pro-social nudges and its impact on policy implications: Retrospecting 'break the chain' campaign of Kerala, India. *SSRN.* https://doi.org/10.2139/ssrn.4010816

Tiwari, R., & Herstatt, C. (2012). Frugal innovation: A global networks' perspective. *Die Unternehmung, 66*(3), 245–274.

UNICEF. (2018). *Demand for health services field guide: A human-centered approach.* https://www.unicef.org/innovation/sites/unicef.org.innovation/files/2018-11/demand_for_healthservices_fieldguide.pdf

Webber, C. M., Martínez-Gálvez, G., Higuita, M. L., Ben-Abraham, E. I., Berry, B. M., Porras, M. A. G., et al. (2020). Developing strategies for sustainable medical equipment maintenance in under-resourced settings. *Annals of Global Health, 86*, 39. https://doi.org/10.5334/aogh.2584

Weyrauch, T., & Herstatt, C. (2017). What is frugal innovation? Three defining criteria. *Journal of Frugal Innovation, 2*, 1. https://doi.org/10.1186/s40669-016-0005-y

World Health Organization. (2010). *Medical devices: Managing the mismatch.* WHO Press. http://whqlibdoc.who.int/publications/2010/9789241564045_eng.pdf

PART III

Knowledge in Action: Asian Experiences

CHAPTER 8

Care Systems in Crisis and Innovative Welfare Technologies: Stakeholders' Views Regarding Care Robots in Hong Kong SAR (China), Ireland and Japan

Naonori Kodate, Mei-chun Cheung, Akiyo Yumoto, Sarah Donnelly, Yurie Maeda, Mayuko Tsujimura, Hasheem Mannan, Wenwei Yu, Sayuri Suwa, Kazuko Obayashi, Shigeru Masuyama, W. C. H. Chan, Boris Hauray, and Diarmuid O'Shea

N. Kodate (✉) · S. Donnelly · H. Mannan
University College Dublin, Dublin, Ireland
e-mail: naonori.kodate@ucd.ie

M.-c. Cheung
The Chinese University of Hong Kong, Hong Kong, Hong Kong

A. Yumoto
Kawasaki City College of Nursing, Kawasaki, Japan

Y. Maeda
Technological University Dublin, Dublin, Ireland

M. Tsujimura
Shiga University of Medical Science, Otsu, Japan

S. Lechevalier et al. (eds.), *Capitalism, Innovations, and Health after Covid-19*,
https://doi.org/10.1007/978-3-032-24479-6_8

Abstract Innovative welfare technologies are frequently presented as the solution to global ageing. Using care robots as an example, this chapter asks: what is the perceived use of care robots in long-term care settings in Western Europe and East Asia, and what do stakeholders in different jurisdictions think of facilitators and barriers to a wider rollout of digital welfare technologies in their own care systems? Our previous research demonstrated that narratives in newspapers regarding care robots are more nuanced in Western Europe than in East Asia. We also found that Japan has been portrayed (in newspapers outside Japan) as the land of robot. For this study, we selected one country (Ireland) from Western Europe and one jurisdiction from East Asia (Hong Kong SAR (China)) where the development of public care provision has been relatively recent. We compared and contrasted these with Japan, where a universal public care system has been in place and care robots have been promoted both by the government and the market. Semi-structured in-depth interviews were conducted with 50 stakeholders in total in Hong Kong, Ireland and Japan. The participants included care professionals, service providers, technology developers, researchers and policymakers. The questions explored their knowledge of and views regarding the current use of assistive technologies in long-term care systems. The findings indicate that there is a sense of urgency in these jurisdictions that more welfare technologies, including care robots, should be utilised to ease the pressures on carers and systems. In recent years, the government's investment in this domain has stepped

W. Yu · S. Suwa
Chiba University, Chiba, Japan

K. Obayashi
Nihon Fukushi University, Mihama, Japan

S. Masuyama
Tokyo Medical University Hospital, Shinjuku, Japan

W. C. H. Chan
Northumbria University, Tyne, England

B. Hauray
Inserm, Paris, France

D. O'Shea
Royal Colleage of Physician of Ireland, Dublin, Ireland

up in Hong Kong, and a more general eHealth agenda has been adopted within the government's planned care reform in Ireland. Japan has been an early adopter of robotics in the world, and the government's robot strategy supports a wider rollout within the long-term care insurance scheme. Although the uptakes of care robots have been slow and falling short of stakeholders' expectations, a degree of optimism was noted for technological leapfrogging after the pandemic, particularly in Hong Kong. Considering the implementation of care robots has only begun in many countries, longitudinal and comparative research is necessary to establish how the characteristics of care systems and policies can promote user-oriented innovation and affect the diffusion of such innovation.

8.1 Introduction

The Covid-19 pandemic challenged health and social care systems across the globe, and reinforced the view that building capacity in care systems should be one of the health policy priorities. Throughout the pandemic, long-term care in particular was negatively impacted, and the lives of older people and people with disabilities, including people living with dementia, have been harshly affected. Even before the pandemic, many advanced economies have been facing major challenges due to global ageing (Organisation for Economic Co-operation and Development, 2011; World Health Organization, 2015) and efforts were made to ensure that health and social care systems are ready for this demographic shift (Greer et al., 2021; Greve, 2017; Wildman et al., 2021).

Against this background, innovative welfare technologies, including the use of AI and robotics, began to be deployed in care settings and are now seen as part of the policy solution to tackle the workforce shortage and promote ageing in place (Zigante, 2020). In parallel, increasing attention has been paid on the global stage to the role of assistive technologies in supporting healthy ageing and vulnerable populations (World Health Organization and United Nations Children's Fund, 2022).

Assistive technologies are designed to promote and support the well-being of people in need, by enabling them to live a healthy, productive and independent life (World Health Organization, 2018). Welfare technologies (WTs) can therefore be defined as 'assistive technologies that provide physical, social and cognitive assistance for older adults and persons at risk of disability, designed to increase their safety, participation and independence, and to improve care delivery and the work environment of healthcare professionals' (Kuoppamäki, 2021: 3). WTs include wheelchairs, walkers, lifts, exoskeletons, prostheses, braille display, screen magnifier, hearing aids, memory aids, in-home monitoring, care robots and wearable technology (World Health Organization, 2018).

Care robots are a type of WT, considering that they are designed to enable active ageing as well as ageing in place by supporting older persons, their families, and care professionals. They take many different forms (e.g. powered exoskeletons, mobile arm support, humanoid communication robot). This fast-growing area in industrially advanced economies is driven by research and development (R&D), which is closely associated with economic and industrial policy (Charisi et al., 2021; Wright, 2020). This is the conventional type of innovation, questioned and discussed in other chapters of this book (Gorry & Montalban, 2026; Lechevalier, 2026; Madhavan & Gaudilliere, 2026; Shiroyama et al., 2026).

In the European context, care robots have been developed as WTs to address ageing issues, while they are also strongly supported by national governments and the European Union. Policy initiatives such as Industry 4.0 (European Parliament, 2016) and the Partnership for Robotics in Europe (SPARC, 2015) supported the development of robots such as Robot-Era, Care-O-bot and Giraffe through the H2020 funding scheme. At the national level, for example, in Germany, the Federal Ministry of Education and Research has been funding R&D projects for robotic support of care under the banner of "Robotic Systems for Care" (Robotische Systeme für die Pflege) (Hülsken-Giesler et al., 2025). In East Asia, Japan and South Korea have been leading in this area, while now China leads in total operational robot stock. In 2019, the South Korean government announced an investment of 231 million EUR in developing service-oriented robots for health care, rehabilitation, and disaster response. As mentioned in the previous chapter, in Japan, the government's Revitalisation Strategy in 2015 (Cabinet Office, Japan, 2015) led to the establishment of the "Care Robot Development and Promotion Office" under the Ministry of Health, Labour, and Welfare (MHLW). The Ministry of Economy, Trade and Industry and the Ministry of Internal Affairs and Communications both provide funding and support R&D from the perspective of smart network robots and ICT innovation. Certainly, the USA and China are the two major producers of service robots (International Federation of Robotics, 2021).

Despite these efforts and investment, the diffusion of care robots as WTs has been relatively slow and limited even among 'early adopter' countries such as Denmark, Sweden and Japan (Frennert et al., 2021; Nickelsen, 2018; Wright, 2020; Bender, 2024). Several facilitators for and barriers to a greater use of care robots have been identified (Pekkarinen et al., 2020). Frennert et al. (2021) used the concept of 'technological frame', underlining the importance of society collectively shaping congruent technological frames among different stakeholders and aligning technological development accordingly. Pekkarinen et al. (2020) highlighted political, socio-economical, legal and practice-based issues as both enablers and barriers, examining three European countries (Germany, Sweden and Finland). Valokivi et al. (2021) also discussed generally positive attitudes towards the applications of eHealth, digitalisation and WTs in tackling ageing issues in Europe, while indicating a limited understanding of the complexity of the digital landscape. Therefore, it has been noted by several researchers across the world (Carlotta et al., 2018; Frennert et al., 2021; Jasanoff & Kim, 2015; Lee, 2025) that the diffusion of innovation in the case of care robots is not as straightforward as suggested by Davis (1989) and Rogers (2010). These studies point to the fact that gaps currently exist between policymaking and policy implementation in the case of care robots. In the care sector, realizing social and human well-being is the ultimate goal of innovation, and unless the positive impact of technological innovation is achieved among the target population (e.g. care recipients, vulnerable groups, people with disabilities), it cannot be regarded as user-centered innovation. Furthermore, social interactions and ethical use need to be properly considered in the process of deployment (Ide et al., 2024; Obayashi et al., 2024; Kodate, 2025).

Other studies (Bentley et al., 2018; Greenhalgh et al., 2015) have analysed and made policy recommendations on social implementation of WTs, particularly telemedicine/telecare. The framework proposed by Greenhalgh et al. (2015) presents six principles abbreviated as ARCHIE (an acronym for Anchored, Realistic, Co-creative, Human, Integrated, Evaluated). These are: (1) Design and development have to be rooted in a shared understanding of what is important to users; (2) Understand the natural history of the disease and the disabilities that accompany it (because it is progressive), and have a realistic recognition that it is not something that can be solved by technology or care; (3) Co-creative, evolutionary, and adaptive solutions with users are important; (4) Human relations and social networks affect the success of technology solutions; (5) Technology-based services need to be integrated by maximizing mutual recognition, coordination and mobilisation of expertise; (6) Continuous evaluation is essential to promoting system learning (Greenhalgh et al., 2015). As indicated by the critical perspective, people's trust (or the lack thereof) in digital technology has been underlined as an important factor (Bradford et al., 2018; Kania-Lundholm & Torres, 2018; Lie et al., 2016). While these previous studies highlight where these policy implementation gaps can emerge, the studies have not examined the nexus between the system in which care is provided and the role of actors working within it, and their interplay effects on implementation. Would diffusion be better facilitated by a universal care system, compared with a more fragmented, market-oriented system? Moreover, little is known regarding the use of care robots in emergent economies in Europe and Asia where the role of the state in welfare provision has been limited. The impact of institutional design (i.e. formal long-term care systems) on the diffusion of innovation such as care robots has been under-researched from a comparative perspective. Therefore, the research questions for this study were two-fold. First, what is the knowledge about and perceived use of care robots in long-term care settings in different jurisdictions in Western Europe and East Asia? Second, what are the systems' characteristics that facilitate or hinder the diffusion of innovation in the care sector? One assumption to be tested here is that a strong public policy initiative, combined with a universal public care system, would lead to a smoother and faster diffusion than a fragmented and market-oriented care system.

This study examines these questions by ascertaining the views of stakeholders concerning care robots in Hong Kong SAR, China (hereinafter "Hong Kong"), Ireland and Japan (Kodate, 2024). The three jurisdictions were selected based on the institutional designs of long-term care services (Abdul Karim et al., 2010; Aspalter, 2006; Esping-Andersen, 1999; Walker & Wong, 2005), with a strong commitment from each government to WTs and digitalisation of care. All three jurisdictions have a historically strong tendency to rely on family (predominantly women) carers in long-term care provision as the common feature (Kodate & Timonen, 2017; Lolich et al., 2022; Nyqvist et al., 2019). With regard to care robots, Japan is one of the early adopters in the world, and the country has formal long-term care insurance. On the other hand, Hong Kong and Ireland have a mix of public and private care systems, with the latter having as yet no universal access. While care robots are developed in both countries, their actual use is relatively new to care settings.

8.2 Tri-jurisdiction Comparison—Welfare Regimes, Health and Social Care and Key Policy Developments Around Welfare Technologies in Hong Kong, Ireland and Japan

The characteristics of the three jurisdictions are summarised in Table 8.1.

Thus the three selected jurisdictions share a commonality (i.e. traditionally strong family-oriented care model) while displaying differences (population size, demographic profile, formal long-term care insurance vs. statutory nursing home support scheme). Of the three jurisdictions, Japan is the only country with a clear long-term government commitment to care robots in health. Using the robot density figures (International Federation of Robotics, 2021) as a proxy, the sample of these three jurisdictions has a spread, with low and high robot production levels. As previously noted, it was hypothesised that we would find a greater sense of integration of care robots into Japanese welfare services (i.e. examples and policy enablers) than in the other two jurisdictions.

8.2.1 Methods

To elicit stakeholders' views in the three jurisdictions selected, the qualitative method was adopted, using semi-structured in-depth interviews.

8.2.2 Participants

In total, 50 stakeholders took part in the interviews (Table 8.2). We adopted a purposive sampling method and recruited the participants from academic and professional networks to begin with, and in some cases, a snowball sampling method was used. The inclusion criteria are that they have worked and are working closely in the domain of or with WTs. Three categories of stakeholders were targeted. These were: (1) technology developers (primarily roboticists) and researchers working in the area of WTs; (2) care providers (e.g. managers or owners of care facilities) and professionals who use WTs; and (3) policymakers and policy advisors in the area of WTs and digitalisation of health care.

Table 8.1 Profiles of three jurisdictions

	Hong Kong	*Ireland*	*Japan*
Population	7,474,200 (2020)	4,977,400 (2020)	125,710,000 (2020)
Proportion of older people (aged 65 or older)	19.1% (2020)	14.5% (2020)	28.4% (2020)
Welfare regimes	Productive/East Asian.	Liberal/Anglo-Saxon.	Conservative/East Asian.
Health and social care	Traditionally, family played the key role in LTC provision. Universal access to health care. No public long-term care insurance. Comprehensive Social Security Assistance Scheme (CSSA). Elderly Health Care Voucher (EHCV) since 2009. Long waiting lists for subsidised residential facilities.	Traditionally, family played the key role in LTC provision. No universal access to health care. No public long-term care insurance, but service provision under the health service system (the Nursing Home Support Scheme) and income supports for carers (e.g. Carer's Allowance). Home Care Packages (no statutory entitlement). Long waiting lists for both schemes.	Traditionally, family played the key role in LTC provision. Universal access to health care. Formal long-term Care Insurance since 2001. The coinsurance rate was increased from 10% for all, to 20% in 2015, and to 30% in 2018 for those in the highest income and/or asset level.
Key policy developments regarding WTs	The government established the "Innovation and Technology Fund for Application in Elderly and Rehabilitation Care". The fund opened two rounds of application and has	There has not yet been government-wide coordination around AI & robotics in connection with health or social care. Department of Health initiated a blue skies policy	The government set out Society 5.0. The Cabinet Office published the "New Robot Strategy" (2015). In 2015, the MHLW introduced a subsidy to allay costs for insured.

(continued)

Table 8.1 (continued)

	Hong Kong	*Ireland*	*Japan*
	granted about \$140 million to subsidise 770 elderly and rehabilitation service units, to procure or rent over 2900 technology products. In 2020, Legislative Council of HKSAR issued "Application of gerontechnology in elderly care services".	project looking at the potential for AI & Robotics to transform the health workforce and health services. The national health reform programme "SláinteCare" (2018): eHealth, digitalisation and the use of ICT form one major component. At European level, the European Commission published a report 'Ethics Guidelines for Trustworthy Artificial Intelligence' in April 2019.	care facilities in introducing care robots. Funding schemes began with the Japan Agency for Medical Research and Development and the METI. The "AI Network Society Promotion Council" established by the MIC in 2016. In 2018, the Office for Nursing Care Robot Development and Promotion established in the MHLW.
Examples of care robots	Grace.	Stevie, Mylo, Mario.	Paro, Pepper, HAL.
Robot density in the manufacturing industry, 2020 (robots installed per 10,000 employees)	275	The second-lowest density in the EU-15 member states.	390

(Demography: Census and Statistics Department, The Government of the Hong Kong Special Administrative Region, n.d.; Central Statistics Office, Ireland, n.d.; Statistics Bureau of Japan, n.d.). Robot density: International Federation of Robotics, 2021)

8.2.3 *Interviews*

Semi-structured interviews were conducted in three jurisdictions between September 2020 and April 2022. The interviews were carried out in local languages (Cantonese, English and Japanese) by native speakers, and due

Table 8.2 Background data of the interviewees

	Tech developers/ Researchers (TR)	*Care providers/ Practitioners (CP)*	*Policymakers/ Advisors (PA)*	*Total*
Hong Kong	5	7	3	15
Ireland	7	8	2	17
Japan	6	7	5	18
Total	18	22	10	50

to the pandemic, they were conducted online. Information sheets and consent forms were provided, with the latter signed by interviewees. The interviews were audio-recorded and transcribed. To ensure the consistency of the study in the three jurisdictions, an interview topic guide with common questions and general instructions was developed. The interview topic guide included the following: the interviewees' personal profiles (occupation, role and responsibilities, their relationship with WTs, and their familiarity with robots); their views regarding the use of WTs in social care, strengths and weaknesses of each jurisdiction's long-term care system; their views on facilitators/barriers to a wider rollout of care robots; and their future vision for independent living in old age (supported by WTs). The average interview durations for each jurisdiction were: 49:02 mins (Hong Kong SAR), 41:46 mins (Ireland) and 69:07 mins (Japan). The overall average duration therefore was 53:40 mins.

8.2.4 *Data Analysis*

Thematic analysis was used with a two-stage (deductive and inductive) approach (Braun & Clarke, 2006). Firstly, after the transcripts were translated into English, the data from the three jurisdictions were coded thematically along the lines of the topic guide, and checked by two coders (NK and YM). Subsequently, common themes were sought across all participants' answers from the three jurisdictions. The inductive approach was adopted because appropriate theoretical frameworks have not yet been found for this relatively new area of research. The data were split into three sets (one set from each jurisdiction), and we investigated whether there were any common themes within each set. These themes were then compared and contrasted between the three jurisdictions.

We also checked whether there are characteristic responses in relation to the participants' views on facilitators/barriers to a wider rollout of care robots which depend on their professional categories (technology developers/researchers (TR), care providers/professionals (CP) and policymakers/advisors (PA)).

8.3 Results

8.3.1 Familiarity With Care Robots

Except in Japan, it was confirmed that the use of robots in the care sector is new, although the seal robot *PARO*, the humanoid robots *Pepper* and *Nao*, and the AI-assisted personal assistant robot *Temi* were mentioned by many respondents in all three jurisdictions (Fig. 8.1). Respondents in Japan and Hong Kong SAR were much more familiar with different types of care robots than those in Ireland.

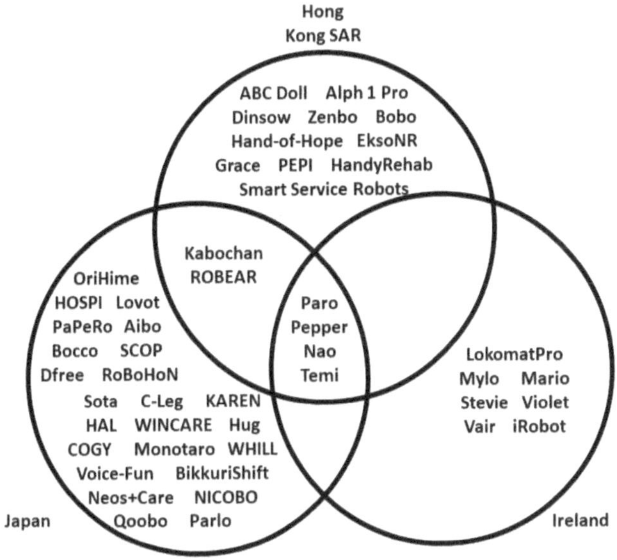

Fig. 8.1 Robots mentioned in the interviews

8.3.2 Common Themes—Lack of Resources and High Expectations for WTs

Despite the different demographic profiles of the three jurisdictions, almost all respondents expressed concern for their respective long-term care systems. For example, older adults and carers in Hong Kong and Ireland are believed to receive insufficient care and services, and many respondents stated that care robots are most needed in order to fill the gaps (e.g. safety monitoring, mobility support).

> In the current system, using technology is not common among service provision. Technology may come into place in aspects such as administrative and management systems, medicine delivery or care plan. However, for daily care provision, I think the use of care robots is minimal (. . .) we should be able to use more. (Researcher, Dementia Care, Hong Kong)

> For older people in particular there's the home care scheme (. . .) bringing home care in terms of carers and hours into the home. I think they (the government) need to look at that with the use of technology. (Technology Developer, Ireland)

In Japan, staff shortage was frequently mentioned, but many respondents went further, highlighting the complexity of implementing WTs in care settings.

> I don't think the purpose is to use technology per se. Such technology is utilised as a means to fulfil demands arising in the care sector. (. . .) There is already not enough manpower. Installing monitoring equipment in all rooms in a nursing home, for example, then, as a caregiver, you could be notified all at once from all the rooms, and if only two care professionals are on shift that night, who could respond to all those alerts? So understanding operational issues of technology in practice is critical. (Policy Advisor, Japan)

Overall, high expectations regarding the use of care robots and WTs were noted, and closely associated with the lack of resources in the sector, irrespective of the differing degrees of demographic pressure.

8.3.3 Key Policies and Actors in Three Jurisdictions

Key stakeholders mentioned in the interviews are shown in Table 8.3.

Table 8.3 Key stakeholders mentioned in the interviews

	Hong Kong	*Ireland*	*Japan*
Government & agencies	Hong Kong Council of Social Service (HKCSS) Social Welfare Department (SWD) Innovation and Technology Bureau Electrical and Mechanical Services Department (EMSD) Hospital Authority Hong Kong Productivity Council	Health Service Executive (HSE) Department of the Taoiseach Health Information and Quality Authority (HIQA) Health Products Regulatory Authority (HPRA) National Integrated Care Programme for Older Persons (NICPOP) Enterprise Ireland European Union	Ministry of Health, Labour and Welfare (MHLW) Ministry of Economy, Trade and Industry (METI) Ministry of Internal Affairs and Communications (MIC) Cabinet Office, Japan (CAO) Japan Agency for Medical Research and Development (AMED) Pharmaceuticals and Medical Devices Agency (PMDA)
Care providers and professional groups	TWGHs Jockey Club Rehabilitation Complex	Irish Society of Chartered Physiotherapists (ISCP) National Rehabilitation Hospital (NRH)	Japan Medical Association (JMA) Japanese Association of Occupational Therapists (JAOT)
Support and community groups	Dementia Link	Alzheimer Society of Ireland (ASI) Age Friendly Ireland Programme An Garda Síochána (Police)	Elderly Service Providers Association Association for Technical Aids
Research & Development, and enterprises	N/A	Fujitsu Ireland, IBM, etc	National Institute of Advanced Industrial Science and Technology (AIST) New Energy and Industrial Technology Development Organization (NEDO) Panasonic, Omron, Fujisoft

8.3.4 Prominent Features in the Three Jurisdictions

In each jurisdiction, key policy milestones in both social care and WT support were addressed.

Hong Kong SAR, China
In Hong Kong, the year 2017 has seen a lot of policy initiatives.

> Gerontechnology is a new topic which has gained increasing attention since 2017. (Researcher, Hong Kong)

This was the year when the Hong Kong Council of Social Service (HKCSS) hosted the Gerontech and Innovation Expo cum Summit (GIES). In 2021, the Social Innovation and Entrepreneurship Development Fund (SIE Fund) established the Gerontechnology Platform, where stakeholders from both the supply and demand sides come together and exchange information. Additionally, the then Secretary for Labour and Welfare earmarked 1 billion HKD for setting up the Innovation and Technology Fund for Application in Elderly and Rehabilitation Care (I&T Fund). Also in 2017, 4 billion HKD was allocated to supporting a fund for caregiving. The government formatted the Elderly Services Programme Plan (ESPP). In order to incentivise older persons to use private services, the government has been looking into the use of Residential Care Service Voucher (RCSV) and Community Care Service Voucher (CCSV).

Ireland
In Ireland in the last decade, there have been several policies and projects in support of older people's care. The main drivers in Ireland have been voluntary organisations and charity bodies, and major research initiatives have been financially supported by Atlantic Philanthropies.

> In Ireland we have a huge amount of NGO's providing supports for older people. (Support Organisation, Ireland)

However, as the country underwent a rapid economic growth period (the "Celtic Tiger"), government involvement steadily grew. In 2012, the National Positive Ageing Strategy and the National Carers' Strategy were published. This was followed by the National Dementia Strategy, which led to the establishment of the National Dementia Office. A national campaign called "Under-Stand Together" was launched. The Memory Technology Resource Room (MTRR) began to be rolled out across the country in 2017. The MTRR offers access to WTs for anybody who has concerns about their memory, and is primarily used by people with dementia, or family carers. The major policy milestone is the national Health Reform Programme, Sláintecare, which was published in 2018. It is designed to bring universal access to health and social care for the first time, and eHealth is one of the key enablers for achieving the goal. Progress has been slow but respondents were positive towards the development.

> For a long time we talked about home based care, and everybody was in agreement that all the national policies are to support people to live at home, but we never really saw a real commitment to that in terms of financing (. . .) now everybody seems to be singing off the same hymn sheet. And not just saying the same things actually, there's action behind it. (Policymaker, Ireland)

Japan

In Japan, the dominant discourse was the sustainability of its long-term care insurance scheme and bureaucratic sectionalism. As one of the fastest ageing countries in the world, Japan has had a much longer history of developing policies around social care for older people and WTs. In 1993, the Act on the Promotion of Research, Development and Dissemination of Welfare Equipment was passed. The Act was an attempt to bring two Ministries (METI (formerly MITI) and MHLW) together to overcome bureaucratic sectionalism in preparation for increasing demand for WTs.

> Broadly speaking, the development is the remit of the METI, and the clinical issues, evaluation, and dissemination in the care sector are covered by the MHLW, which was the role assigned to it. It continues to be like that up to the present. (Care provider, Japan)

In 2000, the policy of long-term care insurance was implemented, and this ensured older people's access to care, depending on their needs, not ability to pay. While this accomplished and has continued to provide universal access, the long-term care market in Japan has been operated under a highly standardised and heavily regulated market. Care providers make decisions in response to changes in the unit price set by the government. In the last two decades, this dynamic and institutional design have been sustained even as the resources became increasingly constrained. Technological innovation, including the development and procurement of care robots, was encouraged under this quasi-market mechanism. In 2015, the New Robot Strategy was published by the CAO, and the MHLW introduced a subsidy of 100,000 JPY per device to allay costs for insured care facilities in introducing care robots. Funding schemes were provided by the AMED under the auspices of the METI for pilot studies on care robots with communication and social support functions for older people. The "AI Network Society Promotion Council" was established by the MIC in 2016, and in 2018, the Office for Nursing Care Robot Development and Promotion was established in the MHLW.

8.3.5 *Different Sets of Issues Surrounding Three Long-term Care Systems and the Use of WTs*

Some issues unique to their own systems were discussed.

Hong Kong SAR, China

In Hong Kong SAR, the restrictions of capacity, particularly physical space were raised by several respondents as obstacles to expanding care services.

> The biggest challenges of Hong Kong's social care system must be the increase in demand and the inadequacy in supporting measures. There is always a long waiting list. (Care provider, Hong Kong)

> There is not enough land, people who work on (. . .) so, 'no money', 'no land', 'no people' (. . .). (Researcher, Hong Kong)

This physical space limitation, on the other hand, meant that there was no real demand for telemedicine.

> You rarely need three hours to reach a hospital in Hong Kong, so telemedicine is limited here. (Policymaker, Hong Kong)

The pandemic changed this landscape, and video calls based on the concept of a 'hospital without walls' were tested and rolled out in local hospitals. Hong Kong's unique public-private mix was also highlighted by some respondents.

> Hong Kong has a double-tier system, so health care is run both publicly and privately. Hong Kong is unique in the way that the public system has a leading role. Even if we are middle or lower class, we may still use the public services unless you have health insurance or have money (. . .) Another possibility is a mixed-mode system, for example, one may go for private services for basic health care needs, and may go for public services for long-term care or hospitalisation. (Policy advisor, Hong Kong)

The public-private divide creates discordance between the two sectors.

> Resources are not divided equally between the public and private sectors, and there is still a lot of capacity for the private sector to take care of more patients. Yet, the charges are too high, and not everyone can afford to go for private services. (Care professional, Hong Kong)

In the private sector in particular, technology use is on the increase, but its effectiveness is questioned.

> When the government rolled out the Innovation & Technology Fund, so many technologies became available. But are all products practical to use? We think it may not be the case. Some of them are more of a gimmick, a toy with new technology. But can they really help the care services or reduce the workload of the staff? That may not be the case. (Care provider, Hong Kong)

Ireland

One prominent feature in Ireland is advocacy groups' initiatives to fill the gaps in the current provision of care and services. One respondent spoke about a pendant-style digital alert scheme that is subsidised by the government.

> We are using pendants (. . .) sharing it with the HSE where you can geo-map. So the older person gives their permission and they might have Alzheimer's and they are comfortable within their own geo thing and so we geo-map and maybe an alarm goes off but we can sign forms in such a way that the government is not totally responsible if somebody falls and

> every risk … we don't over-medicalise it. What a joy that is I know mam is safe, she goes as far as you know the church, but if she falls or went further we'd know about it. (Care provider, Ireland)

In addition, Ireland has been actively involved in international projects such as WHO's Age-Friendly Cities. All 31 local authorities in the country implemented age-friendly programs, which made Ireland the first country in the world that achieved full, country-wide membership in the World Health Organization's Global Network of Age Friendly Cities and Communities. Through these programs, some WTs have been trialed (e.g. tele-consultation on chronic conditions).

> We're working with libraries (…) to make sure that older people can digitally access, borrow a book and that they can connect with their grandchildren. (Care provider, Ireland)

Japan

In Japan, while the government-led, long-term care scheme has a lot of advantages, the universal system has some weaknesses, particularly around person-centeredness and preventive medicine.

> It's public health insurance after all, so it's, to a certain degree, one size fits all. I wouldn't say it's standardised completely, but it's there to offer a certain level … (Policymaker, Japan)

> Since the system is built in such a manner that a greater premium is paid to a care recipient when the degree of care required becomes greater. So there is no subsidy for a care robot in order to prevent the condition from getting worse. (Policymaker, Japan)

The top-down system was also linked to the lack of speed.

> The laws and regulations governing medical devices are extremely strict in Japan. (Care provider, Japan)

> Technology is evolving too fast to keep up with legislation. (Care provider, Japan)

> In Japan, it will take 5 to 10 years to implement it due to PMDA (Pharmaceutical Affairs Law) (Policy advisor, Japan)

Bureaucratic sectionalism can get in the way.

> There is a vertical division of the ministries. Let's say I hurt my back as a carer. When we decide to introduce robots as a preventive measure for such back pain, the current universal insurance system does not allow that, as it recognises only productivity as a sign of benefits for long-term care facilities. Unless you have the evidence of being productive, you won't get any subsidies for a robot, however much your back hurts. (...) Therefore, even if a good robot is produced to prevent back pain, introducing that robot is a challenge. (Policy advisor, Japan)

> The METI will simply promote care robots and dive for it (from the perspective of economic and market growth), while the MHLW will go steady, trying not to increase the budget and total cost of long-term care, so it appears (...) It's not that the vertical division is bad, but that the coordination and communication between the horizontal parts is not good. That may be the problem ... (Technology developer, Japan)

8.3.6 Facilitators and Barriers in the Three Jurisdictions

The tables below (Tables 8.4 and 8.5) summarise the facilitating and hindering factors that were mentioned by the participants in relation to the diffusion of care robots in each jurisdiction.

Where three or more interviewees referred to the item, this is shown in the tables by two ticks next to the item.

Funding and subsidies for purchasing and renting care robots were raised in Hong Kong and Ireland as critical elements for facilitating increased use of care robots. In Japan, incentivisation through the long-term care system and intensified use of care robots within the system (i.e. building critical mass) were mentioned by all three types of stakeholders.

The hindering factors indicate some remarkable differences between Hong Kong and Ireland on the one hand, and Japan on the other. Cost, and the lack of familiarity with and training in the use of care robots featured prominently in the former, and insufficient coordination among technology developers (seeds) and users and care systems (needs) was frequently mentioned by the respondents in the latter. As previously highlighted, fragmented government policy (bureaucratic sectionalism) was one of the hindering factors that the respondents observed (technology developers and researchers, in particular).

Table 8.4 Facilitating factors for the diffusion of care robots

	Hong Kong			*Ireland*			*Japan*		
	TR	*CP*	*PA*	*TR*	*CP*	*PA*	*TR*	*CP*	*PA*
Funding for care robots (purchase/rental)	✓✓	✓✓			✓✓		✓		✓
Low-cost products (market solutions)	✓			✓	✓		✓		✓
User-centred design, needs-driven R&D and usability of care robots	✓	✓	✓	✓				✓	
Promotion, public debates and publicity of care robots (e.g. exhibition)	✓	✓		✓	✓	✓	✓	✓	
Increased use of care robots (critical mass)							✓	✓	✓
Knowledge of benefits of using care robots	✓	✓✓		✓		✓	✓	✓	
Further trials and research evidence (e.g. living lab)	✓		✓		✓			✓	
Government commitment to care robots (e.g. political will)	✓	✓		✓		✓		✓	
Single government office devoted to digitalisation & care robots		✓			✓		✓		✓
Government support for care system enhancement	✓	✓			✓				
Incentivisation through long-term care system							✓	✓	✓
Regulation and risk management	✓	✓			✓		✓		✓
Education, training and support for older people & carers	✓	✓	✓	✓		✓	✓	✓	✓
Coordination between health and social care services		✓	✓	✓	✓			✓	

(continued)

Table 8.4 (continued)

	Hong Kong			*Ireland*			*Japan*		
	TR	*CP*	*PA*	*TR*	*CP*	*PA*	*TR*	*CP*	*PA*
Coordination among stakeholders (e.g. government, tech firms, care providers)	✓	✓	✓				✓		
Knowledge of ecosystem around care services and care robots	✓		✓	✓					
Mindsets and attitudes (e.g. openness to change)		✓	✓	✓	✓		✓	✓	✓
Human resources (e.g. cross-disciplinary technologist, gerontechnology champion)				✓	✓		✓	✓	✓
Infrastructure and digitalisation		✓			✓				✓
Demographic change and external pressure (e.g. labour shortage)	✓						✓		✓

TR: Technology developers & Researchers; CP: Care providers & Practitioners; PA: Policymakers & Advisors

Table 8.5 Hindering factors for the diffusion of care robots

	Hong Kong			*Ireland*			*Japan*		
	TR	*CP*	*PA*	*TR*	*CP*	*PA*	*TR*	*CP*	*PA*
Lack of funding/funding model	✓			✓	✓		✓		✓
Cost	✓✓	✓	✓	✓	✓✓	✓	✓	✓	✓
Lack of familiarity, acceptance, attitudes, technophobia	✓	✓✓	✓	✓✓	✓	✓	✓	✓	
Fear of losing jobs and staff's resistance to change of care practice	✓	✓	✓		✓		✓✓	✓	✓
Perception of robots in society (e.g. luxury goods, only in fiction)				✓		✓	✓	✓	
Lack of knowledge, literacy, training and skills	✓	✓	✓	✓	✓		✓	✓	
Lack of R&D capacity and testbeds (e.g. living labs)		✓	✓		✓			✓	
Difficulty of conducting research with older adults and creating market				✓			✓	✓	✓
Limited functionalities and usability of care robots	✓	✓	✓	✓	✓		✓	✓	
Difficulty of personalising/localising care robots (e.g. language)		✓	✓					✓	
Lack of resources (e.g. staff, space, time, extra money)	✓	✓✓	✓	✓	✓		✓	✓	
Lack of infrastructure (e.g. WiFi)	✓			✓	✓	✓			
Lack of government commitment				✓	✓				

(continued)

Table 8.5 (continued)

	Hong Kong			*Ireland*			*Japan*		
	TR	*CP*	*PA*	*TR*	*CP*	*PA*	*TR*	*CP*	*PA*
Fragmented government policy (e.g. bureaucratic sectionalism)							✓✓	✓	✓
General trend of lagging behind in digitalisation in social care							✓		✓
Lack of guidelines, regulation and risk management (e.g. fear of legal cases)	✓	✓	✓	✓✓	✓	✓	✓	✓	✓
Insufficient coordination among stakeholders (e.g. tech developers, users)	✓	✓	✓				✓	✓✓	✓✓
Mismatch between care systems and technology	✓		✓	✓	✓		✓✓	✓	
Adverse impact of institutional design (long-term care system)							✓	✓	✓
Mistrust in data use and privacy	✓			✓			✓		

TR: Technology developers & Researchers; CP: Care providers & Practitioners; PA: Policymakers & Advisors

8.3.7 *Pace of Diffusion and Prospects of a Wider Roll-out of Care Robots*

In terms of each jurisdiction's readiness for care robots, the majority of respondents in Hong Kong answered that they felt that people in Hong Kong are ready for a greater roll out of WTs including care robots, those in Ireland are sceptical, mainly due to the lack of familiarity (with robotics-aided devices) and proper infrastructure, particularly in rural areas.

> It just has to work, it has to be reliable, it has to be branded, it has to be something that has the infrastructure behind it to say these are functional devices you can put in your home and they're not just novelties, but they are actually going to do something useful. And I think once it gets to that kind of stage, people can trust them … (Care provider, Ireland)

In Japan, due to the longest and strongest policy push from various ministries and agencies in the last ten years, there is a shared understanding that the implementation by all types of stakeholder could have been better, faster and smoother.

> Because there is financial support, and it does not cost us anything, let's introduce them for the time being. When I went to the facility and asked them about the robots, they were not actually using them at all. I have encountered quite a lot of similar cases. (Researcher, Japan)

> Users still show a very strong resistance. There are many people who have intense aversion or feel allergic because they have to change their existing operations, which brings a sense of burden, or because they are machines. (Care provider, Japan).

However, many respondents also believe that a sense of crisis (e.g. staff shortage) on the ground, combined with accumulated knowledge and training, will lead to an increase in the use of care robots in the near future. In 2021, the government also revised the remuneration scheme by introducing an information system called "LIFE" (Long-term care Information system For Evidence). This change will encourage more evidence-based long-term care.

> The way care will change by the introduction of equipment, what kind of results will be produced, what sort of rewards will be generated as a result ... once you can see that clearly, care providers may change their attitudes. (Policymaker, Japan)

Using the same interview topic guide across the three jurisdictions, it became clear that each jurisdiction is at a different stage of accepting care robots in welfare services. The results also highlighted the perceived impact that care systems' characteristics have on technology push and demand pull.

8.4 Discussion and Conclusion

Our findings clearly demonstrated that those stakeholders at the coalface of either providing care for older people using WTs or developing policies and care robots are similarly positive about the use of care robots and WTs to fill the gaps in services and augment the long-term care systems. There are no major differences in this sense across the three jurisdictions. This reflects the challenges and pressures facing the long-term care sector. However, we also found several differences between the three jurisdictions.

Familiarity with care robots varied from jurisdiction to jurisdiction, which was evinced by the concrete examples of robots mentioned by the respondents. The Irish participants were the least knowledgeable and mentioned mostly the robots developed locally. They were also the most unsure about the country's readiness for a large-scale rollout. However, the reason for this was primarily because of the ongoing healthcare reform and the lack of infrastructure in the countryside, not because they doubt the potential transformative impact that WTs can have on care services and the system. The respondents both in Hong Kong and Japan were enthusiastic about a greater use of care robots, although a sense of frustration about the pace of diffusion was expressed from some Japanese participants. As the ARCHIE framework (Greenhalgh et al., 2015) suggests, this reflects the complex and multi-layered processes of policy implementation around WTs in care. The uniform long-term care system can facilitate the government's support for the introduction of care robots, but there can be a mismatch between personalisation of care using such devices and standardisation of minimal care guaranteed under public provision. Moreover, bureaucratic sectionalism can hinder mutual recognition, coordination and mobilisation of expertise, which technology-aided care services require.

When we consider social acceptance of technologies, the perceived usefulness and usability have been considered to be the two crucial factors (Venkatesh et al., 2003). While this may apply to the decision-making of users at individual or family level, the study demonstrates that on a wider social level, other factors also appear to be at play. The study echoes some of the previous and recent findings that include, for example, congruence between the anticipated benefits of care robots and the actual usefulness (Frennert et al., 2021; Che et al., 2025), and coordination among stakeholders (Pekkarinen et al., 2020; Kodate, 2025). Users' trust in technology and data use also matters (Bradford et al., 2018; Lie et al., 2016; Akuta et al., 2026). While these may hold true, this study unearthed different, more systematic features, such as a mismatch between care systems and technology (ecosystem), data management and risk regulation, which affect the speed and process of diffusion.

Our original assumption could not be proven outright by this study. Among the three jurisdictions, Japan has had the longest period of using care robots as a WT and has a formal long-term care system, yet there is consensus that penetration or embedding has not happened. The participants highlighted both strengths and weaknesses of the system for promoting and embedding care robots in practice. On the other hand, in Hong Kong SAR in particular, there was a sense of optimism for technological leapfrogging after the pandemic. Here lies a challenge of striking the right balance between the promotion of user-centered innovation, namely, ethical use of care robots, guided by responsive regulation, and universal access to human care, guaranteed by government.

The limitation of this study consists in the issue of generalisability. However, the in-depth interviews with 50 stakeholders from one European country and two East Asian jurisdictions illustrate how care systems and public policy around the use of WTs can interact with each other. Future studies should critically examine legal, ethical and regulatory arrangements (e.g. health technology assessment) in different jurisdictions, together with the impact of using more WTs on older people, carers, care professionals and society at large from the perspective of equity, wellbeing and human-centered care.

Acknowledgements We would like to thank all participants in the study and the funding body for the project "Harmonisation towards the establishment of Person-centred, Robotics-aided Care System" (HarP:RoCS), 2019–2022. We are also grateful to the CTSH ("Capitalism, Technology, Society, and Health") project team, particularly the four editors of this book.

Author Contribution NK planned the study, collected data, conducted analysis and drafted the paper. MC, AY, SD, YM, MT, HM and WY collected data and assisted in the analysis and contributed to the write-up. SS, KO, SM, WCHC, BH and DOS collaborated in the planning of the study, data collection and analysis, and contributed to the write-up.

Funding details This work was supported by the Toyota Foundation under Grant 'Co-Creating New Society with Advanced Technologies' (D18-ST-0005).

Ethical standards Research ethics approvals were given from two institutions: UCD Human Subjects Ethics Review Committee (HS-20-08-Kodate) and Chiba University Graduate School of Nursing Ethics Review Committee (31–91).

References

Abdul Karim, S., Eikemo, T. A., & Bambra, C. (2010). Welfare state regimes and population health: Integrating the East Asian welfare states. *Health Policy, 94*(1), 45–53.

Akuta, Y., Suwa, S., Kamimoto, T., Ide, H., Inuyama, A., Kodate, N., Shimamura, A., Iida, K., Yumoto, A., Kawakami, N., Jitsuisihi, S., Tsujimura, M., Ishimaru, M., Suzuki, S., Doi, S., Sakai, A., Iwase, S., & Yu, W. (2026). Willingness to use home-care robots and views regarding the provision of personal information in Japan: Comparison between actual or potential users and robot developers. *Computers in Human Behavior, 174*, 108817.

Aspalter, C. (2006). The East Asian welfare model. *International Journal of Social Welfare,15*, 290–301.

Bender, S. (2024). *Feeling machines Japanese robotics and the global entanglements of more-than-human care*. Stanford University Press.

Bentley, C. L., Powell, L. A., Orrell, A., & Mountain, G. A. (2018). Making telecare desirable rather than a last resort. *Ageing & Society, 38*, 926–953.

Braun, V., & Clarke, V. (2006). Using thematic analysis in psychology. *Qualitative Research in Psychology, 3*(2), 77–101.

Bradford, D. K., Van Kasteren, Y., Zhang, Q., & Karunanithi, M. (2018). Watching over me: Positive, negative and neutral perceptions of in-home monitoring held by independent-living older residents in an Australian pilot study. *Ageing & Society, 38*, 1377–1398.

Cabinet Office of Japan, Headquarters for Japan's Economic Revitalization. (2015). *New robot strategy – vision, strategy, action and plan*. Available at https://www.cas.go.jp/jp/seisaku/seicho/pdf/robot_honbun_150210EN.pdf (Accessed 28 January 2026).

Carlotta, B., Rainer, H., & Bechtold, U. (2018). Socially assistive robots diffusion in elderly care. A pre-adoption study by agent-based modelling. *Journal of Strategic Innovation and Sustainability, 13*(5), 58–75.
Central Statistics Office, Ireland. (n.d.). *Population and Migration Estimates*, April 2020. Available at: https://www.cso.ie/en/releasesandpublications/er/pme/populationandmigrationestimatesapril2020/ (Accessed 28 January 2026).
Census and Statistics Department, The Government of the Hong Kong Special Administrative Region. (n.d.). *Population – Overview*. Available at https://www.censtatd.gov.hk/en/ (Accessed 28 January 2026).
Charisi, V., Compañó, R., Duch Brown, N., Gomez Gutierrez, E., Klenert, D., Lutz, M., Marschinski, R., & Torrecilla-Salinas, C. (2021). *JRC conference and workshop report: What future for European robotics? A science for policy perspective*. European Commission. Available at https://publications.jrc.ec.europa.eu/repository/handle/JRC125343 (Accessed 28 January 2026).
Che, R.-P., Ruan, Y.-X., Kodate, N., Shi, Y., Liu, Z., Donnelly, S., Suwa, S., Yu, W., Kong, D., & Cheung, M.-C. (2025). Effectiveness and usability of care robots in supporting older adults living with frailty: A systematic review. *Digital Health*, 11.
Davis, F. D. (1989). Perceived usefulness, perceived ease of use, and user acceptance of information technology. *MIS Quarterly, 13*(3), 319–340.
Esping-Andersen, G. (1999). *Social Foundations of Post-industrial Economies*. Oxford University Press.
European Parliament. (2016). *Industry 4.0. policy department A; economic and scientific policy*.
Frennert, S., Aminoff, H., & Östlund, B. (2021). Technological frames and care robots in eldercare. *International Journal of Social Robotics, 13*, 311–325.
Gorry, P., & Montalban, M. (2026). The crisis of capitalism and health innovation: Symptoms of a crisis or of success? In S. Lechevalier, J.-P. Gaudillière, K. Ibata-Arens, & K. Takuma (Eds.), *Capitalism, innovations, and health after Covid-19. An Asian perspective*. Palgrave MacMillan.
Greer, S. L., Lynch, J., Reeves, A., Falkenbach, M., Gingrich, J., Cylus, J., & Bambra, C. (2021). *Ageing and health: The politics of better policies. European observatory on health systems and policies*. Cambridge University Press.
Greenhalgh, T., Procter, R., Wherton, J., Sugarhood, P., Hinder, S., & Rouncefield, M. (2015). What is quality in assisted living technology? The ARCHIE framework for effective telehealth and telecare services. *BMC Medine, 13*, 91.
Greve, B. (ed.). (2017). *Long-term care for the elderly in Europe: Development and prospects*. Routledge.
Hülsken-Giesler, M., Ackerman, M., Eichelberg, M., Hein, A., Kodate, N., Lienenbrink, S., Meyer, S., Müller, C., & Paluch, R. (2025). Editorial. *International Journal of Social Robotics, 17*, 1633–1634.

Ide, H., Suwa, S., Akuta, Y., Kodate, N., Tsujimura, M., Ishimaru, M., Shimamura, A., Kitinoja, H., Donnelly, S., Hallila, J., Toivonen, M., Bergman-Kärpijoki, C., Takahashi, E., & Yu W. (2024). A comparative study to elucidate factors explaining willingness to use home-care robots in Japan, Ireland, and Finland. *Scientific Reports*, *14*(1), 27656. https://doi.org/10.1038/s41598-024-79414-y

International Federation of Robotics. (2021). Robot density in the manufacturing industry 2020. Available at https://ifr.org/downloads/press2018/World_Robotics_-_Robot_Density_2020_by_nation.jpg. (Accessed August 1, 2022).

Jasanoff, S., & Kim, S.-H. (Eds.). (2015). *Dreamscapes of modernity: Sociotechnical imaginaries and the fabrication of power*. The University of Chicago Press.

Kania-Lundholm, M., & Torres, S. (2018). Ideology, power and inclusion: Using the critical perspective to study how older ICT users make sense of digitisation. *Media Culture and Society*, *40*(8), 1167–1185.

Kodate, N., & Timonen, V. (2017). Bringing the family in through the back door: The stealthy expansion of family care in Asian and European long-term care policy. *Journal of Cross-Cultural Gerontology*, *32*(3), 291–301.

Kodate, N., Maeda, Y., Yumoto, A., Donnelly, S., Tsujimura, M., Mannan, H., Suwa, S., Yu, W., Kohli, P., Obayashi, K., Masuyama, S., & O'Shea, D. (2024). "Welfare technology developers' views concerning responsible innovation and implementation of care robots in Ireland and Japan." In J. Seibt, P. Fazekas, & O. S. Quick. (Eds.) *Social Robots with AI: Prospects, Risks, and Responsible Methods*. Proceedings of Robo-philosophy (pp. 368–377), IOS Press.

Kodate, N. (2025). Achieving a social democratic model and going digital at the same time? Sláintecare, welfare technology and system readiness in Ireland. *Policy Science*, *32*(2), 201–217.

Kodate, N., Kohli, P., Maeda, Y., Obayashi, K., Prendergast, D., & Masuyama, S. (2024). Assembling sociality in caring spaces: Culturally sensitive robot deployment during the pandemic in residential care homes in Ireland and Japan. *Engaging Science, Technology, and Society*, *10*(3), 181–206.

Kuoppamäki, S. (2021). The application and deployment of welfare technology in Swedish municipal care: A qualitative study of procurement practices among municipal actors. *BMC Health Service Research*, *21*(1), 918. https://doi.org/10.1186/s12913-021-06944-w

Lechevalier, S. (2026). Care-led innovation. A new paradigm and an application in the Japanese context of Society 5.0. In S. Lechevalier, J.-P. Gaudillière, K. Ibata-Arens, & K. Takuma (Eds.), *Capitalism, innovations, and health after Covid-19. An Asian perspective*. Palgrave MacMillan.

Lee, S.-H. (2025). "Mapping aging in place through AI and robotics: A system modelling perspective". In Q. Gao & J. Zhou (Eds.) *Human Aspects of IT for the Aged Population*. 11th International Conference, ITAP 2025, the 27th

HCI International Conference, HCII 2025, Gothenburg, Sweden, June 22–27, 2025, Proceedings, Part III (pp. 363–376), Springer.
Lie, M. L., Lindsay, S., & Brittain, K. (2016). Technology and trust: Older people's perspectives of a home monitoring system. *Ageing & Society, 36*, 1501–1525.
Lolich, L., Pirhonen, J., Turja, T., & Timonen, V. (2022). Technology in the home care of older people: Views from Finland and Ireland. *Journal of Cross-Cultural Gerontology, 37*(2), 181–200.
Madhavan, H., & Gaudillière, J.-P. (2026). Frugal innovations and health system resilience. The conceptualization, policy support and forms of frugality during Covid-19 in South India. In S. Lechevalier, J.-P. Gaudillière, K. Ibata-Arens, & K. Takuma (Eds.), *Capitalism, innovations, and health after Covid-19. An Asian perspective*. Palgrave MacMillan.
Nickelsen, N. C. M. (2018). Socio-technical imaginaries and human-robotics proximity: The case of Bestic. In M. Coeckelbergh, J. Loh, M. Funk, J. Seibt, & M. Nørskov (Eds.), *Envisioning robots in society: Power, politics, and public space* (pp. 212–220). IOS Press.
Nyqvist, F., Nygård, M., & Scharf, T. (2019). Loneliness amongst older people in Europe: A comparative study of welfare regimes. *European Journal of Ageing, 16*(2), 133–143.
Obayashi, K., Kodate, N., Ishii, Y., & Masuyama, S. (2024). Assistive technologies and aging in place for people with dementia and disabilities: A proof-of-concept study with in-home passive remote monitoring with interactive communication functions. *Disability and Rehabilitation: Assistive Technology, 19*(6), 2341–2354.
Organisation for Economic Co-operation and Development (OECD). (2011). *Health reform meeting the challenge of ageing and multiple morbidities*. Organisation for Economic Cooperation and Development.
Pekkarinen, S., Hennala, L., Tuisku, O., Gustafsson, C., Johansson-Pajala, R.-M., Thommes, K., Hoppe, J. A., & Melkas, H. (2020, September 22). "Embedding care robots into society and practice: Socio-technical considerations". *Futures*.
Rogers, E. M. (2010). *Diffusion of Innovation*. Simon and Schuster.
Shiroyama, H., Ki, J., Matsuo, M., & Kim, H. (2026). "The mission oriented science, innovation and technology (STI) policies in Japan and Korea with a focus on health". In S. Lechevalier, J.-P. Gaudillière, K. Ibata-Arens, & K. Takuma (Eds.), *Capitalism, innovations, and health after Covid-19. An Asian perspective*. Palgrave MacMillan.
SPARC. (2015). *Robotics 2020 Multi-Annual Roadmap For Robotics in Europe Horizon 2020 Call ICT-2016 (ICT-25 & ICT-26)*. Available at https://www.yumpu.com/en/document/view/56255551/robotics-2020-multi-annual-roadmap (Accessed January 28, 2026).

Statistics Bureau of Japan. (n.d.). Current Population Estimates: As of 1 October, 2019. Available at https://www.stat.go.jp/english/data/jinsui/2019np/index.html (Accessed 28 January 2026).

Valokivi, H., Carlo, S., Kvist, E., & Outila, M. (2021). Digital ageing in Europe: A comparative analysis of Italian, Finnish and Swedish national policies on eHealth. *Ageing & Society*, 1–22.

Venkatesh, V., Morris, M. G., Davis, G. B., & Davis, F. D. (2003). User acceptance of information technology: Toward a unified view. *MIS Quarterly*, *27*(3), 425–478.

Walker, A., & Wong, C.-K. (Eds.). (2005). *East Asian welfare regimes in transition: From confucianism to globalisation.* Policy Press.

Wildman, J. M., Goulding, A., Moffatt, S., Scharf, T., & Stenning, A. (2021). Intergenerational equity, equality and reciprocity in economically and politically turbulent time: Narratives from across generations. *Ageing & Society*, 1–20. https://doi.org/10.1017/S0144686X21000052

World Health Organization (WHO). (2015). *World Report on Ageing and Health.* WHO.

WHO. (2018). *Assistive Technology: key facts.* Available at https://www.who.int/news-room/fact-sheets/detail/assistive-technology. Accessed January 28, 2026.

WHO and United Nations Children's Fund (UNICEF). (2022). *Global report on assistive technology.* Available at https://www.who.int/publications/i/item/9789240049451 (Accessed January 28, 2026).

Wright, J. (2020). *Comparing the Development and Commercialization of Care Robots in the European Union and Japan.* Available at https://hal.archives-ouvertes.fr/FFJ/hal-02527652. Accessed January 28, 2026.

Zigante, V. (2020). *Social situation monitor the role of new technologies in modernising long-term care systems a scoping review.* European Commission/LSE Consulting.

CHAPTER 9

Care-led Innovation. A New Paradigm and an Application in the Japanese Context of Society 5.0

Sébastien Lechevalier

Abstract The purpose of this chapter is to introduce the concept of "care-led innovation" as well as some examples. Although its ambition goes much beyond the Japanese context, we recognize that it has emerged from

I am grateful to the CTSH ("Capitalism, Technology, Society, and Health") project colleagues and to the participants to the Sophia University—DIJ seminar on 20. June 2025, especially Tadashi Kobayashi and Kaori Karasawa for their constructive comments. Special thanks to Jean-Paul Gaudilliere and Kathryn Ibata-Arens for their constructive comments. Numerous discussions with Malo Mofakhami have also been extremely inspiring. This paper is a new version of a previous paper written with Naonori Kodate, to whom I would like to express my gratitude as well. It has been published online as Published as "Care-led innovation. A new paradigm and an application in the Japanese context of Society 5.0" ICDP-02, 2025 ⟨hal-05430004⟩. Usual caveats apply.

S. Lechevalier (✉)
Ecole des Hautes Etudes en Sciences Sociales (EHESS), Paris, France;
German Institute for Japanese Studies (DIJ), Tokyo, Japan
e-mail: sebastien.lechevalier@ehess.fr

S. Lechevalier et al. (eds.), *Capitalism, Innovations, and Health after Covid-19*,
https://doi.org/10.1007/978-3-032-24479-6_9

an in-depth discussion of the transformation of the Japanese models of innovation and of capitalism and its limits. Japan has experienced since the early 1990s a multifold crisis that has led to put in question its former models of capitalism and innovation. After many trials and errors, it seems that from the mid-2010s, new models of capitalism and of innovation are emerging. More precisely, we introduce and critically appraise the Society 5.0 vision promoted by the Japanese government, as a way of overcoming the conventional Neo-Schumpeterian model of innovation that had been in crisis. Society 5.0 marks a potential major break in helping us think about postindustrial economies and societies, beyond industry 4.0. In parallel, but more recently, concepts of sustainable/new capitalism have been introduced by the major employer association and the Japanese government, with the purpose of addressing some of the key challenges of our time. However, we show that some major obstacles remain on the road towards the establishment of Society 5.0 and new/sustainable capitalism. This is why we introduce the new paradigm of care-led innovation as a way to realize Society 5.0 and to make capitalism more sustainable. It allows us specifying the characteristics in the models of innovation and of capitalism that are required to achieve Society 5.0, in general and in health-related issues in particular. While socioeconomics of innovation and STS are the primary disciplinary lenses that are utilized for this chapter, the theoretical perspective is also influenced by the Régulation theory in its analysis of crisis and of capitalism. The chapter proposes a non-Schumpeterian view on innovation, and also incorporates systems thinking. In terms of methodology and sources, we provide an overview of public policy evolution over the last two decades and conducted an institutional analysis of innovation policies in Japan, based on official reports and using theoretical contributions. We also include some case studies of care-led innovation, which we have been directly involved in and/or we could have privileged access to.

9.1 Introduction

The purpose of this chapter is to introduce the concept and the practices of "care-led innovation" as a powerful model to realize Society 5.0 and to allow Japan exiting from crisis. Although the ambition of "care-led innovation" goes much beyond the Japanese context, we recognize that it has emerged from an in-depth discussion of the transformation of the Japanese models of innovation and of capitalism and its limits.

Japan has indeed experienced since the early 1990s a multifold crisis that has led to put in question its former models of capitalism and innovation (Boyer & Yamada, 2000; Lechevalier, 2014). After many trials and errors, it seems that from the mid-2010s, new models of capitalism and of innovation are potentially emerging. They have been respectively labelled as new/sustainable capitalism and Society 5.0 (Whittaker, 2024).

This chapter focuses on the latter one, while not putting aside the model of capitalism, given the complementarities between them. More precisely, we introduce and critically appraise the Society 5.0 vision promoted by the Japanese government from 2015. We are interpreting it as a way of overcoming the limits of the Neo-Schumpeterian[1] model of innovation that is now in crisis. We show the potential of the Society 5.0 vision as a target to be reached but also its limitations. It is partly an unfinished conceptual business as it still corresponds to a techno-centered approach to innovation and it is still influenced by the Neo-Schumpeterian approach. Our argument can be summarized as follows. For about 30 years, the reform of the Japanese innovation system has failed to promote the convergence towards the so-called Silicon Valley model, which is considered as the best possible model of innovation by the Neo-Schumpeterian approach to innovation. However, this is not a major problem if the goal is to solve the innovation crisis *per se*. From this perspective, Society 5.0 marks a potential major break in directing the Japanese system of innovation towards the resolution of a variety of socio-economic issues. In doing so, it helps thinking about postindustrial economies and societies (beyond industry 4.0), including the relationships between science, technology, and society. Although it is not formulated in this way, it may open the door to a non-Schumpeterian perspective on innovation, if the logic of Society 5.0 is pushed towards more coherence.

[1] Neo-Schumpeterian economics is a school of thought that is inspired by the work of Joseph Schumpeter and places technological innovation at the core of economic growth and transformation processes. Strictly speaking, it is a form of evolutionary economics, thus classified among the heterodox approaches to economics, with representative authors such as Christopher Freeman, Richard Nelson or Giovanni Dosi. In the context of this chapter, we do not refer to a specific school of economic thought but rather to any economic thinking that put technological innovation at the center of economic dynamics, while referring to Joseph Schumpeter. From this perspective, a representative work is the one by Aghion et al. (2021), which reinterprets Schumpeter's thinking in a mainstream framework.

After having showed the limited of the Society 5.0 vision, we introduce the new paradigm of care-led innovation, together with some examples inspired by it, as an alternative to the dominant model of innovation. In short, we define care-led innovation as follows: "Care-led Innovation (CLI) refers to the design, experimentation, and adoption of innovations that prioritize care by addressing the expectations, needs, and vulnerabilities of stakeholders in care settings and enhance their capabilities, where possible." (Chetouani et al., 2026). This definition will be further discussed, developed and specified in the Sects. 9.4 and 9.5 of this chapter.

We show this paradigm may be able to unlock the potential of successfully implementing some, if not all, of the visions envisaged by Society 5.0. It allows us specifying the characteristics in the models of innovation and of capitalism that are required to achieve Society 5.0, in general and in health-related issues in particular. This conceptual effort should go hand in hand with: (1) A change in the approach to innovation that should be implemented in STI policies, in thinking about innovation beyond technology; (2) A political debate regarding the costs and the goals of innovation that may lead to a reconnection between technology and society in the context of a new form of capitalism.

The vision of Society 5.0 is of particular interest in the context of this book. First, it is important to recognize the continuity between this vision and the previous ones, which are all influenced by both techno-solutionism and a Schumpeterian vision of innovation. Second, despite this continuity, Society 5.0 was presented at the time when the expression of a new process of innovation is being sought. It should result in new requirements about the relations between science, technology and society; it implicitly recognizes the fact that there is no guarantee that science and technology advancement will be always beneficial to society.

This chapter contributes to Part 3 of the book, as it offers the definition of a possible alternative to the dominant Neo-Schumpeterian mode of innovation. In a complementary way to the chapter by Madhavan & Gaudillière (2026), it deals with technological innovations that are explicit answers to social needs. Also, contrary to the chapters by Ibata-Arens et al. (2026), and Kodate (2026), it focused solely on Japan and does not provide any comparative perspective, even though the concept of care-led innovation was initially developed in the context of a comparison between France and Japan.

This chapter is also connected to Part 1 as it discusses the crises of capitalism and innovation. We interpret the emergence and development of the Society 5.0 vision as the recognition of a crisis (e.g., in the relationship between technology and society) and this is the first (but ongoing and unfinished) attempt to look for alternatives, which echoes the overall purpose of the book.

While the disciplines that are mobilized in this chapter are mainly socio-economics of innovation and Science and Technology Studies (STS), the theoretical perspective is influenced by the Régulation theory in its analysis of crisis and of capitalism[2]. It proposes a non-Schumpeterian view on innovation. Finally, this chapter is also mobilizing the social systems of innovation theory (Amable et al., 1997). In terms of methodology and sources, we propose an institutional and public policy analysis of innovation policies in Japan, in critically examining official reports and theoretical contributions. We also introduce some cases of innovation, in which we have been directly involved or to which we could have a privileged access.

The structure of this chapter is as follows. We first present the twofold crisis of capitalism and innovation in Japan, and then introduce new/sustainable capitalism and Society 5.0 as answers to these crises. Subsequently we outline the notion of care-led innovation as a model that may support the emergence of a Society 5.0, as a way of reconnecting social needs and technological innovation. Finally, we discuss several cases of innovation in health and eldercare from the viewpoint of care-led innovation.

9.2 Innovation and Capitalism: A Twofold Japanese Crisis

This section of the chapter starts with a discussion of the part 1 of the book (especially Boyer and Boylaud (2026) on the one hand a and Gorry and Montalban (2026) on the other hand) in the Japanese context, before moving to the answers given to these crises in the next section.

[2] The analysis of crises is at the heart of the research program of the Régulation theory. Growth regimes in this theoretical perspective emerges from the (constructed or much more often along an unexpected fit) alignment between different institutions, which is nothing but automatic. From this perspective, crisis does correspond to the normal state of the economy, as it corresponds to a period during actors are in conflicts on the institutional hierarchy of the economy (Amable, 2003; Amable & Palombarini, 2009).

9.2.1 *Japanese Capitalism in Crisis*

The nature of the crisis of the Japanese economy since the early 1990s has been the matter of a lively debate. Over the past fifteen years, the explanations focusing on structural factors (such as the end of catch-up area, an aging population and the lingering effects of the financial crisis provoked by the bubble). has achieved dominance. Within this category of explanations, the mainstream view is that this crisis is caused by a lack of structural reforms. In following Lechevalier and Monfort (2017), we argue that this convenient explanation is not validated by facts, given the important number of effective reforms introduced from the 1980s but largely neglected in the literature.

We argue that to understand the crisis of Japanese capitalism, we have to go back to the key characteristic of its "Golden Age" and rephrase the research question about this crisis, which is not limited to growth or productivity outcomes, as follows. Japan has been once characterized as a country that managed to combine high growth and equity (Lechevalier, 2014). Its trajectory, which confirmed that there is no trade-off between efficiency and equality, has been at the origin of the conceptualization of inclusive growth (Lechevalier & Shibata, 2026). However, for many years now (at least from the early 1990s), Japan has been characterized by low growth (below the OECD average) and increasing inequalities. This is the key question to be addressed as it is the core of the crisis of Japanese capitalism.

In this context, digitalization is often presented as the solution and an opportunity to move towards a new model of growth that may solve current social problems: low labour productivity, lack of workforce in a context of ageing (Lechevalier & Monfort, 2025), and restrictive immigration policies (Chiavacci, 2025). Surprisingly, the perception of digitalization as a risk (e.g. that Japan would follow the US path towards impoverishing growth) is not very common and not so much discussed in the Japanese context (Lechevalier & Shibata, 2026).

Digitalization, in the specific Japanese context, is contributing to non-inclusive growth patterns, through its effects on the wage-labour nexus, but it does not correspond to the patterns that have been analysed by the previous literature, in the context of the US or most European countries. This result contradicts two main strands of literature: (1) that which views digitalization as a catalyst of inclusive growth; and (2) that which posits digitalization as a uniform driver of increased inequality converging towards the US model. More precisely, Lechevalier & Shibata (2024) finds a digital divide has emerged in Japan, with an increase of inequalities in several dimensions (income, working conditions, well-being, etc.) but without corresponding growth in labour productivity or wages. The overall result of this trend is that the benefits of digitalization have been very unevenly distributed: while employers have benefited from intensified work and enhanced labour discipline, most workers have experienced stagnating wages and deteriorating working conditions, which can be detected through the analysis of job satisfaction (Lechevalier & Mofakhami, 2025). To put it differently, digitalization has become a crucial part of Japan's neoliberal labour market amidst a labour shortage and an ageing workforce (Shibata & Lechevalier, 2025). The wage-labour nexus under digitalization, which creates more tension between employers' focus on efficiency and a lack of focus on workers' well-being, is therefore likely to contribute to a non-inclusive growth regime.

Moreover, this digital divide differs significantly from those analysed in previous Transatlantic studies. It means that there is no uniform effect of digitalization and, in general, no techno-determinism: not everything is determined by technology, whose impact is embedded in a certain political economy context. From this perspective, the institutional characteristics of the innovation system also deserve a particular attention.

9.2.2 *Which Innovation Crisis in Japan?*

Still, in the 1980s and early 1990s, most of the economists were predicting that the next technological wave would emerge from Japan because of the superiority of its innovation system (Vogel, 1980). The economic crisis from the early 1990s has led to a U-turn in the interpretation of this innovation system, including among those economists who were celebrating its strengths just few years before (Aoki, 2000).

According to a mainstream view (Nezu, 2004), Japan has been facing an innovation crisis from the 1990s because of its backward innovation system. The postwar Japanese innovation system has been successful in promoting the catch-up process but did not adjust quickly enough to the end of the catchup era (when the issue was less to imitate than to innovate) and, even more importantly, to a new technological context, from the end of the 1980s, characterized by the emergence of new technologies more crucially linked to science (as part of the emerging knowledge-economy) with shorter time spans between two innovations in the same sector

(Lechevalier, 2014). In this context, there was no other possibility than to reform the Japanese innovation system to promote the convergence towards the model shown to be the best in this new environment, that of Silicon Valley. This model, supposedly characterized by the important role of entrepreneurship, venture capital, and of the collaboration between firms and universities, is often analysed as the best set of institutions to promote innovation in the new technological environment that has emerged in the 1980s and the 1990s, with key technologies such as Information and communication technologies (ICT) or biotech. In particular, because of the importance of the mechanisms of creative destruction—according to which innovation is based on the emergence of new actors with new ideas and ways of producing, which will ultimately replace the incumbent players—startups are the drivers of innovation and should be the focus of public policies (Lechevalier, 2019; Boyer, 2003).

This is why the relatively small number of startups and the lack of their growth in Japan by comparison to the US is seen as a symbol of the weakness of this innovation system (Anchordoguy, 2000; Ibata-Arens, 2005). As a result, it is often concluded that innovation capabilities in Japan have overall declined (Branstetter & Nakamura, 2003). Various anecdotal (e.g. the trajectory of Sony) and statistical evidence (e.g. the number of breakthrough innovations born in Japan) are then provided to support this view. In short, according to this view, the innovation crisis in Japan is symbolized by its inability to follow a Schumpeterian path and to converge towards the Silicon Valley model.

This analysis is inspired by the dominant Neo-Schumpeterian view regarding innovation and its role in the prosperity of advanced nations (Lechevalier, 2019). By contrast to this mainstream view, our own view, inspired by the Régulation theory (Boyer, 2003; Boyer & Boylaud, 2026; Gorry & Montalban, 2026) and the social system of innovation approach (Amable et al., 1997) emphasizes the necessary diversity of innovation systems. In short, the right "model" for innovation does not exist: it depends on the sector, the technology, etc. More precisely:

- different technologies require different model of innovation: the former Japanese model of innovation (in the 1970s–1980s), has been successful for the development of some technologies used in the car industries and electronics but not so much for biotech and ICT; the SV model have shown some superiority in the field of ICT and biotech but less in others such as mechanics, robotics or nuclear.

- different times of development of a same technology requires different models of innovation, as it is shown by the Schumpeterian approach itself: the early and the mature stages require different resources and strength and often dominated by different types of actors;
- different models of innovation are required in different industries (including when the same technology is considered: robotics in industries and in services requires different models of innovation);
- even more importantly, when innovation is considered beyond technology, a very different type of innovation system, which is able to deliver social innovation, is required (Lechevalier, 2019).

From this perspective, if it is difficult to deny that it is in the North of California that major new technologies have emerged during the 1980s–1990s, this is not the end of history. Back to the Japanese context, the absence of convergence towards the so-called Silicon Valley model is a failure of public policies, which have never questioned their target and continued to follow a direction during three decades that did take account nor the strength of the Japanese innovation system nor its complementarities with other institutions. However, in our view, this is not a major problem, especially in the present context, when ICT and biotech are still major general-purpose technologies: the main issue is to be leading in the next technological wave and to apply these technologies to various domains, where there is a demand.

It does not mean that there is no problem with innovation in Japan. There is indeed an innovation crisis, as in many other countries, but it is not of the same nature as the one delineated by the mainstream view. The notion of innovation crisis might seem a little bit counter-intuitive in a context of numerous major breakthrough technological innovations. Examples are diverse but they range from the quick advance of AI (e.g. the introduction of Chatgpt) to the very rapid and simultaneous launch of several vaccines against Covid-19. Nonetheless, in our view, the crisis is of different nature and more about the relationship between technological innovation and society. Some components of this crisis are indeed quite universal and not specific to Japan:

- Gap between the increasing resources dedicated to innovation and decreasing well-being observed in many cases (e.g. evolution of well-being of patients and nurses in European hospitals, where the investment in up-to-date technologies goes hand in hand budget cut and downsizing of the staff);

- Contribution of innovation to rising inequalities in different dimensions (e.g. digital divide);
- Various technology related scandals (e.g. in chemical or pharmaceutical industries);
- Some problems related to the use of technologies (e.g. use of personal data in different fields).

In short, while several technologies are potentially extremely beneficial to the society, their negative externalities (either real or only perceived as change is associated to disturbance) are not always properly taken into account, which shed doubts on their positive impact. Ex-post effort in making them more acceptable is clearly not enough, and if (scientific) education is certainly useful to rebuild the link between society and technology, there is no doubt that *ex ante* participation of citizen to the definition of priorities and limits to innovation would have much better outcome less in terms of acceptability than in the direction and the nature of innovation.

Although this crisis is global, there are also some characteristics that are specific to Japan. This country, which is among the most technophile and techno-centered, has been shaken by several events that have shed light on the inability of engineers to guarantee safety. The nuclear accident that has followed the Tohoku earthquake in 2011 is certainly a turning point from this perspective. This has been understood by several key players of the Japanese innovation system, as we observe for about one decade the creation of social sciences and humanities departments in institutions such as the Japan and Science Technology agency (JST), RIKEN or Tokyo Institute of Technology (renamed the Institute of Science Tokyo from 2024).

Another dimension of the crisis is also more Japan specific: the Japanese firms have forgotten the sources of their past success: organizational rather than technological innovation (Aoki & Dore, 1994). Since the early 1990s, they have committed to a technological race, with massive investments in R&D, and a HRM race-to-the-bottom, including wage reductions, in the context of competitive pressures from countries characterized by lower labour costs, with poor results (Lechevalier, 2019).

9.3 New/sustainable Capitalism and Society 5.0 as Answers to the Crises: Some Progress with Limitation Because an Overall Lack of Coherence

In the context of this twofold crisis (models of innovation and of capitalism), solutions have gradually emerged on the governmental side, in collaboration mainly with the private sector, and less with parts of the society. In this section, we argue that it corresponds to a first significant step but it is not enough because some obstacles remain and the whole set of answers to the crisis lacks coherence.

9.3.1 Society 5.0 as an Answer to the Innovation Crisis: Reconnection Between Technology and Society

Society 5.0 is a concept that has been proposed in the 5th Science and Technology Basic Plan (December 2015) as a future society that Japan should aspire to. According to this vision, thanks to advanced digitalization, it will be possible to promote "a human-centered society that balances economic advancement with the resolution of social problem by a system that highly integrates cyberspace and physical space"[3]. In short, in order for Japan to regain its Science, Technology & Innovation (STI) edge, it is proposed to apply digital technologies not only to (manufacturing) industries but also to a wide range of services and dimensions of the social life (Fig. 9.1).

The 5th Science and Technology Basic Plan is partly in continuity with previous Basic plans but also introduces a discontinuity in emphasizing social targets rather than numerical targets of increased R&D expenditures. In general terms, in trying to better connect social needs and (mainly) technological innovation, Society 5.0 can be considered as an attempt to propose solutions to the innovation crisis that has been described above. It corresponds to a major progress in helping to think postindustrial economies and societies (beyond industry 4.0) and the potential of digitalization. It is worth noting here that, although Society 5.0 is mainly a concept pushed by the Japanese government, it incorporates some voices coming from the academia and the civil society that are represented within the Council for Science, technology, and innovation, but with a bias favourable to the business side. This is not specific to the field of science and technology policy, but, in the case of Society 5.0, as

[3] https://www8.cao.go.jp/cstp/english/society5_0/index.html. Retrieved on 11. August 2023.

Fig. 9.1 A bird-eye view on Society 5.0. *Source* Cabinet office

well shown by Whittaker (2024), the business side itself has promoted ideas that show that a form of bottom-up process is at work in Japan. It indicates a possible path towards changes in the state-civil society relationship: the reconnection between technology and society is not decided only from the top but is a much more complex process. To put it differently: "Japan is seeking to steer a path between market and state over-reach, aiming for a new balance of state-market-civil society relations, and promoting socially constructive rather than destructive forms of innovation (Whittaker, 2024: 7).

The example of what is expected from digitalization in the fields of healthcare and caregiving, in a general context of an ageing society, is very telling from this viewpoint (Fig. 9.2). The emphasis is put on the role of AI analysis of big data (including personal real-time physiological data, healthcare-site information, or treatment/infection information). Concrete example of innovation (and associated problem solving) includes: using robots to provide living support and conversation partners and to promote an autonomous way of living (with an individualistic flavour that do not emphasize the importance of interactions between people); using robots to ease the on-site burden of healthcare and caregiving; promoting healthy living and early detection of illnesses through real-time automatic health checkups; providing optimal treatment anywhere through the sharing of physiological and medical data. Moreover, it is worth emphasizing that these solutions are also presented as ways to help reduce the social costs associated with healthcare and caregiving and solving labour-shortage problems at healthcare sites.

In our view, the concept of Society 5.0 is now well established and serves as an essential reference to innovation policy and beyond, although it is not popular in the society. This is why this concept is still central in the 6th STI Basic Plan (2021–25), in which social sciences and humanities started to feature more prominently. It is more generally a signal for a wide set of actors, from firms to government through research institutions. The Society 5.0 vision has inspired the STI policies, which have been redirected towards a mission-based type (Mazzucato, 2018), as it is visible in the moonshot program. From this perspective, Society 5.0 is not only a vision as it has led to the implementation of concrete policies, with some benefits and limitations (Shiroyama et al., 2026).

To summarize our argument, in trying to better connect social needs and (mainly) technological innovation, Society 5.0 can be considered as an attempt to propose solutions to the innovation crisis. Moreover,

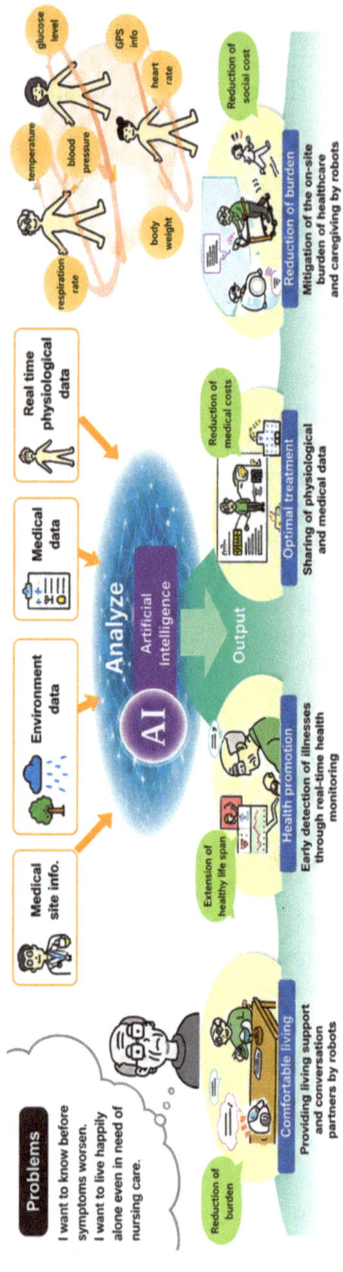

Fig. 9.2 Health related-issues in Society 5.0. *Source* Cabinet office

if considered seriously, society 5.0 may correspond to a new vision not only of STI policies and of economic development driven by digital technologies (beyond Industry 4.0) but also of capitalism. In this new model of capitalism, the priority is no more mainly GDP growth but improvement of well-being. In promoting the emergence of a Society 5.0 since the mid-2010s, the Japanese government has not only encouraged the use of digital technologies outside the plants for different aspects of social life but also elaborated a vision which is not without relation with the idea of an "anthropogenetic" model of development (Boyer, 2019; Boyer & Boylaud, 2026).

However, it seems that it has stopped half-way in this direction, as the concept of Society 5.0 is still very much techno-centered and techno-solutionist. Moreover, it has not been able to propose coherent visions regarding the innovation system and the model of capitalism: there is a disconnection between the society 5.0 vision and the underlying model of innovation attached to both sustainable/new capitalism 2.0 (as promoted by Keidanren and then PM Kishida) and STI policies in Japan (e.g. moonshot program), which are still dominated by a Neo-Schumpeterian vision (Lechevalier, 2024). These points are developed in the next session.

9.3.2 *Sustainable/new Capitalism: How Can Social Challenges Become Engines of Growth?*

The Society 5.0 vision finds an echo, few years later, in the concept of "sustainable capitalism" promoted by the Japanese employers' association, the Keidanren, in its 2020 "New growth strategy" report[4] as well as in the program of Prime Minister Kishida (2021–2024) that promotes the emergence of a "new capitalism" (Whittaker, 2024; Whittaker & Nakata, 2024). As well shown by Whittaker (2024), it should be taken seriously as it possibly reflects a new social compromise. To put it briefly, while "new capitalism" is partly a slogan by a Japanese politician seeking to distinguish himself from his influential predecessor (Shinzo Abe, and its "Abenomics", its relation with the concept of "sustainable capitalism" pushed by the Japanese employers' association confirms an effort to reassemble the socio-economic framework after years of neoliberalism, which destabilized the old model without fully establishing a new one.

[4] https://www.keidanren.or.jp/en/policy/2020/108_proposal.html. Retrieved on 11th August 2023.

The best expression of how "new capitalism" looks like certainly appears in May 5th, 2022 PM Kishida's speech in London: "Why does capitalism need upgrading? Because we need to solve two crucial present-day challenges. One is the problem of economic externalities, such as widening inequality, climate change and issues deriving from urbanization. (...) Under this new form of capitalism, social challenges can become engines of growth." The coherence with Society 5.0 is here striking. It also corresponds to some deeply rooted ideas in the Japanese context—for example promoted by the "Godfather" of Japanese capitalism, Eiichi Shibusawa (1840–1931), according to whom "Entrepreneurial spirit is not in contradiction with social inclusion".

However, after some successful lobbying from the most conservative members of the political and economic elite, this program has become more standard from a conservative viewpoint and partly disconnected from the Society 5.0 vision. This has been visible during the discussion within the "Council of New Form of Capitalism Realization". In reading the minutes of this council that has been published[5], it is possible to identify a narrower vision with an exclusive focus on the promotion of startups, which is the signal of a form of ideological backlash, dominated by the Neo-Schumpeterian vision of innovation and economic growth (Lechevalier, 2024).

Does it mean that its importance should be neglected, and we may predict that its legacy will be very limited? As Whittaker (2024), we do not think so, mainly because of Keidanren's commitment to the sustainable capitalism vision, despite some internal debates. As a whole, these two answers—Society 5.0 and "sustainable/new" capitalism—go in the same direction of a human-centered mode of development. However, it does not go without tensions and conflicts, especially within Keidanren and Liberal Democratic Party. This is why it is important to analyse the contradictions or dissonances that should be overcome in order to realize the potential of Society 5.0, once it is detached from the techno-centered view on innovation.

[5] See for example https://www.kantei.go.jp/jp/101_kishida/actions/202304/25shihon.html. Retrieved on 3rd August 2023.

9.3.3 *Obstacles on the Road Towards the Establishment of Society 5.0 and New/sustainable Capitalism*

If these two visions—Society 5.0 and sustainable/new capitalism—are logically connected, how can we summarize their relation? We cannot disagree with the following image: "As a simplification, if DX [Digital transformation] and GX [Green transformation] are wheels of a cart, and Society 5.0 is the destination, capitalism is the cart itself" (Whittaker, 2024: 105).

If it is correct, then we can identify a series of (logical and practical) obstacles on the road towards the establishment of Society 5.0. In what follows, we emphasize one of them, the legacy of a Schumpeterian vision on innovation, which should be overcome in order to reach the destination of Society 5.0. To put it differently, the major obstacle is not the technology itself: as shown by Shibata and Lechevalier (2025), the major issue is the lack of institutional conditions associated to a techno-determinist view, which is at the core of the Neo-Schumpeterian approach to innovation.

Society 5.0 requires to be achieved a clear departure from the Schumpeterian view on innovation and of capitalism, as it is the major cause of the innovation crisis (see 2.1). This is not yet the case, as it is visible with the emphasis on startups as the core of innovation policy and of the promotion of new capitalism. Startups as a whole are one of the major contributors to innovation but what is required to reach Society 5.0 is of different nature: the key is less decentralized breakthrough innovation that could become *ex post* acceptable to the public, thanks to various efforts, including marketing, than a coordinated effort to promote innovation that increases wellbeing and that is well diffused in order to increase its impact, if possible in an inclusive way.

This inadaptation—due to the persistence of a Neo-Schumpeterian approach to innovation for different goals and industries—between the destination and the vehicle is also visible in the way the STI policies inspired by Society 5.0 is organized. Namely, the Moonshot program is the core of this STI policy and, as a mission-based STI policy framework, it is connected to the goals of Society 5.0 (Shiroyama et al., 2026). However, although it is organized in 9 goals that cover different social challenges, it is obvious that the drivers are technological rather than social, as it can be seen in the management by different agencies that cover different technological fields. More precisely, among these 9 goals, 3 are directly related to health issues:

- Moonshot Goal 2 = Realization of ultra-early disease prediction and intervention by 2050 (JST)
- Moonshot Goal 7: Realization of sustainable care systems to overcome major diseases by 2040, for enjoying one's life with relief and release from health concerns until 100 years old (AMED)
- Moonshot Goal 9: Realization of a mentally healthy and dynamic society by increasing peace of mind and vitality by 2050 (JST)

The analysis of the goals reveals the limitations of this program. For example, in the case of goal 7 (see Fig. 9.3), the image of ageing does not incorporate some recent advances in the sociology of ageing (Watanabe, 2021). It is indeed particularly important to pay attention to individuals beyond statistics on ageing society (with fixed categories such as 65 years

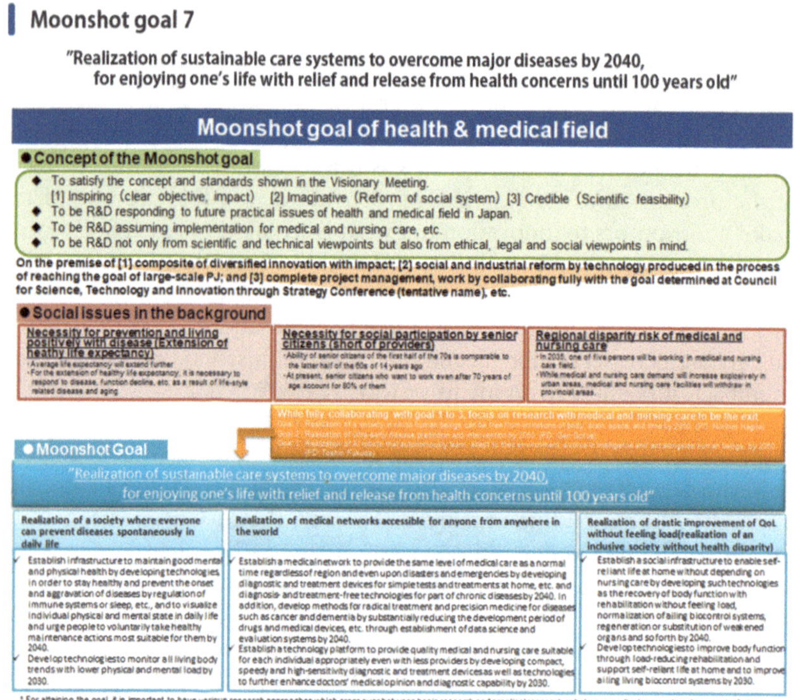

Fig. 9.3 Moonshot goal 7. *Source* AMED

old and above), and thus to emphasize the necessity to understand the diversity and the evolution of individual needs. In the Japanese context, the long-term care system (*kaigo hoken*) has been designed to cover the costs of social answers to them; it can be complemented by the contribution of non-profit organizations, which may ultimately lead to an 'imagined community'.

In short, in order to reach Society 5.0, it is necessary to develop and implement an alternative approach to the Schumpeterian view on innovation. This is what is proposed in the next two sections.

9.4 Care-led Innovation as a Way to Realize Society 5.0 and to Make Capitalism More Sustainable: Origin and Concept

In this section, we introduce the concept of care-led innovation as a way to achieve Society 5.0 and to make capitalism more sustainable. Although it is presented in the Japanese context, it goes beyond it and is generalized as an alternative to the Neo-Schumpeterian model of innovation.

9.4.1 *From the Identification of Social Issues Related to Ageing Society to the Framing of Care-Led Innovation to Realize Society 5.0 and to Make Capitalism More Sustainable*

Society 5.0 is orienting the innovation system towards the search for solution to social problems. Among the various social problems, which Japan is facing, ageing society is by far the most crucial (Lechevalier et al., 2026), as emphasized in many governmental reports, such as the *Annual Reports on the Ageing Society* published by the Cabinet Office[6]. Some forecasts such as the ones issued by the National Institute of Population

[6] See https://www8.cao.go.jp/kourei/english/annualreport/index-wh.html. Without denying the fact that ageing has been well identified by Japanese public policies as a major issue for the future of Japan, it is worth adding two nuances. First, it is often used as an argument mobilized to promote reforms that are not directly related to ageing issues, as it has been done for globalization and new wave of technical progress used as pretext to reform the Japanese capitalism along a Neoliberal agenda (Lechevalier, 2014). Second, despite the fact that ageing is very present in the public policy space, one should not neglect the fact that it has been consistently underestimated, either because of forecast errors or because of difficulty to incorporate demographic variables in economic model (Lechevalier & Monfort, 2025; Monfort, 2026).

and Social Security Research in 2023 have attracted attention: it is predicted that the share of the 65 years old people + will exceed 40% of the total population by 2050. The other side of the coin is that new needs emerge, as ageing is partly the outcome of increasing longevity[7]: from 80 years old on average, the probability of facing a loss of autonomy and forms of vulnerability is increasing substantially; it creates new needs in terms of care, which can be only partly answered within families. The sector of eldercare has thus experienced a major development in Japan during the last decades[8].

This is why, without surprise, the ageing issue is central in both the Society 5.0 vision and in its implementation in the Moonshot program, especially the Moonshot Goal 7 ("Realization of sustainable care systems to overcome major diseases by 2040, for enjoying one's life with relief and release from health concerns until 100 years old"), in relation with health issues. In fact, the issue of long-term care has become a privileged area for the application of technologies. This is explained by the fact that pro-natality policies have had a very limited success (see for example Lee & Lee, 2014; Suzuki, 2006), while migration policies that are becoming more open in the context of lack of workforce are not seen as a possible answer to demographic challenges such as ageing and depopulation (Chiavacci, 2025). In this context, technological solutions in the spirit of the Neo-Schumpeterian model if innovation, are presented as the only solutions to the increasing "Care gap": with the ageing of population, the needs for eldercare are increasing while the number of care staff is stable or decreasing, because of hard working conditions and low wages. More precisely, official projections indicate a shortfall of 380,00 care workers by 2025, which might not be compensated by the hiring of foreign workers, in a context of still restrictive immigration policies (Wright, 2020). These developments participate to the expected growth of a "silver economy", partly financed thanks to the introduction of a Long-term Care scheme in 1993, and whose logic is to create a new growth regime. In other words, these are evidence that an anthropogenetic mode of development is potentially at work in Japan (Boyer, 2019; Boyer & Boylaud, 2026).

[7] Partly only. The two other determinants are natality, which is by far the main one (Lechevalier & Monfort, 2025), and migrations.

[8] According to METI, the market size for the ageing care market in Japan is expected to be about $954 billion by 2025—larger than the markets for domestic automobile, finance, and consumer electronics.

The potential contribution of several technologies (notably robotics, artificial intelligence [AI], information and communication technologies [ICT]) has indeed been recognized, as they can partly solve problems of autonomy and vulnerability, whether it concerns communication, mobility or cognitive abilities (see for example Sætra (2020) in the case of robotics). However, at the same time, several important limitations have been emphasized (Wright, 2023; Maibaum et al., 2022) as well as a gap between the promotion of robots in eldercare by public policies and the real social needs, as industrial policy goals are still dominating social policy goals.

In our view, the difficult introduction of technologies in eldercare is not a one-off problem, but a fundamental impasse related to the way in which social needs and technological responses are articulated, in line with the dominant Schumpeterian paradigm of innovation. There is an urgent need to reconnect social and technological dynamics, by proposing concepts and practices of innovation that make well-being the ultimate criterion for innovation, and we believe it is not unachievable in the Japanese context (Lechevalier et al., 2025).

In more general terms, establishing Society 5.0 requires to take very seriously the fundamental study of social and individual needs that cannot be done afterwards, once the technological and non-technological solutions are develop. Moreover, there should be an additional effort to connect needs and solutions, which requires a certain methodological design. These two principles are at the heart of the care-led innovation model (Lechevalier et al., 2025).

9.4.2 *Towards a Care-led Innovation Model?*

More precisely, our argument is that achieving the goal of overcoming the eldercare gap, as other social goals, requires a different approach to innovation than the one that has been at work to promote (mainly manufacturing) competitiveness. The major reason is that there is no best way for innovation (Boyer, 2003). It means it is highly improbable that the innovation model that has been so successful in the late twentieth century to develop information and communication technologies as well as biotechnologies will be as efficient in a different context and with different goals, such as providing appropriate answers to diverse and evolving needs. In short, there is no guarantee that the Silicon Valley model of innovation will be the most efficient to reach the goals of

Society 5.0. As explained by Lechevalier et al. (2025), the prevailing Neo-Schumpeterian paradigm of innovation indeed presents characteristics that are potential obstacles to innovation in the field of eldercare: focus on new technologies to the detriment of social innovation in a given sociotechnical context; an essentially *ex post* consideration of users through the question of acceptability; a vision of innovation as a source of competitiveness through creative destruction (Lechevalier, 2019). This approach to innovation strictly focuses on new technologies as means to differentiate firms from their competitors, while taking into consideration social needs, only *ex post*. In this context, the deployment of "gerontechnologies" responds primarily to the logic of economic growth, which reflects a domination of industrial policy objectives over those of social policies (Lechevalier et al., 2025). In this context, what is required is an alternative to this dominant perspective, through an embodied, situated and distributed approach to innovation.

A possible solution is to put the concept of care at the heart of the innovation process (Lechevalier et al., 2025). It indeed allows us to clarify and specify social needs, focusing on inter-personal and social relationships and to consider both material and affective dimensions of care situations mobilizing innovative technologies. It is also in line with the idea that the major solution to reconnect social and technological dynamics is to promote a concept and practices of innovation that view wellbeing as the ultimate criterion of innovation (Lechevalier, 2019).

It requires defining more precisely the notion of care, which has been (and still is) the object of very rich literature. In what follows, we refer to the work by Paperman & Laugier (2020), without denying that there are many other approaches (Shimohara, 2024). It is a material, technical, emotional, and affective work, which is done within social, sex, class and race relationships between different types of actors: the care givers, the beneficiaries, the relatives (who are often carers themselves), and those who supervise and prescribe the work. Care is not only a caring attitude, but it corresponds to a set of material and relational activities, sometimes intricated with highly specialized curative techniques, whose aim is to give a concrete answer to others' needs. It can be defined as a service, support and assistance relationship, which implies a sense of responsibility vis-à-vis others' well-being.

Bringing users closer to technological innovations is far from being an isolated concern, and the analysis of technological innovations in the field of care for older adults (OAs) has made significant progress in this respect.

However, this approach is still very much influenced by the "acceptability" perspective (Tamaki Welply & Lechevalier, 2024). By contrast, the focus here is not on individual users but on inter-individual and social relations (Tamaki Welply, 2024).

It means that any *care* approach entails moving some distance from the individualistic and liberal definition of autonomy, which is seen as the goal of eldercare and which posits the absence of dependence as an ideal. Autonomy is understood here in a relational sense, with the ethics of *care* assuming interdependence, in the sense of an autonomy 'extended to the collective'. Under these conditions, the enlargement of the network of interdependence, whether of humans or technical artifacts increases the autonomy of individuals. It is then possible to address several dimensions of autonomy: functional, moral, legal, social as well as digital (Lechevalier et al., 2025).

In short, a model of social innovation is needed to realize Society 5.0; care-led innovation can be this model, if it is extended beyond eldercare and long-term care. It does not exclude the use of new technologies but emphasizes the innovation at a given level of technology. In this model, major actors will not be necessarily startups, which are nonetheless an important actor, but a larger set of stakeholders that includes: users, non-users, communities, and any institution that may help to socialize the costs and the risks while acting for the common good (e.g. governments).

9.4.3 Care-led Innovation: a Synthetic Definition

What is care-led innovation? This is not equivalent to user-centered innovation as it is a relational concept. It is also connected to some values (care ethics) and from this perspective, it is closer to the idea of value-based design (Doncieux et al., 2022). In the same way, care-led innovation is not necessarily a social innovation as we do not exclude the technological dimension.

Then, how to define care-led innovation more positively? Besides emphasizing the fact that it is a form of human-centered innovation, it can be done in several complementary ways. First, care-led innovation is a certain model of interaction between technology and society, where innovation is conceived and developed as an answer to social needs that have been defined in relational way. Second, care-led innovation can be defined by the actors that are involved in the process and eventually leading it: while recognizing the importance of engineers and other highly qualified specialists, care-led innovation is promoting the involvement of the concerned persons (i.e. older adults), care workers and relatives, in an effort to democratize innovation.

Third, the following synthetic definition can be proposed based on Chetouani et al. (2026): "Care-led Innovation (CLI) refers to the design, experimentation, and adoption of innovations that prioritize care by addressing the expectations, needs, and vulnerabilities of stakeholders in care settings and enhance their capabilities, where possible. These innovations should be scientifically grounded and subject to systematic evaluation, while acknowledging the inherent challenges of establishing fully evidence-based approaches, due to the significant value of the lived experience of those in the care domain. Rather than being driven solely by technological advancements, organizational efficiency, and economic imperatives, CLI emphasizes throughout the process the meaning and value of practices and relationships of caring. It is a process of innovation led by care to meet the needs of older adults, their carers and care workers, their families, ensuring that, while recognizing that prioritizing one group may place a burden on another, it supports the dignity of actors in care settings".

Several characteristics of care-led innovation emerge from this definition: (1) the priority given to expectations, needs and vulnerabilities; (2) the crucial role played by scientific experimentation and evaluation; (3) the importance of overcoming strict economic criteria of efficiency to incorporate care-related values; (4) the necessity to adopt a holistic approach on stakeholders in order to consider all of them in the evaluation of benefits of a given innovation.

Per se, care-led innovation is in a sense a normative view on innovation; it is also a reality which is already visible in some practices. Thus, it requires a precise analytical characterization in order to be generalized and proposed as an approach to innovation beyond the specific case of eldercare. This is done in the next session.

9.5 Care-led Innovation: An Analytical Grid and Some Examples

9.5.1 Care-led Innovation: An Analytical Grid

The analytical grid that describes the major characteristics of a care-led innovation is presented in Chetouani et al. (2026) and summarized in Table 9.1. Its basic structure reproduces some key features well recognized from the perspective of economics of innovation but we adapt them to identify the key component of care-led innovation.

Table 9.1 The innovcare grid

General information about the technology	*(in green = care criteria)*	
Name of the technology		
Development and design phase	**Details**	**Key characteristics to collect**
Problem addressed	*The specific issue or challenge the solution aims to solve*	Nature of the care problem (physical, cognitive, emotional, organizational) Level of vulnerability addressed (individual, relational, systemic) Existing care gaps or failures Who defines the problem (developers, caregivers, cared persons, institutions)
Technology/Approach Used (description)		Type of technology (digital tool, AI system, device, platform, organizational method) Degree of automation vs human mediation Role of the technology in the care relationship (support, substitute, coordination)
Organisation responsible for development		Type of organizations involved (private firm, startup, public body, NGO, research lab) Experience in care or health sectors Governance structure and accountability
Target population	*Mainly for the cared person/Mainly for the caring person*	Primary beneficiaries (cared persons, professional caregivers, informal carers) Secondary users (institutions, families) Degree of user heterogeneity (age, disability, socio-economic status)
Involvement of End-Users		Forms of user involvement (consultation, co-design, testing) Timing of involvement (early, late, continuous) Representativeness of users

(continued)

Table 9.1 (continued)

General information about the technology	*(in green = care criteria)*	
Name of the technology		
Ethical Procedure/ Approval	*Relative to this phase*	Existence of ethical review or approval Ethical principles considered (autonomy, dignity, non-harm) Attention to care-specific ethics
Expected care outcomes	*Response to vulnerability by compensation/ Response to vulnerability by enhancing capabilities (CA)—empowerment/none*	Type of care response (compensation vs. capability enhancement) Impact on autonomy and empowerment Redistribution of care work
External assessment		Previous characteristics assessed by publication or external institutions Items assessed Level of proof of items assessed
Intellectual property management	*patents, publications, etc.*	Type of IP protection (patents, copyrights, open-source) Ownership of data and algorithms Accessibility constraints created by IP
Structure of collaborative development	*Alone, in partnership, etc.*	Presence of partnerships (care institutions, user groups, public actors) Degree of interdisciplinarity Power balance between partners
Economic model/ origin of the funding		Funding sources (public, private, mixed) Profit vs care-oriented objectives Economic sustainability assumptions
care-led evaluation step 1		

(continued)

Table 9.1 (continued)

General information about the technology	*(in green = care criteria)*	
Name of the technology		
Implementation and experimentation phase		
Characteristics of implementation (Organisation/actors responsible for implementation)	*Organizations involved, expected outcomes, duration, etc.*	Contexts of use (institutional, home-based, experimental) Duration and scale of implementation Actors coordinating implementation
Actors responsible for regular maintenance	*i.e. for providing 'care' for the technologies, including setting up and charging, etc.,*	Responsibility for technical upkeep Care-related maintenance tasks (charging, updates, monitoring) Burden placed on caregivers or users
Involvement of End-Users	*integration of user feedback*	Feedback mechanisms Responsiveness to care-related issues Power of users to influence changes
Participation of the development initiative structure	*Involved or not*	Continued involvement of developers Responsiveness to care contexts Long-term commitment
Ethical Procedure/ Approval	*Relative to this phase*	Ethical monitoring during use Handling of incidents or harm Consent and privacy in real-life conditions
Expected (care) outcomes	*Response to vulnerability by compensation/ Response to vulnerability by enhancing capabilities (CA)—empowerment/none*	Observed effects on care quality (compensation vs enhancing) Changes in caregiver workload User empowerment or dependency
External assessement		Previous characteristics assessed by publication or external institutions Items assessed Level of proof of items assessed

(continued)

Table 9.1 (continued)

General information about the technology	*(in green = care criteria)*	
Name of the technology		
Intellectual property management		IP constraints during experimentation Limits on modification or repair (and new IP outcomes) Data ownership in practice
Economic model/ origin of the funding (equity)		Costs borne by users or care institutions Financial accessibility Risk of exclusion
care-led evaluation step 2		
Dissemination and adoption phase		
Type of adopters	*Organization type*	Nature of adopting organizations Care orientation of adopters Scale of adoption
Status of the adopters in the previous phases	*On the initiative of technology, in collaboration or independent*	Degree of prior involvement Knowledge of care context Ownership of innovation process
Type of innovation	*Product, process or organizational innovation*	Nature of innovation (product, process, organizational) Disruption of care practices
Degree of novelty	*New to the organization, new to the market*	Novelty relative to existing technologies and work organization practices Distance from the technology frontieer (new to the organization, to the market—domestic or even worldwide)
Reason(s) for adoption	*Productivity, quality of product, care objective*	Dominant motivation (efficiency, quality, care, cost) Alignment with care values
(Observed) care outcomes	*Response to vulnerability by compensation/ Response to vulnerability by enhancing capabilities (CA)—empowerment/none*	Long-term impact on vulnerability Capability enhancement versus substitution Sustainability of care improvements

(continued)

Table 9.1 (continued)

General information about the technology	*(in green = care criteria)*	
Name of the technology		
Ethical guarantees	*Data management, privacy, human rights, etc.*	Data and privacy protection measures Respect for dignity and rights Transparency and accountability
External assessment		Previous characteristics assessed by publication or external institutions Items assessed Level of proof of items assessed
Externalties		Effects on aggregate labour markets Social and institutional impacts Environmental impacts
care-led evaluation step 3		

Source Chetouani et al. (2026)

More precisely, we decompose the characteristics of each technology in distinguishing 3 major phases: Development and design phase; implementation and experimentation phase; dissemination and adoption phase. In doing so, not only we incorporate major findings from economics of innovation but we allow for the possibility that an innovation that is care-led during the phase 1 may lose this characteristic in the phase 2 for whatever reason that should be specified in the table. Being care-led or not is not an intrinsic characteristic for innovation but rather the result of several factors that may change over time. For example, there is always the possibility of a "bifurcation" for an innovation that had care-led features in the development and design phase but not in the subsequent phases. Consequently, we propose an evaluation of the care-led nature of the innovation at the end of each phase.

As for the characteristics that are taken into account to analyse a given innovation, it is impossible to be exhaustive during each of the three phases. However, we build the grid to collect information on two categories of indicator: general and descriptive characteristics of the innovation; what is specifically related to its care-led nature. As for the first category, it includes indicators such as “Problem addressed”, “Technology/Approach Used (description)”, “Organization/actors responsible for development”, “Target population”, “Actors responsible for regular maintenance”, “Type of Adopters”, “Status of the adopters in the previous phases”, “Type of innovation”, “Degree of novelty”. These indicators are not exhaustive but, in our view, they are enough to give a comprehensive description of each innovation that is analysed through this grid.

As for the second category of indicators, it is more difficult to identify because there is necessarily a trade-off between the necessity to capture the complexity of care-led innovation with many diverse indicators and the requirement for parsimony associated to pragmatic approach to focus on indicators for which there is a possibility to gather information. Among all these care-led indicators, we have retained the following ones. A first sub-category includes indicators that directly capture some aspects of the care-led nature of the innovation through the “Involvement of end-users in the development”, “Ethical procedure and approval”, “(expected and *ex post* measured) Care outcomes”, “Participation of the development initiative structure”, “Ethical guarantees”, or “External assessment”. A second sub-category refers to economic characteristics such as “Intellectual property management”, “Structure of collaborative development”, “Economic model/origin of the funding (equity)”, “Reasons for adoption”, or “Externalities”. Some of these categories are more or less present in each phase while others are specific to a given phase (e.g. Development and design phase).

In short, this second category of indicators allows us to capture characteristics that are not purely driven by economic or/and technological objectives. Without being exhaustive, we assume that this set of characteristics that are considered at different phases allows us capturing the essence of care-led innovation. This is confirmed in practice, when we mobilize them to analyse concrete examples.

9.5.2 *Examples of Care-led Innovation in the Eldercare Sector*

Examples of care-led innovation can be drawn from the care sector in Japan where assistive technologies (e.g., communication robots, remote monitoring, sleep sensors) have been actively introduced and implemented. It may sound tautological to use ‘care-led’ innovation in the care sector, as one assumes that not only innovation, but every other aspect of the sector should be driven by care. However, it is far from being always the case, as explained in the previous section and in Wright (2023):

there are indeed plenty of innovation initiatives in the eldercare sector that are not led by care consideration, but rather industrial policy or commercial logics, with poor results in terms of increasing well-being.

In this section, we focus on two examples, one (POTARO) that has the characteristics of care-led innovation, and another one (HomeAssist), which was initially designed from a care-led perspective but has experienced a bifurcation at some point. This second non-Japan related example shows in any case that, of course, care-led innovation goes much beyond the Japanese experience of innovation.

The case of POTARO

Potaro is a hospital medication delivery robot that transports dispensed medications specific to individual patients. It was introduced in 2023 alongside the construction of a new ward at Toyota Memorial Hospital in Toyota City, which is operated by Toyota Motor Corporation. Development of the robot dates back to early 2019, and its medication delivery service started almost simultaneously with the opening of the new ward in May 2023. The robot itself is based on a model developed by Toyota for another service-oriented project. The robot development team sought an application for this technology within their own hospital and eventually relocated to the hospital premises. It delivers medications five times daily from the hospital pharmacy to nurses' stations on other floors. Currently, around 20 robots are in daily use.

The developers collaborated with future users working at the hospital (nurses, pharmacists, laboratory technicians, medical equipment department staff, etc.) on both service implementation and the delivery robot's design. However, according to a report for internal use only, to which we had access, the path to this collaboration was not straightforward. Initially, there were differences in perspective between the developers and hospital staff, as well as discrepancies in how value was defined. Furthermore, qualitative data from focus groups, primarily involving technical developers, revealed that the divergence between the two parties remained significant throughout the development and implementation phases. Qualitative data from focus groups including hospital staff such as nurses indicates that, initially, the robots were not considered particularly valuable as manual transport by dedicated staff was deemed faster and more reliable. However, it is now evident that the robots are considered indispensable and their use is recognized as highly valuable.

When this medication delivery robot was evaluated based on the care-led innovation criteria, it was found that the robots had been developed to reduce the burden on nurses of transporting medication, particularly at night. A research centre at Toyota led the entire process, from development and implementation to adoption, providing financial support and service planning. Although there was collaboration with other companies (primarily within the group), the development process was fundamentally centered within the company. As they were part of the same Toyota Group, users were involved in the development and implementation processes from an early stage. However, for this same reason, ethical approval was scarcely required (also due to Japan's unique circumstances regarding personal data handling). Regarding intellectual property rights, internal reports indicate that approximately 50 patents have been applied for. Following the introduction of the robot, nurses' time spent moving around the hospital decreased due to the robot's night-time medication delivery. This freed up time for nurses to spend with patients, bringing them closer to their ideal working conditions. It should not be forgotten that this was made possible by a unique and privileged environment, in which the robot's maintenance was handled by a team of nearby dedicated developers and former factory workers tasked with improving hospital efficiency.

As a whole, is the innovation process at the origin of Potaro a care-led one? At this stage, it remains difficult to draw firm conclusions and further investigation is ongoing. The innovation process has obviously some care-led characteristics that are shown in Table 9.2, such as the (expected and real) care outcomes or the involvement of end-users. However, the case of Potaro shows how much care-led innovation is fragile and can be put into question, when the balance of power between different stakeholders evolves and leads to changes in the hierarchy of the objectives that are pursued. For example, the imperative of cost reduction may interfere in the process and leads to a deterioration of the working conditions of care workers. Care-led innovation is costly and its successful implementation is conditioned by a long-term and continuous investment.

HomeAssist

HomeAssist (HA° is an Assisted Living Platform for aging in place that has been conceived, and developed in France by an interdisciplinary team in Bordeaux (Consel et al., 2017; Sauzéon et al., 2022). It has also been evaluated by several studies that have been already published, thus has

Table 9.2 The innovcare grid—applied to the analysis of Potaro

		Cas 1
General information about the technology	(in green = care criteria)	
Name of the technology		*POTARO*
Development and design phase		
Problem addressed	*The specific issue or challenge the solution aims to solve*	This transportation robot aims at facilitating the delivery of drugs and medical devices within the Toyota Memorial hospital
Technology/Approach Used (description)		Robot with a system of ceiling cameras in the hopsital, analysing the environment
Organisation responsible for development		Toyota (@Toyota memorial hospital)
Target population	*Mainly for the cared person/Mainly for the caring person*	Mainly for nurses
Intellactual property management	*patents, publications, etc.*	Not known
Structure of collaborative dveloppment	*Alone, in partnership, etc.*	No collaboration (to be confirmed)
End-Users Involved in Development?		yes, nurses and different sections of the hospital have been involved)
Ethical Procedure/ Approval	*Relative to this phase*	Not known
Economic model/ origin of the funding		100% funded by Toyota (to be confirmed)
Excpected care outcomes	*Response to vulnerability by compensation/ Response to vulnerability by enhancing capabilities (CA)—empowerment/none*	The key idea is to allow nurses to dedicate more time to care activities; at the same time, it is also obvious that the introduction of POTARO aims at increasing the efficiency and transform the organization of work at the hospital in replicating the results obtained by Toyota in car plants
care-led evaluation step 1		

(continued)

Table 9.2 (continued)

		Cas 1
General information about the technology	(in green = care criteria)	
Name of the technology		*POTARO*
Implementation and experimentation phase		
Characteristics of implementation—> Organisation/actors responsible for implementation	*Organizations involved, excpected outcomes, duration, etc.*	3 groups of key players have been involved: (1) engineers from the Frontier research; (2) hospital staff and management (to be certainly decomposed); (3) a kaizen team which is involved in the implementation phase
Actors responsible for regular maintenance	*i.e. for providing 'care' for the technologies, including setting up and charging, etc.,*	Engineers at site
End-Users Involved	*integration of user feedback*	yes but to be specified
Intellactual property management		not known
Participation of the development initiative structure	*Involved or not*	Yes
Ethical Procedure/ Approval	*Relative to this phase*	not known
Economic model/ origin of the funding (equity)		100% funded by Toyota (estimation of the cost to be identified)
Care outcomes	*Response to vulnerability by compensation/ Response to vulnerability by enhancing capabilities (CA)—empowerment/none*	Increased efficiency (a nurse can take care of more patients within one hour); no clear impact on the care received by the patients; mixed results regarding the working conditions of nurses and their satisfaction
care-led evaluation step 2		

(continued)

Table 9.2 (continued)

		Cas 1
General information about the technology	(in green = care criteria)	
Name of the technology		*POTARO*
Dissemination and adoption phase		
Type of adopters	*Organization type*	So far, limited to TMH
Statute of the adopters in the previous phases	*On the initiative of technology, in collaboration or independent*	Fully Toyota (internal)
Statute of the innovation	*Product, process or organizational innovation*	Product, Process and organizational innovation
Degree of novelty	*New to the organization, new to the market*	New to the organization but maybe not new to the market (see additional information sent to Yuko and Malo)
Reason of adoption	*Productivity, quality of product, care objective*	Officially only to improve the quality of care and the quality of jobs of nurses but the goal to increase productivity is obvious
Care outcomes	*Response to vulnerability by compensation/ Response to vulnerability by enhancing capabilities (CA)—empowerment/none*	NA
Ethical guarantees	*Data management, privacy, human rights, etc.*	Not known
Externalties		Not identified at this stage
care-led evaluation step 3		Yet to be done

Source Chetouani et al. (2026)

beneficiated from evidence-based analysis, in the spirit of the requirements emphasized in the above synthetic definition of care-led innovation. It has been the object of a quasi-experimental study with a relatively large sample size, over several months, which has led to several publications.

In this version of the grid, we separate the innovation description from the care-led analysis in the three phases. It allows us to emphasize the flexibility and plasticity of this grid (Tables 9.3a & 9.3b).

HomeAssist offers multi-domain and monitoring services at home for supporting self-determined behaviours related to independent living capabilities of pre-frail and frail older adults (according to multidimensional criteria of frailty). This an ambient assisted living platform that offers personalized monitoring and assisted services on tablets for older adults and on phone for caregivers, through a user-centered design. In short, it proposes an ecosystemic human-centered approach for introducing a personalized AAL platform dedicated to frailed older adults and their caregivers. It has been designed to monitor the good running of daily living routines and to provide assistive services and caregiver alarms. It offers a large set of apps for 3 main age-related need domains (activities of daily-living, safety, and social participation).

HomeAssist has obviously some care-led innovation characteristics, which are confirmed in each of the three phases we have distinguished. In phase 1, which has followed an ethical procedure, HomeAssist has been conceived and designed by a pluri-disciplinary research consortium (computer science, psychology, public health) in collaboration with public and private home services for aging in place, as well as disability and aging units of department councils, it has involved end-users with the following expected care outcomes that are well and explicitly defined: reducing or controlling the frailty process for maintaining aging in place while reducing or controlling the caregiver burden. More precisely, the primary targeting outcome are aging in place-related measures through functional status (IADL scale measure). Secondary criteria of HA efficacy include institutionalization and hospitalization as well as measures of health scales (self-efficacy, quality of life, routinization, etc.), general cognitive status, memory, and executive functioning. In addition, caregiver-related measures are used to assess the impact of HA on the daily delivery of services (e.g., feeling of burden assessment and psychological health of caregivers) and reassurance regarding the situation of the older person. As emphasized above, this is another important characteristic of a care-led innovation.

During the phase 2, along the same ethical procedures and with the same collaborative framework, the expected care outcomes have been confirmed. More precisely, some expected outcomes have been confirmed during this phase. First, improvement or non-deterioration in the ability of conducting instrumental activities of daily life (IADLs) has been confirmed. Second, a positive effect of HA intervention for prolonging aging

Table 9.3a The innovcare grid—an alternative version and an application to the analysis of HomeAssist

a Description		
Innovation Description		
General information		
Solution Name	The name or title of the innovative solution	HomeAssist
Problem Addressed	The specific issue or challenge the solution aims to solve	To support aging in place of older adults having high risks to autonomy loss
Target Population	Who benefits from the solution (e.g., elderly people with specific needs, caregivers)	Pre-frail and frail older adults (according to the multidimensional critera of frailty, SEGA scale)
Scenarios	The context in which the solution is applied (home, healthcare, public spaces)	Personal home of individuals living alone
Type of Innovation	Technological, service-oriented, policy change// Products (goods or service), process, organization	Multi-domain assistive and monitoring services at home for supporting self-deterrmined behaviours related to independent living capabilities
Technology/ Approach Used	Description of the core technology or method used (AI, IoT, robots …)	Ambient assisted living platform based on IoT and delivering individualized/ personalized monitoring and assitive services on tablets for older adults and on phone for caregivers/Ecosystemic design approach including iterative participatory design and focus group with the end-users and the stakeholders of aging in place (family, professionnals and public organisations and institutions in charge of issue of aging in place/

(continued)

Table 9.3a (continued)

a Description		
Innovation Description		
Aim of Innovation	Product-oriented (new goods or services) or Process-oriented (improvement of production of goods or services)	To monitor the good running of daily living routines (daytime activities, eating, bathing, dressing, etc) and to provide assistive services (reminders of daily living routines, appointment, occupational and communication activities, etc) and caregiver alarms (abnormal activities)
Degree of Novelty	Technology new to the company or new to the market (adoption versus creation of new technologies)	Fully new because leveraging from both a knowledge-driven approach (rather than machine-learning) of everyday functioning of older adult and a technology design driven by self-determination (self-choose services among services identified by individual and/or caregivers as relevant for the individual' needs)
Country	In what country was the solution developed or implemented?	France
Phase 1: Conception and design phase		
Organisation/Enterprise/Entity responsible for initiative		Inria (French national institute of digital sciences)/ Industrial tranfer by UT4H startup
Phase 2: Development, implementation and experimentation		
Characteristics of implementation—> Organisation/actors responsible for implementation	Organizations involved, excpected outcomes, duration, etc.	Implementation by private and public local home services for aging in place supervised by the Aging units of departmental Councils.

(continued)

Table 9.3a (continued)

a Description		
Innovation Description		
		Duration: from 12 to 24 months/Twofold expectation: (1) Increase individual's self-determination and their capability to live at home while exhibiting a spared quality of live (2) to deal the objective and subjective (informal and formal) caregiver burden
Phase 3: Dissemination and adoption		
Actors responsible for regular maintenance	i.e. for providing 'care' for the technologies, including setting up and charging, etc.,	Project's team including 5 psychogeriatric clinicians, 1 domotician, 2 engineers
Status	Prototype, pilot phase, fully implemented, etc. at the time of the assessment or the publishing of the article	Fully implemented
Future Potential	What are the possible improvements, scalability, or adaptation to other contexts?	Startup creation of UT4H (but stopping)/Transfer to the first-access to independent living in youths with down syndrome (Landuran et al., 2023)
Type of adopters	Organization type	Public and private home-nursing services and the French association of Down syndrome

Source Chetouani et al. (2026)

in place of frail individual living alone has been found, through improved cognitive and mental health, leading to reduced institutionalization and hospitalization. Also, a positive effect on caregivers' health has been confirmed. In addition, owing to the personalization of HA services and their user-centered design, a positive user experience on pragmatic criteria

Table 9.3b Care-led Innovation Analysis (CLIA)

Care-Led Innovation Analysis (CLIA)		
Phase 1: Conception and design phase		
Structure of collaborative development (who is involved)	The parties involved: academics, industrials, institutions	Pludisciplinary research corsortium (informatics, psychology and health) + intersectorial professionals interwining with private and public home services for aging in place + Disability & Aging units of departmental councils (Girandes, Landes, Pyrénées Atlantiques, Dordogne)
End-Users Involvement	Yes/No. If yes, describe their role (1-requirements gathering and design ideation; 2-technology development and (re)design; 3-prototype test and evaluation)	Yes (1-co-design of HomeAssist /2—user studies/ 3-pilot study)
Intellectual property management	Patents, publications, etc	3 Licences + ten years of computer studies and ergonomics studies (More than 35 papers)
Ethical Procedure/ Approval	Yes/No. If yes, describe the ethical procedure or provide the approval reference	YES (the French Southwest and Overseas Protection of Persons Committee deemed the study to be outside the scope of the provisions governing biomedical research and routine care (DC 2015/2066). The study protocol was also approved by the National Commission of Informatics and Liberty (Comission Nationale Informatique & Libertés- French name) and the Ethics COERLE (Comité Operationel d'Evaluation des Risques Légaux et Ethiques) committee of the French National Institute of

(continued)

Table 9.3b (continued)

Care-Led Innovation Analysis (CLIA)		
		Informatics and Mathematics (Inria), as protecting participants and data accordingly
Economic model and/or origin of the funding		Be-to-Be model/Inria Funds + Regional council of Aquitania
Expected care outcomes	Response to vulnerability by compensation Response to vulnerability by enhancing capabilities (CA)—empowerment None	Stakeholders' and indinvidual's acceptability and use behaviours + Elicited self-determination + Reduce or control the frailty process for maintaining aging in place + Reduce or control the caregiver burden
Care-led evaluation step 1		
Phase 2: Development, implementation and experimentation		
End-Users Involvement	Yes/No. If yes, describe their role (1-requirements gathering and design ideation; 2-technology development and (re)design; 3-prototype test and evaluation)	Yes/3—Field studiy with 131 older adults
Intellectual property management	Patents, publications, etc	Sauzéon et al. (2022)
Participation of the development initiative structure	Involved or not	Yes
Ethical Procedure/ Approval	Relative to this phase	YES (the French Southwest and Overseas Protection of Persons Committee deemed the study to be outside the scope of the provisions governing biomedical research and routine care (DC 2015/2066). The study protocol was also approved by the National

(continued)

Table 9.3b (continued)

Care-Led Innovation Analysis (CLIA)		
		Commission of Informatics and Liberty (Comission Nationale Informatique & Libertés-French name) and the Ethics COERLE (Comité Operationel d'Evaluation des Risques Légaux et Ethiques) committee of the French National Institute of Informatics and Mathematics (Inria), as protecting participants and data accordingly. For the control group from the 2 cohorts, an ethics committee approved the research according to the principles embodied in the Declaration of Helsinki: for 3C, the Ethical Committee of the University Hospital of Kremlin-Bicêtre (Paris, France) and Sud-Méditerranée 3 (Nîmes, France) and for AMI, the committee of the University Hospital of Bordeaux (France). All the participants provided written informed consent.)
Economic model/ origin of the funding		Be-to-Be model/FEDER Funds + FRM fundation
Care outcomes	Response to vulnerability by compensation/Response to vulnerability by enhancing capabilities (CA)—empowerment/none	The benefit from HomeAssist with a user-centered design is effective for aging in place for frail older adults in terms of everyday functioning (instrumental activities of daily-life scale). In addition, our secondary expected outcomes are that such an AAL decreases or neutralizes the frailty process and reduces the rates of institutionalization and hospitalization and that it

(continued)

Table 9.3b (continued)

Care-Led Innovation Analysis (CLIA)		
		improves the psychosocial health of participants and their caregivers when compared with the control condition. We also assume that a large proportion of equipped participants will have a satisfactory experience and will accept a subscription to an internet connection to prolong their participation
Care-led evaluation step 2		
Phase 3: Dissemination and adoption		
Type of adopters		Public and private home-nursing services
Status of adopters in the previous phase		Co-designers of the solution
Status of innovation		New to the market
Reason of adoption	Productivity, quality of product, care objective	Proven effectiveness in previous a pilot study (Dupuy, et al., 2016, 2017)
Care outcomes	Response to vulnerability by compensation/Response to vulnerability by enhancing capabilities (CA)—empowerment/none	Increased self-determination, neutralization of functional losses and neutralisation of caregiver burden at 6 and 9 months of use
Ethical guarantees	Data management, privacy, human rights, etc.	Yes
Externalties		Not available today
Care-led evaluation step 3		

Source Chetouani et al. (2026)

(perceived usability, usefulness, ease of use, learnability, etc.) and hedonic criteria (pleasure, satisfaction, perceived attractiveness, etc.) has been confirmed. However, it is worth noting that, at this stage, the business model is unknown.

This is only during the phase 3 that a possible bifurcation has been observed due to divergences of view among different stakeholders: while the ones who have developed HomeAssist from the beginning were trying to keep the spirit and framework of the phase 1, others have pushed for new approaches to intellectual property rights for the benefits of commercialization but with risks of losing the care-led orientation. Namely, to our limited knowledge, it seems that the business model proposed by a startup to market the technology has led to a simplification of the features of HA. It explains it has not been yet disseminated and adopted, despite the excellent prospects of phases 1 and 2. Moreover, public policy actors (such as the French Public Investment Bank, BPI) has promoted a development that would emphasize short-term economic benefits, in separating the different functions, instead of keeping the initial holistic view.

9.6 Conclusion

In this chapter, we have introduced the concept of "care-led innovation" as well as some examples, in arguing that this approach, which is born in the Japanese context in order to overcome the limitations of the previous and reformed systems of innovation in Japan, can be mobilized, beyond the Japanese case, as an alternative to transatlantic models dominated by a Neo-Schumpeterian view on innovation.

In proposing an interpretation of Society 5.0 as a response to the innovation crisis in Japan, this chapter has introduced a critical view on the models of innovation and capitalism that are promoted in order to implement this vision. It has then depicted the notion of care-led innovation as a model that may support the emergence of a Society 5.0, as a way of reconnecting social needs to technological development and deployment.

To put it differently, this article has investigated the condition for the implementation of Society 5.0, a vision that has been introduced in Japan, as part of the 5th Science and Technology Basic Plan (2015). This is in theory an adequate answer to the innovation crisis, but it requires additional efforts to be implemented. We indeed argue that the discussion on Society 5.0 may open the door to the emergence of alternative models of capitalism—such "Anthropogenetic" mode of development—and of innovation. Namely, a model of non-Schumpeterian innovation is needed to realize Society 5.0, in order to move from a concept of innovation as a tool for competitiveness to a concept of innovation as a source of well-being.

Care-led innovation can be this model. It does not exclude the use of new technologies but emphasizes the innovation at a given level of technology, as shown through different examples. Care-led innovation is indeed already at work in various care-settings but it requires a systematization in order to be generalized and extended to other spheres, where the concept of care can be successfully applied.

Beyond the Japanese case of Society 5.0, the concept and the practice of care-led innovation is meaningful in helping us to overcome the limitation of the Neo-Schumpeterian model. What can be learnt from the history of the emergence of new regime is that top/down visions are not enough. A participation from various stakeholders is required in order to promote unexpected fits that are the major conditions for this emergence. Major actors will not be necessarily startups but a larger set of stakeholders that includes: users, non-users, communities, and any institution that may help to socialize the costs and the risks while acting for the common good (e.g. governments).

References

Aghion, P., Antonin, C., & Bunel, S. (2021). *The power of creative destruction: Economic upheaval and the wealth of nations.* Harvard University Press.

Amable, B., Barré, R., & Boyer, R. (1997). *Systèmes nationaux d'innovations.* Economica.

Amable, B. (2003). *The diversity of modern capitalism.* Oxford University Press.

Amable, B., & Palombarini, S. (2009). A neorealist approach to institutional change and the diversity of capitalism. *Socio-economic Review, 7*(1), 123–143.

Anchordoguy, M. (2000). Japan's software industry: A failure of institutions. *Research Policy, 29*(3), 391–408.

Aoki, M. (2000). *Information, corporate governance, and institutional diversity: Competitiveness in Japan, the USA, and the transitional economies.* Oxford University Press.

Aoki, M., & Dore, R. (Eds.). (1994). *The Japanese firm: Sources of competitive strength.* Oxford University Press.

Boyer, R. (2019). How scientific breakthroughs and social innovations shape the evolution of the healthcare sector. In S. Lechevalier (Ed.), *Innovation beyond technology: Science for society and interdisciplinary approaches* (pp. 89–119). Springer.

Boyer, R., & Boylaud, O. (2026). Anthropogenetic development: Long unnoticed and already in crisis. In S. Lechevalier, J.-P. Gaudillière, K. Ibata-Arens, & K. Takuma (Eds.), *Capitalism, innovations, and health after Covid-19. An Asian perspective.* Palgrave MacMillan.

Boyer, R. (2003). The embedded innovation systems of Germany and Japan: Distinctive features and futures. In K. Yamamura & W. Streeck (Eds.), *The end of diversity? Prospects for German and Japanese capitalism* (pp. 147–183). Cornell University Press.

Boyer, R., & Yamada, T. (Eds.). (2000). *Japanese Capitalism in crisis.* Routledge.

Branstetter, L. G., & Nakamura, Y. (2003). Is Japan's innovative capacity in decline? In M. Blomström, J. Corbett, F. Hayashi, & A. Kashyap (Eds.), *Structural impediments to growth in Japan* (pp. 191–224). University of Chicago Press.

Chetouani, M., Harzo, C., Lechevalier, S., Mofakhami, M., Sauzéon, H., & Welply, Y. T. (2026). "What is Care-led innovation? A definition and an analytical grid", *FFJ Discussion Paper Series*, forthcoming.

Chiavacci, D. (2025). Dam break in Japan's immigration policy: The 2018 reform in a long-term perspective. *Social Science Japan Journal, 28*(1), jyae033.

Consel, C., Dupuy, L., & Sauzéon, H. (2017). HomeAssist: An assisted living platform for aging in place based on an interdisciplinary approach. In *International conference on applied human factors and ergonomics* (pp. 129–140). Springer International Publishing.

Doncieux, S., Chatila, R., Straube, S., & Kirchner, F. (2022). Human-centered AI and robotics. *AI Perspectives, 4*(1).

Gorry, P., & Montalban, M. (2026). The crisis of capitalism and health innovation: Symptoms of a crisis or of success? In S. Lechevalier, J.-P. Gaudillière, K. Ibata-Arens, & K. Takuma (Eds.), *Capitalism, innovations, and health after Covid-19. An Asian perspective.* Palgrave MacMillan.

Ibata-Arens, K. (2005). *Innovation and entrepreneurship in Japan: Politics, organizations, and high technology firms.* Cambridge University Press.

Ibata-Arens, K., Gaudillière, J.-P., Madhavan, H., & Nouguez, E. (2026). Commons and the political economy of access: Generics, neo traditional formulations and the dominant intellectual property regime of medicine. In S. Lechevalier, J.-P. Gaudillière, K. Ibata-Arens, & K. Takuma (Eds.), *Capitalism, innovations, and health after Covid-19. An Asian perspective.* Palgrave MacMillan.

Kodate, N. (2026). Institutional design, welfare technologies and diffusion of innovation: Stakeholders' views regarding care robots in Hong Kong SAR (China), Ireland and Japan. In S. Lechevalier, J.-P. Gaudillière, K. Ibata-Arens, K. Takuma, et al. (Eds.), *Capitalism, innovations, and health after Covid-19. An Asian perspective.* Palgrave MacMillan.

Lechevalier, S. (2024). Society 5.0 and new capitalism: Complementarities and contradictions. *Asia Pacific Business Review, 30*(3), 467–484.

Lechevalier, S. (ed.). (2019). *Innovation beyond technology: Science for society and interdisciplinary approaches.* Springer.

Lechevalier, S. (2014). *The great transformation of Japanese capitalism.* Routledge.

Lechevalier, S., d'Albis, H., Hoshi, T., & Monfort, B. (2026). Economics of Ageing, Japan in a comparative perspective: An introduction. *The Journal of the Economics of Ageing*, Special Issue, forthcoming.

Lechevalier, S., & Mofakhami, M. (2025). Assessing job satisfaction in the era of digital transformation: A comparative study of the first wave of tasks digitalization in Japan and France. *Eurasian Business Review*, *15*, 93–129.

Lechevalier, S., & Monfort, B. (2025). Japan at the forefront of the economics of aging? A Bibliometric analysis. *The Journal of the Economics of Ageing*, *32*, 100601.

Lechevalier, S., & Monfort, B. (2017). Abenomics: Has it worked? Will it ultimately fail? *Japan Forum*, *30*(2), 277–302.

Lechevalier, S., & Shibata, S. (2026). The contribution of digitalization to non-inclusive growth in Japan. A Régulationist perspective on post-industrial dynamics. *Competition & Change*, *30*(1), 11–37.

Lechevalier, S., Tamaki Welply, Y., Humbert, C., Shimohara, K., & Robine, J.-M. (2025). Care-led innovation: The case of eldercare in France and in Japan. *International Journal of Care and Caring*, *9*(4), 817–824.

Lee, G. H., & Lee, S. P. (2014). Childcare availability, fertility and female labor force participation in Japan. *Journal of the Japanese and International Economies*, *32*, 71–85.

Madhavan, H., & Gaudillière, J.-P (2026). Frugal innovations and health system resilience. The conceptualization, policy support and forms of frugality during Covid-19 in South India. In S. Lechevalier, J.-P. Gaudillière, K. Ibata-Arens, & K. Takuma (Eds.), *Capitalism, innovations, and health after Covid-19. An Asian perspective*. Palgrave MacMillan.

Maibaum, A., Bischof, A., Hergesell, J., et al. (2022). A critique of robotics in health care. *AI & Society*, *37*, 467–477.

Mazzucato, M. (2018). Mission-oriented innovation policies: Challenges and opportunities. *Industrial and Corporate Change*, *27*(5), 803–815.

Monfort, B. (2026). "The future is now: Reviewing the accuracy of aging forecasts", *FFJ Discussion Paper Series*, forthcoming.

Nezu, R. (2004). Why did Japanese industry lose out in the global competition during the 1990s? *The Japanese Economy*, *32*(1), 45–75.

Paperman, P., & Laugier, S. (Eds.). (2020). *Le souci des autres: éthique et politique du care*. Éditions de l'École des hautes études en sciences sociales

Sauzéon, H., Edjolo, A., Amieva, H., Consel, C., & Pérès, K. (2022). Effectiveness of an ambient assisted living (HomeAssist) platform for supporting aging in place of older adults with frailty: Protocol for a quasi-experimental study. *JMIR Research Protocols*, *11*(10), e33351.

Sætra, H. S. (2020). The foundations of a policy for the use of social robots in care. *Technology in Society*, *63*, 101383.

Shibata, S., & Lechevalier, S. (2025). Hampered digitalization: Institutional failure and new instability in Japan. *The Japanese Political Economy*, *51*(1–2), 180–207.

Shimohara, K. (2024). *Relationality design with a remote-controlled robot as enacting media: Beyond the dichotomy of autonomy and dependency*. INNOVCARE Discussion Paper Series N°2024-01.

Shiroyama, H., Ki, J., & Matsuo, M. (2026). The mission-oriented science, innovation and technology (STI) policies in Japan and Korea with a focus on health. In S. Lechevalier, J.-P. Gaudillière, K. Ibata-Arens, & K. Takuma (Eds.), *Capitalism, innovations, and health after Covid-19. An Asian perspective*. Palgrave MacMillan.

Suzuki, T. (2006). Fertility decline and policy development in Japan. *The Japanese Journal of Population*, *4*(1), 1–32.

Tamaki Welply, Y., & Lechevalier, S. (2024). 'Social' robot and social relations in care settings: Undefined positionality and fixed temporality. *Technology in Society*, *77*, 102559.

Tamaki Welply, Y. (2024). Whose needs and what needs? Social robots in eldercare settings in Japan. *Gérontologie Et Société*, *46/175*(3), I–XVIII.

Vogel, E. (1980). *Japan as number one: Lessons for America*. Harpercollins.

Watanabe, D. (2021). Understanding diversity in later life and a new culture of aging: Sociology of aging in Japan. *International Sociology*, *36*(2), 243–253.

Whittaker, H. (2024). *Building a new economy: Japan's digital and green transformation*. Oxford University Press.

Whittaker, D. H., & Nakata, Y. (2024). Reforming Japanese capitalism: Introduction. *Asia Pacific Business Review*, *30*(3), 421–432.

Wright, J. (2020). Comparing the development and commercialization of care robots in the European Union and Japan. *Fondation France-Japon Discussion Paper Series* n°2020-01.

Wright, J. (2023). *Robots won't save Japan: An ethnography of eldercare automation*. Cornell University Press.

CHAPTER 10

Appropriate Technologies, Primary Health Care and the Integration of Traditional Medicines in India

Jean-Paul Gaudillière and Harilal Madhavan

Abstract The purpose of this chapter is to discuss the relationship between social and technological innovations and their specificity in the health sector by taking the benefit of the long history of discussions about appropriate technologies, social policies and development in international health since the 1970s. The chapter thus looks at a configuration of alternatives to the dominant biomedical model of innovation, namely the primary health care strategy to meet basic health needs that the WHO and UNICEF promoted up to the 1990s. It focuses on one dimension of the strategy, namely the idea that traditional medical knowledge and practices are resources to be integrated in the health systems, following the way India, its health authorities and actors—have articulated social and technological innovations to fostering the integration and

J.-P. Gaudillière (✉)
Inserm & EHESS, Paris, France
e-mail: jean-paul.gaudilliere@cnrs.fr

H. Madhavan
CHRIST University, Bengaluru, India

S. Lechevalier et al. (eds.), *Capitalism, Innovations, and Health after Covid-19*,
https://doi.org/10.1007/978-3-032-24479-6_10

access to Ayurveda. The chapter thus argues that the modernization of ayurvedic medical practice has followed two different logics: first, a model of institutional juxtaposition, which prevailed until the late 1990s; second, a model of industrialization, dominating since the early 2000s. By recounting and analyzing this trajectory, the chapter therefore contributes to two discussions. The first one is about the meanings the notion of appropriate technologies has taken, showing the *boundary work* through which health actors define both the boundary and the interplay between social and technological innovations. The second debate concerns the problematic consequences of the successful industrialization of Ayurveda. Scaling-up the production of plant-based remedies to enlarge access has indeed created novel tensions typical of the Anthropocene. Industrial Ayurveda fosters a massive consumption of medicinal plants, which threatens their mere reproducibility, and therefore the sustainability of a model of continuous growth based on the supply of unlimited resources. The mere successes of the Indian's path toward appropriate technologies therefore urges for urgent adaptations of the anthropogenic mode of development in order to face the mounting issues of ecological sustainability.

10.1 Introduction

The purpose of this chapter is to discuss the relationship between social and technological innovations and their specificity in the health sector by taking the benefit of the long history of discussions about appropriate technologies, social policies and development in international health since the 1970s. The focus is therefore the status of social medicine in the global South, and more precisely a peculiar configuration of alternatives to the dominant biomedical model of innovation, namely the primary health care strategy to meet basic health needs that the WHO and UNICEF promoted up to the 1990s as a form of social medicine for what was then called the Third World. One key dimension of the strategy was the claim that what developing countries needed was less more technology transfer than the regional, national, and local design of "appropriate technologies"; appropriate in this context meaning not only low cost, but also simple, targeting basic health needs, and socially acceptable.

Exploring the relations between forms of innovation and forms of care, the chapter more precisely looks at one dimension of the primary health care strategy, namely the idea that traditional medical knowledge and practices are resources to be integrated in the health systems of the global South. Rather than applying a WHO centered perspective, thus retelling the well-known inquiries into the making of the strategy and its relations to the Cold War on the one hand, the development agenda of newly independent nation-states on the other hand, the chapter follows the ways in which one key Asian country—India, its health authorities and actors—have articulated social and technological innovations while fostering primary health care and trying to institutionalize and scale-up Ayurveda—one of the so-called and officially recognized "Indian systems of medicine". The chapter thus argues that the modernization of Ayurveda has followed two different models: first, a model of institutional juxtaposition, which prevailed until the late 1990s; second, a model of industrialization, dominating since the early 2000s.

By recounting and analyzing this trajectory, the chapter is therefore a contribution to two discussions. The first one is about the meanings the notion of appropriate technologies has taken and what meaning it may have in the future. This notion is indeed a way to reflect upon the articulation of the "social" and the "technological" when health innovation is considered. The really-existing trajectory of Ayurveda integration reveals shifting hierarchies of aims and practices, documenting what may be called the ***boundary work*** through which health actors define both the boundary and the interplay between social and technological innovations. The second concerns more recent issues originating in the successful industrialization of Ayurveda. Scaling-up the production of plant-based remedies to enlarge access has indeed created novel tensions this time between the "technical" and the "ecological". Industrial Ayurveda fosters a massive consumption of medicinal plants, which threatens their mere reproducibility, and therefore the sustainability of a model of continuous growth based on the supply of unlimited resources. The mere successes of primary health care in India are therefore pressing for a reinvention of appropriateness in order to address mounting issues of ecological sustainability.

10.2 Primary Health Care, Appropriate Technologies and the Integration of Traditional Medicine at WHO

At the end of the 1978, the WHO and the UNICEF organized in Alma-Ata (USSR) one of these major international conferences UN institutions like. As the final declaration or the meeting explained the aim was to adopt an innovative strategy to achieve "health for all in 2000". More precisely, the target was to find better adjustments between health needs, the organization of local health systems, the state financial means and the contribution of international development aid. To this effect, Alma-Ata adopted the so-called "primary health care strategy" whose originality was in defining and claiming for a form of social medicine adapted to the situation of Third World countries. As historians have pointed out, Alma Ata was a major moment of redefinition of what health meant at the international level, a moment rooted in the then hefty debates about the Cold War geopolitical order, the hegemony of industrial countries and the attempts to foster a more balanced and just "international economic order" (Birn & Krementsov, 2018).

As overarching health and development strategy, primary health care (PHC) has often been described as horizontal and integrative, in contrast to the postcolonial vertical programs of the 1950s–1960s, which targeted just one disease on the basis of a narrow set of technological interventions (Birn & Krementsov, 2018; Brown et al., 2006; Packard, 2016). Within this context horizontal meant that the strategy claimed: (a) a broad definition of health as a state of wellbeing and development, rather than its medical understanding as mere absence of diseases; (b) the integration of the national health systems the newly independent Third World countries were constructing within an overall planification of social and economic development; (c) the prioritization of the most needy segments of the population, often meaning the people living in rural rather than urban areas (Cueto et al., 2019).

The program discussed during the Alma-Ata conference thus proposed that the core unit of such health systems should be the local dispensaries and their dedicated health personnel. The WHO of the 1970s indeed looked suspiciously at the commitment of many postcolonial health administration to the construction of new hospitals, the training of physicians, and the import of frontier technologies from Europe and North America. These were considered problematic in two ways: first socially, as they reproduce existing inequalities of access to healthcare since they favored the upper urban classes given the limited number of hospitals actually opened there in majority located in cities; second medically, as they implied heavy investments since they relied on skills and machines that were at the same time costly, imported, and difficult to maintain.

The result of Alma-Ata was an action program for countries without large public health infrastructures, facing urgent and multiple needs, and in possession of limited budgetary resources. In the eyes of both experts and political leaders, targeting investments and defining priority needs was therefore not a matter of choice but of necessity. In contrast to what the slogan "health for all" suggested, the PHC strategy did not aim at organizing the *access of all to all* medically thinkable interventions, but at informing the choice of priorities (Chabrol & Gaudillière, 2023).

The final document nonetheless defined a rather broad perimeter of targets: health education, the access to adequate food and nutrition, the access to clean water and sanitation, mother and child healthcare including family planning, vaccination against the most frequent infectious disorders, the control of major endemic communicable disorders, the appropriate treatment of the most frequent pathologies and accidents, the promotion of mental health, and the supply of essential drugs (WHO, 1978a). Even if the country delegates did not want to draw a list of pathologies—this was to remain the jurisdiction of national states—they did make a clear-cut choice, excluding all non-communicable disorders apart from mental health. Interestingly, the very sensitive question of who was legitimate in making such choices was handled in a relatively open way: although bureaucrats and health personnel were paramount, the PHC strategy also mentioned the need for some democracy with the reference to community involvement, an ambiguous notion that meant community members support (financial, logistic) to "their" local healthier as well as the ability to influence the forms of care and the selection of priority diseases.

It is within this context that appropriate technology, one of the most original notion the PHC strategy claimed to back made sense (Gaudillière et al., 2022). As the 1978 final report of the Alma-Ata conference explained:

> "An important factor for the success of primary health care is the use of appropriate health technology. The word technology means an association of methods, techniques and equipment, which together with the people using them, can contribute significantly to solving a health problem. Appropriate means that besides being scientifically sound the technology is also acceptable to those who apply it and to those for whom it is used. This implies that technology should be in keeping with the local culture. It must be capable of being adapted and further developed if necessary. In addition, it should preferably be easily understood and applied by community health workers, and in some instances by individuals in the community; although

different forms of technology are appropriate at different stages of development, their simplicity is always desirable. The most productive approach for ensuring that appropriate technology is available is to start with the problem and then to seek, or if necessary to develop, a technology which is relevant to local conditions and resources." (WHO, 1978b).

Primary Health Care thus embodied a critical relationship to technological innovation, which the debates about drug policies and the notion of essential drugs well illustrate. During the preparation of Alma-Ata, H. Mahler, then director general of the WHO and ardent promoter of the strategy, clearly summarized the problem:

> "Developed countries are faced with problems of high expenditure on drugs, often due to over-consumption or misuse, and of avoidable adverse reactions. Expenditure on drugs in developing countries, in both the private and public sectors, is much lower in absolute terms than in the developed countries, but is usually much higher in proportion to the total health expenditure. The need to optimize expenditure on drugs, which is widely felt in the developing countries, is therefore vital. Resources are often wasted in the purchase of expensive drugs that are only marginally useful, or even totally irrelevant to the solution of countries' main health problems, whereas large segments of the population are in urgent need of essential drugs for disease control and primary health care. In many instances, the lack of these essential drugs is an important constraint on the solution of the health problems of the populations in need." (WHA 1975).

The response was not to avoid all technologies but to focus on technologies, which were deemed appropriate because they meet basic needs, because they were simple, cheap and socially acceptable. In the case of pharmaceuticals, this did not mean appropriate drugs but "essential medicines". The policy of the same name was paramount in the health organization, at least for a decade after Alma-Ata. From the late 1970s onward, the drug strategy WHO recommended to the member states included the creation of a national pharmacopoeia, the control of drugs brought in the market, the support of local production, and the establishment of a list of essential drugs. Essential drugs were appropriate because mass-produced, cheap and effective against major health issues (at the level of the population). They were to be made available in all dispensaries and primary health centers. WHO published a reference list of 186 substances in 1977, which made the notion of essential drugs even more specific:

all the drugs listed were generics without any single exception[1], targeting frequent symptoms (like fever or inflammation), infectious disorders (with many antibiotics and vaccines), or some pressing public need (the sex steroids for contraception).

The search for appropriate technologies grounded several other dimensions of the PHC strategy, beginning with the hiring of community health workers, who were non-medical health personnel devoted to the provision of basic care, and to the implementation of public health campaigns. Community health workers ought to benefit from much shorter training than physicians, would be chosen among members of the community they would help and live in. It was also the case of what was at the time perceived as one of the most visible departures from the framing of vertical biomedical programs, namely the claim for an integration of traditional systems of medicine or traditional healing practices in the national health infrastructure. Within the framework of PHC, these were considered as sources of local knowledge (for instance, when the WHO started to promote the inventory and the evaluation of therapeutic preparations based on medicinal plants), as well as sources of key non-medical personnel (for instance, with the launch of programs for the employment and complementary training of traditional birth attendants).

In parallel with the Alma-Ata document, the WHO thus issued guidelines for the integration of traditional medicines into PHC. The main points were: (1) Give recognition to traditional practitioners and incorporating them into community development programs; (2) Retrain traditional practitioners for proper use in PHC; (3) Acquaint professional health personnel and students of modern medicine with the principles of traditional medicine in order to promote communication, dialogue, mutual understanding and eventual integration; (4) Educate the community to believe the provision of traditional remedies is not second-rank medicine; (5) Catalogue all the medicinal plants in a country or region and disseminating the information thus compiled; (6) Retain the traditional names and forms of prescriptions whenever traditional remedies are adopted for use in PHC, and carry out relevant research into the traditional systems of medicine. All these targets of integration originated in national (mostly Asian) experiences taken as reference in the matter, among which the recent transformation (some actors were speaking of

[1] See Chap. 11 in this volume for the importance of generics in the politics of access to care (Ibata-Arens et al., 2026).

the modernization) of the traditional remedies from the Chinese and Indian medicines were paramount (WHO, 1978b).

In Geneva, primary health care was envisioned and discussed as a global strategy for the Third World. Since the WHO had never been a strong operational institution, but in the first place an expertise and advisory body, the origins, practical meanings, and conditions of implementation of PHC remained a matter of local—national or regional—policies. This is well exemplified by the case of India and the ways in which the country's health authorities supported the institutionalization of—and the access to—Ayurveda and other Asian systems of medicine as powerful instantiation of the quest for appropriate technologies.

10.3 Institutionalizing Ayurveda in India: Social Innovation and the First Wave of Integration (1960s–1990s)

A long-phase of studies and debates about experiments of health system strengthening and basic care for rural populations in the Third World preceded Alma-Ata within WHO and UNICEF. An important moment in the framing of the strategy was accordingly, in 1975, the publication of a joint committee's report presenting a series of key examples from China to Nigeria or Yugoslavia (Djukanovic & Mach 1975). Unsurprisingly given its role in decolonization and in the geopolitics of the Third World, India was included among the countries implementing a form of primary health care worth considering. This very notion had indeed first surfaced in the political vocabulary of the state in 1946 as element in the recommendations of the Bhore committee in charge of preparing the health policy of an independent India (Jeffery, 1988).

What PHC could be was however only defined in 1951, in the context of Indian national planning, with the launch of the first Rural Development Program. The creation of 5400 health centers (one per district) with outpatient facilities and 5–6 beds was then envisioned. These would embody the first level of health service with a broad palette of tasks including basic treatments, maternal and child health, nutrition, prevention of communicable diseases, sanitation, school health and vital statistics. Since health was constitutionally a responsibility of regional states (the central government, for its part, organizing the national programs targeting specific diseases like smallpox or malaria eradication, usually with significant inputs of international aid), creation of primary health care centers on a significant scale started in the 1960s only and remained very uneven.

In time, the federal government nonetheless launched three policies which contributed to the specificity of PHC in India. Firstly, it backed the institutionalization of the "Indian systems of medicine", meaning the medical cultures of importance in the country beside Western biomedicine, namely Ayurveda, the Unani indo-persian medicine, Siddha and Homeopathy. The model followed in India was not that of *integration* favored by WHO and promoted by China, but a policy of *juxtaposition* with the creation of parallel institutions mimicking the professional and stately organization of biomedicine, i.e. dispensaries, hospitals, and colleges. Secondly, in 1973, the Katar Singh Committee started the integration of the auxiliary health personnel hired in the malaria, tuberculosis, leprosis, smallpox, and population control programs to become "multipurpose health workers" working in the local centers (Jeffery, 1988). Thirdly, India's commitment to the WHO version of PHC led to the passage of a Village Health Guides scheme in 1977, supporting the hiring and the training of one community health worker per village.

The logic of intervention in favor of Ayurveda focused on what may be called integration. The committee led by Lt. Col. R.N. Chopra—an allopathic doctor and officer in the colonial Indian Medical Service—defined the agenda as combining three targets: (a) the harmonization between the indigenous and modern forms of medical knowledge, the latter providing the background for the evaluation of the former; (b) the need for an encompassing Indian pharmacopoeia, which would include the valuable preparations of indigenous medicine and could be used as resource for the standardization and modern production of these remedies; (c) the creation of a specialization in Ayurveda within the institutional organization of doctors' and pharmacists' training, which would then permit proper registration of experts in "Indian Medicine" (Banerjee, 2009).

The path followed in the following quarter of century proved significantly different because the practitioners of Ayurveda had different views of the future. Rather than straightforward integration, government policies looked for institutionalization and professionalization, meaning the creation of a series of Ayurveda institutions that would co-exist with biomedicine in order to achieve parity in professional status. More than drug development, what was at stake was the transformation of Ayurveda training and practice into those of a new clinical profession, whose jurisdiction and monopoly of action rested on the sanction of academic diplomas. The main achievements of the 1960s–1980s (Banerjee, 2009) were therefore the creation of more than 200 Ayurveda colleges nation-wide in parallel with the opening of hundreds of Ayurveda dispensaries and hospitals where these sanctioned practitioners would work. This does not mean that pharmacy was totally absent of the state's initiatives: the Central Council of Indian Medicine established in 1961 actually kept arguing for innovation in the making of drugs. However, the steps taken in order to create a parallel profession of Ayurveda pharmacists and to organize the production of remedies were minimal, focusing on the inventory of classical formulations—and the testing of some among them—under the patronage of a new AYUSH department creating within the Union Ministry of Health.

Integration of traditional medicine in the Indian context therefore did not mean unification or hybridization of different forms of knowledge as it happened in China where biomedical doctors should learn some Chinese medicine while practitioners of Chinese medicine learned a lot of Western medicine (Scheid, 2002). The Indian model was one of *juxtaposition*. It was all the more so that the central state's involvement was minimal: the hierarchy was clear since the budget the Indian Ministry of Health devoted to the Indian systems of medicine was roughly 1/10 of what was invested in biomedicine. However, since health was in the first place the affair of the regional states (Jeffery, 1988), these were in practice responsible for a process of institutionalization that was—just like the entire PHC policy—highly variable and localized.

Kerala is good example because of its well-known commitment to investments in social development, first of all in health and education, from the creation of the state onward (1957) in spite of the fact that Kerala during the first three decades of its existence only benefited from low economic growth (Drèze & Sen, 1994). This commitment went through three different phases. First, during the 1960s and 1970s, the creation of an important public health service through the integration of the dispensaries opened during the late colonial period in the state infrastructure was followed by the opening of several hundred new ones. This process rested on a rare political consensus between the two political coalitions alternatively ruling the state, respectively led by the Congress party and the local Communist Party of India (Marxist). It was complemented and reinforced by the pursuit of vertical programs targeting malaria, leprosis, tuberculosis, family planning, which were supported by UN and US organizations and administered by New Delhi. The opening—as well as the later strengthening of these local health centers—was critically dependent on the repeated mobilization of the local communities, their governing bodies (the panchayats) and the district doctors who lobbied the state health department, imposing some accountability and political sanction for unfulfilled promises.

Second, during the 1980s and 1980s, the so-called Kerala model of development went through a major fiscal and financial crisis due to the low growth of Kerala economy on the one hand, to a changing redistribution of revenues taxes to regional state on the other hand. Cuts seriously impacted the health system, reducing the quality of care as the prevention and public health control of infectious diseases remained the first priority. As a consequence, people started to shift to private clinics and private hospitals, whose number grew fast.

Finally, since the early 2000s, Kerala has experienced a new phase of reinforcement in the public health sector due to two main features: (a) the growth of revenues resulting from the remittances of millions migrant workers, including the numerous nurses and doctors expatriates (in other words, originating in an extraverted model of development based on the previous investments in education); (b) the 1995 decentralization laws, which organized the transfer of one third of the state's budget to the local panchayats and organized a form of participatory and decentralized planning, which provided a critical opportunity for renewed support to the public health sector, this time on the basis of community involvement (Gaudillière, 2026).

This trajectory has allowed for several specific features of Ayurveda's institutionalization. First, in contrast to the situation at the federal level, in Kerala, the creation of Ayurveda's institutions (medical school, hospitals and dispensaries) has been allocated significant shares of the state's health budget from the late 1960s onward, between 20% and 30% depending on the year. Second, juxtaposition has taken the form of a parallel segment of the health care system whose organization has followed the Kerala model of primary health care, which focused on the opening of local public centers: hence the existence of dense network of Ayurveda dispensaries (one in every panchayat), each staffed with at least one Ayurveda physician. Third, the state's emphasis on the need for industrialization and local production of health goods although not very successful in general has, in the case of Ayurveda, been translated in the creation of one company, Oushadi, mass-producing Ayurveda plant-based formulations and supplying the public dispensaries and hospitals. Oushadi products are in their vast majority classical recipes from the Ayruveda corpus whose modernization does not involve changes in the composition, but a mechanized mode of preparation and packaging. Fourth, just as it had been the case for the opening of many primary health centers, the lobbying of local government and Ayurveda physicians has played an important role in the strengthening of local Ayurveda institutions in the 1980s and 1990s, providing for increases in bed size, staffing of non-medical personnel and regular supply of remedies.

10.4 Industrializing and Reformulating Ayurveda: the Shift Toward Technology and Its Limits (2000s-2010s)

Since the late 1990s, in India, the modernization of Ayurveda has taken a radical industrializing turn with the rise of a pharmaceutical sector mass-producing ready-made therapeutic combinations of plants, which are "reformulated" (often radically simplified) versions of recipes from the official corpus of Ayurveda treaties (Pordié & Gaudilliere, 2014). The firms trading in these remedies range from small local ventures originating in one family to global players with thousand employees, which market products all over Asia using tools of marketing that do not differ from those of any other large capitalistic Western drug company. Their preparations are mostly purchased by consumers from the new urban middle-class as part of a self-management of health, risks and bodies that do not radically depart from what Western consumers/patients critical of biomedicine do when looking for alternative forms of care rooted in "traditional" medical systems.

The reformulation of classical combinations of medicinal plants described in centuries-old reference texts used by Ayurvedic practitioners lies at the heart of this process. Reformulation means at the same time simplifying and standardizing poly-herbal combinations in order to (1) adapt them to mass and mechanized industrial processing; (2) mobilize elements of biomedical experimentation in the laboratory and the clinic to provide evidence of medical value, and (3) link Ayurvedic and biomedical categories to address the health needs of cosmopolitan consumers.

One essential dimension of reformulation is its industrial nature. Industrialization means that the core actors are Indian Ayurvedic drug-producing companies, some of them large enough to operate as global players. It also refers to the manufacturing process, that is, the search for productivity and large-scale output through the use of mechanized processing, automated machinery, standardization, and possibly laboratory-based quality control. The reformulation regime thus produces new compositions of medicinal plants based on unique knowledge-prospecting mechanisms, borrowing from sometimes very distant medical resources, such as modern galenic, biomedicine, or the various Indian traditional medical systems. Reformulation thus feeds the emergence of an autonomous "pharmacy" (in the sense of a social world exclusively devoted to therapeutic substances) that breaks with Ayurvedic clinical practice both from a sociological point of view (preparations are no longer made by doctors but by persons specializing in medicinal plants and their manipulation) and an epistemic point of view (formulations are ready-to-use mixes for specific indications, no longer ad hoc mixes that are part of an individualized treatment regimen).

The invention of industrialized Ayurvedic remedies not only relies on technological work, such as turning compounded powders or oily extracts into ready-made pills but also mobilizes a complex set of experimental, clinical, economical, and legal practices deemed indispensable to build markets and grant the new products a twofold legitimacy, both traditional and modern. When discussing the reformulation practices involved in the invention of new preparations, the Ayurvedic practitioners (*vaidyas*)—for instance at The Himalaya Drug Company—insist on the mining of Ayurvedic classical texts[2]. Such mining actually rests on moves back and forth between the texts and the laboratory, which obey two different logics. The first one is a logic of translation and *materia medica*, focusing on the supposedly stable composition of plants and a series of equivalences between botanical denominations on the one hand, vernacular and Sanskrit names on the other, which have been worked out along two centuries of interactions between pharmacists, botanists and *vaidyas*. This logic makes possible to examine the classical formulations, looking for combinations including plants whose ingredients biomedical as well as Ayurvedic pharmacology has linked with processes responsible for the

[2] This claim is based on interviews, we conducted, will L. Pordié, at the headquarter of the Himalaya Company in 2015.

targeted pathology. The second logic is one of commonalities and clinical knowledge. It focuses on the supposedly stable symptoms of "real" pathologies, mobilizing another series of equivalences, this time between the concepts used in clinical descriptions. This logic makes possible to look for classical formulations targeting the components of the disease or syndrome for which a new combination is sought even if it is a biomedical one without equivalent in Ayurveda.

The emergence of such neo-traditional and to some extent alternative pharmaceutical capitalism should not be viewed simply as the outcome of industrialization, that is to say the existence, growth and operations of Ayurvedic drug companies. Since the late 1990s, the Indian state has played a central role in creating institutions and regulations fostering reformulation and the growth of the Ayurvedic market. The case of the Traditional Knowledge Digital Library[3] is just one example in a palette of initiatives, which include the creation of a National Medicinal Plant Board to address the problems of medicinal plants supply, the establishment of regional and state-based schemes for helping small companies develop "good manufacturing practices" and quality control, or the passage of a new registration act for Ayruvedic proprietary medicines.

Since the early 2000s, Kerala state governments have endorsed this turn toward industrialized Ayurveda. Moreover, they have linked it to the pursuit of health innovations based on botanical knowledge, thus providing for a version of biotechnology and bioprospection alternative to the manipulation of DNA and other macromolecules (Madhavan, 2014). In addition, given the legacy of primary health care in the state and the strong local demands for Ayurveda, the Kerala innovation policies reveal two features radically departing from the national strategy aiming at the development of new formulations and the growth of Ayurvedic products' exports.

The first peculiarity of Kerala's industrial Ayurveda exemplifying the limits of the pharmaceutical/technological turn is the fact that most players in the making of ready-made preparations, including the two most important ones, namely the public company Oushadhi and the Arya Vaidya Sala foundation do not practice the type of "reverse engineering" mentioned above. They rarely search for radically new formulations (eventually targeting biomedically defined disorders unknown in Ayurveda).

[3] On this, see Chap. 11 in this volume (Ibata-Arens et al., 2026).

They mostly produce classical (rather complex) formulations, with the aim of supplying Ayurveda hospitals in the country, and local dispensaries in Kerala.

The second peculiarity is a legacy of the 1990s debates about the "health transition" in Kerala, meaning the epidemiological transition from a burden of diseases dominated by the impact of communicable diseases to a situation such that the most important causes of mortality and morbidity are non-communicable diseases. This shift has been perceived as the paradoxical outcome of the successful public health policy of the first decades after independence and as a source of great tensions for a health system centered on the control of infectious disorders. The health transition has thus been identified as source of new demands, which contributed to increasing dissatisfaction with the public health infrastructure, recourse to private clinics and mounting health inequalities. From the 2000s onward, given their potential impact on the immune system and various metabolic pathways, Ayurveda and its industrial preparations have in consequence been considered as important resources to improve the situation of patients affected with chronic disorders, for instance in mental health (Lang, 2018). This commitment has contributed to accelerate the design of a list of "essential" Ayurvedic preparations that every Ayurvedic dispensary should store and deliver when prescribed, and that the state health administration should supply.

10.5 New Challenges: the Crisis of Medicinal Plants' Supply and the Limits to Growth

The industrialization of Ayurveda relies on a model of production and economic growth that presupposes the continuous supply of massive and if possible increasing quantities of medicinal plants. Since the vast majority of those used in the poly-herbal preparations—either classical or neotraditional—are collected in the wild (first of all in the forests of India), the changing scale of use in a context of climate change and general threats on biodiversity has resulted in new challenges and difficulties. The crisis of medicinal plants supply is indeed a general feature of industrial Ayurveda. Figures are difficult to obtain but from various inquiries one may say that since 2000 the demand for medicinal plants in Kerala has increased by a factor 2–4 (Dejouhanet, 2012, 2014; Sasidharan et al., 2011). As one member of the Kerala State Medicinal Plant Board explained us:

> "One of the main problems the growth of Ayurvedic drug production has created is that of adulteration. The number of species that are now difficult to find or too expensive for many manufacturers has increased since 2000 and substitution is a widespread phenomenon. It can be legitimate: Ayurveda has always built on local resources and there are many ways to adapt a formulation. But now something else is happening. We don't know the exact extent to which adulteration, illegitimate replacement or deletion of plants, takes place in the Ayurvedic industry but it is massive. More controls and inspections will never get rid of it. Bureaucracy is not the solution the only real solution is that all species used to make Ayurvedic drugs should become cultivated".[4]

As defined by the National Planning Commission (NPC) Task Force, which recommended the above-mentioned reforms aiming at the support of industrial Ayurveda, the increasing difficulty in finding adequate quantities of medicinal plants is a mounting problem and a major bottleneck in any attempt to increase the production of drugs, facilitate the diversification of formulas, and improve the nation's export capacity:

> vii) At present, 90% collection of medicinal plants is from the wild, generating about 40 million man-days employment (part and full) and since 70% of plants collections involve destructive harvesting many plants are endangered or vulnerable or threatened. (...)
> viii) Marketing of medicinal plants is inefficient, informal, secretive and opportunistic. As a result, the raw material supply situation is shaky, unsustainable and exploitative. This results in depletion of resource base, exploitation of rural people (who are the real stewards of the resource), adulteration and non-availability of quality herbal drugs for domestic consumption as well as for exports.
> ix) As the price paid to the gatherers tends to be very low, they often 'mine' the plants, as their main objective is to generate income. (...) As forest habitat disappear and over-harvesting for commercial use reduces the stocks of wild medicinal plant material, there is a corresponding drop in the availability of the plants normally used as the first and last resort for all health care by rural population.[5]

[4] Interview with Dr K., botanist, member of the Kerala State Medicinal Plant Board, March 2013.

[5] Planning Commission Task Force 2000, p. 6.

The central response to problems of supply was the creation of a new agency under the AYUSH department called the National Medicinal Plants Board. In 2002 this NMPB published a list of 32 medicinal plants considered as a high priority for the development of cultivation methods. The existence of this list was a major sign that a new kind of federal policy was emerging, targeting the management of the plants used in Indian traditional therapeutic formulations, and claiming to integrate health, industrial pharmacy, agriculture, and forestry. The NMPB had indeed been established to coordinate initiatives of the relevant ministries and foster an all-embracing strategy to increase the supply of medicinal plants.

The first significance of the 2002 list of prioritized plants was to deliver a framework sheet for what initially seemed the main function of the board: providing subsidies in the form of contracts with medicinal-plant producers or collectors. Priority also meant that these plants should become targets of initiatives for their conservation (*in situ* and *ex situ*) on the one hand, for the standardization of cultivation and manufacturing protocols on the other hand.

But how were these 32 plants selected out of the presumed thousand species used by the industry and sold on the local or regional markets? The logic of the NMPB was not a medical but an industrial and market-based one. Rather than collecting health-related data, NMPB experts focused on market indicators as main proxy for 'demand', and for the benefits of the various species. The first list thus echoed another, tacit, selection made by the 2000 Planning Commission Task Force, which had been based on the documentation of plants in high demand according to a preliminary inquiry on the traded quantities. This involved half a dozen large companies.[6] A critical feature of the NMPB list is the fact that 25 out of the 32 prioritized plants were already being cultivated in 2002. This does not necessarily imply that consumption was exclusively based on field production but that protocols for this production had been developed and were to some extent used routinely.[7]

[6] NMPB, Minutes of the First Board Meeting 2001, Annex. Unfortunately, due to a change of policy, this document like many others from the early nears of the board is no longer accessible on line.

[7] The cultivated species include: amla, ashwagandha, ashoka, atis, bael, brahmi, chandan, chirata, giloe, guggal, *Berberis aristata*, isabgol, jatamansi, kalmegh, kalihari, kutki, kokum, kerth, liquorice, pippali, shatavari, safed musli, senna, and tulsi.

Between 2002 and 2010, NMPB prioritization focused on the agricultural production of already cultivated medicinal plants (Gaudilliere 2014). The basic scheme negotiated between the three ministries (health, agriculture, and industry) was that individual farmers, cooperatives, or clusters committing to the cultivation of prioritized plants on a minimal acreage would receive 30% of their costs as a subsidy. Priority was also a matter of 'promotional activities', which were less a matter of education or awareness than development initiatives ranging from the establishment of nurseries to provide enough planting material, to the standardization of cultivation protocols, or the definition of morphological and biochemical quality-control procedures.

What are the consequences of the NMPB cultivation policy? In 2008, with the launch of a new five years plan, a considerable increase in funding for contractual farming became available (it was more than tripled) and a new scheme was put in place. The task of evaluating thousands of proposals every year could barely be achieved with the allocated staff and resources available during the first five years of the NMPB. Rather than turning the board into a larger administration of its own, the choice was made to transfer the selection and administration of projects to regional states and their State Medicinal Plant Boards (SMPBs) while integrating the cultivation of medicinal plants into the framework of a national rural mission 'covering production, postharvest management, processing and marketing'. Within this organization, the NMPB was only to review the yearly state action plans prepared by the SMPBs and the state Horticultural Mission.

State bodies thus started to participate in the selection of a whole palette of plants, the organization of farmers, and industry into clusters, the building of facilities, i.e. nurseries to produce enough 'high quality' planting material on the one hand, and infrastructures for storage, processing and transportation on the other. In the process, a new list of prioritized plants was established. There are now 116 species, including a great majority of the species in high trade. Moreover, in addition to this list, the SMPBs got specific leverage to include other species as part of their own local, priority lists.

However, this growth in funding and the diversification of priorities do not seem to have been matched with an equivalent extension of cultivation targets. The 20 state action plans agreed upon in the early 2010s involved the cultivation of only 50 highly prioritized species, with 11 species appearing in most plans and representing three-quarters of the associated surface areas. These eleven plants were already in high production during the first years of existence of the NMPB, namely amla, bael, ashwagandha, sarpagandha, ghritkumari, shatavari, kalihari, neem, senna, tulsi, and madhukari.[8]

NMPB and SMPB have therefore handled the crisis of collection through a typical scaling-up strategy, focusing on a market-based plantation approach. Three characteristics of the boards practices are typical of it: (1) measures have predominantly addressed the growth in supply of species already cultivated rather than look for more radical changes associated with the substitution of collected forest products by cultivated plants; (2) if organic farming is officially on the agenda, cultivation remains bound to an understanding of agricultural systems dominated by monoculture (at least for the species which are the targets of administratively-approved good cultivation practices); (3) prioritization, i.e. the selection of species to be included in NMPB lists, has not taken into account indicators of use value, clinical utility or farmers' evaluation, it has operated through market surveys and a ranking of species according to quantities traded and/or average prices.

Other—and less technological—responses to the threat of exhaustion are therefore sought for outside the medicinal plant boards network, for instance within the premises of these new institutions typical of the Anthropocene that are the national and state's biodiversity boards. Initially created in the context of the 2000s debates on biopiracy with the aim of helping in the management of forests and conservation areas, the biodiversity boards have since then enlarged their purpose to a broad palette of issues regarding conservation and the "sustainable use" of natural resources. According to the most recent report of the Kerala State Biodiversity Board, roughly 1/3 of the 3–500 medicinal plants species currently employed in the state for the making of Ayurveda formulations are at risk of extinction and therefore require strict limitations of the quantities collected in the wild.[9]

[8] This computation is based on the plan descriptions included in the documentation for the National Medicinal Plants Mission, Standing Finance Committee Meetings of June 2010, June 2011, and July 2011.

[9] Kerala State Biodiversity Board. (2023) *Tradable/Commercially Potential Floral Bioresources of Kerala*. Thiruvananthapuram: KSSB. Accessible with:https://keralabiodiversity.org/wp-content/uploads/2023/02/4_Tradable_floral_bioresources_of_Kerala_opt.pdf.

Beyond conservation, Kerala responses to the crisis of supply rest on two sets of social and technological innovations aiming at a less extractive use of medicinal plants. The first package, the most technological one, focuses on production, looking at ways of avoiding wastes and reducing the quantities processes by implementing modified—more *frugal*—protocols[10]. To foster R&D in this direction, the state administration sought to involve *Care Keralam*—the regional cluster of support services helping small biotech enterprises.

The cluster unit was located in the Kerala State Industrial Infrastructure Development Corporation (KINFRA) Park, a small industrial area in Koratty (Thrissur district). The project had registered 150 ayurvedic manufacturers and entrepreneurs. Care Keralam is defined as an 'innovation cluster'. The project, a public-private venture funded by the Kerala state, connected private-sector companies through a regional network. One of the objectives of Care Keralam was to ensure manufacturers about the safety of the medicinal raw material. As a government-approved structure, the cluster was entitled to certify the quality of raw material provided by the companies or sold to them through an evaluation of purity, contamination checks for pesticides, and metal contents etc. It used modern methods of standardization like high-performance liquid chromatography (HPLC) equipment or gas chromatography-mass spectrometry (GC-MS), for example to analyze the organic compounds and chemical contaminants of the plants. In 2013, Care-Keralam supplied 65 different species to manufacturers and marketed an average of 20 tons per item in the year. It also attempted to offer rare medicinal plants through the collectors' network it created (Dejouhanet, 2014). This public service facility reorganized the supply channels to major pharmacies in Kerala; at least for a few years before its collapse in 2018 due to problems of governance, disinterest among the small and tiny producers, and mismanagement of finances (Madhavan & Soman, 2022). For a while, the cluster nonetheless worked as a one-point solution for small and medium entrepreneurs by providing raw materials of better quality, production support with simple mechanization, marketing and IPR advice, but also offered a sense of surety and security contrasting the usual short-term management of supply.

[10] On frugality and its relations to the notion of appropriate technology, see Chap. 7 in this volume (Madhavan, 2026).

A second—more radical—package of responses tries to renew the initial—and unfulfilled mandate of the NMPB—by shifting the supply of critical plants from collection to cultivation at the local level. In the social and political context of Kerala, organizing such transition has taken the form of a *cooperative farming strategy* whose operations may be illustrated with the trajectory of the Matthatur Labour Cooperative Society (Thrissur district).

The MLCS was created in 2008 as a district-level non-profit organization aiming at the rejuvenation of Mattathur's agricultural sector by means of pay-back agreements with farmers. The cooperative would negotiate supply contracts with firms or institutional consumers and would—on that basis—guarantee a minimum price to the farmers, who would engage in the production of the agricultural product considered with the material and technical support of the society. Medicinal plants were not part of the initial plan. Until 2013, the MLCS produced bananas for a large temple in the vicinity, an uncertain practice which resulted in regular penalties when the daily supply did not meet the temple demand. In 2013, the MLCS administrators contacted Oushadi to discuss the possibility of including medicinal plants in their crops. The public firm listed 10 species in limited supply it would regularly buy. The MLCS organized pilot cultivation and one third of the plants only proved profitable, meaning being purchased at an average price clearly above production costs. Kurunthotti (*Sida alnifolia*) was among these and the best farmer's choice because it could be grown in six months, and therefore could be included in two-harvests-a year rotation schemes.

Kurunthotti is used in a few dozen preparations, which target chronic symptoms like inflammation or joint pain, and respiratory disorders. The supply problem mostly affects South India since Ayurveda practitioners in North India use another species, *Sida cordifolia*, which is still abundant in the wild. Turning Kurunthotti into a crop was a premiere although (according to MLCS administrators) the cultivation process was not difficult to design as it was adapted from that of Kochalam (*Kaempferia galanga*). The main issue was that of choosing "a good habitat", meaning that buy-back contracts were only signed after a site visit with farmers living in areas where the plant was native and where cultivation could take place in dry soil at the border of the forest. In a decade, the number of farmers involved has reached 250, who provide for 60–70 tons yearly with Oushadi remaining the main buyer.

For the staff of MLCS, the scarcity of Kurunthotti is not a problem of too big a demand, it is a problem of market organization and bad collection practices[11]. As members of a cooperative society, they argue for fair commercial practices and state regulation of the market with guaranteed minimum prices. To them, scarcity is artificially induced by the extreme fluctuations of the market and the speculative storage of greedy intermediaries. When prices are very high, collectors seek the benefit of the situation and uproot the plant even if it has not yet produced flowers and seeds, thus endangering reproduction. MLCS also collect Kurunthotti through a network of 600 registered collectors whose majority live in the "scheduled tribes' areas".

Enlarging the scope of medicinal plants cultivation is therefore not apprehended as a big challenge. From a local farming perspective, the number of species used in Ayurveda and the strength of the demand create many opportunities. The MLCS staff thus considers that expanding production is sustainable if done in a proper way. If the society is currently cultivating 3 species, it conducts field trials on 2 (Chittaratha and Orela) and is considering the development of 4 others. The aim is to define new associations between the farmers and some medicinal plants that adjust to the local ecosystem, the farmers' knowledge and the social and economic needs of the community. This implies a form of integrative and local innovation based on the experience of Kurunthotti cultivation with the cooperative society organizing the testing and choice of "appropriate" cultivation techniques, the production of seeds or shoots, and the balancing of budgets through the negotiations of long-term contracts with trustable buyers.

The crisis of medicinal plants supply in Ayurveda didn't emerge from the blue in 2000. It is more ancient: concerns regarding the difficulty at finding the ingredients of Ayurveda poly-herbal formulations have been mounting since the 1970s. They are rooted in the changes of last 50 years in the practice of Indian traditional medicines, i.e. their institutionalization, but also in changes of forest management, agricultural practices, as well as in the mounting pressure on ecosystems the urbanization of Kerala has induced. There are however little doubts that the accelerated industrialization of Ayurveda has deeply aggravated the crisis, leading to the current situation with one third to half the plants commonly used in

[11] The following description relies on interviews conducted at MLCS in October 2014.

Kerala being officially (by the IUCN or the KSBB) recognized as in need of protection; and with multiple manifestations of scarcity affecting plants' trade, production operations, as well as clinical care.

Scaling up, meaning increasing the three core practices of industrial/pharmaceutical Ayurveda, i.e. collection, manufacturing, and prescription—is the core pattern responsible for the deterioration of medicinal plants' survival abilities and for the fundamental tensions 'Ayurveda for all' is experiencing. Based on Kerala multiple response to the crisis, one may consider two integrative ways out of it, respectively focusing on conservation, care of ecosystems and *descaling* on the one hand; or on a different model of industrialization leading to the replacement of collections by cultivation on the other hand. The utopia at stakes in the latter is that the pressure on wild ecosystems can be replaced by appropriate cultivation through the interplay of domestication and agroecological farming, thus opposing the plantation/monoculture model the medicinal plant boards have defended so far.

10.6 Conclusion

The divide between social versus technological innovation is a pervasive as well as contingent aspect of the twentieth century debates on science, health, and policies. It has been worked out by social analysts as well as social actors with unstable meanings depending on time, and place. The boundaries thus drawn define porous frontiers with entities moving back and forth.

In the more specific context of the international government of health and development, the articulation of the social and technological dimensions of innovation has revolved around the notion of *appropriate technologies* as delineated in WHO 1978 primary health care strategy and the various regional/national experiences that informed it. One pivotal aspect of the social/technological boundary work performed in relation with the implementation of primary health care policies, was the quest for the integration of traditional medical knowledge in the national/regional health care systems. These have been of critical importance in South and East Asia.

The trajectory of integration of Ayurveda in India (both at the national level and in the state of Kerala) reveals hierarchies of the social and the technological shifting: (a) in time with the difference between the institutional phase of the 1960s/1980s and the industrial/pharmaceutical phase after 2000; (b) in place with the continuity of vertical and technological development initiatives at the center while Kerala has maintained its strong policies of investments in social medicine and technologies alternative to biomedicine albeit with significant adaptation.

The question of finding more appropriate innovations to respond un— or poorly met health needs has recently been broadened to include requirements of sustainability and the Anthropocene challenges to health practices.[12] The mounting concerns regarding the exhaustion of a majority of medicinal plants used in a scaled-up and newly industrialized Ayurveda indeed point to the limits of the growth model underlying most innovation policies, whether they are deemed social or not. Beyond, the highly significant case of medicinal plants and the biodiversity crisis, ecological sustainability is indeed a major risk for the future of health systems and the putative advent of a more anthropogenic economic model (see Chapter X in this volume).

References

Banerjee, M. (2009). *Power, Knowledge, Medicine. Ayurvedic Pharmaceuticals at Home and in the World.* Hyderabad: Orient Blackswan.

Birn, A. E., & Krementsov, N. (2018). Socialising primary care? The Soviet Union, WHO and the Alma-Ata Conference. *BMJ Global Health*, e000992. https://doi.org/10.1136/bmjgh-2018-000992

Brown, T. M., Cueto, M., & Fee, E. (2006). The World Health Organization and the transition from 'international' to 'global' public health. *American Journal of Public Health, 96*(1), 62–72.

Chabrol, F., & Gaudillière, J.-P. (2023). *Introduction à la santé globale.* La Découverte.

Cueto, M., Brown, T. M., & Fee, E. (2019). *The World Health Organization. A history.* Cambridge University Press.

Dejouhanet, L. (2012). *'Unclear Occupation'. La filière des plantes ayurvédiques. Paradoxes et limites de la gestion publique des ressources forestières au Kerala (Inde).* PhD thesis in Geography submitted at the University Paris Ouest Nanterre.

Dejouhanet, L. (2014). Supply of medicinal raw materials: The Achillee's Heeal of today manufacturing sector for ayurvedic drugs in Kerala. *Asian Medicine, 9*(3), 206–235.

[12] On sustainability and frugal innovation, see Chap. 7 in this volume (Madhavan & Gaudillière, 2026).

Djukanovic, J., & Mach, E.P. (1975). *Alternative approaches to meeting basic health needs in developing countries*. World Health Organization.
Drèze, J., & Sen, A. (1994). *India. Economic development and social opportunity*. Clarendon Press.
Gaudillière, J.-P. (2014). 'Herbalised Ayurveda?'. Reformulation, plant management, and the Pharmaceuticalisation of Indian 'Traditional' Medicine. *Asian Medicine*, *9*(3), 171–205.
Gaudillière, J.-P., McDowell, A., Lang, C., & Beaudevin, C. (2022). *Global health for all. Knowledge, politics, practices*. Rutgers University Press.
Gaudillière, J.-P. (2026). Local planning, democracy and health in Kerala (1970–2020). Social development without growth? In Y. Sintomer & L. Cordier (Eds.), *Handbook of participatory democracy*. Edward Elgar Publishers.
Ibata-Arens, K., Gaudillière, J.-P., Madhavan, H., & Nouguez, E. (2026). Commons and the political economy of access: Generics, neo traditional formulations and the dominant intellectual property regime of medicine. In S. Lechevalier, J.-P. Gaudillière, K. Ibata-Arens, & K. Takuma (Eds.), *Capitalism, innovations, and health after Covid-19. An Asian perspective*. Palgrave MacMillan.
Jeffery, R. (1988). *The politics of health in India*. University of California Press.
Lang, C. (2018). Depression in Kerala. In *Ayurveda and mental health care in the twenty-first century*. Routledge.
Madhavan, H. (2014). Innovation systems and increasing reformulation practices in the ayurvedic pharmaceutical sector. *Asian Medicine*, *9*(1–2), 236–271.
Madhavan, H., & Gaudillière, J.-P. (2026). Frugal innovations and health system resilience. The conceptualization, policy support and forms of frugality during COVID-19 in South India. In S. Lechevalier, J.-P. Gaudillière, K. Ibata-Arens, & K. Takuma (Eds.), *Capitalism, innovations, and health after COVID-19. An Asian perspective*. Palgrave MacMillan.
Madhavan, H., & Soman, S. (2022). Industry dynamics and clustering in ayurvedic pharmaceuticals in South India. In S. Kloos & C. Blaikie Eds., *Asian medical industries: Contemporory perspectives on traditional pharmaceuticals* (pp. 169–193). Routledge.
Packard, R. (2016). *A history of global health. Interventions into the lifes of other peoples*. Johns Hopkins University Press.
Pordié, L., & Gaudillière, J.-P. (2014). The reformulation regime in drug discovery: Revisiting polyherbals and property rights in the Ayurvedic industry. *East Asian Science Technology and Society*, *8*(1), 57–79.
Sasidharan, N., Muraleedharan, P. K., & Sreedhar, S. (2011). Consumption of raw drugs by the Ayurvedic medicine manufacturing industry in Kerala. *Journal of Non-Timber Forest Products*, *18*(3), 205–220. https://doi.org/10.54207/bsmps2000-2011-2EE5W1

Scheid, V. (2002). Chinese medicine in contemporary China. In *Plurality and Synthesis*. Duke University Press.
World Health Assembly (1975). *28th World Health Assembly. Report of the general director*. The World Health Organization.
WHO (1978a) *Primary Health Care. Report on the International Conference on Primary Health Care. Alma-Ata, USSR, 6–12 September 1978*. The World Health Organization.
WHO (1978b) *The promotion and development of traditional medicine. A report of a WHO meeting*. The World Health Organization.

CHAPTER 11

Commons and the Political Economy of Access: Generics, Neo-traditional Formulations and the Dominant Intellectual Property Regime of Medicines

Kathryn Ibata Arens, Jean-Paul Gaudillière, Harilal Madhavan, and Etienne Nouguez

Abstract This chapter scrutinizes the entrenched intellectual property rights (IPRs) regime, a cornerstone of contemporary pharmaceutical capitalism, questioning the assumed indispensability of patents for incentivizing

Ibata-Arens acknowledges research assistance from Ms. Nicky Taghert and is grateful for support from the France-Japan Foundation (FFJ) of the Ecole des Hautes Etudes en Sciences Sociales (EHESS).

K. I. Arens (✉)
DePaul University, Chicago, USA
e-mail: k.ibata-arens@depaul.edu

J.-P. Gaudillière
Inserm & EHESS, Paris, France

H. Madhavan
CHRIST University, Bengaluru, India

E. Nouguez
Sciences Po-CNRS, Paris, France

S. Lechevalier et al. (eds.), *Capitalism, Innovations, and Health after Covid-19*,
https://doi.org/10.1007/978-3-032-24479-6_11

innovation. Historically, the monopoly of IPRs in drug invention and production, particularly evident between the 1930s and 1960s, marked a significant shift, reorienting drug production into a capitalistic, industrial process rooted in chemical knowledge. This period's paradigmatic shift was not definitive; alternative drug-making regimes persist, reflecting the diverse facets of pharmaceutical capitalism. This chapter develops a "commons" framework in knowledge and access to essential medicines, a concept encompassing alternative production arrangements and experiences that challenge the IPRs' dominance, proposing a recalibration of the moral compass for the global intellectual property rights regime. The chapter delves into two notable instances of such arrangements: generics and neo-traditional (Sometimes referred to as "poly-herbal" or "natural medicinal" formulations). preparations, the latter stemming from Asian medical traditions. These are analyzed through exploring how these collective resources are established and sustained as public goods by the state. This reflects tensions within pharmaceutical capitalism between innovations driven by human-health needs (see the concept of care-led innovation in Lechevalier, 2026) and by profit-motivated private companies. The exploration begins with generics, pivotal in ensuring drug access since the late 1960s, both in the global North and South. For example, while French generics emerge from expired patents, maintaining the status quo of the extant global IPR system, they nonetheless offer an alternative to the innovation system, providing institutional legitimacy and cheaper access for proven drugs. Indian generics, conversely, are borne out of significant legal and social conflicts, challenging and reinterpreting IPRs to address public health emergencies, thus constituting a different form of commons. The subsequent section navigates the terrain of neo-traditional medicinal formulations within globalized Asian medicine. It focuses on the industrialized production and distribution of classical remedies and newly invented compositions targeting contemporary ailments. Cases from China, India, and Japan underscore the complex interplay between traditional knowledge and the forces of industrialization and globalization. In sum, the chapter posits that the moral economy of drugs, through generics and neo-traditional formulations, embodies a multifaceted response to the monolithic IPR regime, signifying the coexistence of diverse drug-making regimes within the overarching structure of pharmaceutical capitalism. This diversity is reflected in how states, through different processes of innovation and contestation within pharmaceutical capitalism have made essential medicines accessible by transforming private goods into (commons adjacent) public goods.

11.1 Introduction

Are medicines a private good, a public good or a commons good? This question, which was already being asked in nineteenth-century European countries, took on new vigor with the deployment of the TRIPS agreements by the WTO in the mid-1990s. Although in 2001 the WTO recognized "*a right of WTO members to protect public health and, in particular, to promote access to medicines for all*", following the Pretoria trial pitting the South African government against 39 pharmaceutical companies from the North (Dix-Neuf, 2003), private appropriation continued to extend to new areas and new countries, mortgaging people's access to medicines (Ibata-Arens, 2021). At the same time, activists' movements and some states, especially in the Global South, have mobilized to protect a body of knowledge and medicines against such private appropriation, in the name of protecting public health. Tensions have been persistent between sharing and private appropriation of knowledge, the promotion of innovation and access to affordable medicines, industrial development and public health. These conflicts over the status of medicines have resulted in highly variable configurations and alliances across periods and countries, despite mounting pressure for global harmonization. This chapter reflects on the nature of these arrangements, focusing on two emblematic cases: generic medicines in France and India, and traditional medicines in India, China and Japan.

At first glance, medicines have all the characteristics of a *private good* or commodity, if we follow the definition given by economists (Musgrave & Musgrave, 1973): they are rival goods (each drug can only be used by one person) and exclusive goods (consumers can be denied access to these goods). The vast majority of medicines are developed, produced and marketed by private companies and sold to individual consumers. While medicines are private goods, the same cannot be said of knowledge about their effects and production processes, which have the characteristics of a pure, non-rival, non-exclusive public good. It is patents which, by granting manufacturers a temporary monopoly on this knowledge, help to reinforce the private appropriation of knowledge and then medicines. Since the early twentieth century, private sector demands have led to national government legitimization of monopoly profiting via patents-based intellectual property rights (IPRs) on active substances, processes of synthesis, and indications. This manifests both nationally and supranationally, for example, via the WTO TRIPS sanctioned global system of pharmaceutical capitalism, wherein health has been capitalized and optimized for value extraction (Gaudilliere, 2021; Gaudilliere & Sunder Rajan, 2021). The system of pharmaceutical capitalism, comprising the production, distribution, and consumption of medicines, is driven by profit-maximizing drug-selling firms enjoying global market power and concomitant political influence (Stiglitz, 2007).

But this status of private good is far from being a constant throughout history and the world. The application of intellectual property laws to medicines has long been contested in many countries (including those of the North) and continues to be so in various countries of the South (notably India and Brazil), despite the deployment of TRIPS. Nor is the development and production by private companies a constant: from 1981 to 1986, the largest French pharmaceutical producer was nationalized; and in China or Brazil, state-owned generics companies are major players. In fact, because public health issues and state sovereign power are at stake (Fassin, 2023), medicines are also *a public good*, placed in many countries under the close control of the State. Moreover, in many countries, the development of national health insurance schemes throughout the twentieth century contributed to the socialization of drug expenditure, by making individual consumers solvent and enabling them to access these goods whatever their budget. At the same time, governments have become increasingly involved in the research and development of new treatments, through funding for universities and start-ups, as well as in production, through financial support for producers and even the creation of a nationalized industry.

Finally, in the wake of Elinor Ostrom's work (1990), various researchers and social movements have attempted to define medicines as a *commons good* (Dolcerocca & Coriat, 2016; Abecassis et al., 2019). In her work on Common Pool Resources, Ostrom (1990) maintains that a commons is an efficient and long-lasting institution only when it meets several conditions: (1) the existence of clear boundaries for both the resource considered and the community concerned; (2) an efficient convergence between local conditions and rules of appropriation; (3) the definition of mechanisms for collective choices engaging most people concerned; (4) the existence of institutions to resolve conflicts; (5) a surveillance of appropriation patterns and a system of sanctions in case of infringement; (6) the recognition of the common by broader (political) institutions. This work has inspired research and social movements that have challenged the private appropriation of common and community knowledge, or other key dimensions of pharmaceutical capitalism, such as access to medicines, drug pricing and, more recently, industrial production (Cassier & Correa, 2003; Abbas et al., 2020; Bourgeron & Geiger, 2024). As Olivier Weinstein (2021) points out, the status of medicines (private, public or commons goods) therefore has less to do with the nature of these goods than with the political and economic institutions that ensure their development, production, exchange and consumption. This chapter extends this idea by showing how the three statuses of drugs, private, public and commons, co-exist and participate in different varieties of capitalism (Hall and Soskice, 2001). We analyze these varieties of capitalism through the three issues of accessibility, sustainability and collective (democratic) governance.

This chapter therefore looks at a set of experiences that challenge the hegemony of IPRs and reflect the diversity of drug making regimes. It focuses on arrangements, which have attracted great public attention because of their economic and medical importance: generics and neo-traditional poly-herbal preparations originating in Asian systems of medicine. It approaches these experiences at organizing production and access from the perspective of commons, namely commons goods—as examples of existing alternatives to the dominant economy of the patent-IPR regime (Lechevalier et al, 2026).

The first section of the chapter focuses on generics. Since the late 1960s, these have become a prominent mode of access to drugs and medicines for the disadvantaged, uninsured, and poor, in the Global North as well as the Global South. The section contrasts their rise and relations to IPRs in France and India. If humans have the fundamental right to health, it follows that medicines essential for basic health should be accessible at fair and reasonable prices. In France, generics are a market solution for a market problem. They do not challenge the IPRs system since they result from the mere application of patent laws: when a patent expires a new generic is born. However, generics challenge the innovation system in a different way. They provide an alternative to planned obsolescence and permanent molecular turnover by providing cheaper access as well as institutional and social legitimacy to the use of copies and drugs of well-proven efficacy through socialized purchase and a logic that one may compare to WHO list of essential medicines. A critical component of the generics as commons is therefore the universal (or quasi) national health insurance. In the case of India, generics have acquired a different meaning since they do not simply originate in the exhaustion of patent rights but have also emerged from major social and legal conflicts to authorize the copy of patented brand drugs. The Indian generic commons thus rests on two original pillars: (a) the limitations of IPRs inscribed in the patent law, even after its revision in the context of the TRIPS negotiations—these limitations have for instance rendered possible the local production of anti-HIV drugs; (b) the jurisprudence which has used these restrictions to foster the lawfulness of copying innovative costly drugs in case of public health emergency.

The second section of the chapter discusses the making of commons for alternative medicinal plants formulations. Within the world of globalized and industrialized Asian medicines, such neo-traditional remedies may take two forms: (a) compositions following the classical, written recipes of the traditional reference books of Asian medical systems (Traditional Chinese Medicine, Japanese Kampo, Indian Ayurveda, Unani, etc) although production as well as distribution have been industrialized; (b) newly invented compositions targeting biomedically defined ailments, which are claimed to stem from the corpus of plants used in the tradition. In both instances one may speak of reformulated drugs. The chapter discusses the knowledge basis and the access arrangements characterizing these remedies in China, India, and Japan revealing a continuum from commons to anti-commons as well as a significant contrast between the status of formulations and the regulation of access. This includes an emerging *sui* generis IP regime in China, challenging the rules of Western pharmaceutical capitalism (Ibata-Arens, 2021).

11.2 Generics

11.2.1 Generics in France—From Alternative to Complement to Pharmaceutical Capitalism

Until the mid-1990s, generic drugs were a foreign curiosity to the French. While debates raged over the development of these products in southern countries during the AIDS epidemic, generics did not seem to be a French issue where they represented less than 1% of total market shares. Indeed, in the mid-1990s, France was characterized by its socialized health insurance system, tightly controlled drug prices limited to low levels, and high drug consumption—three characteristics that were hardly conducive to the development of these copies. Unlike in southern countries, where generics may have been an alternative to pharmaceutical capitalism, in France they emerged as a complementary tool at a time when the country was converting to pharmaceutical capitalism, accepting extensive patent regimes, and deciding to reward innovative medicines with high prices. To understand the role of generics in France, and more generally in the Western countries,[1] we need to look at French policy on patents, drug prices, industrial development and access.

11.2.1.1 From Alternative to Complement to Patents

From 1844 to 1959, France, like many other European countries,[2] has taken the view that medicines, because of their importance to public health, should be exempt from the ordinary law governing the protection of inventions, and that their formulas should not be subject to private appropriation (Chauveau, 1999, 2007; Cassier, 2004). In the past, as in the present, there have been two lines of discussion between those in favor and those opposed to the patentability of medicines. The first concerns the effects of patents on public health. While opponents of drug patentability insist on the need to fight against private monopolies, in order to provide access to quality medicines for all, patent advocates emphasize the incentives to improve treatments, and therefore ultimately public health, that private appropriation of inventions via patents would provide. However, these public health arguments often mask industrial considerations: the refusal to patent medicines in France at the beginning of the twentieth century, as well as in India at the beginning of the twenty-first century, has often enabled the development of a powerful pharmaceutical industry based on copying or improving products patented in foreign countries, and then developing its own innovations; conversely, the recognition of patents has gradually appeared as a strong incentive to industrial innovation and a protection against competition in a context of globalization.

[1] The story of the development of generic drugs in the USA from the 1960s onwards, traced by Greene (2016), bears a strong resemblance to that of France thirty years later.

[2] France prohibited patenting the active ingredients of drugs from 1844 to 1959, and Germany from 1877 to 1967 (although this prohibition did not apply to drug manufacturing processes). Similarly, Switzerland, Italy and Spain only allowed the patenting of medicines in 1977, 1978 and 1992.

The end of the Second World War marked the first appearance of generic drugs in France. In 1946, a law prohibited the sale of drugs manufactured abroad and authorized the marketing of "sealed products" ("produits sous cachet"), copies of original specialties bearing on their packaging the common name of the product and the manufacturer's stamp. The aim of this law was to encourage large-scale production of penicillin in the face of major epidemic risks, and to enable the French pharmaceutical industry to rebuild itself by appropriating American discoveries (Chauveau, 1999).

However, with the improvement in living conditions, the development of a national social security system, the affirmation of a national pharmaceutical industry and France's integration into the European common market, this protectionist rationale gradually gave way to the reintegration of medicines into common patent law, through the Ordinance of February 4, 1959, that introduced the Special Patent for Medicinal Products and the Law of January 2, 1968, that recognized possibility of patenting a molecule for pharmaceutical use for twenty years. Both those laws also created the principle—placing people before profit—of a compulsory license "whenever the interests of public health so require". But this compulsory licensing system has never been used in France since it was introduced, even though it is regularly mentioned by patent activists as an instrument to fight against high drug prices.

11.2.1.2 From Alternative to Complement to High-priced Drugs

Although France accepted the patentability of medicines as early as the 1960s, generic drugs did not develop until thirty years later. One explanation for this absence is the pricing policy adopted in France from the 1940s to the 1990s (Chauveau, 1999; Nouguez & Benoît, 2017). From 1948 to the mid-1990s, the prices of drugs reimbursed by Social Security were set directly by the State on the basis of their industrial cost price (ICP), a fixed margin (decreasing in line with the ICP) intended to remunerate the company's research effort, financial and administrative costs and advertising expenditure, and finally, indexation to inflation. Although regularly manipulated by companies and amended on several occasions by the government, this price control has proved extremely effective in keeping prices low, which has slowed or even prevented the development of generic drugs in France. In countries where prices were set administratively, such as Italy and France, the introduction of generic drugs might seem superfluous as long as the public authorities control price trends; the issue was rather how to control prescription and consumption volumes. On the other hand, in markets where prices were freely set, such as Germany, the Netherlands or the UK, generics were a central instrument for limiting the growth of prices and drug expenditure (Le Pen, 1996; Lecomte & Paris, 1998).

The introduction of generic drugs in France was precisely the result of a change in the pricing regime adopted by the public authorities in the mid-1990s (Nouguez, 2017; Nouguez & Benoît, 2017). Fearing that the emergence of a single European drugs market, symbolized by the creation of the European Medicines Agency in 1995, would result in a loss of competitiveness for the French pharmaceutical industry and administration, the government set up the Drug Economic Committee, a committee bringing together representatives from various ministerial departments and the National Health Insurance administration, to negotiate drug prices with pharmaceutical companies. The first framework agreement signed in 1994 by the Committee and the representatives of the French pharmaceutical industry (SNIP) introduced a new principle for setting drug prices: new drugs with high therapeutic added value would receive high prices in return for limited sales volumes or the repayment of a portion of sales in the form of a rebate. In addition, companies would have to commit to lowering the cost of older drugs in their portfolio, either by accepting delisting or by developing generics. Generic drug prices have been set by the Drug Economic Committee on the principle of a discount to the price of the original drug, rising from – 20% in the mid-1990s to – 65% in the mid-2000s.

Whereas the price administration system in force for 50 years had favored the formation of a flat price architecture (Chauvin, 2011) in which the prices of both old and innovative drugs varied relatively little according to production and R&D costs, the drug pricing negotiation policy between the State and the companies implemented from the mid-1990s onwards led to a polarized price architecture in which the very high prices of innovations with a high therapeutic contribution were offset by the low prices of old drugs and generics (Nouguez & Benoît, 2017).

11.2.1.3 From Alternative to Complement to Big Pharma

As we have just seen, the introduction of generic drugs in France in the late 1990s was not so much about building an alternative pharmaceutical industry as it was about boosting the competitiveness of French pharmaceutical companies investing in R&D for new drugs.[3]

French companies have adopted very different and changing attitudes to the development of a generics offering. In the 2000s, some companies, such as the medium-sized family-owned Servier with its subsidiary Biogaran, moved into the generics sector, making it its main source of revenue on the French market. This company's business model differed from that of its competitors in that it had no industrial production facilities of its own, relying instead on manufacturing contracts with companies producing the original drugs, or with their former manufacturers. Other companies, such as Aventis or Sanofi, developed generics, then abandoned them when they merged, before resuming it once the merger was completed, and abandoning it again after the new management decided to concentrate all its investment in R&D for innovative drugs. The French market has also been gradually penetrated by world leaders in generics, such as the Israeli company Teva, the Swiss Novartis subsidiary Sandoz, the German company Merck KgaA replaced by the American company Mylan in the 2010s. Unlike Biogaran, these international generics companies had their own factories in Asia, Eastern Europe or the USA, producing generics for numerous international markets. Indian generics companies, on the other hand, have never been able to gain a real foothold in France, not only because of regulatory barriers, but also because of the difficulty in implementing them in pharmacies.

In the early 2020s, the French generics market was dominated by a handful of companies. With the Covid-19 pandemic and the multiplication of supply disruptions, since 2020 the French government has asserted its determination to relocate the production of essential medicines to France. However, the government has come up against the consequences of its drug policy, which is essentially focused on promoting innovation and large capitalist pharmaceutical companies. Servier's announcement that it intends to sell its Biogaran subsidiary to refocus on the innovation market in 2024 was a bombshell, revealing the complementary or even secondary nature of the creation of a generics industry in France.

[3] There were two previous attempts by French companies to launch generics (Clin-Midy in 1979 and Sanofi in 1983, even though the company had been nationalized by the French government in 1981). Both failed and were stopped after a few months.

11.2.1.4 From Alternative to Complement to Universal Access to Drugs
Generic drugs have also been used in France to reorganize the French healthcare system by making prices an important determinant of drug prescribing and consumption. Generic drugs accounted for less than 3% of medical prescriptions in France, compared with 40% in Germany and 43% in the UK in the mid-1990s (Lecomte & Paris, 1998). In both countries, reforms had been carried out during the 1980s to turn doctors, pharmacists and, to a lesser extent, patients into informed buyers, by linking their income negatively to the price of drugs prescribed or purchased. Such mechanisms did not exist in France: doctors did not have to manage a prescription budget, and were subject to the influence of pharmaceutical company sales representatives; pharmacists received a margin based on the price of the drug dispensed, and therefore lost money if they dispensed a generic; patients did not necessarily have an interest in preferring the least expensive drug, since most of their drug expenditure was reimbursed by Social Security and their private insurance. By the mid-1990s, this "no price" system had resulted in high per-capita drug consumption (the highest among OECD countries) and a prescribing structure geared towards the latest, most expensive drugs.

The French government introduced a series of measures throughout the 2000s and 2010s to make healthcare professionals and patients more sensitive to the price of medicines and thus enable the development of generic drugs. The main measure was to give pharmacists the right to substitute a generic drug for the original prescribed by the doctor, through the 1999 Social Security Financing Act. Despite their commitment, pharmacists have encountered resistance from some private practitioners and patients who doubt the quality of generics. Public authorities introduced financial measures in the 2000s to encourage the prescription and acceptance of generic drugs: doctors who prescribe generics receive a premium from the National Health Insurance, while patients who refuse generics must pay the price difference out of pocket and accept delayed reimbursements. In this way, generics have enabled the public authorities to make drug prices a factor in prescribing and consumption, while preserving the system of socialization of drug expenditure by the National Health Insurance.

Generic drugs in France could have been an alternative to pharmaceutical capitalism at the end of the Second World War, with the development of so-called "sealed products" and the use of compulsory licenses. But the development of Social Security and administrative price controls from the 1950s to the 1990s rendered them useless for French public authorities. Their development since the end of the 1990s is therefore more in line with a regime of complementarity to pharmaceutical capitalism. Far from being a substitute for patented drugs sold at high prices, they have emerged at a time when patent law was being strengthened and, above all, when state price controls were giving way to negotiations with pharmaceutical companies on the price of innovative drugs, leading to a sharp rise in these prices that generics were supposed to compensate. India's generic drug history began similarly, placing public health before private profit.

11.2.2 Indian Generics: From Import Substitution to Public Health Instrument

The Indian regulatory policies reiterate that the prices of lifesaving drugs shouldn't be set by market forces only. In a country where very few people have health insurance, 60% of Indians pay their healthcare expenses out of their own pockets. When it comes to the drugs for cancer treatments, the problem is even more acute. This made India seeks that drugs—including expensive ones—are available to the larger public at affordable rates, without jeopardizing the growth of the pharmaceutical sector.

11.2.2.1 Indian Pharmaceutical Sector Rise to the "Pharmacy of the World"
The Indian pharmaceutical industry, valued at US $33 billion in 2017, is currently the largest global supplier of cost-effective generic drugs accounting for 20% of the global exports (Racherla, 2019) and is expected to reach around $120 billion by the end of 2030. The drugs made in India are exported to more than 200 countries around the world, with the United States of America (USA) being India's biggest market. According to *India Brand Equity Foundation* (IBEF), in 2016–2017, around 40.6% of India's pharmaceutical exports (US$ 16.8 billion) were to the American continent, followed by 19.7% to Europe, 19.1% to Africa, and 18.8% to the Asian continent. The Indian pharmaceutical companies meet over 50% of the global demand for various vaccines, 40% of the generic demand in the USA, and 25% of demand for all the medicines in the UK. In addition, India supplies over 80% of the antiretroviral drugs needed globally for AIDS (*acquired immunodeficiency syndrome*). In 2022, USFDA granted 1181 market authorizations of the Abbreviated New Drug Application (ANDA) approvals and out of these, Indian companies bagged 493 which accounted for 41.74% of total authorizations, which continued in the following years.

A main factor of the industry's success has been the Indian government's move in 1970 to exclude pharmaceutical drugs from product patenting. This paved the way for local companies to produce generic versions of the expensive foreign medicines and within a few decades they had taken over 80% of the local market, while also supplying cheap medicines abroad (Chaudhuri, 2005) as in the case of generic antiretroviral drugs for the treatment of AIDS.

During the "colonization" phase, the Indian Patents and Designs Act of 1911—drafted by the British—enacted India's first patent statutes. At the time of independence in 1947, India's pharmaceutical market was dominated by Western MNCs that controlled between 80 and 90% of the market primarily through importation (Chaudhuri, 2014). Approximately 99% of all pharmaceutical products under patent in India at the time were held by foreign companies and domestic Indian drug prices were among the highest in the world. During the "post-independence" phase, the British-imposed, foreigner-favoring patent laws stunted the development of the Indian pharmaceutical industry and forced independent India to import even basic medicines at unaffordable prices.

The 1949, Bakshi Tek Chand headed committee formed by the government to review the 1911 Patent Act, completed an intensive review, which concluded that the existing patent laws are highly biased in favor of the MNCs and the new Patents Act should contain clear indication to ensure that medicine and surgical and curative devices are made available to the public at the cheapest price commensurate with giving reasonable compensation to the patentee. The following committee headed by justice Rajagopala Ayyangar in 1959 paved the way for a larger reform in the Indian patent sector. It materialized with the Patents Act of 1970, which (a) prohibited patents on products useful as medicines and food, (b) shortened the term of chemical process patents, and (c) significantly expanded the availability of compulsory licensing. This led to the birth and growth of the powerful Indian pharmaceutical generic drugs industry (Racherla, 2019). Thus, the Indian pharmaceutical market that remained import-dependent through the 1960s until these government- initiated policies, slowly began to take a self-reliant path through local production.

To quote one of the major observations of the Ayyangar committee:

> Where the patentee has no intention of working the invention in this country either because he considers that this is not profitable or because he prefers to expand the production in his home country so as to achieve

> their greater efficiency and more production or is otherwise not interested in working the invention in India, the grant of the Indian patent might tend to improve the economy of the patentee's home country but offers little advantage to us. Unless therefore the law provides for measures to be taken to compel the patentees to work the invention within the country, and these measures are effective to achieve their purpose, the social cost involved in the grant of the patent is not offset by any benefit to the community. (Ayyangar, 1959, p. 18)

After 1970, the patent regime in India underwent significant transformations aimed at promoting domestic innovation and ensuring access to essential products, particularly in the pharmaceutical sector. The basic purpose is to balance patent protection with public interest, emphasizing the need for affordable medicines and promoting indigenous industries. It excluded product patents for pharmaceuticals, chemicals, and food items while process patents were allowed in these sectors for seven years instead of the usual fifteen years. The policy thus encouraged domestic companies to reverse-engineer patented products and develop alternative manufacturing processes. As MNCs began to exit the Indian market due to significantly diminished IP protection, the Indian pharmaceutical companies began to fill the void.

The best example of how India's alternative regime benefited the developing countries is the antiretroviral drug case. From the late 1990s onward, the Indian company Cipla produced HIV/AIDS generic medicines that could treat a patient for $300 a year, far cheaper than the branded product's cost of $10,000 a patient a year then prevailin. At present the Indian drug cost has been cut further to below $80. Without doubt, the pricing has enabled millions of AIDS patients to afford the treatment (UNAIDS, 2023). India currently supplies 70% of the HIV/AIDS medicines obtained by UNICEF, the Global Fund and Clinton Foundation for developing countries.

India, thus probably produced one of the best alternatives to Western pharmaceutical capitalism in terms of giving some space to the domestic producers to make generic medicines. But it is also true that the extension of this policy has been partially ruined because of the application of the TRIPS agreement.

11.2.2.2 The 2005 Act and the Definition of New Flexibilities

To meet its TRIPS obligations, India amended its patent law on March 22, 2005, abolishing its process patents law and reintroducing product patents for pharmaceuticals, food, and chemicals. This action stipulated that Indian companies selling generic drugs must pay foreign patent holders a 'reasonable' royalty for copies sold in the Indian market. The amendment made reverse engineering of patented drugs illegal after January 1, 1995. The Act allowed for only two types of generic drugs in the Indian market: *off-patent generic drugs* and *generic versions of drugs patented before 1995*. As of 2024, nearly 97% of all drugs manufactured in India were off-patent and therefore not affected by this Act.

However, TRIPS offers some flexibility for the developing countries, which were hotly debated through different negotiating rounds in the early 2000s. These flexibilities enable some WTO member states to alleviate hardships resulting from the need to modify patent laws to TRIPS standards. For example, they allow countries to determine the criteria for an invention that can be granted a patent, and governments to grant a compulsory license to local companies to produce the patented products if the latter's requests to patent owners for a voluntary license does not succeed.

India has significantly made use of these mechanisms for creating some space for leveraging the defense of new product patents. While finally allowing the patent protection for pharmaceutical products, India's patent law, Section 3(d), in particular, limits the number of patents that can protect a drug, providing two important exclusions from the scope of that protection. It excludes discoveries of (1) new forms of known substances—unless there is an enhancement of the known efficacy of that substance, and (2) new uses for known substances. In addition, the amendment provides a list of substances that would be considered a new form of the same substance unless they differ significantly in properties with regard to efficacy. The Indian law also contains more strict criteria for patentability (trivial changes to a patent-expired product would not qualify for a new patent), allowance for public opposition to a patent application before a decision is made, and the possibility of compulsory licensing.

To protect consumers and its pharmaceutical industry, Indian patent law aims to curtail a process known as 'evergreening,' in which pharmaceutical companies make sometimes minor improvements to an old medicine, allowing them to renew their patent. Through the famous case of Novartis' Glivec medicine, the Indian courts reasserted the preference for generic competition, stating that if a patented drug in the Indian marketplace is not made widely available at a reasonable price, then generic manufacturers are entitled to make their own versions of the drug and pay a royalty to the patent holder.

Glivec was awarded a patent for minor improvements in the US and the attempts to patent Glivec were rejected in India because it was considered to be an improved version of an existing Novartis drug, and hence doesn't qualify for patent protection (Rajan, 2017).

11.2.2.3 Complementary Policies of Affordability

In India, out of pocket (OOP) healthcare expenditure is one of the major causes for a large number of households falling into poverty (Krishna, 2010). The shifting burden of diseases to individuals has been aggravated by the epidemiological transition from communicable to non-communicable diseases since it is largely met from OOP expenditures (Motkuri & Mishra, 2020). In 2008, the Department of Pharmaceuticals, Ministry of Chemicals & Fertilizers, Government of India launched the *Pradhan Mantri Bhartiya Janaushadhi Pariyojana* (PMBJP) to ensure the availability of quality generic medicines at affordable prices to all citizens (Singh et al., 2020). Under this scheme, the government opened a number of public pharmacy shops (*Janaushadhi Kendras*) that offer generic medicines, consumable and surgical items at an affordable rate. As of December 2025, more than 16,000 medical shops are functional across the country.

Another direct intervention is implementing the price controls on essential drugs, which date back to 1962. The National Pharmaceutical pricing authority of India intervenes with the policies of price control at various points. Through the Drug Price Control Order (DPCO) of 2013, the authority capped the prices of 871 essential drugs listed in National List of Essential Medicine (NLEM) 2015, besides regulating prices of 642 drugs classified as 'new' ones. Exorbitant prices of medical devices prompted the government to extend the price policy for the same. This is for instance the case of coronary stents and knee implants. Drug price controls have facilitated the access to medicines, even though there are debates regarding the dominance of market-based pricing strategies against cost-based pricing strategies.

Indian companies have therefore been engaged in the manufacture of generics and development of non-infringing processes rather than in new drug development for decades (Joseph, 2011). The process patent regime under the Patents Act 1970 was a decisive step in facilitating this commitment. Although the TRIPS regime of intellectual property rights has made the transformation of drugs into generics more difficult, India has massively used its TRIPS "flexibilities" as well as the power of its courts to pursue its policy.

Viewed from the perspective of Ostrom's "Governing the Commons," (1990) both India and France have developed robust systems to manage their pharmaceutical industries as common resources, but with distinct approaches. India's focus on generics and its flexible IP regime has allowed it to provide affordable medicines not only domestically, but also, to some extent, globally, while France's regulated pharmaceutical market ensured healthcare access through centralized price controls and negotiations. Both countries demonstrate how collective action and national governance structures can manage pharmaceutical resources, ensuring public health remains a policy target. In France, generics were adopted as a tool to regulate drug pricing and healthcare costs while maintaining a capitalist pharmaceutical structure with its monopolies. France saw generics as complementary to patented drugs, balancing high innovation costs with budget constraints. India's generic drug industry thrived by rejecting strict patent laws for decades, and of late even appropriating the loop holes within the dominant structure of IPR, prioritizing public health over pharmaceutical profits. While generics were complementary to pharmaceutical capitalism in France, they represented a direct alternative to it in India. Asian traditional medicines' relationship with pharmaceutical capitalism has been more complex and varied across Asian countries including China, India and Japan.

11.3 Asian Medicines

11.3.1 The Indian Ayurveda Common(s), Patents, and the Appropriation of Indigenous Knowledge

Since the 1990s, the modernization of Ayurveda has meant industrialization (Banerjee, 2009; Bode, 2008). It has gone hand-in-hand with the rise of a pharmaceutical sector mass-producing ready-made therapeutic combinations of plants, which are "reformulated" (often radically simplified) versions of recipes from the official corpus of Ayurveda treaties (Pordié & Gaudillière, 2014). The firms trading in these remedies range from small local ventures originating in one family to global players with thousands of employees, which market products throughout Asia using "scientific marketing" tools exactly like those of any large capitalistic Western drug company.

The reformulation of classical combinations of medicinal plants described in centuries-old reference texts used by Ayurvedic practitioners means simultaneously simplifying and standardizing poly-herbal combinations in order to (1) adapt them to mass and mechanized industrial processing; (2) draw on elements of biomedical experimentation in the laboratory and clinical medicine to provide evidence of medical value, and (3) combine Ayurvedic and biomedical categories in order to address the health needs of cosmopolitan consumers (Gaudillière et al., 2022).

Intellectual property rights play a peculiar role in the reformulation strategy since Ayurvedic formulas are viewed on the one hand (when they more or less replicate the classical combinations described in Ayurvedic treatises) as collective resources that must be protected from private ownership to ensure further mining of classical texts, and on the other hand (when they significantly differ in ingredients or proportions from the classical preparations) as innovative products that can be appropriated through trademarks and patents.

11.3.1.1 Creating a Common to Facilitate Private Industrial Innovation? The Indian Traditional Knowledge Digital Library.

The status and operations of the Traditional Knowledge Digital Library (TKDL) established by the Indian government in 2000 in order to oppose the patenting of poly-herbal therapeutic preparations, which originate in Indian traditional knowledge, powerfully illustrates this conundrum (Gaudillière, 2014).

The TKDL official status is that of a database gathering all the medical texts composing the Ayurveda (and other systems of Indian medicine) written corpuses and translating their recipes into English since it was conceived as a resource in intellectual property disputes. To be useful to patent examiners, the whole collection must be searchable on the basis of legal intellectual property categories. By arranging the knowledge according to composition, production process, and usage, the TKDL descriptions of therapeutic mixtures closely follow the structure of patents, focusing on the combination of matter rather than on the medical context and the clinical meaning of the original texts. Borrowing the patent-derived notion of "composition of matter", the digital library is however not only a means in intellectual property disputes but also a powerful instrument in the "pharmaceuticalization" of Ayurveda (Chap. 10 in this volume).

Given the TKDL's official aim of resisting the appropriation of Indian knowledge, contractual access agreements have been signed only with the intellectual property agencies of the global North. The European Patent Office has been authorized to consult the TKDL since February 2009. An access agreement with the USPTO was reached a year later, in 2010. The impact of this access on legal practices seems to be significant, at least in the European context. Since 2009, dozens of patent applications have been denied on the basis of "prior art" information provided by the TKDL and its lawyers. However, not all contested patents are canceled. The EPO is recognizing not only the prior art status of traditional knowledge but also its importance as a resource to be mined and valued: newly defined poly-herbals are also deemed patentable, at least when associated with standardization and biological evaluation of their effects. In other words, the price paid by TKDL architects for their success at the international level is the juxtaposition of two contradictory results: a reinforced protection of the compendia of classical formulas, and a reinforced industrial appropriation of reformulated compositions. On the one hand, tradition is being stabilized through the reference corpus and its translation; on the other, the path is open for the inscription of some reformulations into the proprietary drug economy.

The claimed function of the TKDL is to preserve the status of "common" knowledge granted to the classical formulas. "Common" in this context is synonymous with "national." The classical formulas are viewed as an Indian heritage, and the TKDL's first official goal is to avoid foreign (meaning Western) appropriation. With this national dimension it is all the more important that the existence of the TKDL does not preclude the possibility of patenting new formulations, in addition to their mandatory registration. The Indian Patent Office has accordingly granted hundreds of patents protecting reformulated preparations in the past ten years, most of them with no international status.

11.3.1.2 Reformulation Beyond the Common. Patents and the Appropriation of Local Traditional Knowledge

The neo-traditional remedies of industrial Ayurveda are approached as innovative products because they do not simply originate in the official corpus of *classical* formulas but in the mobilization of heterogeneous bodies of knowledge including the pharmacological and biomedical clinical knowledge taught in Ayurveda Medical Colleges, and—eventually—other forms of "traditional knowledge" developed outside the realm of codified traditions for instance in the so-called tribal communities of India.

This is the case of Jeevani (Madhavan et al., 2020), a polyherbal preparation sold by Arya Vaidya Pharmacy (AVP), a company based in North Kerala. It is a simple formula made out of four plants: *Trichopus zeylanicus, Withania somnifera, Piper longum and Evolvulus alsinoides.* It is advertised as a restorative, immune-enhancing, anti-stress and anti-fatigue medication. This drug is registered as an 'Ayurvedic Proprietary Medicine', which means that it is marketed under a name registered as a trademark. This form of intellectual property is based on the recognition that this drug is not a formulation mentioned in the classical medical texts, but a modified preparation. Although three of the ingredients in the composition of Jeevani are well-known Ayurveda plants, the first, *Trichopus zeylanicus* (or 'arogyapacha' in Malayalam, which means 'the green that gives strength') is not part of this tradition. Jeevani has double origins in Ayurveda and in the traditional medical knowledge of the Kani people who live in the forests of North Kerala.

Jeevani is indeed the outcome of an encounter between the Kanis and the researchers from a state institution, the Jawaharlal Nehru Tropical Botanical Garden and Research Institute (JNTBGRI). In the late 1980s, these botanists were involved in a general survey of tribal knowledge of forest plants that focused on plants used as food and/or healing agents, the All India Coordinated Project on Ethnobiology (AICRPE) (Pushpangadan & Pradeep, 2008). The first survey lasted until 1992, but the JNTBGRI researchers learned about arogyapacha anti-fatigue properties from their Kani guides at an early stage, in 1987. The first scientific paper on arogyapacha was published in 1988 in *Ancient Science of Life*, an Ayurvedic research journal edited with the support of the Arya Vaidya Pharmacy Company (AVP). The aim was not to grant the plant new botanical or pharmacological properties, but to argue for a specific Ayurvedic identity, taking into account its description as well as its anti-fatigue and rejuvenating potency. The botanists then joined Ayurvedic practitioners to explain that the plant had already been described in one important text in Ayurveda, the Sushruta Samhita (written during 1st millennium BCE).

Linking arogyapacha and Ayurveda did not only mean taking the plant away from oral, indigenous, tribal knowledge to bring it into the realm of a written, scholarly, and institutionalized system of medicine, it also implied changing the materiality of its uses by turning it into a formulation. The JNTBGRI scientists thus made little effort in the direction of searching the (active) ingredients of arogyapacha and no attempt to isolate and purify them. They looked for a new therapeutic combination including arogyapacha and a few additional plants. Kani knowledge did not help to solve this problem because the locals used T. zeylanicus in isolation. Analogous to a form of screening, their testing of a dozen preparations provided the basis for the registration of Jeevani as Ayurvedic proprietary medicine, but also for its patenting without any specific mention of the Kani knowledge.

This appropriation of Jeevani generated a novel and fundamental type of inequality between the Kani people and the JNTBGRI scientists, which was reflected in the latters' ability to negotiate a licensing agreement with AVP. In the 1980s-1990s, AVP emerged as one of the major firms in the field of Ayurvedic manufacturing, promoting integrative research with an associated foundation hosting a hospital and the establishment of a scholarly journal, Ancient Science of Life (published in English). Jeevani was one of its earliest commercialization of proprietary products with the establishment of a large capacity production line and mass promotion. AVP marketed Jeevani for seven years but the process was plagued with major issues of raw-material availability and limited collection of arogyapacha (Chap. 10 in this volume). Towards the end of the patent-protection period, AVP could produce only 2000 bottles per month when the capacity of its production line was 30,000 bottles per day. The company then started to sell another formulation, Punarjeevani, targeting the same indications and using the same composition as Jeevani but excluding its key ingredient, T. zeylanicus!

The Kani contribution was however not simply overlooked. Its recognition took another form with a verbal contract between the botanists and some Kanis, defining how the sharing of benefits would be organized. JNTBGRI scientists formed a trust namely the Kerala Kani Samudaya Kshema Trust (KKSKT) administered by a majority of community members. The Trust had power to decide on the ways of utilizing the accrued interests but not the capital provided by the license fee and the royalty installment from AVP. With the help of these funds, the Kanis were able to start a school and a hospital and also a store (namely 'arogyapacha') room and vehicle for timber transportation.

Such benefit-sharing agreements (BSA) are indeed the form of protection for traditional knowledge favored by international regulation. The role of the Jeevani agreement in hindering the appropriation of Kani knowledge has been rather limited because of the tensions they inevitably create. To take just one example, coming up with a proper definition of the community proved an arduous task with serious conflicts regarding who was entitled to benefits. Thus, when the JNTBGRI officially interacted primarily with the Kanis from one panchayat (the local government unit in Kerala), those who lived in the other two panchayats were offended by what they saw as the JNTBGRI's cultural insensitivity, bias and exclusion policy. Several village-level leaders then boycotted the meetings organized to administer the agreement, arguing that the Trust was neither representative nor participatory.

The existence of a commons to maintain the access to Indian traditional medical knowledge is relatively well known due to the visibility of the TKDL and its international role in opposing foreign appropriation. Beyond the operations of this state-supported commons, the interests of Ayurveda pharmaceutical firms for the invention of neo-traditional remedies (new herbal composition targeting biomedical disorders) reveal deeply entrenched patterns of appropriation. Entrepreneurs rely in the first place on other means than patents including branding, technical monopoly, and legal certification. As the case of the anti-fatigue remedy Jeevani shows, practices aiming at the creation of monopolies on reformulated preparations have been extended to indigenous medical knowledge, mobilizing the signature of benefit-sharing agreements in order to access and facilitate the integration of indigenous knowledge in the world of industrial Ayurveda. Through these dynamics, the invention of neo-traditional formulations does not only rest on the defense of the Ayurveda commons focusing on the classical formulas but also mandates the unmaking of other—less national and more local—commons.

The case of reformulated traditional medical remedies in India makes visible a fundamental tension in the ways in which pharmaceutical commons are approached. There is indeed a strong contrast between the policies of access, governance and maintenance of commons goods: the first set focuses on the access to and the openness of knowledge, the second set focuses on the access to—and the public status of—drugs themselves. The paradox of neo-traditional remedies in India is that the former has a real existence in spite of mounting practices of appropriation while the latter has not in spite of local policies of free distribution. The cases of Japan and China show that very different hierarchies are at play in other Asian countries.

11.4 Traditional and Neo-traditional Medicines in China and Japan

This section compares the ways in which China and Japan have pursued non-global IPR regime conforming alternatives that demonstrate that there is another way to ensure access to essential medicines. These alternatives have involved the integration of traditional medicines and neo-traditional medicines first, into the national health insurance schemes and, second, into institutional frameworks of care, thus challenging the dominant discourse of Western pharmaceutical care—i.e. limiting what is defined as a "medicine" to synthetic pharmaceutical drugs.

With the advent of intellectual property rights regime creep into biotechnology and biopharmaceuticals since the 1980s (see Ibata-Arens, 2021 on US Supreme Court case precedents allowing the patenting of biological materials)—the separation between "standard" or standardized (produced on a mass scale with identical composition), and natural medicines (e.g. comprised of whole plants and compounds of organic materials sourced from the living world) has become blurred. Neo-traditional medicines have an intermediate position between the patented Western standard conforming pharmaceutical drugs and the shared global intellectual commons of medicines derived from traditional formulations. For example, Japan has moved to incorporate "pharmaceutical grade" quality assurance into its certification of neo-traditional medicines while China has a more formal national level certification regime (seal of approval) signaling quality control of formulations.

The relative openness in both China and Japan to incorporating neo-traditional medicines into national IPR and access frameworks can in part be explained by the continuity of care from pre-modern systems of health to the present, as well as the relative lack of Big Pharma lobbies in the domestic political economies that have led to regulatory capture in the United States, for example.

The global intellectual property rights regime has yet to fully recognize traditional health knowledge (THK) at the same level as patented drugs (Gorry & Montalban, 2026). Explanations for this disparity often refer to a lack of definitive criteria and measurements for traditional medicines and other neo-traditional drugs, as well as poor performance in clinical trials under so-called evidence-based methodologies (i.e. double-blind human subjects clinical testing with control groups). Since traditional Asian medicines have been shared in the commons for millennia, the Western IP standard of identify-novelty-then-patent has lacked resonance in Asian countries with long-standing traditional medicine practices. Since the international framework for recognizing neo-traditional medicines is underdeveloped,[4] Asian traditional medicines have been extracted and expropriated by western pharmaceutical companies with virtual impunity (Ibata-Arens, 2021). China and Japan have responded differently in the aim of upholding the intellectual property of domestic traditional and neo-traditional medicines, reflecting their domestic markets for traditional medicines and the related burden on government sponsored universal healthcare insurance.

11.4.1 Neo-Traditional Medicines in China

Traditional Chinese Medicine (TCM), documented since the third century BCE, encompasses a medical system that includes natural medicines and related therapies. While TCM lost favor for a time after China's encounter with western imperialism in the nineteenth and early twentieth century—after the mid twentieth century (during the Mao era) it slowly regained its place in China's domestic health system (Liu, 2023). It remains important today in China and was, for example, recognized in the clinical literature for its contributions to COVID-19 treatment (Wang et al., 2021). In 2021 the domestic TCM market size in China was USD $18.8 billion (Xu & Wang, 2023), based on 48,000 documented formulations (Zhang, et. al. 2023).

11.4.1.1 Intellectual Property (IP) Rights and Traditional Chinese Medicine (TCM)

IP protections for TCMs in China emerged in the 1980s. For example, China's TCM Law, Article 43, established certain IP protections for TCM formulations. Even so, findings indicate that 61.8% of enterprises prefer trade secret protection as TCM trade secrets are eligible for IP protection

[4] The United Nations Convention on Biodiversity (CBD) minimally addresses the need to conserve and protect traditional knowledge, including medicinal knowledge particularly that emerging from indigenous communities in biodiverse spaces.

under Chinese law. As a result, domestic pharmaceutical firms often apply for IP protection within China but not abroad (Xu & Wang, 2023). Even though China has in recent decades pursued a more techno-national framework (Ibata-Arens, 2019) for protecting its domestic intellectual property arising from its traditional medicine industry, these protections have not yet matched that of patented drugs. Further, TCM recipes are often seen as "collective wisdom" (Xu & Wang, 2023), which is inconsistent with the western first-to-invent framework of referencing prior art, since the prior art of most traditional Asian medicines is already a part of the global knowledge commons, as mentioned in the previous section on Indian Ayurveda.

Analogous to the TKDL in India, initiated in the 2010s, the Nationwide Survey and Registration for Traditional Knowledge of Traditional Chinese Medicine in China (NRTCM), which is not publicly available as of December 2024, comprises (as of 2020) more than 6000 validated formulations.[5] The majority of these previously uncodified formulations were collected from practitioners in indigenous communities. Subsequently designated by the Chinese government as national protected assets, access to the NRTCM has been severely restricted under China's emerging *sui generis* IP regime securitizing TCM as state assets to be protected. China has thus been enclosing access from these historically commons goods (Ibata-Arens, 2021).

11.4.1.2 National Health Insurance and Access

According to Wang et al. (2021) as recently as 2017, research indicated urban and rural disparities in access to TCMs. For example, "around 80% of TCM practitioners serve in urban areas while only 20% are in rural areas" (Wang et al., 2021), reflecting a lack of healthcare infrastructure in general in rural areas. Under Xi Jinping, China's national government support for a resurgence in TCM accelerated, evidenced in its 12th (2011), 13th (2016), and 14th (2021) Five-year plans. These plans have sought to develop regulatory frameworks, support research and development (e.g. into neo-traditional formulations consistent with evidence-based medicine techniques) and improve the integration of TCMs into the national healthcare scheme. For example, the national health insurance scheme covers more than 1300 Chinese medicines (and about the same

[5] See Ibata-Arens 2021, pp. 87–91 for a discussion of the political factors in China driving the creation of the NRTCM, and subsequently limiting its impact.

number of Western medicines) and among these the greatest coverage is for a proportion categorized as "Class A", indicating their necessary use in clinical treatments (nearly 400 Western medicines and just over 240 Chinese) (Ibata-Arens, 2021, p. 71). Relatedly, China's "Healthy China 2030" (2016), seeks to pay "equal attention to traditional Chinese and Western medicine" as well as "promote the complementary and coordinated development of traditional Chinese medicine and western medicine" (Tan, et. al. 2017).

Despite this renewed support for TCM through increasing domestic IP protections, challenges remain in ensuring access to them beyond urban centers. The Chinese government has claimed that 95% of all Chinese citizens are covered by basic medical insurance or BMI according to a 2020 government report (Yi, 2021). However, of those surveyed about their care, 30% were uninsured, with only 70% having some kind of government health insurance[6] (Chung et al., 2013; Su et al., (2018); Peratello, 2025; Yi, 2021). Some of the conclusions made from the study were that older people tend to use more traditional aspects of TCMs, like acupuncture and massage therapy, and that those who are uninsured have a higher use of TCMs, due to them being less expensive than modern medicine alternatives.

In sum, through such government plans Healthy China 2030 and 5-year plans, since 2011 China has steadily increased investment and grants to grow China's TCM industry within an increasingly techno-national intellectual property rights regime (Ibata-Arens, 2019). Likewise, government fiscal appropriation to TCM agencies has increased more than twofold from 2012 to 2017 (202 to 460 hundred million RMB), resulting in an expansion of government bureaucracies concerned with TCM and increasing the number of TCM practitioners, and subsidies for TCM hospitals (Wang et al., 2021). Despite the national government push for TCMs, they have not been universally embraced by the Chinese public, citing quality concerns and complaints about high prices resulting in the fact that those of lower income are less likely to purchase TCMs if the cost burden was entirely out-of-pocket (Meng et al., 2020). In addition to the urban-rural divide, there exists regional inequity in

[6] These include Urban Employee Basic Medical Insurance (UEBMI) and Urban Resident Basic Medical insurance (URBMI). EBMI (both urban and rural) covers around 337 million individuals in China. RBMI covers 1.014 billion people. Only UEBMI of China's basic medical insurance covers TCMs (Peratello, 2025).

TCM resources, specifically in Eastern regions benefiting from government largesse more so than the western and southern regions of China (Zhu et al., 2020). Nevertheless, China has shifted towards a *sui generis* domestic IP protection system tailored to its vast traditional medicine corpus and growing evidence-based recognition of their efficacy, especially since the COVID-19 pandemic (Ibata-Arens, 2021). Japan, in contrast, has leaned somewhat but not entirely, towards the western dominant patent-based IP system.

11.4.2 Neo-Traditional Medicines in Japan

Kampo medicine (formally *Kampoyaku*)[7] was brought to Japan from China in the sixth century CE. After the Meiji Restoration in 1868, Japan's national government embraced western medical practice, modeling its modernization in medical education on the German system and outlawing the prescription of Kampo medicines in 1883 (Shibata et al., 2022). However, even during the *sakoku* isolation initiated by the Tokugawa Shogunate in the early seventeenth century, western (Dutch) medical practices had some presence, particularly in the southwestern parts of Japan. Kampo medicine was re-integrated into the Japanese health care system officially in the 1970s, following the modernization in research and development and clinical studies of efficacy conforming to international standards in manufacturing (Yamamoto, 2022). Efforts to establish Kampo medicines as evidence-based medicine (EBM) have been underway since the mid-twentieth century, led by such neo-traditional pharmaceutical companies as JPS Pharmaceutical and Tsumura.[8] By 2011 Japan imported 80% of natural medicinal ingredients, typically plant materials from China, declining from a historical peak of more than 95% dependency. Only a handful of herbal medicinal plants for Kampo are grown in Japan (Fuyuno, 2011). "Kampo medicines accounted for approximately 2.4% of Japan's total pharmaceutical sales in 2015, and the majority were dry extract products for prescription (Arai &

[7] For a list of Kampo related terminology, see Kampō Shōyaku Jōhō, Nihon Kampō Shōyaku Seizai Kyōkai.

[8] Tsumura & Co. is a pharmaceutical company founded in 1893 and is the leading Kampo producer, with a 83.2% market share of Japan's Kampo industry. Additionally holding 129/148 of Japan's registered Kampo formulas. Their executives hold many leadership roles in the JKMA, or Japan Kampo Medicines Manufacturers Association. (tsumura.co.jp).

Kawahara, 2019)". Japan's neo-traditional medicine market is a fraction of the size of China's, comprising no more than 200 formulations, with fewer than 150 approved for national health insurance coverage.

11.4.2.1 Intellectual Property Rights and Kampo

In Japan, Kampo and other neo-traditional medicines have been integrated into Covid relief in 2020 and previously as treatment for the SARS epidemic in 2002–2003 (Hofer, 2020). The compounds used in Japanese Kampo are based on so-called good manufacturing practices (GMP), and most Kampo herbal remedies have been standardized under government regulation and thus covered by national health insurance (Park et al., 2012). Unlike China, Japan's national government has not made its traditional medicines a centerpiece of intellectual property or industrial promotion policy. In fact, Japan's domestic intellectual property rights framework has aligned over time with international patenting standards and the TRIPS Agreement. This has caused some consternation in China as Japan was accused in 2023 of applying "for 210 patents internationally based on ancient recipes recorded by classical Chinese treaties" (Xu & Wang, 2023).

IP and quality are regulated in Japan by the Ministry of Health Labour and Welfare under the Pharmaceutical and Medical Device Act (PMD Act, 1943)[9] and the Health Promotion Act (HPA, 2002). Further, under Japan's Patent Act, while original Kampo formulations (of TCM) cannot be patented, if these are modified in a so-called novel way then patents can be granted on such "new" formulations. Likewise novel techniques for extraction of chemical compounds from plants can be patented under Japanese law, and there are government grants available to help inventors pursue these patents. Once a Kampo medicine has been listed as prescribable in the Japanese pharmacopeia, it is covered by the national insurance scheme.[10] Estimates indicate that at least 80% of medical doctors in Japan use Kampo in their practices (Motoo et al., 2011). By 2020, prescribed Kampo formulas made for a domestic market size of 162 billion yen. In addition to prescribed Kampo medicines, the market for over the

[9] The PMD Act was enacted originally in 1943 as the Pharmaceutical Affairs Law (PAL) and earlier under regulations on the sales of medicines (1889).

[10] Japanese government attempts to contain costs by delisting a combo formulation have been met with public outcry, and citizen LED social media campaigns to shame the government for denying care (Ibata-Arens, 2021).

counter (OTC) Kampo formulas (294 were officially recognized by the government) reached 50 billion yen in 2020 (Yoshino et al, 2023).

11.4.2.2 National Health Insurance and Medicine Access

In China, TCM (care and treatments) is covered, while the reimbursement for TCM and neo-traditional medicine formulations is not covered under the national health insurance scheme to the same extent as in Japan, though as mentioned above Japan's overall market for neo-traditional remedies is a fraction of the size of China's. Universal health insurance was created in Japan in 1961 (Yoshino et al, 2023) and coverage is determined by employment status and age. However, as of 2015 only 58.7% of the population was covered by a government insurance scheme (EHI, NHI, and late-stage care) (Matsuda, 2019).[11] Like China, there are also regional disparities in quality of care provided and the numbers of practitioners and hospitals in certain regions. Due to rural depopulation, there exists a de facto urban concentration in access to traditional medicine care.[12]

Further comparing China and Japan to each other elicits interesting nuances. For example, China's traditional medicine industry is well-developed and rich in diversity, from small-scale producers in the provinces to major mass market and branded industrial-scale manufacturers in places like Beijing and Shanghai. As such, its domestic lobby of TCM makers is strong and provides a counterbalance to the influence of Western pharmaceuticals in its national healthcare system. Japan, on the other hand, lacks a significant domestic traditional medicine industrial base (and too few large-scale producers, save Tsumura). Prescribing physicians have significant influence in national health policymaking, represented by the very powerful Japan Medical Association (JMA) and therefore limit the influence of any drug maker, synthetic pharmaceutical or natural medicine, domestic, or foreign.

China, India, and Japan can be said to occupy positions along a continuum; at one end is a fully open commons characterized by

[11] Employees' Health Insurance (EHI): employees and their dependents, premium of about 10–13% of salary, employer paying half; National Health Insurance (NHI): for the self-employed, farmers, retirees, and their dependents, monthly premiums set by local governments, about half of the cost is subsidized by the government. Late-Stage Medical Care: the elderly pay only 10% of total monthly cost.

[12] For an historical overview see Liu et al. (2022).

communally shared access and benefit sharing in natural essential medicines (neo-traditional formulations), represented by India, at least into the early 1990s. Japan occupies an intermediate position, a middle-ground between a "commons" approach and adhering to the Western IP-paradigm of monopoly patents. At the other end of the continuum is China, which has increasingly pursued both a techno-national strategy of prioritizing the needs of domestic industry over the demands of foreign and a sui generis domestic IP regime, identifying neo-traditional medicines as national assets to be protected accordingly under the law.

11.5 General Conclusion

Inequalities of access to health goods play a paramount role in the governance of health-related innovations as well as in the governance of health systems. The tensions originating in what are perceived as unfair configurations of production and distribution of goods and services have for instance played a central role in the rise of global health from the early 2000s campaigns for the access to antiretroviral therapies to the creation of numerous alliances and partnerships to foster research targeting neglected disorders in the 2010s. The search for pragmatic responses to the lack of access has resulted in a peculiar framing of the problem shared by private actors like the Bill and Melinda Gates Foundation or quasi-public actors like the Global Fund Share. It focuses on the idea that access is a problem of "charity", that is donation and philanthropy, while innovation and production are best achieved by private companies incentivized by patents and other IPRs. In other words, the discourse about essential medicine access dances around the off-limit proprietary IP and profit-driven core of pharmaceutical capitalism. The initiatives to support the access to the vaccines against Covid-19 and their controversial impact since 2020 are a further illustration of the strength and limitations of this paradigm.

This chapter has sought to avoid the pitfalls of a framing looking at access to health goods and services as an autonomous, bottom of the line, coverage problem by linking it with issues of invention and production. Focusing on the monopole originating in IPRs, which have dominated the political economy of Western industrial pharmacy since the mid-twentieth century, the chapter discusses the emergence of two alternative ways of regulating access, invention, and production: those associated with generic drugs on the one hand, neo-traditional poly-herbal preparations originating in Asian medical systems on the other hand.

As outlined in the introduction, Ostrom's approach of the relationship between commons goods, public goods and private goods articulates issues of accessibility, sustainability and collective (democratic) government. All the experiences analyzed in the chapter fit some of Ostrom's conditions but not others.

Our analysis of the rise of generics as response to the access deficit, and alternative to the patent-dominated regime thus shows that this is a market-based response to a market-framed problem. This response is no alternative since in the vast majority of generic drugs development projects the generic status is a normal second life in the after-patent existence of a therapeutic substance. Even in India where the opposition to patents has led to spectacular legal proceedings pleading health emergencies and resulting in the transformation of major new pharmaceuticals into cheap affordable goods, the generic market remains a parallel one, mostly providing old drugs. Considering the triangle between private, public and commons goods introduced above, one may consider generics as powerful illustrations of the public-private basis of the system. Our comparison between India and France furthermore suggests that national differences consist in slightly different hierarchies in analogous mixes placing for instance the latter closer to the public good side than the former since generics help France to balance the public health insurance budget covering costs of most pharmaceuticals.

In contrast, the case of Indian neo-traditional remedies presents a commons of knowledge providing—under close state supervision—access to—and preservation of—the written formulas of Indian systems of medicine. Even in this case however, the commons is closely circumscribed by the proprietary regime since the close collaborations between scientists in public institutions and the industrial companies inventing and producing new formulas rest on heterogeneous means of appropriation including national patents, while—even more importantly—the number of neo-traditional remedies produced as public goods remains limited. The situation in China and Japan is no exception to this assessment even if the coverage of costs by the insurance system is more systematic in the Chinese case.

Generics and neo-traditional remedies reflect misalignments between the fundamental dimensions of a "commons" good, and the fact that—in practice—health products or services most often combine features typical of public- and private- goods without being a full-fledged commons good. They also show that—just like the famous Global Fund against tuberculosis, HIV, and malaria—a majority of the initiatives implemented to enforce access to pharmaceutical products have originated in—or relied on—national state institutions and global regulation with the consequence that commons as empowering and more democratic forms of governance are the exception.

These existing politics of access to drugs are therefore strong reminders that pharmaceutical capitalism cannot be equated with the patents-centered regime of the current health economy. The firms making generics or neo-traditional remedies in Asia and the innovation systems within which they operate are equally extractive and capitalistic as the former even if they function without patent monopoly or without chemical expertise. At the same time, there are signs for optimism. Certain states, for different reasons and via different processes have provided essential medicines as a public good, acknowledging the fundamental human right to health. States have likewise mitigated deficiencies in the collective governance of medicines as a commons good, in cases where the logic of pharmaceutical capitalism has failed to serve the common good.

References

Abbas, N., Hasan, S. S., & Curley, L. (2020). Access to medicines-a systematic review of the literature. *Research in Social and Administrative Pharmacy, 16*(9), 1166–1176.

Abecassis, P., Alesandrini, J. F., Coriat, B., Coutinet, N., & Leyronas, S. (2019). DNDi, a distinctive illustration of commons in the area of public health. *AFD Research Papers Series, 93*

Arai, I., & Kawahara, N. (2019). Kampo pharmaceutical products in the Japanese health-care system: Legal status and quality assurance. *Traditional & Kampo Medicine*, *6*(1), 3–11.

Ayyangar, R. (1959). *The report on the revision of Indian patent law*, Available online https://ipindia.gov.in/writereaddata/Portal/Images/pdf/1959-_Justice_N_R_Ayyangar_committee_report.pdf

Banerjee, M. (2009). *Power, knowledge, medicine: Ayurvedic pharmaceuticals at home and in the world.* Orient Blackswan.

Bode, M. (2008). *Taking traditional knowledge to the market.* Orient Longman.

Bourgeron, T., & Geiger, S. (2024). Counter-movements from the core: The assetization of pharmaceuticals, transparency activism and the access to medicines movement. *Socio-Economic Review*, *22*(4), 1755–1782.

Cassier, M., & Correa, M. (2003). Patents, innovation and public health: Brazilian public-sector laboratories' experience in copying Aids drugs. *Economics of AIDS and Access to HIV/AIDS Care in Developing Countries. Issues and Challenge.*

Cassier, M. (2004). Brevets pharmaceutiques et santé publique en France: Opposition et dispositifs spécifiques d'appropriation des médicaments entre 1791 et 2004. *Entreprises Et Histoire, 36*(2), 29–47.

Chaudhuri, S. (2005). *The WTO and India's pharmaceutical industry: Patent protection, TRIPS, and developing countries.* Oxford University Press.

Chaudhuri, S. (2014). *Intellectual property rights and innovation: MNCs in pharmaceutical industry in India after TRIPS*, ISID Working Paper. 170.

Chauveau, S.(1999). *L'invention pharmaceutique. La pharmacie française entre l'État et la société au XXe siècle.*Les empêcheurs de penser en rond.

Chauveau, S. (2007). Le statut légal du médicament en France, XIXe et XXe siècles. *Revue Française Des Affaires Sociales, 3*, 87–113.

Chauvin, P. M. (2011). Architecture des prix et morphologie sociale du marché: Le cas des Grands crus de Bordeaux. *Revue Française de Sociologie, 52*(2), 277–309.

Chung, V. C., Ma, P. H., Wang, H. H., Wang, J. J., Hong, L. C., Wei, X., Wong, S. Y., Tang, J. L., & Griffiths, S. M. (2013). Integrating traditional chinese medicine services in community health centers: Insights into utilization patterns in the pearl river region of china. *Evidence-Based Complementary and Alternative Medicine.*

Dixneuf, M. (2003). Au-delà de la santé publique: les médicaments génériques entre perturbation et contrôle de la politique mondiale. *Revue française de science politique, 53*(2), 277–304.

Dolcerocca, A., & Coriat, B. (2016). Commons and the public domain: A review article and a tentative research agenda. *Review of Radical Political Economics, 48*(1), 127–139.

Fassin, D. (2023). *The worlds of public health: Anthropological excursions.* John Wiley & Sons.

Fuyuno, I. (2011). Japan: Will the sun set on Kampo? *Nature, 480*, S96.

Gaudillière, J.-P. (2014). An Indian path to biocapital: The traditional knowledge digital library (TKDL), drug patents, and the reformulation regime of contemporary ayurveda. *East Asian Science Technology and Society, 8*, 391–415.

Gaudillière, J.-P., McDowell, A., Lang, C., & Beaudevin, C. (2022). *Global health for all: Knowledge, politics, and practices.* Rutgers University Press.

Greene, J. (2016). *Generic: The unbranding of modern medicine.* John Hopkins University Press.

Gaudilliere, J. P., & Sunder Rajan, K. (2021). Making valuable health: Pharmaceuticals, global capital and alternative political economies. *BioSocieties, 16*(3), 313–322.

Gaudilliere, J. P. (2021). Pharmaceutical innovation and its crisis: Drug markets, screening, and the dialectics of value. *BioSocieties, 16*(3), 411–432.

Gorry, P., & Montalban, M. (2026). The crisis of capitalism and health innovation: Symptoms of a crisis or of success? In S. Lechevalier, J.-P. Gaudillière, K. Ibata-Arens, & K. Takuma (Eds.), *Capitalism, innovations, and health after Covid-19. An Asian perspective*. Palgrave MacMillan.

Hall, P. A., & Soskice, D. (2001). An introduction to varieties of capitalism. *Debating Varieties of Capitalism: A Reader*, 21–74.

Hofer, T. (2020, June 23). *The invisible Mask: Kampo pharmaceuticals and Chinese medical practitioners during the coronavirus crisis 2020 in Japan.* Society for Cultural Anthropology.

Ibata-Arens, K. C. (2019). *Beyond Technonationalism: Biomedical innovation and entrepreneurship in Asia.* Stanford University Press.

Ibata-Arens, K. C. (2021). *Pandemic medicine: Why the global innovation system is broken, and how we can fix it.* Lynne Rienner Publishers.

Joseph, R. K. (2011). The R&D Scenario in Indian pharmaceutical industry, *RIS Discussion series No.* 176.

Kanpō Shōyaku Jōhō, Nihon Kanpō Shōyaku Seizai Kyōkai. https://www.nikkankyo.org/seihin/yougo/explanation01.htm. Accessed 10 March 2024.

Krishna, A. (2010). *One illness away: Why people become poor and how they escape poverty.* OUP Oxford.

Lechevalier, S. (2026). Care-led innovation. A new paradigm and an application in the Japanese context of Society 5.0. In S. Lechevalier, J.-P. Gaudillière, K. Ibata-Arens, & K. Takuma (Eds.), *Capitalism, innovations, and health after Covid-19. An Asian perspective.* Palgrave MacMillan.

Lechevalier, S., Gaudillière, J.-P., Ibata-Arens, K., & Takuma, K. (2026). Capitalism, innovations, and health after Covid-19. An Asian perspective: An introduction. In S. Lechevalier, J.-P. Gaudillière, K. Ibata-Arens, & K. Takuma (Eds.), *Capitalism, innovations, and health after Covid-19. An Asian perspective.* Palgrave MacMillan.

Lecomte, T., & Paris, V. (1998). Le contrôle des dépenses en médicament en Allemagne, en France et au Royaume-Uni. *Économie Et Statistique, 312*(1), 109–124.

Le Pen, C. (1996). Drug pricing and reimbursement in France. *Pharmacoeconomics, 10*(2), 26–36.

Liu, S., Matsuo, T., Matsuo, C., & Abe, T. (2022). Traditional Chinese medicines and prescriptions brought from China to Japan by a monk (Jianzhen, Japanese: Ganjin): A historical review. *Compounds, 2*(4), 267–284.

Liu, R. (2023). Conflict and integration of Chinese and Western medicine in Chinese literature, 1906–1946. *Advances in Literary Study, 11*(1), 1–14.

Madhavan, H., & Gaudillière, J.-P. (2020). Reformulation and appropriation of traditional knowledge in industrial ayurveda: The trajectory of Jeevani. *East Science Technology and Society*, *14*(4), 603–621.

Matsuda, S. (2019, March 4). Health policy in Japan—Current situation and future challenges. *JMA Journal*, *2*(1), 1–10.

Meng, F., Ji, Z., Song, F., Bai, T., Fan, X., & Wang, D. (2020). Patients' familiarity with, trust in and willingness to pay for traditional Chinese medicine in Chinese community health care centres. *European Journal of Integrative Medicine*, *36*, 101118.

Motkuri, V., & Mishra, R. N. (2020). Pharmaceutical market and drug price policy in India. *Review of Development and Change*, *25*(1), 30–53. Madras Institute of Development Studies

Motoo, Y., Seki, T., & Tsutani, K. (2011). Traditional Japanese medicine, Kampo: Its history and current status. *Chinese Journal of Integrative Medicine*, *17*, 85–87.

Musgrave, R. A. & Musgrave P. B. (1973), *Public finance in theory and practice*. McGraw-Hill.

Nouguez, É. (2017). *Des médicaments à tout prix. Sociologie des génériques en France*. Presses de Sciences Po.

Nouguez, É., & Benoit, C. (2017). Governing (through) Prices: The state and pharmaceutical pricing in France. *Revue Française de Sociologie* (English Edition), *58*(3), 1–23.

Ostrom, E. (1990). *Governing the commons: The evolution of institutions for collective action*. Cambridge University Press.

Park, H. L., Lee, H. S., Shin, B. C., Liu, J. P., Shang, Q., Yamashita, H., & Lim, B. (2012). Traditional medicine in China, Korea, and Japan: A brief introduction and comparison. *Evidence-Based Complementary and Alternative Medicine 2012*, *1*, 429103.

Peratello, G. (2025, December) *China healthcare system, explained*. Wise. https://wise.com/us/blog/china-healthcare-system

Pordié, L., & Gaudillière, J.-P. (2014). The reformulation regime in drug discovery: Revisiting poly-herbals and property rights in the Ayurvedic industry. *East Science Technology and Society*, *8*, 57–79.

Pushpangadan, P., & Pradeep, P. R. J. (2008). *An All India coordinated research project on ethnobiology and genesis of ethnopharmacology*. Amity Institute for Herbal and Biotech Products Development.

Racherla, S. (2019). Historical evolution of India's patent regime and its impact on innovation in the Indian pharmaceutical industry. In K. Liu & S. Racherla (Eds.), *Innovation, economic development, and intellectual property in India and China*. Springer open. https://doi.org/10.1007/978-981-13-8102-7_12

Rajan, K. S. (2017). *Pharmacocracy: Value, politics, and knowledge in global biomedicine*. Duke University Press.

Shibata, R., Chu, G. X., Lin, X., & Fu, J. R. (2022, March). Development and future trends of traditional kampo medicine in Japan. *Chinese Medicine and Culture*, *5*(1), 58–64.

Singh, P., Ravi, S., & Dam, D. (2020). Medicines in India: Accessibility, affordability and quality (Brookings India Research Paper No. 032020–01). Brookings Institution India Center. https://www.brookings.edu/wp-content/uploads/2020/03/Medicines-in-India_for-web-1-1.pdf

Stiglitz, J. (2007). Prizes, not patents. *Project Syndicate.*

Su, M., Zhongliang, S., Zhou, Z., Si, Y., Wei, X., Xu, Y., Fan, X., & Chen, G. (2018). Comparing the effects of China's three basic health insurance schemes on the equity of health-related quality of life: Using the method of coarsened exact matching. *Health and Quality of Life Outcomes*, *16*, 1–12.

Tan, X., Liu, X., & Shao, H. (2017, May). Healthy China 2030: A vision for health care. *Value Health Regional Issues*, *12*, 112–114. https://doi.org/10.1016/j.vhri.2017.04.001

UNAIDS. (2023). *The path that ends AIDS: UNAIDS global AIDS update 2023.* Joint United Nations Programme on HIV/AIDS. Licence: CC BY-NC-SA 3.0 IGO

Wang, W. Y., Zhou, H., Wang, Y. F., Sang, B. S., & Liu, L. (2021). Current policies and measures on the development of traditional Chinese medicine in China. *Pharmacological Research, 163.*

Weinstein, O. (2021). Bien public (approche économique). In: Cornu, M., Orsi, F. & Rochfeld, J.(Eds.), *Dictionnaire des biens communs.* PUF.

World Health Organization (WHO) (n.d.) *"Essential medicines" and "model list of essential medicines"*. Accessed 14, June 2024.

Xu, Y., & Wang, Y. (2023). *IP protection of traditional knowledge: A dilemma faced by the Chinese traditional medicine in global competition.* https://www.intechopen.com/chapters/1131810

Yamamoto, M. (2022). KAMPOmics: A framework for multidisciplinary and comprehensive research on Japanese traditional medicine. *Gene*, *831*, 146555.

Yi, B. (2021). An overview of the Chinese healthcare system. *Hepatobiliary Surgery and Nutrition*, *10*(1), 93.

Yoshino, T., Kashio, A., Terasawa, Y., Hachiki, M., Yoshinaga, R., & Arita, R. (2023). The integration of traditional medicine with conventional biomedicine: A narrative review of the Japanese perspective. *Journal of Integrative and Complementary Medicine*, *29*(6–7), 372–379.

Zhang, X., Zimmerman, A., Zhang, Y., Ogbuoji, O., & Tang, S. (2023, December 19). Rapid growth of private hospitals in China: Emerging challenges and opportunities to health sector management. *The Lancet Regional Health–Western Pacific*, *44*(100991). https://doi.org/10.1016/j.lanwpc.2023.100991

Zhu, D., Shi, X., Nicholas, S., & He, P. (2020). Regional disparities in health care resources in traditional Chinese medicine county hospitals in China. *PloS One*, *15*(1), e0227956.

CHAPTER 12

General Conclusion

Sébastien Lechevalier, Jean-Paul Gaudillière, Kathryn Ibata-Arens, and Kayo Takuma

Abstract This book has interrogated the dual crisis in innovation, especially with technology and society, and capitalism as arbiter of societal needs specifically during and after the Covid-19 pandemic. The crisis of innovation, is a failure to produce new and novel solutions to health problems whether they are infectious, chronic or environmental, for the many rather than the few. It also a crisis in capitalism, as a profit-oriented arbiter of societal needs including the fundamental human right to health. Part of the problem has been limitations in the techno-innovation paradigm of neo-Schumpeterian approaches. An approach less technological and more social has been proposed in the spirit of Regulation theory (RT)

S. Lechevalier (✉)
Ecole des Hautes Etudes en Sciences Sociales (EHESS), Paris, France;
German Institute for Japanese Studies (DIJ), Tokyo, Japan
e-mail: sebastien.lechevalier@ehess.fr

J.-P. Gaudillière
Inserm & EHESS, Paris, France

K. Ibata-Arens
DePaul University, Chicago, IL, USA

K. Takuma
Keio University, Tokyo, Japan

S. Lechevalier et al. (eds.), *Capitalism, Innovations, and Health after Covid-19*,
https://doi.org/10.1007/978-3-032-24479-6_12

as response to the difficulties the dual crises in innovation and capitalism raised during the Covid-19 pandemic. However, there exists no response that fits all needs, no single best system of innovation even if experience shows that Asian alternatives have often been more effective at improving healthcare beyond access to products, at reducing mortality as well as morbidity One key result of this book is to recognize there are alternative drivers of innovation, including care-, commons- and frugal- innovation oriented healthcare systems. These alternatives were identified and defined in empirical context of Asian countries, offering a narrative of possible responses to the dual crises of innovation and capitalism. These narratives highlight the paramount role of comprehensive and socially-embedded approaches of health needs, the inclusion of key state and non-state stakeholders, and trial-and-errors reflexive assessment. They are present in Asian countries, but also, to a lesser extent, in European countries. In short, contributors proposed that health needs can and should be drivers of innovation and regulation of capitalism.

12.1 Dual Crises of Innovation and Capitalism

This book has interrogated the dual crisis in *innovation*, especially with technology and society, and *capitalism* as arbiter of societal needs specifically during and after the Covid-19 Pandemic. However, it is evident from historical-institutional analysis by Gaudillère et al. (2021) the dual crisis manifested over time in the late twentieth and early twenty-first century. Our contributors reflect on this long-wave of innovation and capitalism, beginning with Boyer & Boylaud in chapter two on the "anthropogenetic" logic centering health as key driver (Boyer & Boylaud, 2026). As such, Boyer chapter two (Boyer & Boylaud, 2026) and chapter three (Gorry & Montalban, 2026) argue that health is an end to be achieved rather than a means to productivity and profit. If health is integral to the long-term development of society, then the Covid-19 Pandemic exposed both the relative success and the poverty of the dominant Western market-based paradigm in developing accessible medicines and treatments in the form of mass-produced, proprietary, pharmaceutical products. Subsequent chapters achieve two goals. First, they examine more closely the diversity of responses involved during the pandemic and the ways in which these have—especially in Asia—challenged the dominant paradigm and its role in global health. Second, they demonstrate the richness of alternative experiences of health innovations in Asia, demonstrating how these frameworks explore ways of innovating in health considered organizational, care-led, appropriate, frugal, or based on commons show potential as avenues of inquiry based on greater attention for health needs. Further, the dual crisis is evident in the limitations of the neo-Schumpeterian approach reviewed in chapter one (Lechevalier et al., 2026) and elaborated in chapters two (Boyer & Boylaud, 2026) and three (Gorry & Montalban, 2026).

For example, Boyer and Boylaud (2026), citing Lechevalier (2019) and Gaudillière et al. (2021), noted that despite rapid developments in science and technology in response to health crisis the Covid-19 Pandemic, the failure of the techno-innovation paradigm to deliver vaccines and treatments accessibly revealed health as a global public good. Gorry and Montalban (2026) finds failure in the duty of care caused by neo-liberal cost-cutting within "medical Fordism" that had been underway for decades in Europe and the United States. This period witnessed increases in intellectual property holdings by private firms, even while productivity continued to decline. Generic medicines in the Global North would prove to be a perfect example of medical Fordism. Generics, once introduced to global markets at affordable prices, only become available upon patent expiry after 20-years of monopoly profit by the IP holder. After patent-expiry this medicine knowledge is supposed to be diffused into the global knowledge commons (Ibata-Arens et al., 2026). Gorry and Montalban trace this through the application of EROOM's Law and observe the shift in pharmaceutical industry strategies from blockbuster (drugs for many) to niche busters (highly profitable drugs for the few who can pay).

An approach less technological and more social is proposed in the spirit of Regulation theory (RT) as response to the difficulties the dual crises in innovation and capitalism raised during the Covid-19 Pandemic. As noted in this book's introduction and above, the crisis of innovation, is a failure to produce new and novel solutions to health problems whether they are infectious, chronic or environmental, for the many rather than the few. It also a crisis in capitalism, as a profit-oriented arbiter of societal needs including the fundamental human right to health. Part of the problem has been limitations in the techno-innovation paradigm of neo-Schumpeterian approaches (Lechevalier, 2026).

The limits of a neo-Schumpeterian approach are most evident in its assumptions of techno-determinism, that technology is the solution to any problem, meanwhile distributional or democratic concerns had been underexamined (Gorry & Montalban, 2026). In retrospect, should we really have been encouraging "creative destruction" or "destructive creation" when human lives, health, wellbeing, were at stake?

Beyond situation of acute crisis like the Covid-19, the limits of the technology-centered paradigm are strongly visible with the consequences of the pharmaceuticalization of care, social science and STS observers have analyzed (Biehl, 2007; Dummit, 2012; Gaudillère & Chabrol, 2026b). Pharmaceuticalization originates in the dominant role large capitalistic ventures have acquired in health R&D with its well-investigated consequences in terms of access and global inequalities. However, pharmaceuticalization as innovation model is also a question of forms of knowledge recognized and targeted needs. Major health issues beginning the world-wide heavy burden of chronic diseases as well as the health problems of aging populations have thus proved recalcitrant to a molecularized and product-oriented biomedical approach of innovation at pain to take into account the fact that care is a deeply social and relational activity (Lechevalier, 2026). Hence, the choice of this book to explore not only the double crisis of innovation and capitalism, but also different framings of health practices and policies, focusing on the Asian context.

As Boyer & Boylaud indicate in chapter two, in a crisis scenario such as the world faced in 2020–2023, applying a RT/anthropogenetic frame exposes the destabilized fissures in the systems of innovation and capitalism. Under crisis, these fissures and associated pressures on the institutions underlying governance regimes, lead to fractures in previous regulation modes. This fracturing presents an opportunity to consider alternative regulatory and governance modes, potentially transforming innovation and capitalist systems: returning human concerns, including the fundamental right to health, to the core.

The authors in this volume foreground Boyer & Boylaud's concept of anthropogenetic mode of development and some of the key concepts elaborated by the RT, although not all the authors recognize themselves in this theoretical approach, given their diversity. In particular, we all agree there exists no universal model of capitalism. Rather, the twentieth century revealed variations on a continuum of neo-liberal capitalist systems dominant in the West (UK, US) and a socially embedded ethos governing markets generally and S&T innovation activities specifically that persists in the East (evidenced by countries examined herein: China, Hong Kong, India, Japan, and South Korea). Likewise, there exists no response that fits all needs, no single best system of innovation even if experience shows that Asian alternatives have often been more effective at improving healthcare beyond access to products, at reducing mortality as well as morbidity.

The book's three sections explored this seeming contradiction with novel conceptual frameworks and extensive original fieldwork in Asian countries. The first section laid out the historical-institutional origins of the dual crisis in innovation and capitalism, while centering health at the core of drivers of innovation. The second section illuminated how the Covid pandemic pushed the limits of existing institutions and practices to a breaking point. The third section, through grounded theorizing presents these alternative innovation frameworks indicating a way forward in terms of actionable policies and how these frameworks offer interesting lines of inquiry in the future.

12.2 Comparing Approaches to Health Innovation: Value, Governance, Evaluation

Alternative approaches to health innovation can be compared on three core dimensions: their value orientation, their governance and coordination, and how they are evaluated (Lechevalier, 2019; Godin et al., 2021). First, for whose benefit are these innovations pursued? This is an indication of what is valued within the dominant systems of innovation and of capitalism for health goods and services. Chapters in this volume have demonstrated that what was valued in the Global North during and after the COVID-19 Pandemic was, and remains the profits of pharmaceutical companies, within which human disease conditions were capitalized upon. Unsurprisingly, this resulted in unprecedented levels of profit for companies including Pfizer, as shown in chapter five (Storz et al., 2026).

Second, the chapters have provided evidence for better practices in governance and coordination of health innovation to bring accessible solutions, including but not limited to specific national government policies and their implementation (Shiroyama et al., 2026; Storz et al., 2026), evident in governing the processes of innovation in the context of health crisis. Further contributors have shared evidence of success at the local (Madhavan and Gaudillère, 2026) national and international (Kuo & Takuma, 2026) levels of health policy and governance.

Third, the chapters have discussed successes versus failures in health innovations, allowing for comparisons of approaches and evaluation patterns. If the main drivers of innovation should be and have been—as the anthropogenetic hypotheses suggests—the health and wellbeing of humans individually, and humanity writ large, then it makes sense to explore cases where governments have had the political will (Gorry & Montalban, 2026) to introduce policy and organizational innovations to challenge the neo-liberal health as cost center—and disease as profit center—under pharmaceutical capitalism (Gaudillère et al., 2021). This political will is on a national level in Shiroyama et al. (2026) (chapter 4), in which social measures of policy success were introduced in Japan's and South Korea's Society 5.0 and at a local level in chapter seven (Madhavan and Gaudillère, 2026), which discusses the Kerela, India frugal innovation ecosystem successes in mitigating morbidity and mortality better than other Indian regions during Covid-19.

Chapter 9 (Lechevalier, 2026) shows care-led innovation—which refers to the design, experimentation, and adoption of innovations that prioritize care by addressing the expectations, needs, and vulnerabilities of stakeholders in care settings and enhance their capabilities, where possible—is a possible approach to overcome the inability of the neo-Schumpeterian model of innovation to focus on competitiveness rather than well-being. It is appropriate in the context of population ageing, which is particularly acute in the East Asian context. It is also shown that care-led innovation is "fragile", in the sense that an innovation which is led by the care during the conception phase can experience a bifurcation in later phases, for example during the development phase. To be properly analyzed, it thus requires a type of evaluation that respects its complexity.

Chapter 11 (Ibata-Arens et al., 2026) shows how China, India, and Japan have integrated less-expensive natural, so-called traditional medicines into national health insurance schemes, improving access on the one hand, and creating market demand driving innovations for "neo-traditional" medicines. In doing so, traditional medicines have been a commons good transformed by the state into a public good: as neo-traditional medicines. National governments have intervened in the provision of essential medicines as a public good, theretofore they have been reluctant to challenge the dominant IP regime of monopoly patents, with, to some extent, the exception of China and India (Ibata-Arens, 2021, Ibata-Arens et al., 2026).

12.3 Drivers and New Challenges of Health Innovations in Asia: Care, Commons, Frugal

One key result of this book is to recognize there are alternative drivers of innovation, including care- (Lechevalier, 2026, Chapter 9) commons- (Ibata-Arens et al., 2026, Chapter 11) and frugal-innovation oriented healthcare systems (Madhaven & Gaudillère, 2026, Chapter 7). These alternatives were identified and defined in empirical context of Asian countries, offering a narrative of possible responses to the dual crises of innovation and capitalism. These narratives highlight the paramount role of comprehensive and socially-embedded approaches of health needs, the inclusion of key state and non-state stakeholders, and trial-and-errors reflexive assessment. They are present in Asian countries, but also, to a lesser extent, in European countries.

The notion of care-led innovation places at the center the fact that health is a social and relation property. Health systems—and therefore innovation within them—of course imply the use and the provision of goods, but these can only perform as part of a relation of service, which is a personal one, a relation based on human work and interactions between people. Care-led therefore points to a way of thinking about innovation that places at the center the conditions permitting these interactions to meet health needs, for instance those of aging populations affected by chronic disorders.

The importance of institutional or political prioritization mentioned above is evidently echoed in the idea of the commons as basis for socially more adequate organization of research, production, and use of health goods and services. The commons however bring in much more emphasis on the more or less democratic decision-making processes involved when choosing priorities and programs and therefore on the need for new and more empowering forms of needs' recognition and people's participation. After all, in the classical scheme proposed by Ostrom, the commons are the result of a community setting the rules and boundaries of appropriate (re)production and use of resources, or services.

Finally, frugal innovation, the category most discussed in the global South and a kind of reinvention of the notion of (socially) appropriate technology which was once high in currency among development experts (Gaudillière & Madhavan, 2026), captures many of the above as it resonates with low cost or affordable, with technological simplicity, and with adaptation to local needs and means. Moreover, in a context where health, and more generally, production systems are confronted with the consequences of multiple ecological crises (climate, biodiversity, mass-pollution) frugality has acquired a new layer of meaning, becoming synonymous of, or criteria for, sustainability.

Beyond the discussion of frugal innovation, the question of the relations between the Anthropocene and the limits to growth is indeed a source of new tensions affecting the dominant model of innovation and capitalism, and a major challenge for the anthropogenetic mode of development. Chapter 2 (Boyer & Boylaud, 2026) thus discusses the consequences of climate change and biodiversity loss on global health policies, insisting on the very contrasted ways in which the existing institutional arrangements have addressed the non-sustainability issue and their poor results in terms of habitability. Such assessment evidently calls for an update of the anthropogenetic mode of development.

12.4 Alternative Innovation Frameworks: Concepts in Empirical Context.

At its core, this book outlined potential alternative innovation frameworks as a new health-centered model for innovation. As such we present the potential for resolving the neo-Schumpeterian conundrum evident in Western approaches that have produced advanced S&T innovations, but made them accessible only by select populations within certain Global North countries while failing to meet the more complex health needs associated with aging or chronic disorders.

In parallel with the broad alternatives it highlights, the book offers applied and specific contexts within which health has been the aim of innovation activity: organizational innovations for example in Japan and South Korea's centering of the challenge for national government-level mission-oriented STI around concerns for Society 5.0 of the safety and security of people including their happiness and well-being. (Shiroyama et al., 2026; Lechevalier, 2026). Organizational innovations were evident in the harnessing of public-private-partnerships (PPPs) in "glocal' health governance during Covid. This included local, politically nuanced decisions taken in Taiwan, ahead of the WHO and involving adroit moves by diplomats and foreign ministers (Kuo & Takuma, 2026). Others have examined sectoral innovations in the global private sector race to make COVID-19 vaccines available to the general public worldwide. (Storz et al., 2026).

Chapter 5 (Storz et al., 2026) outlined how private pharmaceutical firms in Europe and the U.S. used the urgency of the COVID crisis to obtain unprecedented government funding, successful in the rapid development of vaccines, but ultimately failing to make them accessible worldwide, exposing the limits of a neo-Schumpeterian techno-innovation approach to driving innovation activity.

Contributors have carefully considered the role of the state at national, regional and local levels in responsible governance including during public health crisis interventions, and also structuring the parameters of frugal health innovation as in the case of Kerela, India and its stakeholder-driven COVID pandemic response, including the key role of women's self-help groups (Madhavan and Gaudillère, 2026).

We also noted that certain states, including Japan and South Korea demonstrated the political will to transform the way S&T innovation output is evaluated, incorporating social impact as a key criterion of success. Meanwhile, the organizational innovations "provincializing the WHO" and glocalizing global health governance noted in chapter 6 (Kuo & Takuma, 2026) point to the need to *de-politicize* health crisis response in light of the way in which the WHO was caught between China and the U.S. and thus limited by this inter-state rivalry. This de-politicization involved diplomatic finesse by state and multilateral actors. The result was innovative ways PPPs including COVAX were created and harnessed in the goal of jointly developing and deploying vaccines—circumventing the geopolitics of technonationalism prevalent in the vaccine nationalism at the time (Ibata-Arens, 2021).

The findings herein resonate with other scholarship identifying advances in health technologies including essential medicines, vaccines against polio and measles, and robotic technology that emerged resulting from scientific innovations shared in the knowledge commons (Ibata-Arens, 2021).

Kodate et al. (2026) in chapter eight on the adoption of care robots in Hong Kong, Ireland, and Japan, as well as Lechevalier (2026), in his chapter (9) on care-led innovation, find that although there have been significant advances in robotic technologies introduced in Hong Kong, Japan and South Korea in response to shortages in health care workers particularly for the elderly, these technologies have neither been fully embraced nor widely adopted even in such advanced industrialized economies as the aforementioned. One factor in their limited adoption has been lack of trust, resulting from technology introductions into caregiver spaces without sufficient consultation with neither caregivers, nor patients themselves.

Finally, looking at the Indian context and focusing on a peculiar dimension of the latter, Gaudillière and Madhavan (2026) converge with the conclusion of chapter 2 (Boyer & Boylaud, 2026) about the anthropogenetic mode of development and the need for an update taking account the challenge of habitability as they document both the successful industrialization and growth of Ayurvedic medicine, and its adverse consequences on the supply of medicinal plants, and their ability to survive in their natural ecosystems.

12.5 Emerging Themes and Beyond

Through deep empirical research in Asian countries, this volume presented alternative health innovation frameworks to the Western model of (techno) innovation and (pharmaceutical) capitalism. These systems have been in crisis, not least of which for failing to ensure equitable access to essential medicines and vaccines during and following the COVID-19 Pandemic. They have also been in crisis generally, evidenced by declining economic productivity and worsening public health outcomes, while private IP holdings—the ownership and control over access to medicines and treatments—has grown significantly.

Five critical themes thus emerge from our book. First, we offered a conceptually provocative and empirically grounded critique of the dominant systems of innovation and capitalism. Second, we observed how the real economies of social and human factors are central in concrete examples of health innovation. Third, we documented these alternative models looking for better ways of articulating policies, practices, and unmet health needs like chronic diseases, problems of age, or emerging infectious disorders through examining Asian, public-private, and most importantly, beyond techno-deterministic approaches. We have done so through addressing not only cost and access, but also the appropriateness of products and services advancing human health. Fourth, we examined the challenges of governance and institutional change to solving health crises that necessitate institutional and political reform. Further, we find that despite neo-liberal and neo-Schumpeterian assumptions, technological breakthroughs themselves have real but limited impact. Fifth, we present a comparative, transnational, and global health lens, revealing the specifity of experiences in East Asia (China, India, Hong Kong, Japan, Korea, Taiwan). The dual crisis of innovation and capitalism thus reveals fissures in these systems but also creates openings for transformative change.

Contributors proposed that health needs can and should be drivers of innovation and regulation of capitalism. We offered two normative frameworks for consideration, reflecting on the anthropogenetic nature of innovations for health and the role of the Regulation theory and related works in comparative political economy and the study of science technology and innovation. These normative frameworks provide a guiding vision for a way forward of transformative change in the way we go about and the structures within which we engage in health innovations. In sum, authors have demonstrated that centering human health and well-being as the core aim of innovation activity, that is health as the end goal not the means to profit.

In retrospect, through our grounded theorizing, incorporating Asian perspectives and deeply researched empirical findings, this is a move towards a better understanding of alternative innovation models and an evolved form of capitalism in health economies. We believe this to be a worthwhile pursuit as a line of inquiry, and further, for improving human health.

References

Biehl, J. (2007). Pharmaceuticalization: AIDS treatment and global health politics. *Anthropological Quarterly, 80*(4), 1083–1126.

Boyer, R., & Boylaud, O. (2026). Anthropogenetic development: Long unnoticed and already in crisis. In S. Lechevalier, J.-P. Gaudillière, K. Ibata-Arens, & K. Takuma (Eds.), *Capitalism, innovations, and health after Covid-19. An Asian perspective*. Palgrave MacMillan.

Dumit, J. (2012). *Drugs for Life. How Pharmaceutical Companies Define Our Health*. Duke University Press.

Gaudillière, J.-P., & Madhavan, H. (2026). Appropriate technologies, primary health care and the integration of traditional medicines in India. In S. Lechevalier, J.-P. Gaudillière, K. Ibata-Arens, & K. Takuma (Eds.), *Capitalism, innovations, and health after Covid-19. An Asian perspective*. Palgrave MacMillan.

Gaudillère, J.-P., & Chabrol, F. (2026b). Pharmaceuticals from and for the Global. South. In D. Conor, S. Geiger, T. Kleinhout-Vliek, P. Martin, & S. Wadman (Eds.), *Handbook of global pharmaceuticals, biotechnology, and society studies*. Edward Eldgar Publishing.

Gaudillière, J. P., Izambert, C., & Juven, P. A. (2021). *Pandémopolitique: Réinventer la santé en commun*. La Découverte.

Godin, B., Gaglio, G., & Vinck, D. (2021). *Handbook on alternative theories of innovation*. Edward Elgar Publishing.

Gorry, P., & Montalban, M. (2026). The crisis of capitalism and health innovation: Symptoms of a crisis or of success? In S. Lechevalier, J.-P. Gaudillière, K. Ibata-Arens, & K. Takuma (Eds), *Capitalism, innovations, and health after Covid-19. An Asian perspective*. Palgrave MacMillan.

Ibata-Arens, K. C. (2021). *Pandemic medicine: Why the global innovation system is broken, and how we can fix it*. Lynne Rienner Publishers.

Ibata Arens, K., Gaudillière, J.-P., Madhavan, H., & Nouguez, E. (2026). Commons and the political economy of access: Generics, neo traditional formulations and the dominant intellectual property regime of medicines. In S. Lechevalier, J.-P. Gaudillière, K. Ibata-Arens, & K. Takuma (Eds.), *Capitalism, innovations, and health after Covid-19. An Asian perspective*. Palgrave MacMillan.

Kodate, N., Cheung, M. C., Yumoto, A., Donnelly, S., Maeda, Y., Tsujimura, M., Mannan, H., Yu, W., Suwa, S., Obayashi, K., Masuyama, S., Chan, W. C. H., Hauray, B., & O'Shea, D. (2026). Institutional design, welfare technologies and diffusion of innovation: Stakeholders' views regarding care robots in Hong Kong SAR (China), Ireland and Japan. In S. Lechevalier, J.-P. Gaudillière, K. Ibata-Arens, & K. Takuma (Eds.), *Capitalism, innovations, and health after Covid-19. An Asian perspective*. Palgrave MacMillan.

Kuo, W., & Takuma, K. (2026). Global health governance: Organizational innovations in the era of Covid-19. In S. Lechevalier, J.-P. Gaudillière, K. Ibata-Arens, & K. Takuma (Eds.), *Capitalism, innovations, and health after Covid-19. An Asian perspective*. Palgrave MacMillan.

Lechevalier, S. (Ed.). (2019). *Innovation beyond technology. Science for society and interdisciplinary*. Springer.

Lechevalier, S. (2026). Care-led innovation. A new paradigm and an application in the Japanese context of Society 5.0. In S. Lechevalier, J.-P. Gaudillière, K. Ibata-Arens, & K. Takuma (Eds.), *Capitalism, innovations, and health after Covid-19. An Asian perspective*. Palgrave MacMillan.

Lechevalier, S., Gaudillière, J.-P., Ibata-Arens, K., & Takuma, K. (2026). Introduction to capitalism, innovations, and health after Covid-19. An Asian perspective. In S. Lechevalier, J.-P. Gaudillière, K. Ibata-Arens, & K. Takuma (Eds.), *Capitalism, innovations, and health after Covid-19. An Asian perspective*. Palgrave MacMillan.

Madhavan, H., & Gaudillière, J.-P. (2026). Frugal innovations and health system resilience. The conceptualization, policy support and forms of frugality during Covid-19 in South India. In S. Lechevalier, J.-P. Gaudillière, K. Ibata-Arens, & K. Takuma (Eds.), *Capitalism, innovations, and health after Covid-19. An Asian perspective.* Palgrave MacMillan.

Shiroyama, H., Ki, J., Matsuo, M., & Kim, H. (2026). The mission oriented science, innovation and technology (STI) policies in Japan and Korea with a focus on health. In S. Lechevalier, J.-P. Gaudillière, K. Ibata-Arens, & K. Takuma (Eds.), *Capitalism, innovations, and health after Covid-19. An Asian perspective.* Palgrave MacMillan.

Storz, C., Lee, K., Kuo, W., & Velte, F. (2026). Covid-19 and successful vaccine development: Comparative lessons for innovation and policy from east Asia and Europe. In S. Lechevalier, J.-P. Gaudillière, K. Ibata-Arens, & K. Takuma (Eds.), *Capitalism, innovations, and health after Covid-19. An Asian perspective.* Palgrave MacMillan.

Glossary

Anthropogenetic Refers to something generated or caused by humans. An anthropogenic mode of development has as its starting point and end goal the creation of human beings. Education, health, and culture are the conditions for the mobilization of economic resources. In turn, their transformation enables the financing of investments and activities that shape human beings. This mode can take various forms depending on whether it is shaped by the market, the state, or civil society. Furthermore, certain configurations are not viable and are in crisis due to the inconsistency between human creation and economic organization (see Chap. 2).

Care-led Innovation The design, experimentation, and adoption of innovations that prioritize care by addressing the expectations, needs, and vulnerabilities of stakeholders in care settings and enhancing their capabilities, where possible (See Chaps. 1, 3, 9 and 12).

Commons good A non-excludable, but rivalrous resource, typically shared by a community and requiring governance for sustainable use. Elinor Ostrom introduced the notion of common-pool resources (CPLs) and their governance to counteract the tendency to deplete natural resources and result in a "tragedy of the commons." Examples: clean water, marine resources (See Chaps. 11 and 12).

S. Lechevalier et al. (eds.), *Capitalism, Innovations, and Health after Covid-19*,
https://doi.org/10.1007/978-3-032-24479-6

Costs disease In economics, Baumol's cost disease is the growing share of some activities in the GDP or budget related to the low productivity gains of such activities, leading to an increase of their relative price. Health services are typical examples that can suffer from costs disease. Another example is the growing cost to innovate in the pharmaceutical sector, or so called 'Eroom law' (see Chap. 3).

Epidemiologic transition A theory of the epidemiology of demographic transition. It explains the changes of pathologies related to economic development and the shift from a demographic regime with high mortality and fertility to a regime with low mortality and low fertility. The epidemiologic transition results in major changes in health needs since it implies that chronic disorders replace or dominate infectious diseases as main causes of morbidity and mortality (see Chaps. 1, 2, 9 and 10).

Frugal innovation A concept widely discussed in development economics with a peculiar bearing on the specific needs of low-and-middle income countries. The concept of frugal innovation is not only a matter of low-cost. It is an approach of innovation beyond technology as it takes into account issues of simplicity, adaptability, collective appropriation, and sustainability. Frugal innovations originate in local situations and experiences, displaying a strong community-oriented perspective but they heavily depend on the innovation (eco)system, i.e. regional and state-wise social and economic policies (See Chaps. 1 and 7).

Innovation system A set of (local, regional, national) public and private sector institutions and actors within a socio-economic space, interacting to produce and diffuse new and novel knowledge and technologies. Christopher Freeman and Bengt-Åke Lundvall advanced scholarship about national-level innovation systems, emphasizing the role of systemic coordination and the role of networks. A **health innovation system,** comprised of producers (e.g. pharmaceutical and medical device makers), regulators (governments), and users (i.e. hospitals, patients) of health and healthcare technologies is focused on the creation, regulation, and application of new and novel medical and medicine discoveries for the purpose of improving human health (See Chaps. 1, 5, 7 and 9).

Neo-Schumpeterian Is a school of economic thought that is inspired by the work of Joseph Schumpeter and places technological innovation at the core of economic growth and transformation processes. Strictly speaking, it is a form of evolutionary economics, thus classified among the heterodox approaches to economics, with representative authors such as Christopher Freeman, Richard Nelson or Giovanni Dosi. In the context of this book, we do not refer to a specific school of economic thought but rather to any economic thinking that puts technological innovation at the center of economic dynamics, while referring to Joseph Schumpeter. From this perspective, a representative work is the one by Aghion et al. (2021), which reinterprets Schumpeter's thinking in a mainstream framework (See Chaps. 1, 9, and 12).

Pharmaceuticalization The concept has emerged in social studies of health and medicine as an analog to medicalization, focusing on the mounting importance the prescription of pharmaceuticals has acquired in late twentieth century health innovation and health care. This pattern has been especially strong in the context of a mounting burden of chronic diseases. In the global South however, pharmaceuticalization has rather focused on epidemics, meaning massive global health investments in the access to drugs like antiretrovirals or anti-malarials. This volume considers pharmaceuticalization in relation with pharmaceutical capitalism and its innovation system, which is centered on industrial goods, their IP status and financial value, and tends to reduce the progress in people's health to the growth of drug markets (See Chaps. 1, 3, 10 and 11).

Public good A non-excludable and non-rivalrous resource, sometimes involving provision by a government ensuring access. Examples: clean air, essential medicines (See Chaps. 2, 3, 7, 11 and 12).

Reference

Aghion, P., Antonin, C., & Bunel, S. (2021). *The power of creative destruction: Economic upheaval and the wealth of nations*. Harvard University Press.